VOICES OF HOPE
IN THE STRUGGLE
TO SAVE THE PLANET

About the Authors

Marjorie Hope and James Young are professors emeriti at Wilmington College, a Quaker-affiliated institution in Ohio.

Separately or together, they have published over 135 articles in general and scholarly magazines. Their four books include *Youth Against the World* (1970), *The Struggle for Humanity: Agents of Nonviolent Change in a Violent World* (1977), *The South African Churches in a Revolutionary Situation* (1982), and *The Faces of Homelessness* (1986).

Marjorie Hope has a master's degree in sociology from Columbia University, and another master's degree from New York University in social work. James Young has a master's degree in sociology from Montclair State University, and completed his pre-doctoral work in sociology at SUNY-Binghamton.

They have traveled extensively in over 80 countries on five continents, speak and/or read several languages, and write about the people, the social problems, and the ecological stress in countries where they have lived or traveled.

Prior to publication of *Voices of Hope in the Struggle to Save the Planet*, they published 23 articles excerpted from (or related to themes in) the book.

A Note on Capitalization in This Book:

Because we have followed custom in various religious traditions, as well as usuage by the different sources, capitalization of some terms is not consistent throughout the book.

VOICES OF HOPE
IN THE STRUGGLE
TO SAVE THE PLANET

Marjorie Hope
James Young

The Apex Press
New York

Published by The Apex Press, an imprint of the Council on
International and Public Affairs, Suite 3C, 777 United Nations Plaza,
New York, NY 10017 (800-316-2739), www.cipa-apex.org.

Portions of Chapter 4 first appeared in "Faith and Ecology on the *S.S. Dostovevsky*" by Marjorie Hope and James Young. Copyright 1992 Christian Century Foundation. Reprinted with permission from the February 26, 1992 issue of *The Christian Century*. Portions of Chapter 1 first appeared in "Thomas Berry and a New Creation Story." Copyright 1989 Christian Century Foundation. Reprinted with permission from the June 3-10, 1989 issue of *The Christian Century*. Portions of Chapter 5 first appeared in "Islam and Ecology" in the Summer 1994 issue of *Cross Currents*. Reprinted with permission. Portions of the following three pieces reprinted with permission from *EarthLight Magazine*: (1) "Keeping the Sacred Fire," Summer 1995 issue; (2) "Contrasting Perspectives: Seyyed Hossein Nasr and Thomas Berry," Winter 1995 issue; (3) "Experiencing Sufi Spirituality," Fall 1993 issue. Portions of Chapter 3 first appeared in "Student Ecologists Stir Up Things to Ease the Earth" in the October 9, 1992 issue of *The National Catholic Reporter*. Reprinted with permission. Portions of Chapter 6 first appeared in "Keeping the Sacred Fire" in the May/June 1995 issue of *Resurgence*. Reprinted with permission. Portions of the Introduction first appeared in "Environmental Concerns and Actions of Six Faith Groups" in the March/April 1991 issue of *Sequoia*. Portions of Chapter 3 first appeared in "Awe and Wonder" in the September/October 1995 issue of *Sojourners*. Reprinted with permission.

Library of Congress Cataloging-in-Publication Data

Hope, Marjorie.
  Voices of hope in the struggle to save the planet / Marjorie Hope,
James Young.
    p. cm.
  Includes bibliographical references and index.
  ISBN 0-945257-91-0 (hardcover : alk. paper)—ISBN 0-945257-97-X
  (softcover : alk. paper).
    1. Nature—Religious aspects. 2. Human ecology—Religious aspects.
  3. Religions. I. Young, James, 1916- . II. Title.

BL65.N35 H66 2000   99-027651
291.1'78362—dc21

Typeset by Carol Marino
Cover design by Warren Hurley
Printed in the United States of America

For T. Canby Jones:

mentor, religious scholar, steadfast one

Contents

ACKNOWLEDGEMENTS

In the course of working on this book, we met and talked with hundreds of people in 16 countries. It would have been impossible to write this without the insights and ideas of these generous people. Unfortunately, it is also impossible to name them all. We can only cite some whose observations and experiences had particular meaning in our quest. The following does not include people whose names occur in the text. It does include some in countries—England, Italy, Switzerland, Turkey, Nepal—which space considerations forced us to omit from the text. Their insights, however, helped to round out the "big picture."

We remember and thank especially:

Egypt: Abdel Fattah el Kasas • Samir Ghabbour • Aida Hussein. *England*: Ibrahim Abaza • Roger Martin • Marcelle Papworth • Sheikh Zahran. *India*: Ausaf Ali • Swami Gulukananda • Acharaya Majaraj (Guruji) • Devi Prasad • Padma Seth • Mohinder Singh. *Israel*: Shoshana Gabbay. *Italy*: Sergio Andreis • Gianfranco Bologna • Anna Donato. *Japan*: Shojun Bando • David Howenstein • Masao Ichishima • David Kubiak • Maggie Suzuki. *Kenya*: Aneesa Kassam • Davinder Lamba • Diana Lee-Smith. *Nepal*: Chung Mo • P.B. Thapa. *Pakistan*: Inamullah Khan • Ikramullah Khan. *Palestine*: Lesley Abukhater • Victor Batarse • Ghassan Khatab. *Russia*: Olga Bazhenour. *Switzerland*: Gordon Shepherd. *Taiwan*: Ching Hang • Xiang Sun Meng • Denis Tsinan-Tsai. *Thailand*: Siri Buddasuk • Nay Htun • Pisit na Patalong • Mae Chee Suddhama. Turkey: Celal Ertug • Semra Somersan. *United States*: Azizah al-Hibri • Elizabeth Dyson • Virginia Frost • Riffat Hassan • Azadeh Jahanbegloo • Bill Jerman • John Kolars • Letty Lincoln • Daniel Martin. State of Hawaii: Paul Achitoff • Louis Agard • Hank and Helen Chapin.

Special thanks go to Anna Bellisari, Paul Burks, Elizabeth Desan, Louise Detweiler, Cynthia Hope, Craig Ilgenfritz, Bob Schutz, Nasrin Shahinpoor, and Sabha Shah for reading parts of the manuscript. Their comments added to the rich experience we have found working on this to be.

We are deeply grateful to our editor, Cynthia Morehouse. We admire her patience and mastery of detail, her nimble handling of copy-editing, layout planning, and many other production tasks.

Our heartfelt thanks to Donna McClughen, our dauntless and unfailingly cheerful typist, with her command of computer mysteries and her imaginative solutions.

But how can we convey our deepest gratitude of all—our gratitude to the presences in our corner of this still-beautiful Earth that have brought joy and laughter and meaning to our lives? The myriad birds who transform our feeding stations into small communities, the family of geese on a neighbor's pond, the grace and unfathomable moods of our cats, the trees that surround and sustain us, the wild storms that often light up our sky and remind us of other presences, other forces, beyond our understanding.

IN THE BEGINNING

There is *A W E* and *W O N D E R*. . . . . .

There was at first no Being—nor blank.
There was no air, nor sky beyond.
What was in it? Where?
In whose protection?
Was water there, deep beyond measure?. . . .
Love began, at first; desire was the seed of mind.
Sages and poets, searching within
Saw the link of Being in non-Being.
But who really knows? Who can tell—
How it was born, where Creation began?. . . .
                    —Opening of the Hindu *Rig Veda*
The hills break forth into singing,
and all the trees of the field clap their hands.
                              —Isaiah 55:12

. . . the world is a mirror from head to foot
in every atom are a hundred blazing suns.
If you cleave the heart of one drop of water
A hundred pure oceans emerge from it.
If you examine closely each grain of sand
A thousand Adams may be seen in it. . . .
            —Mahmud Shabastari (Persian Sufi)
        "Gul-shan-i-raz," *The Garden of Mystery*

A — U — M. . . . . .
                    —Tibetan Buddhist Mantra

Let this seed amaze the ground again!
            —Roberta Hill, Wisconsin Oneida Nation

On the return trip home, gazing through 240,000 miles of
space toward the stars and the planet from which I had come,
I suddenly experienced the universe as intelligent, loving, harmonious.

—Edgar Mitchell, astronaut

The mole thought his happiness was complete, when as he me-
andered aimlessly along, suddenly he stood by the edge of a
full-fed river. Never in his life had he seen a river before—this
sleek, sinuous, full-bodied animal, chasing and chuckling,
gripping things with a gurgle and leaving them with a laugh to
fling itself on fresh playmates that shook themselves free and
were caught and held again. All was a-shake and a-shiver—
glints and gleams and sparkles, rustle and swirl, chatter and
bubble. The mole was bewitched, entranced, fascinated. By the
side of the river he trotted as one trots, when very small, by
the side of a man who holds one spellbound by exciting stories;
and when tired at last, he sat on the bank, while the river still
chattered on to him, a babbling procession of the best stories
in the world, sent from the heart of the earth to be told at last
to the insatiable sea.

—Kenneth Grahame, *The Wind in the Willows*

Rainbows are surprises that smile in the sky after a rainstorm.

—Gerry Espinoza, age 11

INTRODUCTION

Picture a planet without the wonders of the natural world that we like to call "our environment." Could we experience the sacred as we do now? What would Judaism be without images of green pastures, still waters, vineyards, the Ark built of gopher wood to house every living thing? What would Christianity be without the wooden cross, the Mount of Olives, or donkeys joining with shepherds and kings to worship an infant born in a manger intended for animals? Islam, without its images of date palms and pure water, its promise of fertile gardens in the hereafter? Buddhism, without the Bo-Tree where Gautama Buddha found enlightenment?

This book explores connections between the biosphere—that all-pervasive presence both immanent and transcendent to our being—and beliefs about who we are and where we come from and where we are going. Between faith and ecology.

Our major focus is on people. We portray the lives of individual women and men who are searching to give life to a new—or renewed—vision of humans' relationship to the earth, and we describe action launched by faith-based environmental groups.

None of these men and women could be called optimistic, in the sense of firmly believing that things will surely turn out for the better. All of them have experienced deep despair. Yet they are people of hope. Many take inspiration from some heroic figure in their faith tradition. But more often they look to the present, and to the life force within themselves. They no longer believe that probable chances of success must precede action. On the contrary, it is when they *do* something, even one small step, in response to overwhelming odds that they begin to feel hopeful. Struggle gives birth to hope.

1

These are the voices of a growing movement that we have witnessed unfolding in Judaism, Western Christianity, Eastern Christianity, Islam, Buddhism, Taoism, Shinto, Native American traditions, and religions of other indigenous cultures. The movement has also penetrated faiths—from Baha'ism to Zoroastrianism—which we cannot explore here. It has even touched some of the highly diverse "new religions," which range from Ananda Marga to various forms of Goddess religion. Some of these groups, it is argued, are not religious at all. But who can precisely define what is religious?

Today many people, particularly in the West, call themselves "not religious, but spiritual." What they generally mean by this is that they are turned off by highly institutionalized religion, and seek a more individual path. They tend to overlook the fact that every religion harbors a prophetic wing, where those with discomfiting and farsighted views gather together, in the interstices of the system. Restless seekers need not leave a tradition entirely.

Hence our book focuses on established religions, even while its compass extends to the unchurched as well as the more orthodox faithful. All of us, deep down, share the urge to believe in something larger than our own small selves. It is what makes us human. Even though we try to forget it, all of us sense that there is a greater, mysterious force within and around us. All of us yearn to rediscover a spiritual center.

The actions and thought of the people portrayed here are rooted in particular places, situations, and cultures. Yet at a time when transnational corporations invade even once-remote ecological niches of the globe, and pollution steals across geographical boundaries, activists working to preserve their corner of Planet Earth from further devastation confront similar problems. Their responses emerge from particular places, but are remarkably parallel.

Our subjects range from those who see themselves as stewards of God's Creation to people who have encountered a new sense of "self." This is an age when the personal search for meaning and self-discovery has become a dominant theme. But the new sense of self that some of these women and men have discovered is not "self-fulfillment" in the usual sense. They have expanded their sense of living-in-relationship to include other forms of life in the world.

How deep is the connection between ecology and religion? Glimmerings of an answer lie in the words themselves. "Religion" comes from the Latin *ligare*, to bind or bond or join together, and from *re*, which in Latin or French means back, again, anew. Re-connecting. At its best, then, religion can be the blessed tie that binds a community of believers.

Less happily, history has shown that religion can split us asunder as well. Yet humankind cannot seem to do without it.

Ecology implies wholeness. One definition is the study of the network of interrelationships among organisms and between them and other aspects of their natural environment. "Eco" derives from the Greek *oikos* (house). Hence ecology, in a broad sense, can be interpreted as Creation imaged as one public household. As "public household," ecology, like religion, points to a bound-togetherness.

Every religion deals in varying measure with the same themes: love, compassion, wise use of wealth, reverence, fear, service, sacrifice, joy, community, humility, arrogance. It also addresses ultimate questions such as good and evil, and "What does immortality mean?" It is concerned with questions of ethics and power: relationships between men and women, rich and poor, authorities and ordinary folk, the Almighty and humans—and with the limits of human power and the temptations that encircle the oppressed once they have tasted power. Woven into the teaching of every faith, too, is recognition of the sacredness of life.

Ultimately, the choices we make in dealing with the ecological crisis are ethical ones. Yet ironically, many scientists, including a sizeable number who do not adhere to any organized faith, have been far more aware than most church leaders that saving the planet is not only a technological, but an ethical and spiritual problem. Biologist Paul Ehrlich asserts that "scientific analysis points, curiously, toward the need for a quasireligious transformation of contemporary cultures."[1] In a 1990 "Open Letter to the Religious Community," 34 internationally renowned scientists, led by astronomer Carl Sagan and Nobel Prize-winning physicist Hans Bethe, declared:

> As scientists, many of us have profound experiences of awe and reverence before the universe. We understand that what is regarded as sacred is more likely to be treated with care and respect. Our planetary home should be so treated. Efforts to safeguard and cherish the environment need to be infused with a vision of the sacred.[2]

Humans have trod heavily on the earth for thousands of years. Even in ancient China, empire-building came into conflict with the earth-loving ethic of Taoism. By 1800 industrial pollution in Europe had increased to the point where Samuel Coleridge was moved to observe:

> The River Rhine, it is well-known
>   Doth wash your city of Cologne;
> But tell me, nymphs, what power divine
>   Shall henceforth wash the River Rhine?

But today the problem is more, far more, than one of water, soil, or air pollution. It is hard to imagine that a great deal of the damage is irreversible, for we have always managed to patch things up, or move away. The idea that some day spring might be silent, that the land we have always planted might instead be repeatedly flooded, or scorched, seems to defy the logic of our experience. And it is hard to *feel* the connection between flooding and global warming, between global warming and carbon dioxide, between the lethality of carbon dioxide and the emissions from automobiles, which neither we, nor increasing numbers of people in developing countries, can envision doing without.

It is harder still to sense connections across the world and across the centuries. When the Vatican affirms the "right to life" by denouncing contraception and abortion, it ignores the effect on others' "right to life": the life of other species we are crowding off the planet, the life of humans seven or seventy generations to come. When American farmers sell fertile land for development because farming no longer "pays," they do not see the "China connection": in the near future more pressure will be exerted on remaining American cropland in order to feed more Chinese, because today their farmers, too, are finding that it "pays" to quit their land to make way for factories and roads. Nor does the Chinese farmer perceive the "U.S. connection": the worldwide push to "keep up with the Americans."

The connections are there, but we rarely ponder them in our hearts. For the first time in human history, we are called on to think about *everything*—and then make responsible decisions.

Western Faiths and Alienation from Nature

Are Western mainstream religions a part—perhaps a significant part—of the problem? Have they been largely responsible for our estrangement from the natural world? These have become central questions in the debates over the prospects for an environmental ethic. They are questions that startle many pious believers.

What seems clear is that alienation from nature is comparatively recent in the life story of homo sapiens. It seems clear, too, that a sense of closeness to the world of nature does not insure active care for preserving it.

Nevertheless, that sense does impart an awareness of human limits, and lay the base for a framework of values that can serve as a guide for a community's perception of reality. To recapture connectedness with all forms of life might seem like an impossible dream in an age we often experience as chaotic, secular, normless, and isolating.

Paradoxically, it may be the right time to turn toward a new vision. As we are constantly reminded by advertising, this is an age of change. We learn from machines rather than elders. The old Thomistic question of "How many angels can dance on the head of a pin?" is replaced by "How many million circuits can be squeezed onto a microchip the size of a thumbnail?" We possess unimaginable means of power, yet feel powerless before tropical storms, computer viruses, radiation, invasions of microbes, inundations of throwaway mail inviting us to consume new! new! new! products.

Moreover, old religious boundaries are crumbling. Earth-goddess religions are taken seriously by increasing numbers of women and men who would never describe themselves as "New Agers." At conferences of Women-Church Convergence: Weavers of Change, booths offer literature about Catholics for a Free Choice, refugee rights, and economic justice issues; worship services range from Protestant, Buddhist, and Sufi observances to Earth Mother rituals, a Holocaust remembrance, a Native American pipe ceremony, and a Catholic-rooted feminist Eucharist.

We question traditional religious frameworks more openly. An eminent Protestant bishop admits he is more comfortable among spiritual seekers than the "safely convinced" in his own family of faith. A survey of theology faculties reveals that sizeable numbers of Protestant and Catholic clerics do not believe in hell or even an afterlife.[3] Churchgoing Christians and devout Jews, many in response to the television dialogues between Bill Moyers and comparative mythologist Joseph Campbell, seek ways to recognize the power of myths in their lives. Almost everywhere we focus increasingly on the ways we *experience* the divine.

Are we ready to experience the earth, indeed the universe, in a new way?

Signs of change in that direction are emerging.

There are mutations within what might be called the inner dimension of our reality. We are discovering that there are other beings on earth with the capacity for thought, emotions, even altruism. Scientists have found ways to record the conversation of creatures who speak in decibels of sound so high or so low that we cannot hear it; hence we have arrogantly assumed it could not exist. A few rare humans have learned to communicate with animals in their language.

As authorities like entomologist E.O. Wilson remind us that nearly four species are disappearing *every hour*, we begin to sense that their extinction endangers our own health, and that somehow the world would be a smaller, duller, poorer place without them. It would be robbed of a wholeness, of what many religious people call "the integrity of creation."

Growth of a Movement

Stirrings in the inner dimension of reality do not necessarily eventuate in organized action in the outer dimension. Such action has been slow. Nevertheless, the ecospiritual movement is unfolding even under the roof of organized faith.

Its potential is enormous. Like no other force, religious faith has the power to fire passions, mold values, inspire sacrifice, draw people into new paradigms of experiencing the world. Religion in its institutional expression has the power to mobilize community concern.

By its very nature, the movement is diffuse, for it touches almost every level of human activity and experience. It is ecumenical in spirit. Moreover, its literature is drawn almost as much from the work of biologists, poets, nature writers, and economists as from sacred scriptures. Literature on the topic—whether it be known as ecotheology, creation theology, theology of ecology, or simply environmental ethics—is growing.

Although there had been scattered conferences earlier, it was in the 1980s that the movement finally took off, spurred in part by the United Nations General Assembly's passage in 1982 of the World Charter for Nature.

To cite only a few of the important international ecumenical events:

In 1986 the World Wide Fund for Nature (formerly World Wildlife Fund) combined a conservation conference and a multi-faith cultural and religious festival in Assisi, the home of Saint Francis, "the patron saint of ecology." The five world religions represented—Hinduism, Buddhism, Judaism, Christianity, and Islam—presented evidence of ecological concern in their scriptures, and committed themselves to renewing and acting upon their heritage. In 1987 the Fund's Conservation and Religion Network began publishing *The New Road*, devoted to news about the environmental work of secular and religious groups all over the world. The year 1988 saw the first Global Forum of Spiritual and Parliamentary Leaders on Human Survival—a gathering in Oxford, England, of 200 eminent persons, ranging from the Dalai Lama, Orthodox Metropolitan Paulos Mar Gregorios of India, Mother Teresa, astronomer Carl Sagan, Kenyan Greenbelt founder Wangari Maathai, Iroquois chief Oren Lyons, Soviet scientist Evgeni Velikhov, and geologian Thomas Berry. Every year since 1983, groups within the World Council of Churches have sponsored conferences on Justice, Peace, and the Integrity of Creation.

In this country, members of a broad spectrum of churches gathered for the first North American Conference on Christianity and Ecology (NACCE) in 1987. In 1989 another, more broadly based group emerged: the North American Conference on Religion and Ecology (NACRE), which is preponderantly Christian but has attracted a sprinkling of Jews, Muslims, Hindus, Jains, Baha'is, Sikhs, Buddhists, and Native Americans to its meetings. In 1990 representatives of several world religions gathered at Middlebury College for a symposium (documented by Bill Moyers) on "Spirit and Nature." Intermingled with poetry, art, and music, an Islamic scholar, a Protestant feminist theologian, a Jewish rabbi, a social ethicist, a Native American woman elder, and a Buddhist holy man (the Dalai Lama) portrayed the ecological dimension of their traditions. Religious conferences that include concern for the fate of Planet Earth now number in the hundreds.

Philosophies and Patterns of Action

The approaches of the thinkers and doers in the ecospiritual movement are influenced not only by religious paradigms, but also by schools of thought within the broader environmental movement. The following appear to dominate the scene today:

- reform environmentalism, which aims at improving natural resource policies, but is basically a human-centered concept of managing the earth, seen as treasury of sustainable resources for human benefit;

- political action and political education;

- social ecology, which sees ecological exploitation as rooted in capitalism, patriarchy, and hierarchy;

- ecofeminism, which links the mistreatment of women with mistreatment of the earth, and envisions a world in which domination, excessive competition, and war are replaced with interdependence, cooperation, and peace;

- deep ecology, which embraces a strong spiritual component in the sense of seeking a connection with something greater than one's ego.

  The goal is to develop an "ecological self," embedded deep in the natural world, and based on an all-encompassing identification with all other beings and the ecosphere itself. The core belief is that human beings have no right to reduce the rich diversity of life, except to satisfy basic needs. Hence the emphasis on preserving true wilderness, where humans may intuit "organic wholeness" and other species may live unhindered. Of all these approaches, deep ecology represents the strongest opposition to the human-dominant perspective, the strongest support of a paradigm shift to an earth community.

The ecospiritual movement is far from unified. Debates flourish. Will only the intervention of humans save nature? Does justice require that the poorer nations catch up with the more affluent before fully committing themselves to the struggle? Is it right to put spotted owls before the jobs of humans—or is that not the real question? Is the concept of good stewardship a sufficient answer? Should our chief source of inspiration be the written Scriptures?

How We Came to Write This Book

Sometimes it seems that this is the book we were compelled to write. Sociologists by training, generalists by bent, inveterate readers and inquisitive travelers by nature, we had long wanted to draw the larger picture of the world that we had begun to sense. We already had written four books on the problems of human beings in society—problems like homelessness and apartheid—which required examining the complex and interrelated causes of these forms of violence. But we came to realize that they did not give enough attention to another kind of violence we were witnessing: despoliation of the earth. All these oppressions were connected in some way. Nevertheless, arriving at the point where we could begin putting it all together was a process of evolution.

Reflecting back, we realized that it all began long ago, when we were very young. Children of the city, both of us spent long vacations in rustic settings, with no electricity, gas, or running water. Both of us remembered the excitement of fetching water from springs, making up our own games, blazing trails in what to us was unexplored "wilderness." Both of us remembered long days mapping our special worlds, and mysterious nights listening to the soft ker-*plunk* of a frog into the pond, the *whip-poor-will* calling, the vibrant *z-z-z-z* of the crickets, the sky thick with stars.

Inspiring professors at our respective colleges opened the world of nature writers. Marjorie was particularly fortunate to study with comparative mythologist Joseph Campbell, who introduced the wisdom traditions of Asia and the first peoples of the Americas and the Pacific.

None of this prepared us for the 1960s, when young and old across the globe rose up to challenge militarism, Third World exploitation, racism, the remoteness of government, the growing power of big corporations, and the manipulation of human consciousness through instruments of the Establishment, especially the mass media. We were active in that movement, and traveled far to talk with young social revolutionaries in other countries and then write about it.

By the 1980s it was clear that the problems they had combated were not only alive, but more oppressive than ever. At the same time we were witnessing—and experiencing—the progressive deterioration of the beautiful planet that is home to all human beings. Were the goals of that "movement of the sixties" not basically similar to those of the movement to preserve the planet? we asked ourselves. How could social and environmental justice be separated?

In our travels we had seen that the poor suffer most from environmental degradation. Returning to some of the world's great cities, we were shocked by the rapidity of decay. In New York's Harlem—where Marjorie once worked as a social worker, and Jim worked with Ella Collins, sister of slain black radical Malcolm X, on a Quaker conflict resolution team—we encountered growing despair among the young who sit on the stoops, staring at the refuse that the city failed to collect. In the words of a young woman whose job had just been declared "redundant": "I'm like the throwaways there in the streets." In Capetown we saw how businessmen were driving mixed-race "Coloreds" from their communities, where their ancestors had lived for centuries, to desolate shanty town areas. In parts of Leningrad that were relatively clean in the sixties, aging factories were emitting sulfur dioxide, and endangering workers' health.

By 1988 we began to follow the work of the organizations and people portrayed here. In 1989-1990 we took a four-month trip around the world. In Hawaii, Japan, Taiwan, Thailand, Nepal, India, Pakistan, Kenya, Egypt, Israel/Palestine, Turkey, Greece, Italy, Switzerland, and England, we observed what was happening to the land and talked with faith leaders, secular environmentalists, and religiously oriented activists about their efforts to prevent further destruction.

We have kept in touch with these new friends, at home and abroad, by letter, fax, and telephone, but it has not been easy. Hence in the winter of 1995-1996, we returned to talk in person with some of the key people in Greece, Egypt, Israel/Palestine, Thailand, Taiwan, Japan, and the U.S. It was a good opportunity to see with our own eyes how these activists were managing to stay out there, fighting, in the face of obstacles that were daunting, even dangerous. Since then, we have continued our conversations with our subjects at home and abroad. Thus this is the story of the development of faith-oriented ecological activists and organizations over a decade.

A Brief Overview

The book begins with "a prophetic voice," that of Thomas Berry. Why have we focused our primary attention on Berry and his ideas? A cultural historian with a deep knowledge of both science and world religions, he has shaped a vision that challenges long-standing assumptions about our relationship to the natural world. The "new creation story" that he conceived, and later expanded in collaboration with physicist/cosmologist Brian Swimme, has evoked angry rejoinders, as well as passionate support among those who see it as lending a framework for a vision of ecological balance. Throughout the book his controversial ideas recur in various places; sometimes we introduce them in our conversations with others as background for understanding their thinking more fully. It is not that we find this thought to be the only true way of perceiving the world; like Berry himself, we believe that there can be many valid approaches. We do believe that his "new story" is so radical (in the original sense of going to the roots, the *radices*) that it serves as a base or point of departure.

The central chapters focus on the faith traditions discussed in the book. Each includes a brief synopsis of some key tenets of the tradition considered, and an analysis of its ecological perspectives, as reflected in its scripture and practices. The main part of each is devoted to portraits and mini-portraits of religiously oriented people who are actively trying to shape a more promising future. Some disagree with each other. They are real people, not abstract theorists or preachers of some noble statement of unity.

We begin with Judaism, the first of the three great Abrahamic faiths. The chapter examines the growing ecospiritual movement in the United States and, more briefly, a parallel awareness that is developing in England and Israel, the latter a tiny, troubled country with some of the strongest environmental laws in the world.

Western Christianity appears before the Eastern branch of the faith because our focus is on present-day activity, not history. Taken as a whole, Roman Catholicism and Protestantism have been the leaders in promoting discussion of an environmental ethic. One reason may be that Western cultures have been most destructive of the earth's ecosystem, and Christianity, in its Western forms, manifests a certain burden of guilt for its long association with exploitative capitalism. Western churches also possess more material means to cope with the problem.

Eastern Christianity (commonly known as Orthodoxy) follows the Western branch, although chronologically the Eastern branch could be seen as the original church, and still considers itself to be the bearer of an uninterrupted tradition of true Christianity. It is both more mystical and more tradition-bound than its Western counterpart, yet today it has begun to articulate an eloquent ecological ethic and has spawned small groups of green activists; it is evolving in ways that could never have been predicted 10 or 15 years ago.

Islam, the subject of the succeeding chapter, has been suspicious of environmental movements. But today change is occurring. Green parties have formed in Turkey and Egypt, for example, and women's groups in many countries have expanded environmental activities. The following chapter, on Native Americans, focuses principally on the Iroquois, a fiercely independent group that has been among the most eloquent in voicing the necessity of living in harmony with nature. The next chapter looks briefly at the way Buddhists, as well as Native Hawaiians, indigenous Kenyans, Taoists, and Shintoists, have traditionally seen their relationship with the natural world and what they are doing to preserve that bond. The penultimate chapter, "A Global Perspective," describes our return round-the-world trip, and the Conclusion sums up trends in the present and reflects on the future.

Since no idea can be understood apart from its setting, our own observations of the ecological, political, and economic situation confronting these thinkers and doers are included, as well as the views of concerned secular people.

Our subjects frequently endure bitter criticism, and sometimes, outright persecution. But like the people Archbishop Dom Helder Camara once called "Abrahamic minorities," and today could be called "creative minorities," they represent increasingly important trends within their traditions. Fully aware that religion alone cannot provide a solution to the complex problems confronting us, they believe nonetheless that it can offer guidance, a sense of boundaries, direction, and a responsive community. It represents the spirit animating all life.

Fire

Across the millennia human beings have gathered together around campfires. Inspired by the flames, they have recounted stories of birth and death, noble exploits, wondrous encounters, the miraculous powers of water, the meanings of fire itself.

It is still true today. Generation to generation, person to person, narratives journey on.

Environmental scientist Calvin De Witt tells the story of listening to a talk by conservation biologist Susan Bratton, who in turn told the story of what the great naturalist Aldo Leopold described as the story of his conversion experience. Because fewer wolves meant more deer, he had always assumed that no wolves meant more deer—a hunters' paradise. He was still scarcely aware of the interconnections, the delicate ecological balance that nature maintains to perpetuate the life of the whole.

But one day he saw a wolf die. He and his hunting companions had spied a wolf approaching her pups, who had sprung from the willows and joined in a melee of wagging tails and playful maulings to welcome their mother back from her forage. Excitedly, the hunters pumped lead into the pack. As Leopold ran up to the dying mother, something compelled him to look into her green eyes. Suddenly he realized that he was watching "a fierce green fire dying."

As he later told it in "Thinking Like a Mountain,"[4] he understood then that the deer and the mountain knew that a wolfless mountain leads to a surfeit of deer, which in turn leads to a devouring of every edible bit of foliage on the mountain, and in turn to death. In the end the wolf is extinguished, the mountain is shorn of its roots and its foliage, soil washes down the eroded slopes, and the bones of the great deer herd that humans have longed for lie moldering; the herd is dead of its own too-much.

Scientists like Calvin De Witt tell us that the biosphere, the green fire born of sunlight and photosynthesis and metabolism, is dying.

The people you will meet in these pages are trying to keep the sacred flame—the fierce green fire we share with all other creatures—alive.

1

A PROPHETIC VOICE:
THOMAS BERRY

As Thomas Berry looks out on the meadow from his home in the hill country near Greensboro, North Carolina, he often thinks of the meadow he watched in his boyhood. He grew up a few miles from his present home, on land with a slope down to a creek and, beyond that, a field of lilies. Even as a child, he was enchanted by the life surging in the meadow, by the "symphony of creatures" at sunset. There was the rejoicing of a great medley of birds, the chorus of crickets and grasshoppers, the burbling of flowing water, the rustling of leaves in the trees. It was all an intimate unity, a community of interacting forms of being. And as the years have gone by, in his mind that living community has come to represent the good economy, the good society.

Greensboro is changing, and the noise and smells of frenetic road-building are moving ever nearer. Yet the earth still brings forth a display of blooming dogwood and redbud in late April, then daisies and honey-suckle in May and June. Berry has returned to this land after a long career of teaching, traveling, and lecturing throughout North America, with occasional journeys to Europe and Asia.

As he contemplates the profusion of beauty that still lingers here, this cultural historian—who calls himself a geologian—also reflects on the disastrous damage humans have wrought on the earth. What is happening today is not just another change, he says. We are changing the

13

very chemistry of the planet, the biosystems, the topography, even the geological structures. Indeed, we are extinguishing many of the major life systems that have emerged in the 67 million years of life of this, the Cenozoic period—a period that has witnessed a spectrum of wonders, including the development of flowers, birds, and insects, the spreading of grass across the land, and the emergence of humans.

The earth is changing, and we ourselves, integral aspects of the earth, are being changed, he says. Religion must now function within this context, at this order of magnitude. But religion, he says, has been assuming little or no responsibility for the state or the fate of the planet.[1] Theology has become dysfunctional today.

Berry knows the institution of religion well, for in 1934 he left his native region to enter a monastery. There he led a life of study and prayer until the mid-1940s, when he began his advanced studies in history at the Catholic University of America. After finishing his studies in 1948 he went to China to prepare for teaching at Fu Jen University in Beijing. This objective was never achieved because of Mao's takeover of China in 1949.

Today, as a geologian, one who has studied Chinese, as well as Sanskrit, the ancient language of Hinduism and much of Buddhism, his intention is to address peoples everywhere in the great variety of cultures. He speaks to people of the human condition and the condition of other beings on this planet. "We have lost our sense of courtesy toward the earth and its inhabitants, our sense of gratitude, our willingness to recognize the sacred character of habitat, our capacity for the awesome, for the numinous quality of every earthly reality,"[2] he observes. The capacity for intensive sharing with the natural world lies deep within each of us, but has become submerged by an addiction to "progress." Arrogantly, we have placed ourselves above other creatures, deluding ourselves with the notion that we always know best what is good for the earth and good for ourselves. Ultimately, custody of the earth belongs to the earth.

In the past the story of the universe has been told in many ways by the peoples of the earth, but today we are without one that is comprehensive. What is needed is nothing short of a new Creation story, a new story of the universe, he asserts. Creation must be perceived and experienced as the emergence of the universe as both a psychic-spiritual and material-physical reality.

Human beings are integral with this emergent process. Indeed, "humans appear as the moment in which the unfolding universe becomes conscious of itself. . . . We bear the universe in our beings as the universe bears us in its being. The two have a total presence to each other and to that deeper mystery out of which the universe and ourselves have emerged."[3]

Everything tells the story of the universe—the wind, trees, birds, stones. They are our cousins. Today it is harder to hear them, for we have become autistic, talking to ourselves. But Thomas Berry can hear them: he has concentrated over the years on listening to the story told by the physical sciences, the story narrated by human cultures, the story recounted through cave paintings, visions of shamans, the pyramids of the Egyptians and Mayans. Each narrative is unique. But ultimately, it is the same story.

We need a narrative that will demonstrate that every aspect of the universe is integral with a single organic whole, he insists. From the beginning of human consciousness, all cultures experienced the cyclical modes of functioning: the ever-renewing sequence of seasons, of life and death. But today scientists and some others have begun to move from that dominant spatial mode of consciousness to a dominant time-developmental mode: time as an evolutionary sequence of irreversible transformations. We are beginning to recognize that our capacity to do temporal damage can become eternal damage.

The new narrative will encompass a new type of history, a new type of science, a new type of economics, a new mode of awareness of the divine—in the very widest sense, a new kind of religious sensitivity.

Such ideas do not always sit well with religious people, especially followers of Abrahamic faiths.

Certainly Berry does not fit the common image of a non-conformist, we realized on our first meeting at the Riverdale Center of Religious Research—a few miles upriver from Manhattan—which he headed at that time. A man with a gentle smile, bright eyes, and tousled whitening hair opened the door and introduced himself simply as "Tom Berry." It was a little hard to imagine that this retiring man, dressed in an old shirt and subdued in his speech, should write so passionately of the dance, song, poetry, and drumbeats through which human beings have expressed their exultation and sense of participating in the universe as a single community. He led us through the house, which appeared to be one vast library with special collections of books, many in the original language on Hindu, Confucian, Buddhist, Shinto, and Native American cultures, and then seated us on the plant-filled, sunny veranda overlooking the Hudson. Despite his shy manner, he began to respond easily to our questions, and sometimes took the initiative.

Noticing that our eyes had been drawn to the majestic oak outside the window, he told us it had endured more than 400 years of nature's buffets, even human-made disasters. To him it stood as a symbol of hope. And it was to this tree that he had dedicated *The Dream of the Earth:* "To the Great Red Oak, beneath whose sheltering branches this book was written."

As we listened, occasionally looking across the Hudson at the Palisades, we sensed that the Center, set in the river valley that had witnessed
a story that included the emergence of the Palisades, the appearance of
trees and birds and bears, then the long habitation by Native Americans,
was a fitting place to contemplate the fate of the earth. It seemed fitting,
too, that scientists, educators, environmentalists, and people of many
faiths from all over the world could gather here, in small groups, to dream
a new vision of the earth into being.

Although reticent about personal matters, he told us that his own life
story began in 1914 in Greensboro. The third of 13 children in a middle-
class Catholic family, he managed to develop a congenial relationship

Thomas Berry. (Photo by Gretchen McHugh)

with his parents, but at the same time a certain distance. (Later, in *Be-friending the Earth*, we got a somewhat fuller glimpse of his early years: "I have always lived marginally. My mother told me once that I was so difficult as a child that by the age of four, my mother and father had a conference one day about me, and my father said, 'We have been nice and sweet and kind to the boy. We have spanked him, we have punished him. Just nothing's going to work. I guess he will have to raise himself.' There seem to be deep, personal gifts or determinations that each of us has. This sense of a certain distance from what was officially happening has never bothered me. I went my way and tried to keep a certain independence.")[4]

This trait of distance, combined with his growing attachment to the land, surfaced often as he told us of his boyhood. The family had a horse, cow, chickens, and dogs; he felt close to the animal world. He often roamed the hills alone, except for the companionship of a collie, sensing the freedom of the woodlands and delighting in the clear streams, the song of the birds, the subtle smells of the meadows. "But even at the age of eight," he recalled, "I saw that development was damaging nature. At nine, I was collecting catalogues for camping equipment, canoes, knives, all the things I'd need to live in the Northwest forest. I felt the confrontation between civilization and wilderness, and I was acting on it."

That fascination with wilderness helped shape his search to find out how people found meaning in life. Always drawn to Native Americans because of their sense of integrity and freedom, their bond with the riches of nature, he came to know many, including Sioux chief Lame Deer, Onondagan leader Oren Lyons, and the poet Paula Gunn Allen. Aided by his knowledge of Sanskrit and Chinese, he deepened his exploration of Eastern religious traditions. Over the years he also published a large number of papers and books on subjects ranging from Buddhism to the creative role of the elderly and the thought of Teilhard de Chardin. Philosophers ranging from Confucius to Thoreau, poet/visionaries from Dante to Chief Seattle, ecologists and scientists from Rachel Carson to Anne and Paul Ehrlich, all came to influence his conception of the earth community.

"But Teilhard had the greatest influence on what might be called your ecological vision?"

"Yes. As a paleontologist as well as philosopher, he had a grasp of the need for healing the rift between science and religion. He appreciated the important role of science as a basic mystical discipline of the West. He was the first great thinker in the modern scientific tradition to describe the universe as having a psychic-spiritual as well as a physical-material dimension. Teilhard had a comprehensive vision of the universe in its evolutionary unfolding. He saw the human as inseparable from the history of the universe. Also, he was keenly aware of the need in Western religious thought to move from excessive concern with redemption to greater emphasis on the creation process."

"And Teilhard's thought inspired you to delve into science?"

He nodded. "But I must emphasize that his framework has limitations. Remember, he died in 1955. He believed in technological 'progress,' and saw the evolutionary process as concentrated in the human, which would ultimately achieve super-human status. He could not understand humans' destructive impact on the earth, even when others pointed it out. Science would discover other forms of life! But his work remains tremendously important. The challenge is to extend Teilhard's principal concerns, to help light the way toward an Ecozoic Age.

"Teilhard posed the greatest challenge of our time: to move from the spatial mode of consciousness to the historical, from being to becoming. The church finds difficulty in recognizing the evolution of the earth. For a long time it wouldn't accept even the evolution of animal forms. As a child I was taught by the catechism that Earth was created in seven days, 5,000 years ago."

"And today the church, again, is lagging instead of leading?"

"There is some concern, but it does not go far enough," he said slowly. "The Vatican makes vague statements on being careful about the environment, but the emphasis is on making the natural world useful to human beings. So far, the most impressive Catholic bishops' statement comes from the Philippines. It's called 'What Is Happening to Our Beautiful Land?'"[5]

Over Greek salad at the Broadway Diner nearby, we learned more about the ever-widening scope of his activities and some of the people who were carrying out his ideas. He told us that he spoke rather often at the ecologically-minded Cathedral of St. John the Divine in New York, and at religiously-based educational centers, such as Genesis Farm, Grailville, the Ontario-based Holy Cross Center, and the Au Sable Institute, all of which emphasized new ways of living in harmony with the natural world. He had participated in many conferences, including the seminal 1988 meeting of the North American Conference on Christianity and Ecology, and the first (1988) Global Conference of Spiritual and Parliamentary Leaders on Human Survival. In Puebla, Mexico, a Jesuit group had founded the Institute for Ecological Personalism, based on his ideas. Letters came in continually from people all over the earth.

During the afternoon our talks continued, touching on animism, Taoism, and Buddhism, including Buddhist ideas for human habitats, which Berry considered models of ecological functioning because they disturb the natural world very little.

The Universe Story

Since that day we have met Berry many times, studied his writings, and gradually gained a clearer picture of the transforming vision he presents.

In 1988 he brought out a collection of his essays entitled *The Dream of the Earth*. In 1991 he and Jesuit priest Thomas Clarke published a dialogue, *Befriending the Earth: A Theology of Reconciliation Between Humans and the Earth*, originally a 13-part series on Canadian television. Years earlier, in 1982, he teamed up with Brian Swimme to work on a daring venture: *The Universe Story: From the Primordial Flaring Forth to the Ecozoic Era*. It appeared in 1992.[6]

Their partnership has been an unusual one. Swimme, a physicist and mathematical cosmologist, is younger and lives thousands of miles away on the West Coast. His early book is entitled *The Universe Is a Green Dragon*.[7] This later collaborative book tells the story of the universe as a single comprehensive story, a narrative of the sequence of transformations that the universe has experienced. Grounded in present-day scientific understanding, it parallels the mythic narratives of the past as they were told in poetry, music, painting, dance, and ritual. Nothing quite like this coupling of science and human history had been published before. Indeed, the authors were both criticized and encouraged as they tested out their ideas with a distinguished group of scientists, cultural historians, religious scholars, anthropologists, and philosophers at symposia sponsored by the Center for the Story of the Universe.

The authors claim no final revelation. While using what they consider the most convincing hypotheses, they are aware that in the future new evidence may well insist that others fill in what is missing, and alternative hypotheses may be adopted.

Today we can begin to understand the story in the full richness of its meaning, they tell us. This is especially true of Earth—surely a mysterious planet. We need only observe how much more brilliant it is than others of our solar system, in the diversity of its manifestations and the complexity of its development. Earth appears to have developed with the simple aim of celebrating the joy of existence.

Through this story they hope that the human community will become present to the larger earth community in a mutually enhancing way. Our role is to enable the entire universe to reflect on and celebrate itself. Today we are making awesome decisions without the sense of awe and humility commensurate with their impact. We need a new mystique as we move into the Ecozoic era, and this will need the participation of all members of the planetary community.

In the first chapters of *The Universe Story*, they demonstrate how the various members of that community have a common genetic line of development, the authors tell us. It begins with the Beginning: the primordial "flaring forth" of the universe some 15 billion years ago. It starts as stupendous energy. Before a millionth of a second has passed, the particles stabilize. From this point on we are carried through the seeding of galaxies, and the appearance of galactic clouds, primal stars, the first elements, supernovas, and galaxies. These are magnificent spiraling moments, carrying the destiny of everything that followed. They are moments of grace. Some five billion years ago a solar cloud begins to evolve in the Orion arm of the Milky Way, a cloud destined to become our solar system. Gradually, Sun is born, plants are formed, Earth brings forth an atmosphere, oceans, and continents, and living Earth emerges. We travel through the Paleozoic era (in which vertebrates, jawed fish, and insects appear); the Mesozoic era (witnessing the first dinosaurs, birds, and mammals); and the Cenozoic (beginning with the emergence of the first rodents and bats), and carrying on through the arrival of later orders of mammals, including humans.

After the emergence of homo habilis, some 2.6 million years ago, it gradually evolves to homo sapiens, with marvelous new gifts of expression—ritual burials, then language, musical instruments, cave paintings, and other skills and artifacts. Homo sapiens continue to evolve through periods of the Neolithic village, classical civilizations, the rise of nations, and the "modern revelation."

The latter refers to a new awareness of how the ultimate mysteries of existence are being manifested in the universe. This revelation is a gradual change from a dominant spatial mode of consciousness, where time is experienced as moving in ever-renewing seasonal cycles, to a dominant time-developmental mode of consciousness. Time is experienced as an evolutionary sequence of irreversible transformations. Our perception moves from"cosmos" to ever-evolving "cosmogenesis." The universe is not "being," but always in the process of "becoming." This awareness begins with the discoveries of Copernicus, and embraces those of Galileo, Francis Bacon, Descartes, Newton, Darwin, Einstein, Rachel Carson, and many other scientists and philosophers.

Throughout, the two men from such differing backgrounds evidence a unified point of view as they present some cardinal principles. Among them, that the birth of the universe was not an event in time; time begins simultaneously with the birth of existence. There was no "before" and there was no "outside." All the energy that would ever exist erupted as a single existence. The stars that later would blaze, the lizards that would crawl on the land, and the actions of the human species would be powered by the same mysterious energy that burst forth at dawn.

Another principle is that the universe holds all things together, and is itself the primary activating power in every activity. Recent scientific work has shown it is not workable to think of a particle or event as completely determined by its immediate vicinity. Although in practical terms their influence may be negligible, events taking place elsewhere in the universe are directly related to the physical parameters of the situation. They conclude that "since the universe blossomed from a seed point, this means that a full understanding of a proton requires a full understanding of the universe."[8]

Articulating the new story so that humans can enter creatively into the web of relationships in the universe will require, to some degree, reinventing the meaning we attach to words. For example: what is gravitation? In classical mechanistic understanding, it is a particular attraction things have to each other. But the bond holding each thing in the universe to everything else is simply the universe acting. To say that gravity pulls the stone to earth implies a mechanism that does not exist. To say that Earth pulls the rock misses the presence of the universe to each of its parts. It is more helpful, say Berry and Swimme, to see Planet Earth and the rock as drawn by the universe into a profound intimacy. "The bonding simply happens; it simply is. The bonding is the perdurable fact of the universe, and happens primevally in each instant, a welling up of an inescapable togetherness of things."[9] Thus gravity is not an independent power; the universe in both its physical and spiritual aspects holds things together and is the primary activating power in every activity. We can begin to understand the idea that the universe acts, that it is not a thing, but a mode of being of everything. Each process, then, is ultimately indivisible. Primal peoples have understood this bonding.

Consider the Milky Way. Its truth cannot be realized by focusing only on its early components, helium and hydrogen. . . . "Unless we also reflect on the fact that the Milky Way in its later modes of being is capable of thinking and feeling and creating, we are failing to confront the galaxy as it is. . . . In this universe the Milky Way expresses its inner depths in Emily Dickinson's poetry, for Emily Dickinson is a dimension of the galaxy's development."[10]

Walt Whitman did not invent his sentience. It is an "intricate creation of the Milky Way; his feelings are an evocation of being, involving thunderstorms, sunlight, grass, history, and death."[11] Poets, then, do not think on the universe; rather, the universe *thinks itself*, in them and through them.

Thus the vibrations and fluctuations in the universe are the music that called forth the galaxies and their powers of weaving elements into life. Our responsibility is to develop our capacity to listen. The eye that searches the Milky Way—the eye of humans or that of telescopes—is itself an eye shaped by the Milky Way. The mind searching for contact with the Milky Way is the very mind of the Milky Way searching for its inner depths.

The appearance of humans brought a consciousness characterized by a sense of wonder and celebration. Even in the period of classical civilizations (3500 BCE to 1600 CE), the human social order was integrated with the cosmological order. Yet there was also great devastation. In the West, particularly, there developed an exaggerated anthropocentrism. When the Black Death struck Europe in 1347, this changed to theocentrism. Since there was no germ theory to explain it, humans concluded they must be too attached to the earth and should commit themselves to salvation from the earth, absorption into the divine. Anthropocentrism and theocentrism, however, both denied the unity of the natural, human, and divine. The mystic bonding of the human with the natural world was becoming progressively weaker. Closely associated with this insensitivity to the natural world has been the insensitivity to women and the reign of patriarchal dominance.

Since the late eighteenth century, the West has considered its most important mission to be that the peoples of the earth achieve their identity within the democratic setting of the nation-state. Nationalism, progress, democratic freedoms, and virtually limitless rights to private property are the four fundamentals to this mystique. It was not even considered that unless their limits are recognized, these might bring catastrophe upon the natural world.

Moving from Cosmos to Cosmogenesis: Its Awesome Implications

The "modern revelation"—characterized as it is by gradual awareness of the universe as an irreversible sequence of transformations that enable it to gain greater complexity in structure and greater variety in its modes of expression—is fraught with significance. Our predicament today is itself the result of a myth—the myth of Wonderland. If only we continue the path of progress, happiness will be ours—happiness virtually equated with the ever-increasing consumption of products that have been taken violently from the earth or react violently with it.

We need a new myth to guide human activity into the future. It should be analogous to the sense of mythic harmonies that suffused the fifteenth-century Renaissance, say Swimme and Berry. At the beginning of the scientific age, the universe was perceived as one in which each mode of being resonates with every other mode. Somehow this sense of an intelligible ordered universe has directed the scientific quest. But only recently have we been able to comprehend the depths of these harmonies, and thus fully recognize the mission of mathematics. The scientific meditation on the structure and functioning of the universe that began centuries ago has yielded, among other insights, a sense of what can be called "the curvature of the universe whereby all things are held together in their intimate presence to each other."[12]

Today we are arriving at the point of entering the Ecozoic era. What will it mean? This is explored in Swimme and Berry in *The Universe Story* and by Berry in *Befriending the Earth*, and in essays on economics, technology, law, bioregionalism, education, and planetary socialism in *The Dream of the Earth*. The basic answer is to begin by questioning some of our implicit assumptions:

- The assumption that we need constant economic growth. How could we believe that human well-being can be attained by diminishing the well-being of the earth? Since the threat to both economics and religion comes from the disruption of the natural world, should economics not also be seen as a religious issue? If the water is polluted, it can neither be drunk nor used for baptism.

- The implicit assumption that we could cure sick people by modern technologies and by focusing on their present problems. How can we have well people on a sick planet?

- The idea that the primary purpose of education is to educate people for jobs. We need jobs, certainly, but is it not more important to be educated for roles and a diversity of functions? Is it not more realistic, in the long run, to see education as knowing the story of the universe, of life-systems, of consciousness as a single story— and to help people understand and fulfill their role in this larger pattern of meaning? Even in the arts, instead of focusing on producing professionals, would it not be better if all of us played music, if all children painted and wrote poetry?

- The conviction that a democracy that is exploiting the natural world is the highest form of governance. Indeed, "demo" refers to people, not to all beings, to beings whose fate we are controlling— in the name of human life, liberty, and happiness. We need a biocracy, a rule that will be concerned with all members of the earth community.

Re-evaluating these assumptions and other "truths" that we hold as "self-evident" should enable us to realize that the earth is primary, the human secondary; that the universe is a communion of subjects, not a collection of objects. Stepping back a little from our efforts to impose our will on life systems, we will be free to listen to the natural world with an attunement that goes beyond scientific perceptions and reaches the spontaneous sensitivities in our own inner being.

Human professions need to recognize that their primary source is the integral functioning of the earth community. The natural world is the primary economic reality, the primary educator, the primary governance, the primary technologist, the primary healer, the primary moral value, the primary presence of the sacred. The professions do not yet have the words for the type of transformation required. For instance, we need to invent a new language in law, then move from the ideal of democracy toward the more comprehensive paradigm of biocracy. One example: a constitution recognizing not only the human on this continent, but the entire North American community, including all beings, geographical structures, and life-systems.

Religion needs to appreciate that the primary sacred community is the universe. Our ethical sensitivities need to expand beyond suicide, homicide, and genocide, to include biocide and geocide.

Changes are already happening. Divisions of learning are beginning to overcome their isolation. The need to limit human population is modifying traditional roles of women and men, indeed, the entire human situation. Fundamental to a real sea-change, however, will be the move from a human-centered to an earth-centered language. Words like good, evil, freedom, society, justice, literacy, progress, praise should be broadened to include other beings of the natural world.

The Cenozoic era emerged independent of human influence, but homo sapiens will enter into virtually every phase of the ecological era or Ecozoic era. We cannot create trees, fish, or birdsong, but they could well disappear unless we choose to exercise our awesome power with humility—unless we follow three basic axioms in our relations with the natural world: acceptance, protection, fostering. Acceptance of the given order of things. Protection of the life-systems at the base of the planetary community. Fostering a sense of active responsibility for the larger earth community, a responsibility conferred through humans' unique capacity for understanding the universe story.

We shall need to recapture the basic principle of balance. Its prototype lies in the awesome reality that the expansive original energy of the primordial "flaring forth" keeps the universe from collapsing, and gravitational attraction holds the parts together, enabling the universe to flourish. So, too, on Earth. The balance of containing and expanding forces keeps it in a state of balanced turbulence. In the industrial age humans have upset the equilibrium. Undisciplined expansion and self-inflation has led to destruction. In the Ecozoic era the task will be to achieve balance between our activities and other forces on this planet.

The Place of Religion

Where does God fit into this story?

It is a word that Berry rarely uses. It has been overused and trivialized, he says. The word has many different meanings to people. His principal concern is to reach the larger society, including people who would not call themselves religious.

Although Berry does not say it in so many words, he implies that in the West we spend too much time arguing over definitions rather than recognizing—in both theological and experiential ways—the ineffable. The term "God," he claims, refers to something beyond that which we can truly comprehend. Many primal peoples experience this as the Great Spirit, a power pervading every aspect of the natural world. Some people dance this experience, some express it in song, some find it in the laughter of children or the sweetness of an apple or the sound of wind through the trees. At every moment we are experiencing the overwhelming mystery of existence.

Berry prefers to speak of the Divine, of the numinous presence in the world about us. This is what all of us—child or elder, Christian or Jew or Buddhist or agnostic—can experience; this is the ground that all of us can truly know. Since the universe story is the way the Divine is revealing itself, humans *become* sacred by participating in this larger sacred community. The gratitude we feel in this experience, we call "religion." For Berry, all this is more real than theology, because it emanates from experience of the emergent universe, an experience so basic that it is shared by other members of the earth community.

With his comprehensive *weltanschauung*, embracing non-theistic faiths, he never speaks of a God who commands, judges, rules over an afterlife, or watches over human actions. He does not go into traditional religious questions like good, evil, heaven, hell, or individual salvation. Yet he points out that his position follows quite directly from Saint Paul's Epistle to the Romans. In the first chapter (of the Jerusalem Bible), Paul declares that "Ever since God created the world, his everlasting power and deity—however invisible—have been there for the mind to see in the things he has made."

In our own discussions with Berry, he has stressed that his primary interest is that humans come to see the visible created world with whatever clarity is available. The first step, as Saint Paul suggests, is perception of the created world. Thus God is not our first clear perception. Rather, the sense of God emerges in and through our perception of the universe. Just how the divine is perceived obviously varies among different peoples. In any case, it seems that the divine is perceived "in the things he has made." The *knowledge of God* emerges in the human mind not directly, but through this manifestation.

As we have seen, Berry is highly critical of many aspects of Christian doctrine and practice, for they have profoundly affected all of Western civilization. Christianity, he says, is involved not as a direct cause of our ecological crisis, but as *creating the context*. To summarize briefly:

First, it emphasizes a transcendent, monotheistic deity, creator of the world with a covenant relationship with a special people. Second, it exalts the human as a spiritual being as against the physical nature of other beings—the human is so special that each human soul has to be created directly by God. Third, it perceives redemption as some kind of out-of-this-world liberation. Fourth is the idea, developed particularly by a devout Christian named Descartes, that the world is a mechanism.

All these "transcendencies"—transcendent God, transcendent human, transcendent redemption, transcendent mind—foster entrancement with a transcendent technology that shall liberate us from following the basic biological laws of the natural world. Thus do we create a transcendent goal, a millennial vision hearkening back to the Book of Revelation, with which to go beyond the human condition.[13]

The Bible, he says, is one of the most sublime books in the world—but perhaps also the most dangerous. In contrast to the perception of most peoples that the primary manifestation of the divine is in the cosmological order, the Bible introduced an emphasis on seeing the divine in historical events, stimulating a dynamism toward a missionary zeal to explore and possess.

Like many other religions, primarily monotheisms, Christianity tends toward narrowness. Among religious people, the more intense the commitment, the more fundamentalist they tend to be. What is needed today is not intensity but expansiveness. Take the traditional Christian hostility to animism. St. Boniface, for example, cut down sacred oak trees. Today that would seem absurd. Could not the future of Christianity actually involve assimilating some elements of paganism?

In view of all this, Berry makes the startling suggestion that we consider putting the Bible on the shelf for perhaps 20 years, so that we can truly listen to Creation. One of the best ways to discover the deep meaning of things, he says, is to give them up for a while. Thus we would be able to recover the ancient Christian view that there are two Scriptures, that of the natural world and that of the Bible. We would be able to create a new language, more adequate to deal with our present revelatory moment. Unfortunately, at present the manifestations of the divine are being lost and we are still reading the book instead of reading the world about us. We will drown reading the book.[14]

Still, we cannot do what needs to be done without the religious traditions. The new story does not replace them; it provides a more comprehensive context, a common Creation story, in which all the earlier stories can find a more expansive role.

It is of pivotal importance, then, to be open to ongoing revelations, including those emerging from the scientific venture, say Swimme and Berry. What we need is a sense of reverence such as we find with the great naturalists or with some of the foremost scientists of our times. Indeed, in a broad sense, scientific understanding is the key to the future of religion. By the same token, there is a belief element at the ultimate reaches of the scientific inquiry into the universe.

The Challenge of Berry's Vision

It is too early to appraise Berry's influence, especially in a period when America is riding high on the intoxication of power: domination of world politics and of the global economy. The full import of his message may not sink in for many years. But already he has stimulated a broad range of women and men, ranging from religious scholars to secular ecologists and even economists, to re-examine the direction of their work. His workshops always draw many young people. He even inspired one member of his own family to take up a new life. After his brother Jim retired from the military, Berry suggested he might want to start an organization to encourage more discussion on the new story and the proper role for humans in the working of the created order. The result was the Center for Reflection on the Second Law, which has sponsored annual conferences and published a newsletter.

Nor can Thomas keep up with speaking requests, although he responds to as many as possible. In small workshops, particularly, he seems to enjoy the opportunity to establish an intimate relationship with his audience. His eyes move back and forth, never leaving his listeners. He chuckles at the stories he uses to illustrate a point, and his face often lights up with the boyish smile of someone who finds zest in life. Demand for his writings grows every year, and his work is being translated into other languages. In our own conversations with people as diverse as Buddhists in Japan, Muslims in Egypt, and agnostics in Russia, speaking of Berry has always provoked great interest and requests for copies of his work.

One criticism of his thought is that he exaggerates the extent to which the Bible provides a context for an exploitative attitude toward the earth. Another is that the challenges we face are more complex than rediscovering an integral relationship with the earth. A frequent objection is that his ecocentric vision denies the chosen status of "man," viceregent of God. Berry listens to such criticisms, sometimes adapts his thought to accommodate them, sometimes answers with a helpful rejoinder. To the objection that the ideas he and Swimme present about gravity, curvatures, and time may prove transitional in the realm of human thought, Berry replies that this may well be; we should always be open to new revelations.

Even critics admire his sweeping synthesis, imaginative insights, and courage in confronting the narrowness of traditional theology. They also respect the fact that although he often uses abstract terms, he lends them a vivid—at times biting—concreteness. He describes ecological, economic, and political problems with down-to-earth examples. When looking to a more promising future, he illustrates his ideas with examples ranging from methods of appropriate technology to bioregionalism or steady-state economics. He even proposes, not entirely tongue-in-check, running every other truck on our highways into a ravine. It is not that he eschews all technological advances. But our technologies must harmonize with the *technologies of the natural world* that operate on self-nourishing, self-healing, self-governing principles.

Like most significant teachers who have possessed a prophetic vision, Berry alternates between pessimism and hope. At conferences on ecology and religion he has often played the role of reconciler in disputes, the one who can find truth in each side.

Still, it is our observation that he is becoming more radical as he advances in years—and sees the time left for saving the planet running out. He is "radical" in the original sense: hearkening back to the Latin word *radices*, roots. It is as if he is driven by the thought: "They just don't get it! They don't comprehend how deeply rooted it is, the crisis that confronts us!"

Sometimes one can hear the anger in this gentle man as he speaks of "the order of magnitude of the present catastrophic situation." It is, he says, "so enormous, so widespread, and we don't know what we are doing. The people who built the automobile, the people who built the nuclear program, the people who dreamed up the Green Revolution in agriculture, were unable to make the connection between their activity and its consequences. Vandana Shiva, one of the most competent people in the Third World, says the Green Revolution initially produced great increases in India's food supply—and in the end, devastated its whole agricultural system. We made 50,000 nuclear bombs, and now we don't know what to do with them!

"We fool ourselves into thinking that recycling cans and papers will do it. Of course we must recycle. But basically that is designed to keep the system going. It can help mitigate the problem, but only till we can do the fundamental changes. Meanwhile, when ecology groups try to protect the last bit of our old-growth forest, the entrepreneur types say these 'radicals' are trying to do away with jobs. If these are the only jobs we can imagine, it is a sick society, and we need cultural therapy. We can't solve this crisis by meliorism."[15]

Yet Berry sees hope in the growth of bioregional movements, Green political organizations, and confrontational movements launched by activist groups such as Greenpeace. He talks of shifts of consciousness revealed in countercultural writers and feminist, anti-patriarchal movements. He has also been encouraged by shifts within the World Bank toward more viable programs and the addition of an environmental department; by the spread of vital information through organizations like the International Union for the Conservation of Nature, the World Resources Institute, and the Worldwatch Institute; and by various United Nations programs.

Our awesome power spells our danger—but it also presents an unparalleled opening to a larger creativity, he observes. The danger lies in the mystique that pervades our patriarchal, plundering industrial society. It is a mystique that could propel us not into an Ecozoic era, but into one that could be called Technozoic, led by people—epitomized in the corporate establishment—who are committed to an even more controlled order. In the future, the dominant struggle will be the struggle between Entrepreneur and Ecologist.

Who will lead us into the future? The intimacy with the cosmic process that is needed describes the shamanic personality. As in earlier cultures, today the shaman may be woman as well as man. Certainly, to fulfill the function of healers, shamans must represent the feminine principle, embodied in the growing scientific perception of our planet as a single organism, alive, self-governing, self-healing. True, nurturance is not the only role for women. Nurturing roles, however, are the key to the future; they are epitomized in the archetype of woman but reside in the capacities of each one of us.

Taking our cues from earlier peoples, we can create, or recreate, renewal ceremonies. We need to celebrate through poetry and song, drama and dance, the great historical moments in the unfolding of the universe, cosmic events that constitute psychic-spiritual as well as physical transformations. Such celebrations might begin with the primordial flaring forth and the supernova implosions, moments of grace that set the pattern for emergence of this planet. They might go on to include the beginning of photosynthesis, followed by the arrival of trees, then flowers, then birds, and other aspects of this wondrous evolution.

Without entrancement, emerging from the immediate communion of humans with the natural world, and the sense that nothing is itself without everything else, it is unlikely that humans will have the psychic energy needed for renewal of the earth.

Berry's shamanic voice raises a challenge. Is the human species viable, or are we careening toward self-destruction, carrying with us our fellow earthlings? Can we move from an anthropocentric to an ecocentric vision? How can we help activate the intercommunion of all members of the earth community? What shall we be leaving the children—the young of our own families, of our own species, of other species whose fate we share?

Can we find the guidance we need in religions as they exist today?

2

JUDAISM

Revitalizing Old Stories: Ellen Bernstein and Shomrei Adamah

When you walk across the fields with your mind pure and holy then from all the stones and all growing things, and all animals, the sparks of their soil come out and cling to you and then they are purified and become a holy fire in you.

—Hasidic saying

If one enjoys the fruits of this world without blessing them . . . it is as though he steals the sparks of the soul of his mother and father.

—The Kabbalah

Unlike many who follow mainstream Jewish theological principles, Ellen Bernstein does not see the animal kingdom as a hierarchy with man on top ruling over all.

Yet her outlook differs in significant ways from Berry's view stressing that human beings are integral aspects of the earth. Nor does she believe we need a new cosmology. Instead, she says, "we need to re-read and revitalize the old stories; science and religion are both needed to understand and value Creation. Science speaks to 'how' questions, religion to 'why.'"

Ellen sees her own mission as one step toward fulfilling that need. A biologist by training, she founded Shomrei Adamah, Guardians of the Earth, to inspire an awareness of nature and promote an active practice of stewardship, based on Jewish traditions and the revelations of modern science. Its first teaching vehicle—a *haggadah* (guide or "telling") for the holiday *Tu B'Sh'vat*, the Jewish New Year of the Trees—is entitled *The Trees' Birthday*: A *Celebration of Nature*.[1] It guides the reader through a four-part ritual seder (which in Hebrew means "order") culled from the Hebrew Bible, the Zohar (the most significant document of the Kabbalah), Taoist scriptures, modern Jewish and non-Jewish poetry, and excerpts from works of environmental scientists.

We first met Ellen at the Reconstructionist Rabbinical College, where she had an office. She was a tall, slender young woman, with long, curly reddish-blond hair, blue eyes, and a lithe athletic build. Her manner was cordial but almost subdued. As she began to talk, the intensity of her convictions seemed to melt her reserve, and she became increasingly animated.

"Most Jews interested in the environmental crisis see it as a social problem," she began slowly, as if choosing her words with care. "That is not my experience. I see the crisis as a spiritual one. The spiritual element is missing in most people's lives. If we didn't have so many material 'needs,' our lives wouldn't focus so much on consumption."

She ran her fingers through her tousled hair. "Development is one reflection of this problem. When I visit my mother in Florida, from Boca Raton to Miami it's wall-to-wall cement, malls, and highrises. In these artificial environments, I feel physically sick. It is truly terrifying to me. And then there's the traffic, another aspect of development. In much of Florida, San Francisco, or along the East Coast, it's so terrible you can't breathe.

"What's beneath all this? That's the question I keep asking myself. I think we've lost our sense of place, of where we belong, and what it means to be human. Without it, we are empty. People don't experience their own roots. It took *me* a long time to find them."

Ellen's family belonged to a Conservative congregation, simply because it was "the only show in town." They had Jewish food and some Jewish values, but no Jewish learning or culture. Looking back, she sees their need to integrate into WASP society as a "function of the time." Living in an immigrant, upwardly mobile milieu in Haverhill, Massachusetts, they were caught up in materialist values.

"Today I realize that my father did have a deep spiritual side. He believed in God and did good things because he knew they were right. Still, our traditions weren't emphasized. I wasn't proud of being Jewish. My friends and I used to make fun of the rituals.

"If you grow up with little religious education, you don't know what you're missing. Still, I felt a vague emptiness inside me, around me. My happiest times were spent outdoors. Even then, I was disturbed by how our culture had forsaken nature for material progress. I was drawn to the Native American idea that the land is sacred. And I began to study all the natural sciences.

"So when I went to UC-Berkeley for a bachelor's in conservation, I studied mysticism for a while. I also went skiing and hiking along nature trails. It was beautiful, walking and listening to nature. But I realize now I was going for solace—I was rebelling from something."

After graduating, Ellen taught high school biology, received her master's in biology and education from Southern Oregon State University, and co-directed the Turtle River Company, guiding people on river trips. It was on the banks of the Colorado, during a river expedition with 10 other geology students, that she had an experience during which she made some significant connections. As she tells it in the preface to *The Trees' Birthday*:

> One Pesach (Passover), about ten years ago, I "got" Judaism. I was backpacking in the Grand Canyon with ten other geology students. Missing the traditional Passover celebration, I suggested a seder. We discussed the symbols of the Holy Days and then we each went out into the desert to collect herbs, bones, trilobites—our *own* symbols for the seder plate.
>
> As the sun set, we gathered together and cooked up a lentil stew feast. We found a beautiful spot where the red canyon wall formed an overhang. There, cradled in the most awesome river canyon, we sat through the night eating, G-D talking, reflecting and singing, as we watched the moon rise overhead.
>
> It was a special moment for me. I realized that the Holy Days were gifts to help us enjoy life more fully.

Concluding the preface, Ellen writes:

> With more study, I found nature alive everywhere in the Jewish tradition. I saw that the global perspective was also inherent in Torah.
>
> It is my hope that through the celebration of the Holy Days, and especially *Tu B'Sh'vat*, we can grow more in love with the land, nourish her and "keep" her as a blessing for ourselves and future generations.[2]

As she began her searching, Ellen discovered Barry Holtz' *Back to the Sources*.[3] "Through it the *meaning* of Judaism opened up for me. It

made me ask, 'Why didn't I study this before, alongside Greek and Roman history?'

"That started me on a long journey. I began to see that Jews had been
divorced from the land for over 2,000 years. Yet Judaism was one of the
first great environmental religions. In biblical times we knew our plants;
we knew where to find water in the desert. We davened—prayed—at
times set by the sun. The rhythm of the moon prescribed our holy days.
Our lives revolved around the seasons. I began digging deeper into the
traditions, especially the festivals that highlight our agricultural roots—
like *Shavuot*, which celebrates the grain harvest, and *Sukkot*, which honors the vegetable harvest, and Pesach, when we're reminded of the
ripening barley as we begin counting the *omer*, the 49 days of mourning
until *Shavuot*.

"I've come to see *Sukkot* as Judaism's holy day par excellence. Today
we tend to rush through our meals, forgetting where the food came from.
Sukkot forces us to slow down long enough—a whole week—to focus on
the source. If you've seen a *Sukkah*, you know it's a simple, open-air,
moveable hut that we build of wooden slats and colorful old material.
It's sort of flimsy, the rain and raccoons can get in, and we can see the
stars through the branch-covered roof. The *Sukkah* draws us into relationships with the four elements: the Earth, Water, Air, and Fire."

"The four worlds that you honor in your *Tu B'Sh'vat* seder."

She nodded. "With its openness and fragility, the *Sukkah* teaches us
the true nature of protection. Today we humans build walls around ourselves, shutting out life and nature. We consume, often maniacally, build
defenses of power and wealth to protect us from the unknown.

"So on *Sukkot*," she continued, "we Jews build a fragile little hut to
remind ourselves of our own vulnerability and humbleness. To remind
ourselves that the only real shelter is under God's wing. We also learn
about limitations of human power. We perform the water-drawing ceremony, and recite the prayer for rain. That reminds us that while agriculture is a human effort, rain is a miracle. Ultimately, our sustenance lies
in the hands of the Creator."

"And, of course, *Sukkot* remembers the Exodus from Egypt."

"That's right. While Passover celebrates the miracle of Exodus, and
its promise of freedom, *Sukkot* commemorates the day-to-day life along
the path of liberation. It teaches that the daily chores of cooking, cleaning up, setting up the tents, walking the way every day, are as worth
celebrating as the exodus event. To me, this tells us that there are no
simple overnight solutions to the environmental crisis. It's made up of
small, day-to-day steps like separating our garbage, making trips to
the recycling center, reading labels, and talking to our friends and communities. I've come to see these as the daily chores our generation must

take on to assure freedom for this planet so that our grandchildren will enjoy it. I like to think that *Sukkot* celebrates stewardship, because it praises—*joyously*—small acts that will assure a better world."

"And *Tu B'Sh'vat*—it has a special meaning for you?"

"Yes, because it's the Jewish new year of the trees and honors the mystical Tree of Life. These are only examples of the great love for the preciousness of life that I began to find all through the Judaic tradition. I thought: why haven't today's Jews come together around the environment issue? It was time."

Shomrei Adamah was established in 1988, five years after Ellen moved from California to Philadelphia. She had come to see the environmental crisis as a "direct result of the consumer products we're creating," which went hand-in-hand with "the imperialistic ideology that we're pushing." But what could she do? Write *Tu B'Sh'vat* seders, and reach out to like-minded Jews. "I started Shomrei Adamah after the great success we had with the first *Tu B'Sh'vat* seder," she recalls. "It was held in a boathouse in Philadelphia overlooking the Schuylkill River. Participants read from the *haggadah* and feasted on fruits and wine. The experience was profoundly moving for everyone."

In 1988, too, Mordechai Liebling, executive director of the Federation of Reconstructionist Congregations and Havurot, offered Ellen a home base from which to begin a national non-denominational Jewish environmental project. For Rabbi Liebling, this was a significant step because he had become increasingly apprehensive about what he saw as a "complete misunderstanding of the Bible and of Jewish teaching on the environment"—the interpretation that humans have dominion over the earth and therefore have a right to exploit it. "Most Jews," he says, "have ignored environmental concerns, and I think it's because for centuries Jews have not only been living in the Diaspora, but in a Diaspora that prohibited them from owning land. For the sake of survival, Jews became the most urbanized people in Europe. But today the Reconstructionists feel it's important to put forth the positive teaching of Judaism about the environment."

Ellen has created her *Tu B'Sh'vat* ceremony in the tradition of the mystical Kabbalists, who lived in Israel in the 1500s. They attempted to show that by deepening our relationship to nature, we deepen our relationship to ourselves. They honored trees by eating three fruit meals and drinking four cups of wine, in between, reciting from Judaic texts on nature.

For the first meal, she says, they ate fruits with a tough outer skin, such as pomegranates, as reminders of the quality of boundaries, the power of limits, and the need for defenses. The second consisted of fruits

Ellen Bernstein, founder of Shomrei Adamah.

with a soft, edible outer part and a pitted inner part, such as peaches, for as we grow stronger and more invincible within, we can soften our protective outer shell. The final meal included fruits soft and edible through and through, such as strawberries and grapes. They teach that a life of total faith in God and surrender to the divine scheme is truly sweet—no pits, no shells, no fears, no obstacles.

The guide that Ellen, building on the Kabbalistic tradition, created for the ceremony attempts to integrate a sense of place with a global perspective. Each of the four worlds celebrated—Earth, Water, Air, and Fire—is to be introduced with music or dance, described in readings from the *haggadah* or one's choosing, and finally honored with blessings of fruit and wine. For example, Earth—*Assiyah*—represents the character of "physical," the direction of "west," and the season of "winter." The fruit to be eaten should be hard on the outside and soft on the inside, while the wine to accompany it should be white.

Such a seder can be varied to fit ideas from the celebrants. "Be creative and have fun as you embrace your worlds!" she says. For example, Congregation Ansche Chesed (Conservative) in New York City planned a *Tu B'Sh'vat* observance that followed its own *haggadah*, blended in modern Israeli songs and poems, and included a program for children on Judaism and the environment (consisting of theater, stories, art, and a special children's seder), as well as a forum covering topics like "Nature in Midrash" and "Trees, CO_2, and the Greenhouse Effect."

Ellen's role in Shomrei Adamah included fundraising, management, publicity, running workshops, writing, networking, and working on national conferences. In her talks and Shomrei Adamah's newsletter *Voice of the Trees*, she has encouraged synagogues to remind Jews of their ecological heritage by taking such steps as installing biblical gardens of plants that reflect the biblical landscape of Israel, as well as with initiatives like banning styrofoam from their premises, converting to paper or glassware, planting trees, using organic lawn products, and hosting conferences on Judaism and the environment.

Shomrei Adamah has published *Judaism and Ecology*,[4] a source book edited by Marc Swetlitz. Together with the Reform movement's social and political arm, the Religious Action Center, Shomrei Adamah has brought out a packet for rabbis to use on Earth Day, comprising a sermon, a liturgical piece, and a tree-planting ceremony, together with recycling information and source material. The packet has also been used by several Conservative congregations. Ellen and Rabbi Dan Fink also published *Let the Earth Teach You Torah*: *A Guide to Teaching Ecological Wisdom*.[5] Geared toward a broad audience, it integrates readings from religious and ecological sources with activities, and can be used in schools, camps, weekend retreats, family programs, rabbinical schools, and college courses in ecology or religion.

In our talks with her, we have come to understand better the many dimensions of Ellen's quest. She rejects Thomas Berry's approach, not because she quarrels with his emphasis on our need for a more ecocentric frame of reference, but because of what she calls "the way he wants to disregard scripture." It makes her distinctly uncomfortable to abandon ancient and sacred texts; her inclination is to see scriptures in the context in which they were written.

Ellen is also impatient with debates over the Genesis story versus the concept of evolution. "To me, evolution is a scientific theory, while Genesis is concerned with religious questions." While some Christians take the Genesis story literally, she says, Jews do not. They are more inclined to look at it interpretively—as a marvelous myth, so to speak. "Does that mean human beings are descended from other species? I have no problem with that,"

While her concept of God appears to be an eclectic one, suggesting influences from the Kabbalah and strands of contemporary progressive Judaism, she says that her basic concept has not changed since childhood; it was only as an adult that she came to know the Kabbalah. "To me, there's godliness everywhere, in everything. I've never seen a God-figure enthroned up there in Heaven, nor a God guiding every human action, orchestrating everything on earth. Rather, I look for a law of nature. I don't have any visual image of God, but rather, a feeling. Other people can look at it differently. They should have any image of God that they like."

In Judaism, she says, much of the Torah does not provide specific answers, but instead offers texts to reflect on. "For practice of principles there are the commentaries. There are tons of commentaries, so you can select from them, synthesize them."

"Roman Catholicism," we once observed, "has a Pope, together with an elaborate hierarchy and a tight codification of what is acceptable to the True Faith."

She nodded. "Judaism is not like that. All can have an opinion. The result is healthy tension. Besides, there are four ways of studying the texts—the mechanical, the psychological, the analytical, and the secret, through the Kabbalah. They can overlap. Like most others who take this seriously, I study all four ways; you can say it's a blend."

"In Judaism there seems to be a greater focus on this world than in Christianity."

Her eyes lit up. "Yes! That, to me, is another strength of our faith. Many Jews don't even believe in resurrection of the body. The Kabbalists do talk a lot about life in the next world. But even then it's different from Christianity's emphasis on salvation through faith. Instead, there's an ethical focus, being rewarded for leading a good life here. In general, it's not a materialist view of Paradise. The holidays do emphasize redemption, but in the here-and-now. It's all more down-to-earth. See how many of our festivals celebrate planting and harvesting!

"On some levels I *am* attracted to Roman Catholicism," she went on. "The liturgical music, the reverence for Mary the Mother, the seasonal celebrations—all these seem vibrant with the feminine and the mystical. They're elements I find in Judaism. Not in Protestantism, which to me is too stiff. It has less vitality.

"But Judaism, with its chanting and prayers in Hebrew!" She sat back and took a deep breath. "When someone dies, the Kaddish is so moving! The words enter you, even if you don't understand Hebrew. The sound is part of the mystery. I need music. It's part of the wholeness."

Out of the Jewish traditions, Ellen selects what is meaningful to her work and her need for wholeness. Denominations have little meaning to her; the differences among them do not seem significant. What interests her, she says, is the core, "Judaism, the religion." For example, although she does not adhere to Orthodoxy, many of its customs, reflecting a sense of wholeness and order, have a strong appeal to her.

"Yet in Orthodox synagogues women are separated from men."

"True. But in Jerusalem, for instance, both men and women go to the Wailing Wall to pray. Separately, of course. Anthropologically speaking, separation is an ancient custom and is found in many cultures."

"It's unusual for a woman to be heading a religious organization within Judaism. Has this caused you any problems?"

"No. I honestly feel that the problems I've faced have not come from being a woman. Most men, especially rabbis, are delighted to talk to me. Those who are not—well, the disagreement is about the relationship between ecology and religion. They don't understand that this is a *values* crisis, a crisis in our relationship with the land."

She fell silent a moment. When she began again, her voice sounded tired. "Some people seem unable to value the work of Shomrei Adamah. They perceive Judaism as only having something to say about urban social issues, not *land*. Too many Jews have not been taking Judaism seriously enough—that is, looking at what it's all about. Even in Israel, where I spent a summer, environmentalists are so secular, they could not understand the work of Shomrei Adamah."

"And your family?"

"I also have some problems with them. They love me, but they still don't understand what I'm doing. I am always thinking about whether life will continue on this planet. They don't understand that."

"Where do you go when you feel frustrated and need to refresh your spirit?"

"I go walking or running in the woods. Sometimes alone, sometimes with a friend. Or I study with a Hevrusah study-companion. I never get enough time for that, and it's so important.

"But there are so many rewards in this work," she added quickly. "Like talking to rabbis. They're good colleagues. And they like talking to me. They have a need to talk about the spirit and the environment. Down deep, they know this is the way to bring back the youth. The big challenge, though, is getting it to filter down into the congregations. I can help, because I can offer a range of concrete ideas."

Over the years Ellen has become convinced that much of the alienation today stems from the way people all over the world have cut themselves loose from traditions. She has been largely motivated by a feeling that she has a particular calling to reach out to Jews who do not feel connected to religion, a calling to intensify their awareness of the tie between ecology and religion.

"Our tradition knows what D. H. Lawrence called 'the way of knowing in terms of togetherness—of the body, the emotions, the passion with earth and sun and stars.' It knows the rituals for the dawn and for sunset, for kindling the lights, purifying with water, breathing in the first breath and breathing out the last. They are still woven into the fabric of daily life, and can help keep us conscious of our relationship with nature and with the divine. If I can get non-affiliated Jews excited about nature, they'll begin looking for wholeness. Our movement tries to integrate intellect, emotion, spirit, and activism."

To Ellen, all religions are sacred; what is important is to dig down into one's roots. But Shomrei Adamah in particular, and Judaism in general, are good models, she feels. On the one hand, they integrate celebration of nature and the holidays with the legal aspects of the Jewish tradition. About a third of the laws in Torah—that is, about 200—could be called environmental laws, she observes. On the other hand, practice of *Tikkun Olam*, repair of the earth, can deepen one's religious joy. And it should be just that—joy. Reconstructionism's founder, Mordecai Kaplan, emphasized that Judaism should be a celebration, not a burden.

"The underlying theme of Jewish thought is the covenant—a binding relationship between human and God, between human and human, and between human and nature. And Judaism is an earth-based religion. 'Ecology' means the study of home. And the earth *is* our home."

Ellen's life has been one of continuous searching. It has brought some serendipitous surprises. One of the most gratifying is the experience of living in the Philadelphia suburb of Mount Airy. When she moved from the Oregon mountains in 1983 to study physical therapy—a career she finally saw was not for her—she expected to leave soon after her training. Cities, she was convinced, were devoid of nature and without beauty. But on her first visit to Philadelphia in the spring of 1982, the azaleas were blooming in dazzling shades of fuchsia, purple, and peach; she was completely overwhelmed at how beautiful it was. Nature is alive in the city if we take the time to notice, she discovered.

After years of keeping her distance from Jewish institutions, she also found community—Jewish community. She became a member of the Germantown Jewish Center, served on its board, and found deep satisfaction in sessions of studying Jewish texts in homes throughout the neighborhood. Today, she says, people may have momentary glimpses of nature when traveling to resorts. But how, she asks, do we consistently maintain a sense that the earth is sacred so that stewarding the earth becomes habitual and normal? What can keep us remembering, acting? "That's where community comes in."

Judaism and Ecology

As we can see in Ellen's story, history is of utmost importance to Judaism and the people who make it their faith. The Jews' own history is full of suffering and persecution, yet also a determination to endure.

More than most other peoples, too, the Jews feel they have experienced God's presence in human history. Hence the great importance of Mount Sinai, where Yahweh (YHWH) gave Moses the Law and established a covenant with him; of Jerusalem, the site of the Temple; and of other places in the Holy Land where they have sensed his "hereness." Hence, too, the great emphasis on Jewish holidays, such as Pesach (Passover), commemorating the Exodus from Egypt, and Rosh ha-Shanah, celebrating God's sovereignty, justice, and mercy.

Like Ellen, virtually all Jews, even those who would not call themselves "religious," find deep meaning in the holy days; they offer a communal identity. Most Jews are not as aware as Ellen of how these festivals are rooted in their ancestors' closeness to the natural world, but they sense that the rituals represent an invisible bond that has helped them endure over the millennia. Judaism's vitality rests largely on the fact that it is not only a religion, but a way of life.

Another bond is the emphasis on ethical behavior and divine law, so evident in the Torah ("teaching"), which is embodied in the first five books of the Hebrew Bible; in the Talmud, the literary expression of oral Torah; and in Halakhah ("process"), which develops legal doctrine and ritual parts of scripture, showing how Torah should be applied in daily life. These and other teachings serve as a center in a tradition that has never had a representative body of world Jewry.

The principal branches (Orthodox, Reform, Conservative, and Reconstructionist) are divided over many questions, such as the definition of "being a Jew," the status of women, proper relationships between Jews and non-Jews, the importance of social action, whether Judaism should be seen principally as an evolving religious civilization, and whether the emphasis should be on traditional beliefs and ritual or on realizing the biblical vision of world peace.

Beneath these differences lies the ongoing tension between exclusivistic and universalistic tendencies, seen by Jews as "the unique and the universal." By virtue of their covenant with Yahweh, Jews see themselves as "a kingdom of priests and a holy nation." But what does this mean today? Some Jews see this unique relationship as conferring less a privileged status than ethical responsibilities. Others pursue a more militant view.

All these varying perspectives influence how Jews perceive their relationship with the natural world, as well as ways they take action to help preserve it.

Among Jews, reactions to the idea that nature is inherently divine are often of anger.

Rabbi Everett Gendler takes vigorous exception to what he sees as Berry's "inflation of Earth." Reacting to this "substitute theology—earthology," Gendler asks, "Is transcendence thus banished, with God renamed Gaia?" Yet Gendler is an ardent supporter of Berry's insistence that we must reintegrate ourselves with the life-sustaining earth processes, and he often emphasizes the mystical and earth-loving elements of Judaism.

The range of Jewish thought on the relationship between humans and God and the earth is wide, for in Judaism diverse viewpoints are encouraged. Steven Bowman, professor of Judaic studies at the University of Cincinnati, observes that the Judaic tradition of scholarly commentaries on the sacred texts is such that "you don't throw anything out; you just keep commenting on commentaries. This is the intergenerational dialogue that defines Judaism." In the case of contemporary discussion of Judaism and ecology, the dialogue is further complicated by the fact that secular writings play an influential role as well. Moreover, younger thinkers who have grown up in an ecologically troubled era are emerging on the scene.

A central debate—one that has also been prominent in Christian circles—is how to interpret Genesis 1:27-28:

> And God created man in his image, in the image of God He created
> him; male and female He created them. God blessed them and God
> said to them: "Be fertile and increase, fill the earth and master it;
> and rule over the fish of the sea, the birds of the sky, and all the liv-
> ing things that creep upon the earth.[6]

Related to this debate there are others. Is God immanent in all nature, or does He transcend the natural world? If He is transcendent and man is created in God's image, does this not mean that man has been licensed to subdue it? After all, Psalms 115:16 does tell us that "the heavens, even the heavens, are the Lord's, but the earth hath he given to the children of man."

At one end of the Jewish spectrum is the anthropocentric conception of humans' place in this world. In contemporary writing it is articulated in the works of those who, like Steven Schwarzschild, feel that unsettled landscapes are to be filled and conquered, and reject all attempts to "re-sacralize nature" as contradicting the Jewish view that nature possesses no value in itself. Schwarzschild declares that despite certain heretical, quasi-pantheistic tendencies that are manifest in medieval Kabbalism and modern Zionism, traditional Judaism holds that nature should be subject to human ends. He does believe in the usefulness of ecology, but only because human survival depends on it. Schwarzschild even argues that as a Jew he is an "unnatural man"; his forebears have been urban dwellers.[7] Schwarzschild's ideas, however, are shared by only a small minority of Jewish thinkers today.

At the other end of the spectrum are Kabbalism and Hasidism, which see all Creation as linked together. The Kabbalah declare that God, being boundless, cannot be known—yet they also stress seeking mystical experience of the Divine. This is not quite mystical union, for even in Jewish mysticism there lingers the sense of creature-Creator difference so central to Judaism. As philosopher Martin Buber once put it, in Judaism there is no union with God—only the unity of God and the *shekina*, the presence of God.[8] Like Kabbalah, Hasidism perceived the immanence of God in this world ("there is no place empty of Him"). It extended the Kabbalistic tradition of seeing the world as a symbol of God, says Norman Lamm. "For Hasidism . . . man* has a kinship with other created beings, a symbiotic relationship with nature, and he should maintain a sense of respect, if not reverence for the natural world."[9]

The great majority of Jewish thinkers strike middle ground, but incline toward the transcendental point of view; nature is to be treated with care, yet is not in itself divine. An insistent refrain is that in contradistinction to paganism and pantheism, Judaism refuses to ascribe holiness to nature. Thus Israeli immunologist David Weiss declares that in Judaism the forces of nature are acknowledged as powerfully real, but denied all autonomy. There is only one embracing authority, and it is illimitably concerned with man. Nevertheless, says Weiss, the forces of nature need not be shut out—nor should the passions of humans. Rather, they must be sanctified.[10]

In the final analysis, as conservation biologist David Ehrenfeld and Rabbi Philip Bentley point out, most Jews believe that every living thing on earth must have some human reference and use. In any comparison of world religions, "Judaism stands at one end of a philosophical spectrum—the human-centered end—in which the human role in the world is that of careful steward."[11]

Does Judaism, then, posit a basic antagonism between humans and the natural world? It is an ongoing question. Certainly Judaism had to

---

* As the reader will note, many of the older writers referred to in this chapter speak of humans as "man"; this is not our preference.

overcome the "idols" of its predecessor religions to establish itself. Nature-worship (which leaders identified with promiscuity) was regarded with implacable enmity by the Jewish monotheist. "You could read the Hebrew Bible as one long polemic against paganism," says Bowman.

Paganism says nature is holy, worships the forces of nature, and thereby unleashes the beast within humans, observes Samuel Dresner. Christianity, he adds, says nature is unholy, denies its forces as sinful, and thus frustrates humans' natural desires. Judaism, however, says nature is neither holy nor unholy, but is *waiting to be made holy*. It is the duty of the good Jew to make everything holy through *mitzvot* (commandments raised to the level of spiritual joy). Blessings are to be offered for virtually everything. For example, one should bless God on awakening because one has been allowed to awaken, and on beginning to use a new house or piece of clothing or tool, because one has been preserved in life to this hour.[12]

Yet today more and more Jews find that wilderness transforms *them*. "Each blessing of Shabbat, each journey into the wild, and each moment in nature can give us an opportunity to participate more fully in the mysteries of the divine world," says Mark Sirinsky, an avid whitewater kayaker and rabbi in Ashland, Oregon.[13]

Growing numbers of Jews believe that only by reconnecting with the natural world can human beings be truly human. Gendler says the separation from the vegetation cycle may have consequences for the spirit that we have scarcely begun to comprehend. He goes so far as to suggest that elements of ancient nature cults persisted as an underground stream of Judaism, mainly in Kabbalah, Hasidism, and certain Jewish poets, as "the reassertion of both the Natural and the Feminine components of religion." Gendler recalls the midrashic *Aboth d'Rabbi Nathan*:

> Whatever the Holy One, blessed be He, created in the world,
>   He created in man . . .
> He created forests in the world and He created forests in man . . .
> He created a wind in the world and He created a wind in man . . .
>   A sun in the world and a sun in man. . . .[14]

And he declares that "the fact that earth and all living beings are bound by covenant to God implies that Judaism takes universal sentience for granted: all of Creation must be alive with feeling." Many are the biblical verses in the vein of Psalm 98:8: "The rivers say: 'Let the rivers clap their hands, let the mountains sing for joy together!'" Could not the sense of nature as holy, but not deity, alive but not necessarily animistic, help reestablish our sense of respect and wonder toward the world around us?[15]

These views carry on Martin Buber's attempts to proclaim the possibility of an I-Thou relationship with all beings in the natural world.[16]

Ecological Principles in Practice

In exploring religions for ecological traditions, we sometimes overlook the reality that centuries ago most human beings could not have
imagined the magnitude of the crisis we face. Hence traditions cannot
always speak directly to the crisis. However, they *can* voice ecological
principles.

So it is with Judaism. It is a faith offering broad precepts that can
become guidelines. The four cardinal principles might be condensed to
read: If humans do evil, nature reacts . . . God ordained a definite order;
nothing is created without a purpose . . . You don't get something for
nothing . . . We humans depend upon nature. . . . Perhaps these four could
be summarized into the principle that all behavior has ecological consequences.

Jewish sacred literature is filled with proverbs, parables, and *halak-
hic* laws that relate to the wonder of the natural world and our duty to
care for it. In the Talmud, for example, it is written "He who goes out in
the spring and views the trees in bloom must recite, 'Blessed is He who
left nothing lacking in His world and created beautiful creatures and
beautiful trees for mankind to glory in.'"

Moreover, the *halakhah*, particularly, goes beyond vague gen-
eralities, providing a concreteness often lacking in writings of other
faiths.[17] For example, every phase of agricultural practice was described
in an order of the *Mishnah* entitled *Seeds*. God's speeches out of the
whirlwind to Job, which imply that humans only take their place among
other beings created by God, can be seen as a religious base for the
inherent rights of animals. In Deuteronomy, farmers are forbidden to
plow with an ox and a donkey yoked together; to do so would cause the
latter to suffer too great a burden. In Exodus, God commands Moses to
rest on the seventh day, "that thine ox and thine ass may rest." Deuteronomy warns against taking a bird with her young.

Indeed, originally Adam was commanded to be a vegetarian. When
Noah was finally permitted to eat meat, he was forbidden to consume
"the flesh with life thereof, which is the blood thereof." The permission
was a compromise, a divine concession to human weakness and human
need. Thus the pious must have reverence for the life that is taken. It is
part of the process proclaimed in *Kashrut* (the Jewish dietary laws),
which prohibit eating blood, and provide for "humane" slaughtering—
that is, killing that minimizes the pain of the animal. The slaughtering
must be performed by a person known for his kindness.[18]

Are laws needed to teach this? Yes, says Dresner, citing the case of
Albert Schweitzer, who wrote volumes about reverence for life, yet

changed the actions of few people. In contrast, Jewish law takes great Bible teachings and fixes them into observances that fashion a meaningful way of life. In eating a slice of bread we can discover God, in drinking a cup of wine, sanctify the Sabbath, and in preparing a piece of meat, learn something of reverence for life.[19]

Jewish views of excessive consumption stem from the principles of *balance* and *restraint*, says Eliezer Diamond. Family and religious celebrations should be restrained so that they do not create pressures on others who are less well off. The concept of Sabbath, too, injects the element of restraint into stewardship, which otherwise might easily become corrupted into subjugation.[20] On the Sabbath," say Bentley and Ehrenfeld, "the traditionally observant Jew does more than rest, pray, and refrain from ordinary work." He creates nothing, destroys nothing, and enjoys the bounty of the earth. Nothing is created, and this reminds him of God's supremacy. Nothing is destroyed, reminding him that the world is not his to ruin. He enjoys earth's bounty, reminding him that God is its ultimate source.[21]

Extensions of this idea are the Sabbatical and the Jubilee years. Leviticus 25 declared that every seventh year one might not tend the field or the vineyard. Only the poor and strangers had the right to produce that grew by itself. Letting the land lie fallow helped regain its fertility. After seven sabbatical years, the 50th year was celebrated as Jubilee. All property sold during the preceding five decades was to be returned to its original owner without compensation, for Leviticus proclaimed that "the land shall not be sold in perpetuity, for all land is Mine, because you are strangers and sojourners before Me." While these laws have virtually ceased to function, even today certain ultra-pious groups, such as members of the Israeli kibbutz Hafetz Hayim, let the land lie fallow every seventh year, and Talmudic law still proclaims an adjusted law of the Jubilee.

The concept of a "Green Belt" was set forth in the Book of Numbers. Cities given to the Levites were to be surrounded by a *migrash*, an inner belt of open space extending 1,000 cubits in every direction, and reserved for animals, moveable possessions, and public amenities. The outer belt of 1,000 cubits was for fields and vineyards.

Environmental pollution, widespread in urban areas even in ancient times, was subject to control. Over 2,000 years ago, the rabbis had formulated planning regulations, such as those governing the location of cemeteries, threshing floors, and slaughter houses. In some towns anyone engaged in noisy work that disturbed neighbors was required to stop or move to a comfortable distance. Tanneries, which produced the most noxious fumes, were located only on the east side of towns, because the prevailing winds in Israel blew from the west.

Bal tashhit (thou shalt not destroy) is often cited. In the Torah only despoiling the fruit-bearing trees outside a beleaguered city, as a tactic of warfare, is specifically criticized: "You shall not destroy trees by wielding an axe against them, for is the tree of the field a man that it should be besieged?" Some scholars extend this to cutting water sources necessary for trees to grow, says Barry Freundel.[22] Moreoever, the injunction against cutting fruit-bearing trees can be interpreted as a "case example" to illustrate a general prohibition against destroying the environment. Today *bal tashhit* is sometimes invoked as a commandment forbidding hunting for sport, and even against using detergents, non-recyclable materials, gasoline, inefficient incinerators—indeed, against a whole host of destructive actions.

These injunctions have not been practiced faithfully in the past. Moreover, rabbinical scholars are skilled in finding exceptions to virtually every rule. Nevertheless, they represent practical guidelines that are remarkably relevant to our time. Looking further, growing numbers of thoughtful Jews today would agree with Aryeh Carmell that the major cause of pollution is the "vicious circle of luxury production and consumption"—and that this means material possessions must be replaced with spiritual goals: kindness, holiness, and pursuit of truth.[23]

Human-Centeredness, God-Centeredness, and Stewardship

The severely anti-pagan tradition of Judaism and the fact that it stands toward the transcendental end of the immanence/transcendence religious spectrum restricts efforts to move from an anthropocentric frame of reference toward a more ecocentric one. On the other hand, the transcendental emphasis can lead away from human-centeredness, pointing toward God and constant awareness of the limits of humans' power.

What *is* clear is that throughout much of Jewish history care of the environment has been an important concern. The underlying assumption—more prevalent in the Jewish than the Christian ethos—is that unbridled individualism must give way to the well-being of the community. That community extends into the future, for the sins of the fathers can be carried into the third and fourth generation (and much further).

The central principle, then, is that of responsible stewardship. Humans are distinct from the rest of God's creation, but they carry responsibility toward the Creator. Nature is not to be used solely for human benefit. But vigilance should ever be exercised against the danger that stewardship become distorted into the belief that humans are lords, not caretakers.

With both Christians and Jews the line between stewardship and control is a tenuous one. The questions persist: Who defines "good stewardship"? Does the "good steward" idea that "man's title to the world is conditional" nonetheless suggest superiority?

The Ambiguities of Dominion

In our own view it comes down to the problem of power. And power wears an eternal face. There is the age-old, apparently innate urge to control objects and people in the world that we know. But today there is also the ever-growing urge to master everything—the world that we know and the world that we fancy we ought to know. Let us decipher the genetic code and produce humans completely devoid of anti-social tendencies! Let us split atoms and produce a brave new world of nuclear energy! Let us smash protons against each other in a supercollider, replicating in a laboratory—safely, of course—the Big Bang, the Genesis story. Let us clone *good* humans, and other creatures useful to humans. The consequences? We'll get a grant to study them later.

Many Jews are acutely—at times painfully—aware of the problem of power and its complexities. For example, in "Environmental Control and the Decline of Reality," biologist/ecologist David Ehrenfeld focuses on the extraordinary proliferation of administration. He perceives in the management explosion several grave consequences: demoralization of the producers, direct appropriation of power through control of the money supply by managers with little direct knowledge of how a product is actually produced, destruction of science in its truest and highest sense. Many of our environmental problems—ranging from use of biological, chemical, and nuclear weapons to the greenhouse effect, the international agricultural crisis, the ozone hole, deforestation, loss of species, and loss of human cultures—need to be addressed quickly and effectively. Bureaucracy is slow and ineffective. All this emerges from an organic growth of a power-worshipping society, almost religiously dedicated to a belief in control. Moreover, overpopulation is partly responsible for all these environmental problems. Does overpopulation make overmanagement inevitable? That is a question to ponder.[24]

In closing, Ehrenfeld quotes two sources. One is urban planner Lewis Mumford, who asserted that our task is to find a way to convert a "power economy to a life economy." The other is Deuteronomy 30:19: "I have set before you life and death, the blessing and the curse; therefore choose life that you might live, you and your seed."[25]

Arthur Waskow, a Reconstructionist rabbi and director of the Shalom Center, brings the problem of dealing with power into a vision of transforming our everyday lives. He suggests a program, founded on Sabbatical and Jubilee principles, that could address our environmental, economic, and emotional woes. It could also empower individuals at the grassroots—while offering, paradoxically, opportunities to reflect on our limits as human beings.

Waskow has a dream. He imagines three major structural reforms as elements of the "Jubilee program":

- Wealth-recycling that could shift massive amounts of investment capital from control of giant corporations to local businesses.

- Halting research and development every seven years, to enable everyone to pause for a "sabbatical" of sacred, reflective time and consider production and technology in the light of their environmental and social effects. Corporate investments beyond a certain amount would be subject to a one-year "sabbatical" to delay pending public review of their environmental impact, and scientific and technological research would halt for a year. These pauses would teach society that there are values other than producing, making, and doing.

- Celebration of neighborhood empowerment. For instance: empower neighborhoods to choose one day a month, or one week a year, for a neighborly celebration. We could create a national Sabbath at least twice a year (Earth Day might be one occasion) when only life-preserving emergency services are open; highways, hotels, offices, and television stations would be closed, and train, bus, and airline services suspended. Thus we could rediscover walking and talking, singing and cooking—we could rediscover our neighbors. Synagogues and churches could initiate this Jubilee program by holding a miniature Jubilee, a festival that would encourage economic renewal by imaginative measures like inviting co-ops and innovative small businesses to explain their work, demonstrating energy conservation, and turning parts of church or synagogue grounds into communal vegetable gardens. At town meetings, people could discuss concerns about jobs, public health, family, the environment. Through it all the people would become bonded through the sharing of food and the joyous celebration of song, storytelling, and dance. The passages on the Jubilee in Leviticus, says Waskow, demonstrate that the most effective politics contains a potential ritual element, engaging not only material interests, but also deep emotional, intellectual, and spiritual energies.[26]

Rabbi Arthur Waskow and 250 worshippers celebrate *Tu B'Sh'vat*, the Jewish New Year of the Trees, in a Californian ancient redwood grove. The event served also as a protest against Maxxam Corporation, headed by Jewish CEO Charles Hurwitz, with the planting of redwood seedlings. (Courtesy *Sierra* magazine; photo by Averie D. Cohen)

To Waskow, then, the emphasis in Jubilee is not on deprivation and gloomy sacrifice, but on empowerment and jubilant sharing. Like Berry, he feels that celebration is essential.

Growing numbers of Jewish religious leaders and their congregations agree that adherents must assume a stronger stewardship role. Yet for the most part, concern has remained on a theological or *halakhah* level. Some observers believe that the reason that Jews have lagged behind Christians in arriving at active environmentalism is that they are newcomers to the power, affluence, and guilt that allow and stimulate people to reflect on the quality of life around them.

Increasingly, however, Jews as a whole are not only experiencing deep concern for the environment, but are translating it into action. Until recently, secular Jews have led the way. Traditionally, liberal Jews have been in the forefront of liberal political movements, and today many have begun to link ecological and political problems.

Religious Jews who share a sense of urgency feel confronted with a great challenge. How can they apply the concern so evident in the *halakhah* to raising popular awareness of Judaism's rich ecological heritage and engaging Jews in action that can protect our Earth-home?

A Brief Look at Other Activity in the U.S. and Britain

In the U.S.

CELEBRATING THE GIFT OF LIFE WHILE POSING HARD QUESTIONS

Everett Gendler, rabbi of Temple Emmanuel (Reform) in Lowell, Massachusetts, and until recently teacher of religion and philosophy at Phillips Andover Academy, attempts to live out his sense of nature as a "primary source of our religious inspiration." He and his wife Mary are part-time farmers on the small acreage where they live. He sometimes takes his congregation outdoors for Friday evening services that emphasize nature elements in the traditional rite and include special readings, periods of silence, meditation on trees and shrubs, and focusing on the varying qualities of the "twilights." The morning services of Sabbaths and festivals, too, are sometimes held out of doors. As congregation members face the sun, says Gendler, they chant together "that part of the service which celebrates the gift of Light and radiance of the luminaries."

He also poses hard questions. "What of our responsibilities towards the natural surroundings that sustain our lives and may exalt our spirits as well? What should be our responses to issues concerning the treatment of our own national parks and forests? What can we say in defense of our neglecting such issues as nuclear waste, chemical dumping, acid rain, or the pollution of our water supplies? If, as seems to me clearly the case, our path to redemption is through Creation, not around it, then the sooner we act decisively in light of this revelation, the better our planetary and human chances for survival and fulfillment."[27]

TRANSFORMING VALUES INTO ACTION

"We are not only trustees, but *partners* in ongoing creation. This means getting involved—Jewish values are built on deed and action," declares James Prosnit, associate rabbi at Congregation Rodeph Sholom (Reform) on New York's Upper West Side at the time we met.

Tall and sturdily built, with an engaging smile and alert dark eyes, Prosnit spoke with the rapid pace of a man engaged in a plethora of activities. He was a founding member of the Religious Leaders Media Project, an interfaith coalition concerned about peace, social justice, and the environment. In addition, Rodeph Sholom had joined the Jewish Environmental Network, a circle of Jewish schools, university groups, and other organizations in New York.

He went on to describe how in the 1980s, the congregation's concern for peace became linked with the planet. They had formed a committee on environmental action, which launched a recycling program and banned styrofoam from the temple. On the religious side, they had begun connecting ecology to Jewish holy days, especially *Sukkot* and *Tu B'Sh'vat.*

"Environmental deterioration is a good preaching issue because everybody can do something," said Prosnit. "I emphasize that we must change our financial structures and life-styles. Some changes are fairly easy, some inherently difficult. But hope is essential if people are to change their ways. A great deal depends on whether government provides structures."

WOMEN EMERGE AS A MORE VISIBLE FORCE

Although traditionally Judaism has been patriarchal, some male scholars and rabbis, such as Gendler, have begun to underline its feminine elements, and women rabbis appear particularly sensitive to the ecological dimensions of the faith. Lynn Gottlieb in Albuquerque, New Mexico; Tierzah Firestone in Boulder, Colorado; Debra Robbins in Dallas; and Laura Geller in Los Angeles are outstanding examples. Other women find imaginative ways to emphasize the feminine elements that Judaism shares with other religions. For example, the Cincinnati-based Fanchon Shur Ceremonial Dance Company has created a two-hour choreographic work, "Tallit: Prayer Shawl," described as "a movement prayer that turns the theater into a sanctuary and an audience into a sacred community." The inspiration for the dance is the *tallit*, a prayer shawl until recently worn only by men, but here opened out as "a sacred mantle joining all." Fanchon Shur says she has taken this holy cloth, used for conversations with one's inner spirit and the Infinite One, and has made it her vehicle to give voice to those who never wore it: thus it expresses all silent prayers. The dance weaves together many elements, including a ceremony celebrating *Mikvah* (a sacred water-immersion place), morning prayers, traditional Hebrew Sabbath candle blessings, and communal celebrations. As dancers and audience gather together in movement to connect the elemental energies of earth, air, fire, and water, the ritual also evokes both Native American and Goddess rites that celebrate humans' links with the earth.

In London: Educating a New Generation

While British Jewish leaders have participated in the 1986 conservation and religious festival at Assisi, the ongoing meetings of the Global

Forum of Spiritual and Parliamentary Leaders, and other such gatherings, environmentalism has not been a predominant concern in the Jewish community. Nevertheless, interest is growing, declared Jonathan Sacks, who was Rabbi of London's Marble Arch Synagogue and principal of the Orthodox seminary Jews' College at the time we met, and is now Chief Rabbi of Great Britain (representing all of British Jewry).

A dark-haired, slimly built, solemn man, he spoke in a measured way. "The environment has always been a matter of concern to Jews," he said after reflecting a long moment. "There are biblical and rabbinical teachings on the environment, and these have been practiced faithfully by all Jews for more than 2,000 years."

"And today?"

"The United Orthodox have not formed an official position. Here we are more traditional than in the States. But I have a personal interest in these questions. At Jews' College we now have a stipulation that one must go outside to smoke. More recently, I ruled that we'd be vegetarian on college grounds. Vegetarianism is not a mainstream tenet in Judaism, but it is one strand in the tradition, and in recent years I've come to vegetarianism myself. So I thought, if students can get along on vegetable protein, so much the better. Also, I lecture on environmental ethics at the college. Just last week the great Israeli expert on Jewish law, Nahum Rakover, spoke to the students on the environment. In Israel, Jews have made the desert bloom. Israel is a living example of the Jewish ecological imperative."

"So education has become a primary focus?"

"Exactly. I'm committed to training young minds for the next generation. Jewish children have also begun to raise money to plant trees after disasters as they have always done for *Tu B'Sh'vat.*"

"And environmental action on the part of the synagogue as a body?" we asked.

He looked a bit uncomfortable. "What can we do but vote for an environmentally conscious government? It's easier to identify it as a religious issue in a religious state like Israel.

"Environmental ethics depends on more than government actions," he added quickly. "It depends on the mindset of individuals. Judaism is particularly strong at teaching individuals to cherish the natural world as God's creation. More people *are* beginning to see this as a religious issue. And in our curricula today, three kinds of commandments are named: between man and man, man and God, and man and Earth. This is not an approach you'd have found a few years ago."

Israel: "Yea, We Wept When We Remembered Zion"

In the early 1900s Zionists often described their vision of Israel in phrases from Deuteronomy: "a land of brooks, of fountains and depths . . . a land of olive trees and honey."

In the late 1940s a popular song promised the new state of Israel: "Oh, our country, we will dress you in cement and asphalt!" Today that promise has been more than fulfilled.

At Tiberias, on the Sea of Galilee, the major source of Israel's dwindling water supply, highrise hotels, fast food parlors, and parking lots pave the shores. At Tel Aviv, another center of Israel's tourist industry, smog smothers drivers crawling their way down the coast. Along the asphalt highways between the Mediterranean and Jerusalem one can still see fertile stretches of olive and orange groves, vineyards, and nature reserves. But in the West Bank, olive trees have become an endangered species. From the Mount of Olives today, virtually none are visible; the landscape is graced by fortress-like apartment blocks erected for Israeli settlers. In the rest of the West Bank, and in Gaza, the land and its sources of life are under siege. Whatever the outcome of peace agreements in the next few years, formidable ecological problems will abide.

The future of both Palestinians and Israelis is threatened. The sources of the water that sustains the Land of Promise have been running so low that many predict an environmental crisis that would engulf not only Israel/Palestine but many other parts of the thirsty Middle East. In the words of former water commissioner Meir Ben-Meir, "Nobody can win this war."

The Land

On first arrival in Israel, it is difficult to understand how poets over the centuries could have rhapsodized over the beauties of Zion. Many parts of the cities look rundown, their architecture "functional" in the drabbest sense. In the countryside there are lush green farm areas and pine forest here and there, but great stretches of land are gray-brown, desolate, forbidding.

Yet the longer you linger in this promised place, the more you become aware of its peculiar beauty. The desert and the semi-desert land can change face from one hour to the next, shifting from amber to rose to ocher to delicate purples and, finally, deep darkness. You remember that the great prophets of the Abrahamic religions—Moses, Jesus, Muhammad—all prayed in the desert. As night falls, the path Jesus took down the Mount of Olives is streaked with gray-green shadows, and a soft golden light suffuses the walls of Jerusalem. On Fridays, Muslims gather at noon for their weekly communal worship; and at sunset, Jews begin to light candles for their Sabbath, activities cease, and a hush falls on the city. You begin to understand why this land is sacred to all three of these great world faiths.

Did it *become* holy through an act of sanctification by some transcendent deity? All three faiths would make such an assertion, although for each of the three, the deity bears a different name. Or could the land possess a primordial sacred quality of its own?

The Many Meanings of Zionism

The place name "Zion" has come to represent symbolically the entire land of Israel whose people had been exiled. Since biblical times, a tension has characterized the Jews' relationship to Zion. It is seen as the "holy land" promised particularly to the Israelites and their descendants, and YHWH can be properly worshipped only on this sanctified territory. On the other hand, the universalistic idea has persisted that God reigns over the whole world and can be worshipped anywhere.[28]

This tension became more complex in the twentieth century. Israel's many political parties include several secular Zionist parties, an anti-Zionist religious group that regards Zionism as preventing the coming of the Messiah, as well as several activist groups, convinced that all Eretz Israel (Greater Israel) is God's gift to Jews, and that it is an act of obedience to drive the Palestinians from their homes in order to establish settlements in the West Bank and Gaza.

Indeed, over the years the myth has persisted, even among non-religious socialist Zionists, that they were "a people without a land" who came to "a land without a people"—despite solid evidence that it had long been inhabited by a people who had produced cities, a culture, and a modest but largely self-sufficient economy.[29]

The tension between religious and secular Zionism dates back to the nineteenth century. The secularists maintained that anti-Semitism could be dealt with only by creating a Jewish homeland, a center for their own national culture. Modern Zionism goes back to Theodore Herzl and the first Zionist Congress in 1897. Like Herzl, most members of the movement were secularized and westernized, but sought to recreate a truly Jewish culture. Labor Zionists, generally more moderate than the right-wing Revisionist Zionists, became the dominant political force after Israel's birth in 1948. Since then, the rapid increase in Sephardic Jews, who did not share in the European Zionist movement or the Holocaust, has further complicated a tangled situation. The debate over whether Israel should be a religious or secular state has intensified. At the same time, the young nation has become the most powerful military state in the Middle East. A century ago, Herzl's great antagonist, Ahad Ha-Am (Asher Ginsburg), argued that a "spiritual center" in Palestine could be accomplished only by a small-scale community of no political importance. He predicted that a larger state would mean seduction of the spirit by the tendency to want material power and political dominion, and Israel would become a client state subject to "the interests" of the Great Powers.[30]

The meaning of Zionism, then, varies from one sect to another. To most Palestinians, it simply means all Jews who want to take the land where Palestinians once lived. The definition of the "promised land" is also ambiguous. Some Israelis have defined it as extending into Lebanon in the North, as far east as the Euphrates, and as far southwest as the Nile. Most leaders simply avoid outlining boundaries. All this adds to the tension one senses everywhere in Israel/Palestine.

Water, Soil, and War

Water is a sacred symbol to all three Abrahamic faiths. The Old Testament/Hebrew Bible prophet Isaiah bids the faithful to "draw water in joy from the wells of salvation," and the Qur'an reminds believers that "the heavens and the earth were of one piece, and We parted them, and We made every living thing of water." Over the millennia in this largely arid region, holy wars have been fought over this most precious of all natural resources.

For years Israel has been using water at between 15 and 20 percent beyond its replenishment rate. Israel (Israel proper and the settlements) has been taking nearly 40 percent of its waters from the West Bank. In doing so, it has been draining up to 87 percent of the West Bank's water table, leaving the small remainder to the Palestinian inhabitants.[31]

Israel has been consuming, per capita, three to four times as much water as the Palestinian entity and neighboring countries. But its reserves are diminishing, and according to water experts like Thomas Naff, desalinization is prohibitively expensive (except for low-lying areas).[32]

The River Jordan bears little resemblance to its description in the Bible. Standing on its banks, visitors may recall that a growing question among clerics today is "How can you baptize someone in water that is polluted?" Yet every year busloads of Christian pilgrims are immersed in this sacred river—and at the point where Jesus is believed to have been baptized, indeed everywhere below the Sea of Galilee, those waters are polluted.

The Israelis divert water from the Sea of Galilee (which they renamed Lake Kinneret) into a country-wide piping system which is also fed by westward-flowing aquifers, mainly those under the West Bank. They also pump saline water from springs near the Sea of Galilee/Lake Kinneret into the Lower Jordan to prevent salinization of Israel's water. Hence, people in Jordan have been getting only a small, saline, contaminated residue from the river that bears its name.

Behind all this lies an Israeli expansionism fueled by fear, distrust, a drive for an American standard of living, and what political scientists blandly refer to as "the hydraulic imperative." Over the years Israel has gained control of the Jordan and its main tributaries. When the Israelis seized the Golan from Syria in the Six-Day War, they clinched their de-facto control of the Hasbani flowing from Lebanon and the Baniyas rising in the Golan. They also seized land along the Yarmuk, which rises in Syria and has become Jordan's chief source of water. For years Israel has also managed to truck in water from the Litani in occupied southern Lebanon.

Despite these efforts, and recent moves to cut water supplies to its farmers, Israel constantly faces potentially disastrous shortages of water in agriculture and industry. Water is only one of its critical environmental problems. But most of them contribute to the worsening quality of acceptable water, which in turn worsens those problems. They are all interconnected.

The Israel Environment Bulletin, official publication of the Israeli Ministry of Environment, tells the story in detached, scientific terms. It describes, for example, the alarming growth of solid wastes, hazardous substances, marine pollution, air pollution, noise pollution, and overuse of pesticides and artificial fertilizers. The most recurrent themes are water scarcity and water quality deterioration, coupled with the problem of inadequate sewer treatment. For example, much of the water in Western Galilee is bacterially polluted, ground water along the coastal strip is so salinated that many wells have been closed, and the coastal aquifer has been contaminated. Some organic pollutants in wells and aquifers are toxic. Every year there are dozens of oil spills on the Sea of Galilee/Lake Kinneret, the Gulf of Eilat, and in the Mediterranean.[33]

Population growth—resulting from the influx of Soviet immigrants and the policy of encouraging Israeli births to compete with the Palestinian population—is rarely noted in the *Bulletin*, although occasionally one can read observations that it increases air, noise, water, and soil pollution, and contributes to the stockpile of wastes as well as the rise in demand for energy. Politicians never describe population as a problem. The environmental deterioration in the West Bank and Gaza is never mentioned by either politicians or the *Bulletin*.

Few Israelis, except settlers and soldiers, go to the West Bank and Gaza. Until recently, most foreign tourists were carefully led by official

Israeli guides to special places, such as Bethlehem, the Mount of Beati-
tudes, and Bethany. The Palestinian people—the "living stones" of Palestine, in the words of Melkite priest Elias Chacour—were rarely
encountered. However, tourists who deviated from the beaten path could
find these "living stones." Even before Palestinians spoke, the uprooted
olive trees, the bulldozed or sealed homes, the hospitals crowded with
wounded stone-throwers, the sparsely irrigated fields, the sight of women
walking miles to an ancient spring because their wells had run dry, the
scene of children playing amid garbage because there was no disposal
system—all these, and more, told the story.

It is a story of rage and retaliation leading to more rage and blood-
letting and revenge. It is not only humans that have been scarred, it is
also the land—the source of their being. Today Israelis and Palestinians
seem to be increasingly aware that this small area of Planet Earth is one
land, a land to be shared. Yet they are still far from a vision of shared
goals.

The Struggle Between the Unique and the Universal

How do present-day Israelis look at their relationship to the land?

This was our question as we sought out the Jerusalem branch of the
Society for the Protection of Nature in Israel (SPNI) during our 1990
visit. Milwaukee-born Peggy Brill, a friendly, dark-haired, green-eyed
Israeli in her 30s, welcomed us into the public relations office and spoke
with pride about efforts to conserve the country's natural heritage. SPNI
was supported by private, government, and American Zionist funding,
and had over 50,000 members. Its field study and research centers served
everyone in Israel (except Palestinians living in the Occupied Territories). The program involved every school, army unit, and immigrant
group. Almost every pupil in the school system spent at least one week
each year in experiential study of nature in Israel; children began with
their immediate surroundings, and later, gradually worked up to hiking
and field trips to all parts of the country. This experience also served to
encourage the national outlook.

We told her that we had already visited a nature center on the Gulf
of Aqaba, at Eilat. From here students made week-long excursions to the
mountains and desert to study flora and fauna. In fall they observed migrating birds. With its well-stocked library, spacious lecture rooms, bunk-
rooms, and trails, it was a beautiful place, and had enhanced our
impression that Israel had one of the most comprehensive and efficient
nature education programs in the world.

"One of SPNI's first projects was to save threatened species," said Peggy. "Wildflowers, for example. The children took the campaign so seriously that they would yell at anyone picking wildflowers—and adults took notice! Water conservation efforts have become much stronger. As you've seen, hotels even put stickers above water faucets saying 'Use no more than is really necessary.' But like other countries we've also moved backwards. For instance, we used to bring our own shopping bags. Now stores provide unlimited plastic bags, free."

She described several major SPNI campaigns: the fight against billboards, which resulted in the Anti-Billboard Law of 1979; a similar campaign culminating in the Anti-Litter Law of 1976; and successful actions to establish Carmel National Park, prevent construction of an oil refinery near a coral reef in the Gulf of Aqaba, halt building in certain wooded areas such as a pine forest of Samaria, and stop development projects in several scenic and historical areas.

"But you must understand that Israel is only now making the transition from a conservation to a real environmental approach," she cautioned. "Today we're concerned about animal and plant life—*and* air quality, the ozone layer, water. The water problem is serious."

We remembered that many Israeli writers asserted that wars had been mainly fought over control of the Jordan River and its sources in the Golan Heights. Most Israelis did not acknowledge this to foreigners, however. We framed our next question carefully. "Would it be better in the long run to work regionally on water-sharing?"

She did not answer directly. "Israel has always been interested in developing technology. Water technologies like desalination are state-of-the-art here. Whether it will prove economic is a question we debate. Another question is whether it would be more rational to export seeds rather than fruits and vegetables, which represent water."

"That could *help* solve the water problem."

"Yes. There are other technologies, too." And she described drip-irrigation and other methods of controlling environmental problems that Israelis had brought to "state-of-the-art."

"Most Israelis have an almost pious devotion to modern technology," we observed. "Yet SPNI is strong, and represents love for the land in itself. Isn't there a certain ambiguity here?"

She nodded, but did not pursue the question. "Israelis are—split—in whether their love for the land could be called 'religious,'" she said slowly. "Many would even have trouble with calling it 'spiritual.' Don't use the word 'ecospiritual' here! Still—if you dig deeper, often that *is* the implication. All this is complicated. Basically, it's important to understand that when most Israelis talk about their 'love for the land,' it's directed toward a particular piece of land and to land reclamation. Biblical references are used a great deal. In essence, it's 'I love *Israel*, and it is sacred.'"

"But this might change toward the more universal statement that the earth is sacred?"

"Well—it interests me to watch and see how much this concern will grow to one beyond its borders. Many things *are* changing. Here, you might want to read this when you get back to the hotel. It's a little essay by S. Izhar-Smolansky, one of our leading writers."

We found his words to be very moving. They spoke of the Zionist movement's urge to conquer the wilderness, to make the desert bloom. The assumptions were that wasteland and desert were bad, while making the desert bloom was good. "But empty places have force," Izhar-Smolansky concluded. "In the desert man learns a measure of humility. He begins to discover things he did not see or hear before. He sees things in the natural setting where there is a slow wisdom that surpasses our hasty wisdom, where there is greater historical harmony."[34]

"Mr. Sierra Club of Israel" and the Zionist Dream

After years of achievement—as founding father of SPNI and editor of the 12-volume *Plant and Animal Life in the Land of Israel*—Azaria Alon was struggling to retain the early vision of the Promised Land.[35]

As he made his way through the noisy Tel Aviv café where we were to find each other—we had not previously met—we saw that he was a short, stocky man apparently in his late 50s, with a tanned face, stubby hands, and graying hair. His brown jacket and loose-fitting, dull plaid shirt contrasted with the opulent attire of most of the other café patrons. It seemed ironic that this man who had dedicated himself to preservation of the natural world had had to choose this glittery world as a place to meet, simply because it was so well-known. Introducing himself, he hastened to tell us that he did not frequent such places. He lived at Beit Hashitta, a kibbutz 60 miles to the north, and came to Tel Aviv only to give lectures and do some administrative work at SPNI.

As he responded, in a reserved way, to our questions, we began to realize how difficult it must be for this pioneer to communicate to others, especially foreigners, the pain, occasional exhilaration, and complexity of his life struggle. He was born in the Ukraine 71 years ago. Not long afterward, the Communists sentenced his father, a socialist Zionist, to 10 years hard labor for "subversive" activities. Somehow the family held together, nurtured by the dream of a homeland. When he was six and his father was still in Siberia, they managed to migrate to Israel, then a land under British mandate where Arabs outnumbered Jews about seven to one.

"I went to school, joined the youth movement, and finally moved to the kibbutz. It was only two years old, and it was a very poor place, where nothing grew. We irrigated, we planted, we transformed the swamp water into fish ponds. We were living in nature. Now it is difficult to close my eyes and see how it was. What was swamp water is now serving several different systems, like the fish ponds. We changed the land-scape!" A note of pride crept into his voice.

"You were trying to make the desert bloom."

"We did make it bloom!"

"But making the desert bloom has created ecological problems?"

He shrugged. "Well—there are problems, like all the world."

"When the state of Israel was founded, many had the image of build-ing a country of concrete and asphalt."

"Many people still have it," he said cryptically. "When the everyday person becomes a decision-maker, he becomes power-hungry."

Sensing he did not want to pursue this topic, we asked about his work in founding SPNI.

He began slowly, but gradually his voice became more animated. Basically, SPNI was a private organization, but they had realized early on how important it was to get fundamental legislation in place. To get it through the Knesset (Parliament) had taken years of persistent effort. But now the country had a strong Nature Reserves Authority, and many regulations. "There is power in *law*—you don't rely on whether a person likes to do the right thing. But if citizens are not aware, laws mean nothing. In the end, power comes from education."

"You must have had to fight hard."

A flickering smile crossed his face. "There are people who respect us, people who fear us, people who hate us."

"But today you have a system that the rest of the world can envy. As for the future, do you think Israel should try to keep as much as possible of its original focus on agriculture, or take the direction of industrial development?"

"I am not a prophet. How can I know how the world will develop?" His voice sounded irritated. After a long pause, he spoke again; his voice was even, but edged with weariness. "Things have changed. Now there are so many people, everywhere. And the kibbutzim are losing money. Today it takes only one-tenth the people to produce food that once took 50 people working from dawn to dusk. Is that progress? I don't know. They do it with chemicals."

We remembered a kibbutz we had visited in 1988, which had built lavish tourist facilities because the community could no longer survive on agriculture. "But on your kibbutz, which is still agricultural, they abstain from chemicals?" we asked.

"Even on my own kibbutz . . . " He let out a scarcely audible sigh.

"Even there, I can't convince the others not to spray poisons on crops."

"And meanwhile, the quality of the soil and water continues to deteriorate, right? To say nothing of the growing shortage of water."

He nodded, without replying.

"We've seen that these problems are widespread throughout the region. Perhaps regional cooperation, including the Palestinians, could offer the greatest promise for the future."

"It is not possible! Who am I to tell Jordan what to do about what Syria is doing to its water supply?"

"What Israel is doing—isn't that where you'd have to start?"

"Look—we were in Sinai 15 years and kept it pristine as a pearl. We didn't let development touch it. We had nature centers where we did research that's never been done since. When we left, Egypt developed Sinai for tourism and the army, totally neglecting the environment."

"Yes, we saw destructive development in Sinai. But we've seen it here, too."

"I will not deny that."

"If your most basic problems are regional, then cooperation—"

Before we could finish, he was shaking his head. "Israel is an island in the Middle East. We're the *only* point where something is being done. I can only work where I am. Let them work on their problems. Americans don't understand that their relations with Canada are not like our relations—our *problems*—with our neighbors."

"They *are* immensely complicated. Even as outsiders, we can see that. But in our travels we've also seen another reality: ecological tragedies don't respect boundaries."

"That is true," he said slowly. "But we do make contributions to the international movement." He began recounting some of the Israelis' achievements. For years they had studied the migratory routes of birds crossing between Africa and Europe. A "glider man" even glided with the birds to the Egyptian border, and volunteers counted them. Israel had signed some international protocols, did research for the International Union for the Conservation of Nature (IUCN), and belonged to the Mediterranean Council, the only body uniting all the Mediterranean countries for the purpose of protecting that historic sea. Israel participated as an observer in the Governing Council meetings of the United Nations Environmental Programme (UNEP), and held seminars to teach other countries about its field research and nature conservation strategies. "That is action enough," he said firmly. "Let others worry about the Brazilian rainforest."

"We were thinking more about problems, like the water shortage, that Israel shares with her neighbors."

He did not answer.

"You have so much feeling for the land of Israel. Would you call it a religious feeling?"

"Religious?" He stiffened. "You told me before we met that you are writing a book on ecology and religion. Ecology in Israel, *that* I can talk about. But if it is religion, you are talking to the wrong person. Your religious conception is far from me."

"Our book concerns religion only in the very broadest definition of 'religion.' It is really concerned with the sense of connection with the land, other creatures, fellow human beings, and that force that many people call God—and others simply call the great mystery. We talk with many people who would never describe themselves as 'believers' in a conventional sense. We want to hear many perspectives. And as you know, better than we, Judaism is more than a religion—it represents a people and their traditions."

He reflected for a long moment. "I feel a deep commitment to the Jewish nation. I *feel* the ties of Jewish history, language, culture. But not to religion. I never based our existence in Israel on a biblical mandate, which means little to a non-believer. Rather, on the inexplicable connection of the Jews to the country through millennia, expressing itself in our return. I feel great pride that we've created a culture that's totally Hebrew and Jewish. In just this last year, 10 new Hebrew books were published *every day*. Already 21,000 people have subscribed to the plant and animal life encyclopedia I've been editing."

"You feel this bond with Jewish history and culture, an inexplicable connection to this country. And perhaps a spiritual feeling for the land?"

"Spiritual?" Again, he stiffened.

"Well, for growing numbers of people today, spiritual feelings emerge from a reverence for nature, and that reverence is not just for one particular piece of land, but for all of nature."

He stirred his cold coffee slowly, staring into the cup. "I am not without such spiritual feelings," he said at last.

After another pause, he added, "Religious, they are not. I do like to read and reread the Bible. Wherever I look, there is a place from the Bible. Tomorrow I will show slides to a group active in maintaining our culture. Some slides show nature as it is expressed in the Song of Solomon."

He seemed to be opening up, and we would have liked to talk with Alon much longer. There was so much about his life and thought that we had not touched on. But the hour was late, and it was becoming even harder to hear him as the clatter level of glasses, dishes, and insistent voices rose around us. To our surprise, he insisted on accompanying us to the bus for Jerusalem.

At the bus, he cleared his throat, then stood there in awkward silence.

We thought of his long, long struggle for the conservation of nature in this tiny country. Even in this dimly-lit, acrid-smelling setting, he stood out as a tough, stalwart figure. But he also looked lonely and tired.

He cleared his throat again. "I just want you to know—I *am* concerned about the rainforest in Brazil."

Working for Peace with the Palestinians, Peace with the Earth

For Conservative Rabbi Jeremy Milgrom, the environmental deterioration in Israel was so intimately connected with political, social, and religious problems that it sometimes seemed almost beyond repair. Yet his buoyant nature refused to accept defeatism. He wore the Yarmulke skullcap and beard we associated with rabbis, but at the same time this lanky, curly-haired six-footer with the boyish smile had a relaxed manner that we encountered only rarely in Israel. Greeting us with a warm handshake, he waved us into his tiny car.

Through friends, we knew he was born in Richmond, Virginia, in 1953, emigrated here in 1968, graduated from Hebrew University, returned to New York to study for the rabbinate at Jewish Theological Seminary, married Hilary Worms from England, and had three children.

"I still like living here," he said as we drove past carefully-tended forest preserves and farmland. "But it's provincial. The ingathering of Jews is a good idea, but it's caused us to become more ingrown. Most Israelis see Palestinians as 'the other,' with a completely different set of mores. They see Palestinians as demonic. You could say our irrational perspective is due to our insecurity. That *is* true. Israelis tend to feel the whole world is against them. But the irrationality only deepens when they keep using the Holocaust to justify more violence. The Holocaust was such a terrible but singular case, it should not be used. Palestinians and Israelis should be working together. That's one reason I became active in Yesh G'vul, soldiers who refuse service in the Occupied Territories and Lebanon. And I helped found Clergy for Peace."

We had read that this was the first truly indigenous clergy dialogue that focused on peace and justice, and included Christian, Jewish, Muslim, and Druze clerics. Unlike past dialogues, where Jews set the agenda, Clergy for Peace focused on present-day events.

The group had already accomplished some unusual things, Jeremy told us. For the first time in recent history, a rabbi had spoken during a church service in Israel—namely, at a Melkite church in that part of the country (the Galilee) where Arabs had Israeli citizenship. "We've set up clergy dialogues, and begun efforts to reach people at the grassroots, through the media, the schools, and study groups. It will be a long road, but we've begun."

"You weren't always so active in peace-making, right?"

"Right. On the contrary, I was pretty military-minded. Briefly, I was raised in a Zionist home. We first came here when I was eight, because my father taught for a year at Hebrew University. When I came back at 15, I was convinced Jews had exclusive rights to Israel. After graduating from high school here, I did three years active service—in the army and the air force, as paratrooper. But little by little I found my way into the peace movement. At Hebrew University, I was a dorm counselor. There were some Israeli Arabs there, and I came to see them as people. Then came the invasion of Lebanon and out of that came Yesh G'vul, which means, 'There is a limit'—in other words, 'That's it—I've had it!' I was drawn to the movement but didn't yet feel a commitment. Then the army sent me to Lebanon. I felt uncomfortable as an occupier. Instead of arguing it out with the officers, which would have been useless, I simply refused to eat or drink, till they finally sent me back. Since then, I've been involved in peace activities."

We knew that Jeremy also worked closely with the Palestinian Center for the Study of Nonviolence, a group that was directed by Palestinian peace activist Mubarak Awad until the Israelis deported him in 1988. We asked about their activities.

"It's a small group, especially now that Mubarak has gone. But there have been many activities. The dialogues between Israelis and Palestinians have been important. But even more important, just *being* together as human beings. Israelis spent a weekend at Beit Sahour, for example—you know the little town near Bethlehem where the people resisted the Israelis non-violently for months, and created an international interest in their cause. Israeli kids are raised in a militaristic environment. For instance, my three-year-old son was crushed when he learned I'd told the army I wouldn't carry a gun. And Palestinian kids think we Jews are all monsters. But there they all were, playing together!

"And we've worked together—Palestinians, Israelis, volunteers from other countries. We've planted hundreds of trees to replace Palestinian trees uprooted by the army and the settlers. There've been demonstrations against expulsions of Palestinians, against demolition of their homes, against depriving them of the right to dig wells as deep as those that settlers have dug. Against shooting so many people—including children—on the slightest suspicion. I do *not* excuse Palestinian violence or Palestinian provocation. But most of the killing, by far, has been done by Israelis. And these actions are laying waste to the land."

"So replanting trees has a special significance."

"Not only because tree-planting is good in itself, especially in a semi-arid country. It's also a symbol of restitution, of reconciliation. But," he added, "you know what all of us should have seen is, trees don't belong to individuals or groups. They are part of the earth."

"So you'd call the deterioration—"

"A common enemy. We should be launching a common war against that—the deterioration. Instead, we war against each other and against the environment itself."

He pondered a long moment. "Today's Zionism is—a kind of redneck ideology. Violence as a means has become an end in itself. We need to develop a new vision of Zionism."

Conclusion

During the 1990s the Jewish world has progressed, albeit fitfully, toward incorporating ecological thought into the life of the individual, the religious community, and the body politic.

In London Jonathan Sacks, now Chief Rabbi of Great Britain, has continued his efforts to encourage environmental teaching in the curricula of Jewish schools. The Board of Deputies has recently issued a book on Jewish environmental ethics.

In Israel Peggy Brill has left SPNI to move into the field of education, where she has a broader audience for environmental teaching. Azaria Alon has officially retired from SPNI, but perseveres in his commitment through seminars and discussions, as well as weekly radio broadcasts on nature conservation. Jeremy Milgrom has become disgusted with politics in his country. He has also taken leave from working as rabbi on the congregational level, has a fellowship on Islam and Judaism at the Shalom Hartman Institute, and gives talks on peace based on justice for occasional stipends. The focus of his life has become to work for sustainable peace with Muslims and peace with the earth on the personal and small group level. This new vision emerged from many sources, especially a close friendship with the family of a Palestinian imam he met on a Clergy for Peace conference in Sweden—a family he describes as "desperately poor, living in a Gazan refugee camp, but somehow held together by a certain joy, by love for each other."

In the United States Rabbi Everett Gendler has been celebrating the liturgical year in a variety of imaginative ways. For example, on the last Friday evening in October, when people recognize so definitively autumn's approaching end, the Sabbath evening service has a "Jacob's Lantern Service"—a somewhat whimsical Hebraization of the traditional American Jack o' Lantern, says Gendler. Congregants bring in carved pumpkins that shed light throughout the traditional service, augmented by poetry and music. At the Friday evening service nearest to each equinox or solstice, there is a ritual spinning of a sun wheel—accompanied by music and poetry—reminding Jews of the ancient once-every-28-years Hebrew ceremony, the Blessing of the Sun. The Eternal Light of the Temple burning perpetually above the Ark containing the Torah scroll has been converted to solar power.

Rabbi James Prosnit has moved to Congregation B'Nai Israel in Bridgeport, Connecticut. A depressed city troubled with urban blight, Bridgeport is plagued by issues of environmental justice, such as toxic dumping in the poorer areas. Rabbi Prosnit has been confronting these problems through Greater Bridgeport Interfaith Action.

Ellen Bernstein has resigned her position as head of Shomrei Adamah because it was consuming all her energies and she needed time to devote to her writing, which has become her most important mission. She took a job at the Jewish Federation of Greater Philadelphia, while concentrating on finishing a book that looks at Genesis 1 from an ecological perspective. Shomrei Adamah headquarters moved to New York, where its primary focus is the Teva Learning Center that integrates study of the natural world with Jewish learning through experiential education programs at the Center and at Jewish camps in the New York-New England-Pennsylvania area. Meanwhile, Ellen has completed and published *Ecology and the Jewish Spirit*. Gathering together the ecological understandings and practices implicit in ancient Jewish texts, it is an extraordinary collection of contributions from a wide range of American Jews. Most of them are rabbinical scholars, but they also speak out of direct experience with the natural world—trekking through wilderness, kayaking, farming, and seeking ways to be good "keepers of the earth."

Increasing numbers of synagogues and temples across the country are celebrating *Tu B'Sh'vat* with seders built around environmental issues and presentations that include plans for action. Children's programs—songs, drama, story-telling, ecofables, special seders for youngsters—always play an important role in these celebrations. More rabbis, too, have introduced environmental themes into their preaching and initiated recycling programs. Like their Christian counterparts, however, many stop short of linking these small local actions to broader social and political issues, or to difficult choices in personal life-style.

One sign of hope in this realm is the ecumenical National Religious Partnership for the Environment (NRPE). All four Jewish branches are represented—a feat in itself, as one spokesperson put it. Together they form the Coalition on the Environment and Jewish Life, an alliance within the Partnership, and have published *To Till and to Tend*: *A Guide to Jewish Environmental Study and Action*. As congregations exchange ideas on ecological prayers, community actions, and reducing personal consumption, Jewish concepts of "stewardship" acquire fresh meaning.[36]

In its worldview Judaism has long stressed the element of law. Early Judaism also stressed the community even more than the individual.

Like other monotheists, Jews have wrestled with the question: If God has all the power, why is it that the people He loves suffer from droughts, famine, and plagues?

Tikva Frymer-Kensky's *In the Wake of the Goddesses* offers a provocative answer—one that could also provide reflection for those who think less in terms of God than "the divine." The Bible, says this scholar of ancient Near Eastern religions, explains disasters in nature and history as God's reaction to human deeds. If the people of Israel pollute the land of Israel, the consequences are inevitable: they will be cast out of the land in order that the land can return to its healthy state.

Paradoxically, the solo power of God over rain and fertility means that, ultimately, it is the people of Israel—individually and collectively—who determine, less by their prayers than their actions, whether rain comes. God's behavior toward nature, then, is reactive. Yet in a sense drought or disaster also present opportunity: time for the people to search out the causes and to pray for compassion with a repentant heart. In the final analysis, what happens to the natural world depends on the behavior of human beings toward nature, toward God, and toward each other. Biblical monotheism, she says, is indeed anthropocentric, but not in the sense that the world exists to serve humanity. Rather, it is on humans' interaction with God that the world depends.[37]

3

WESTERN CHRISTIANITY: ITS TWO GREAT TRADITIONS

Three Catholics in Action

Carrying the Vision to Children

"If you mess around with Mother Nature, expect the worst," Thomas Berry warned an audience of business people, educators, and public officials at a conference on the stately grounds of Wainwright House in Rye, New York.

Berry was quoting environmental activist Christopher Tucker, a 13-year-old member of Kids for the Earth. Soon after the club was formed at Nichols Middle School in Mount Vernon, New York, Christopher contributed a cautionary tale to his group's first newsletter. Entitled "Mother Nature's Revenge," it portrayed the poisonous track of a chemical used by an unthinking farmer as it made its way through the food chain and ultimately back to the farmers' own children. Moral: "If you mess around . . . "

In its first year of existence, Kids for the Earth managed to shake up the establishment to a degree that its founder and advisor, Sister Patricia Monahan, had never anticipated. Members wrote state senator Guy Velella such eloquent letters that he came to the school and addressed the group on how the state was responding—and failing to respond—to the

environmental crisis. The group convinced the city and the management
of a large apartment complex to institute the first multi-dwelling newspaper recycling project in Westchester County. It persuaded the Board of
Education to order that polystyrene products like plates and drinking
cups be replaced by biodegradable utensils. That success upset Amoco
Oil so much that the company issued a formal invitation to the pupils to
visit its factory and inspect its efforts to recycle plastics. "Amoco treated
the kids like VIPs!" recalls Sister Pat with a chuckle.

We first met Sister Pat at the Riverdale Center for Religious Research
during a meeting of the Teilhard Association, a circle concerned with the
convergence of social and spiritual issues. At one point we broke up into
discussion groups to brainstorm ideas for the ideal academic institution.
As our group launched into the ecological aspect, a small woman with
short, brown curly hair, intense hazel eyes, and a quick smile introduced
herself as Pat Monahan and began a fervent description of the creative
ways her seventh- and eighth-grade pupils were responding to the challenge of preserving the earth. Her eyes danced as she recited a poem by
Andrew McPhillips:

America the Beautiful

If America's so beautiful,
How come some parts look so bad?
With all the dirty beaches,
Boy! The Indians would be sad.

Some parts had real nice forests.
But now there's not so many.
And if we don't preserve them,
In a few years there won't be any.

We'd better fix it up
And work on it real soon.
Because if we don't
We'll be settled on the moon!

After the meeting, as people gathered to chat over wine and cheese,
we nabbed her. Pat's eagerness to share ideas and experiences seemed
unlimited. "I've always loved working with kids," she said. "But this past
year, Thomas Berry's ideas have rejuvenated my teaching and opened up
a whole new world to me."

After talking with her several times, a picture of Pat began to emerge.
This is her story, and the story of the first years of Kids for the Earth,
which she continues today at another school.

She sees Thomas Berry as her shaman, the spiritual guide who opens
up a new vision. "The first time I read his work, I got very excited. It

Sister Pat Monahan with members of Kids for the Earth.

was awakening something already in me. I thought a long time. In my computer and English classes, I could implement some of his ideas!"

When Senator Velella addressed the club, Pat stood by, occasionally asking a question, but for the most part letting the youngsters take the lead. Eighth-grader Tara Scullin asked the senator why county officials were asking for an extension of a federal regulation that would ban ocean dumping in two years. The pupils did not seem completely satisfied with his reply that local governments had a hard assignment, but would not get a formal extension unless their plan was in place. When Christopher asked how to lobby for a recycling plant in Westchester County, Senator Velella told him to organize a rally at the County Offices the day the legislators were meeting.

The group rallied, carried signs, sang songs, and gave out its newsletter; some even dressed up as stuffed garbage bags. County Executive Andrew O'Rourke invited them to meet the legislators, and two students addressed them. That day a bill to build a recycling plant was passed.

Students also petitioned the Board of Education to stop using polystyrene in the lunch program. Would students pay five cents extra for the added cost of biodegradable utensils? the Board asked. The club circulated a questionnaire. Over 400 of the 500 students said "Yes!"

Although the poor suffer most from environmental degradation, it is common wisdom that only the middle class will be motivated to act. Yet many pupils at the school come from low socio-economic backgrounds. Over 80 percent are African-American or Hispanic.

"Children who have chosen to spend their free time during lunch and after school working for Kids for the Earth learned that they can make a difference, even in a drug-burdened environment," says Pat. "The club touches a sensitivity that lies deep within every child. They enjoy cleaning up the grounds, recycling, planting flowers around town, learning about the oceans, and feeling a part of the larger Earth community— something mysterious and beautiful. Children have a natural affinity with Earth."

How did Pat's new spiritual journey begin?

"As a child, I loved being outdoors, watching birds, marveling at ant hills and butterflies. My first baby-sitter and companion was Pal, our collie-chow dog. We played together, digging holes in the backyard. My spirituality has always been Earth-inspired. I always loved St. Francis of Assisi, especially his simplicity and love of nature.

"But there is a difference, a big difference," she reflects slowly. "Now I realize the earth continues to unfold within the universe as an expression of mystery. Call it God if you will. I don't use that word because it means we've defined God as a transcendent father rather than an immanent force of radial energy. I'd call it love. Particularly since reading Tom Berry's work, I've come to realize I'm part of the universe in its human expression. I'm a participant in this ongoing event—along with every other being. This is my spirituality! It's what energizes my life!"

After 17 years in various posts, Pat moved to Mount Vernon to be a support to her aging father, and quickly found a position in a public school, teaching computers.

Appropriately enough, a month at Genesis Farm in 1988 marked the genesis of Pat's absorption in Thomas Berry's new cosmology. "I was browsing through the library and found Tom's Riverdale Papers and five audiotapes. Soon I read everything of his I could find.

"For some time I'd begun to feel that institutional religion was losing its inspiration for me. It was frightening. Was I losing my faith? My spiritual director, a Franciscan priest, told me once that while yes, the earth is beautiful, it's on the material level; the time would come when I wouldn't need its inspiration. I couldn't imagine such a time. But now here was someone saying that Earth is the primary scripture, the primary revelatory event.

"I spent a lot of time in meditation, prayer, thought, and study. I was awakening to a new understanding of spirituality, a new relationship to the whole of Creation and the Creator.

"Then Tom came out to the farm and I told him of the inspiration he'd given me. He smiled, so modestly. I was struck by the profound simplicity of this great man.

"Well, he told me about the Riverdale Center, just 15 minutes from where I live. I joined, took an introductory course in ecology at SUNY Purchase/NY, so I could be better informed, and began introducing ecological themes into my writing classes. Students responded so well that we decided to start Kids for the Earth."

When we asked how she introduced these themes, Pat looked pensive. "Well, I write poetry and prose myself. And I've always found that children enjoy writing if the subject really interests them. And I discovered that their concern for the earth is a great motivator for self-expression. For instance, I discussed illegal dumping with them. We sent for material from Clean Ocean Action and the EPA. We linked dumping to depleted species of animals and fish. SoundWaters, a floating classroom on Long Island Sound, invited us on a sail to study sea life and discuss the problem and its solutions. All these experiences went into volumes as a resource for others.

"Students kept an eye out for articles. Like one day we discussed the Exxon Valdez oil spill, after Tajian Jones brought in a story on it from the Science section of the *New York Times*. It gave statistics about the fish, animals, and birds that had been put at risk. We drew a lesson—it's high time to find an alternative to fossil fuels. Here's the story in our newsletter, with sketches showing ocean pollution—illegal dumping, garbage, oil spills, and fish kills."

We thumbed through the newsletter. "They all seem to have imaginative artwork, sketches of harmful household products, vegetables and fruits, marine life, rainstorms."

Pat nodded. "And, as you can see, stories, essays, sketches, crossword puzzles, interviews, cartoons, and poetry.

"Even though many children think they could never write a poem?"

She laughed. "Not these kids, when they write about nature! They've even written Cinquain and Haiku poetry on themes like 'Snowflakes.' Our classroom is full of colorful photographs, bulletins, and the kids' work. I've collected some into an anthology and they love showing it off and reading through its treasures themselves.

"Children feel valued for their ideas and their persons. They appreciate adults who listen and take them seriously. There are no grades, yet everyone's involved. Each one is special, and yet they all work together for the common good. There are gifted children working alongside ones with special needs. What they all have in common is a feeling for the earth."

Throughout this new experience, Thomas Berry was Pat's mentor. He guided her reading, with suggestions from others' works and his own. Particularly meaningful to Pat was an essay he wrote, entitled "Our Children: Their Future," which begins:

> Our children will live not in our world but in their world, a future world that is rapidly taking on its distinctive contours. Our exploitive industrial world, despite all our scientific discoveries, is in a state of decline. Their long-term survival will depend on a new relationship between the human and the natural worlds. A change is taking place from exploitive relationships to a relationship of mutual enhancement between the natural and the human worlds. The type of prosperity known in the better moments of the twentieth century will never again be available. A new prosperity, however, will be available. Our children must activate this prosperity in the great variety of human activities.[1]

Berry then comments on basic needs of the young under the headings of Health and Environment, the Great Society, Literacy, Energy, Food, the Managerial Role, Revelatory Experience, A Sense of History, and America.

Using these ideas, Pat worked out a Children's Bill of Rights for an Ecological Age:

Children have an inalienable right to:

*   a future with fresh air, pure water, and fertile soil;

*   nutritious food which is free of harmful chemicals and preservatives;

*   an education which will prepare them to function with the energy of the sun, wind, and water rather than fossil fuels or nuclear processes;

*   learn about the community of all living and non-living beings of the natural world;

*   learn gardening so that they can actively participate in the deepest mysteries of the universe;

*   nurture and be nurtured in a universe that is always precarious but ultimately benign;

*   become literate in the language of the earth, a language of living

relationships that extend throughout the universe.

"Even though I don't use this wording with children, I must have communicated the principles, because they spontaneously come up with delightful insights. Like one youngster saying, 'The Earth is so special, we should always write it with capital letters.' So now we do!

"And I think of one girl's response to the fill-in 'Earth is—' She wrote: 'Earth is sometimes good, sometimes bad. We could help it by recycling and stopping dumping!' Tom loved it. 'That child is so right!' he said. 'The Earth can often be violent. But it is ultimately benign.'"

She continued to be sustained by Berry's encouragement. For instance, he sent her a note: "Pat, your project for the younger folk is perfect. They can learn writing skills and thinking and civics and cosmology and biology and religion and behavior all together."

"Also, I often checked out specific ideas with him. I'd call and say, 'Hi, Tom, Got a minute?' And he'd say, 'Forget the phone. Want to come over this afternoon?' He's just about the busiest person I know, but he'd drop everything. So we'd go to the Broadway Diner, and we'd talk away. He loved the stories about what the children were doing and he'd lean back and laugh at some of the marvelous things they came up with. Like 'Rainbows are surprises that smile in the sky after a rainstorm.' Or the story called 'It's Tough Being a Turtle,' which started 'How would you feel if some greedy person killed you to make expensive wallets and shoes out of your skin?' Both eventually went into the club newsletter."

After learning that the school was dropping lunchroom polystyrene products, Amoco wrote the club a formal letter, informing it that the company could recycle, and inviting it to visit. Before the trip, Pat discussed with the children some basic facts: plastic, degradable or not, is made from oil, which is polluting and non-renewable; and technology used to convert crude oil into plastic resins creates enormous amounts of hazardous waste. "We must use recyclable products that came from renewable resources. But we must do *more*—we must *reduce* wasteful use. And most important, appreciate the earth not as a resource for humans but as an interdependent community of life; the human is only a part. So even though we listened respectfully during the visit, the children didn't accept Amoco's basic position that we must continue to manufacture plastics because Americans are addicted to convenience."

During Kids for the Earth's first spring, members continued to support the newspaper recycling effort at the Lefrak apartment complex. On Labor Day weekend, that project was publicly recognized at a public ceremony. Among the speakers were the mayor, Westchester's Commissioner of Public Works, and Christopher Tucker. "For recycling to succeed, three things are necessary," he told the crowd. "First, separating out things that *can* be reused or recycled. Second, transporting them, and we thank Mayor Blackwood for helping us with that. Third, a market for recycled newspaper. We need everybody's cooperation, especially the local newspapers. Can you accept that challenge?" Laughter and applause swept through the audience. "Kids for the Earth are here to help," he went on. "We're going to put up posters in the hallways to remind people to separate the newspapers. We'll also distribute our newsletter to all tenants."

THE NEW GROUP GROWS AND SPREADS

Kids for the Earth has acquired a fame that still astonishes Pat. "What I've been trying to do is to actualize Tom Berry's idea that our children need to see themselves as members of the whole life community," she says. "That seems to be just what's happening. Throwing a pebble into a pool starts ripples, circles move out to the edge, then back. Gradually our circle widened from the club to the entire school, to other schools, to the local political and business world. Later, the state, national, and international communities. And still we've remained rooted in our immediate circle, the school—with our eyes on the larger community of life."

Consciousness-raising within the school community expanded. Besides sponsoring poster contests and setting up student forums, they led other pupils in recycling in the lunchroom. They arranged for outside speakers from adult groups like the League of Women Voters and youth groups like the Student Environmental Action Coalition to make presentations at the school. Sometimes they visited classes in other schools to spread the "green word." For example, one group visited a class of third-graders, read them a fable called "The Giving Tree," discussed the contribution that trees make to the planet, taught the pupils a song called "Dear Earth," and suggested they write "thank you" notes to Mother Earth for the many gifts from trees. Then the younger ones were invited to close their eyes, remember one special tree, and draw it at the bottom of the note. A few weeks later, the class had a tree-planting ceremony at which they sang "Dear Earth"; the notes were buried in the ground, and club members helped the younger pupils plant the tree. Since then the youngsters have tended the new life.

Kids for the Earth even succeeded in teaching teachers a lesson or two. Noticing that the adults were using styrofoam cups at faculty meetings because they were "cheaper and convenient," the students decided to give them coffee mugs, placed in a large box marked ADOPT-A-MUG . . . THEY'RE EARTH FRIENDLY! How could teachers say "No"? Especially when the students assured them the mugs would be washed for them after each meeting.

In the local community, club members persevered in their quietly assertive role. Cooperating with the city's beautification committee, they planted flowers at City Hall, outside shops, and along the parkway. Sometimes they formed working alliances with adult organizations like the Audubon Society, League of Women Voters, and the "floating class-room" SoundWaters. Each fall, these young ecologists teamed up with hundreds of adults to clean area beaches.

With all its recognition from establishment organizations, Kids for the Earth continued to "speak truth to power." When the Environmental Protection Agency sent the club a package in an envelope lined with plastic bubbles instead of one made of recycled fibers, indignant members wrote EPA, suggesting a change. It wrote back that plastic-lined envelopes were lighter, hence cheaper to mail. In a tactful rejoinder, Kids for the Earth noted that this was hardly a way for an environmental agency to set an example, especially to young people. EPA's answer was that "further study of the issue" was needed. Months passed. The pupils wrote again: "Why is it taking the EPA so long to make the right decision?" Finally, 10 months after their initial complaint, EPA yielded.

Work on the state level included participation in Cornell University's "Environmental Leadership: Beyond Today," and in the New York State Environmental Competition, where Ramsey Barnes won one first place for his essay "The Life Cycle of a Piece of Paper" and Michelle Henderson, another first place for her poster/essay on "Aluminum Recycling." At the national conference of Future Homemakers of America, Taz Guishard won first place for his illustrated talk on "Vermicomposting." "It's nature's way of recycling organic waste," explained Taz to his audience. "We built a wooden worm bin and added moist newspapers for bedding, a couple of pounds of red worms, then organic food scraps from the students in the lunchroom boycott group. Soon the worms transform the scraps into rich fertilizer. Then it's stored in bags. In spring it's mixed with potting soil and we plant our marigold seeds. Later these plants beautify the community." Taz's work was published in the July 1993 edition of *National Geographic World*.

Moving to the international level, six members joined the Student Environmental Action Coalition to frame an environmental statement from the youth of the world. "They were thrilled," Pat recalls, "when Al Gore addressed them, and even more excited to hear that their statement was included in the final statement at the Global Youth Summit in Costa Rica."

For Pat personally, what she describes as her "most meaningful experience—just speaking as a woman," came when she was chosen by the Global Assembly of Women and the Environment to present her "success story" at its world gathering in Miami in 1991. Two hundred eighteen women, most of them from poor countries, described grassroot projects ranging from designing smokeless stoves and solar cookers to defending the rainforest. All the projects met the criteria of repeatability, affordability, sustainability, visibility. "I can't describe the *gratitude* I felt to be among such brave women," she recalls. "Many wore native dress—absolute elegance! There were beautiful performances of dances from many cultures. But when we all joined in dance, it wasn't Caribbean or Peruvian or African dancing; we were women of the world dancing as one."

"Could you tell us more about the women?" we asked.

"Many live at the edge of disaster, including desertification, poverty, and sickness. They're just like us, but their problems are so much worse. These women are *strong*. I remember a Filipino woman who told of halting highway construction that would cause erosion and flooding, by standing in front of bulldozers. They killed one priest. I met another woman who attached herself to a tuna boat in a campaign to save dolphins that get caught in huge tuna nets, and a Ghanaian woman who spent hours every day fetching wood, until she and her sisters learned to use methane gas from compost. When Mustafa Tolba, the Executive Director of the United Nations Environmental Program, gave the opening address, he said, 'Women are often considered voiceless, but today they're challenging the world to listen to their messages and use their capacities.'"

"What were some of the reactions to your project?"

"Amazement that so much is possible with children of color. And many wanted to repeat the ideas—in their own way, of course. These women were so eager to learn from each other!

"I learned many things. How much women all over the world have in common. How serious the population problem is. We're approaching the carrying capacity of the planet. I realized the power of story. In ancient times story-telling was the most important way of communicating a message within the community, and across time from one generation to another. Story-telling is face-to-face, and reaches deeper levels of the personality than mass communication. It's particularly suitable for women. And children, especially, love stories."

"One wonders what stories *their* children will be able to tell."

She nodded, and a smile that seemed to express both sadness and hope passed over her face. "One wonders. But I know that what these women are doing is for the children, and *their* children and grandchildren."

After the Global Assembly, the world came rippling back to the original circle. A woman who heard Pat talk at the Assembly selected her story for Renew America's *Success Index*. "Students from several states have been in touch with us and we've heard from as far away as Colombia and Palestine," says Pat.

Every year, indeed every week, new opportunities have presented themselves . . . just bubbling up from the imaginations of Pat and her pupils. What happens might be likened to the dynamics of process theology, for it is totally open and responsive. Unfettered by established "Truths," but led by a guide who nurtures the Child in herself, they perceive what needs to be done, and then *do* it. The school yard is regularly junked up with litter and graffiti. So . . . club members clean up the school grounds, paint over the graffiti, and plant trees and flowers. It works! Children can't teach their own parents anything? Well, give it a try! Many club members have convinced their parents to recycle newspapers, not buy non-recyclable juice boxes for school lunches, and most importantly, to *pre*-cycle—that is, reduce waste before it happens.

Pat herself has continued to discover and re-invent new ways of expressing her love for the earth. At Genesis Farm, she and Maureen Wild have responded to requests of parents and teachers for a workshop. They have conducted a two-week workshop for teachers and interested adults entitled "Teaching the Universe Story." Wainwright House hosted Pat and her associate Margarita Urrea for a six-week series entitled "Activating a New Prosperity for Our Children."

"Anybody can do it," Pat insists. "For me, it has snowballed over the years. Tom, Miriam, Margarita, Maureen, and other friends have all worked together. Everyone says 'Yes!' to our requests. It's hard to say 'No' to children speaking the truth. The important thing is, we're not just changing things for the betterment of the human community. As Tom says, 'We are reinventing the human at the species level.' We're discovering our place within the larger life community.

"Adults are becoming increasingly interested in sharing the unfolding story of the universe. Maureen and I discovered that from our adult workshops at Genesis Farm. Retired teachers, grandparents, young parents, single women, college professors . . . they're all open and enthusiastic about spreading the story through their lives in some way."

Her face glows with quiet excitement. "I've made new friends in the most unexpected places. I feel the universe is awakening and finding its voice through me. I feel fully alive."

Do the children actually sense that they belong not just to the human community, but the whole life community? Pat recalls that Ronald Jones confided to her, "I want to begin a Kids for the Earth group at the high school next year. I want people to know that the earth is one big family. A family working together. That's the only way we can make things better."

Celebrating the Earth

Miriam Theresa MacGillis, OP, is a Dominican sister who founded Genesis Farm, a reflection center that seeks to combine global community with ecology and sacred agriculture. In 1977, captivated by Berry's thought, she speaks all over the country on his ideas and the need for our culture to actualize them in everyday life. She possesses a talent for telling the universe story in a way that draws listeners into the experience itself; one can almost sense the evolutionary unfolding of the Creation process.

We first met Miriam, a graceful woman with wavy graying hair, quick expressive hands, and bright blue eyes that connect with you at once, at Calumet College of St. Joseph, where she was keynote speaker for "A Festival of Creation."

She talked easily of her early formative experiences. "I was born in an ethnic neighborhood of Bayonne, New Jersey. We had little money, but my father managed to buy some land in a remote wooded New Jersey area, where I came to know the Musconetcong River and the forest and all its creatures in an intimate way. I didn't realize it then, but my deepest soul experiences were formed in that place. After joining the Dominicans, I studied and taught art.

"But as the Vietnam War dragged on, I became involved in the peace movement. That led to studying world hunger and working with Pat Mische, co-founder of Global Education Associates. Meeting Tom Berry opened up a new world. We published some of his papers. And I began giving talks on his new cosmology."

During the festival weekend, termed "an open, celebrative, liturgical event," we listened to environmentalists, politicians, and religious figures speak of the challenge confronting the human species; participated in workshops; and joined small rituals in which we shared bread and wine and painful personal experiences of witnessing the earth being wounded. And at the end we all gathered together in a great circle to form a "Council of All Beings," a celebration of all the animate and inanimate creatures of the world, each of us taking the part of a species endangered with extinction. Then we sang and danced in the great circle, united in hope.

Miriam's talks were also permeated with hope. Acknowledging her profound debt to Thomas Berry, she spoke of our "disconnectedness." Our definitions of community are so human-centered that they simply cannot give us a full sense of community, she told us. The universe is the basic sacred community! And *we* are the community reflecting on itself. We are the skin, the very tissue of this wondrous earth. Some five billion years ago, the solar system began to evolve, and a billion years later, the beginnings of what we might call "the living earth." One could begin to grasp the five billion years of our solar system by looking at that period as if it were one year. Four months ago, life as we know it began. The human entered Earth only in the last 24 hours. Only in the last half hour did recorded history begin. That should be something for humans, with their hubris, to reflect upon. Yet in these past seconds they have decided to create technologies that are inconsistent with the evolutionary process! They are trying to improve on it to get rid of chaos, death, pain, the mystery. . . . And Miriam continued on with the universe story.

In her talks across the country these themes always emerge. She also emphasizes that unlike Mars, Earth is a water planet. "That is why the earth is alive. Seventy percent of its surface is salt water. One single salt water system. A banana, cat, human, tree—everything is of salt water. These fluids are in the oceans and ponds and rivers—and in *you*. No matter what you weigh, 70 percent of you is salt water. Oceans become clouds, which turn into rain, which is transformed into corn and milk, which are ingested into our bodies. We excrete into the ground and thus eventually into the ocean. It is all one system. And so when we cry, we cry the ocean. When we excrete, we excrete the ocean. We are the earth! And *you*"—Miriam thrusts her hands toward the audience—"you are the child of the fireball!

"But we are also the beings through whom the earth thinks, knows, judges, acts, chooses." she continues. Recalling a piece by liberation theologian Ruben Alves, she offers a challenge: "We can make choices. Like people who live in desert oases, we can choose to plant date palms that will not bear fruit for 80 years or more, beyond our own lifetimes. We can do it for the sake of our grandchildren. Let us live by the love of what we never will see! Let us *plant dates*!"

On our visit to Genesis Farm, 140 acres of gently rolling land in northwestern New Jersey, where deer, foxes, wild turkeys, and an occasional bear still roam the hills, we could see some of the planting. Certain efforts have already borne fruit, but others will not return a visible yield for many years to come. There are the beginnings of permaculture, for instance—a long-term strategy of seeking to learn nature's own design principles and incorporate them into a way of living creatively with the ecosystem. Permaculture seeks to build small, nearly self-sufficient human communities within the larger earth community. Already the farm has constructed houses made with bales of straw, a material that comes from the vicinity, is cheap, and has high insulation value. As with traditional Irish cottages, the bales are bound with wire, and stuccoed together; then the house is completed with a floor and a roof.

Genesis Farm works in various ways with the human community. The gardeners follow the Rudolf Steiner "biodynamic" method, preparing the seed with reverence, sowing them according to cosmic forces like the alignment of stars, and setting the seed out in terms of "companion planting." Local people purchase shares in the community-supported garden, in which 150 people pay in advance for the seeds and the salaries of the four gardeners. Shareholders come every week to pick up the produce, and may also participate in tending the broccoli, beans, squash, tomatoes, and other vegetables. There are horses, beehives, a greenhouse for seedlings, and maple trees that provide sap from which visitors make syrup every spring.

Workshops offer topics ranging from "cooking the natural way" to "parenting for a peaceful earth"; Native Americans speak about the land and the Minsi who inhabited it for at least 7,000 years; local children learn to make connections between nature and the spiritual; and the staff works with local environmental commissions to promote land trusts and other farsighted uses of the land. They also celebrate Celtic planting rituals and maple sugaring festivals, hold Holy Week retreats, and convene workshops on adjusting to the "new cosmology" that will guide humans toward living harmoniously with the natural world. Through affiliation with St. Thomas University, the Ecological Learning Center offers accredited undergraduate and graduate certificate programs.

Perhaps the most central question discussed at Genesis Farm is: How should the traditional Judeo-Christian-Islamic cosmology be reshaped so that Western society can understand recent discoveries about the earth as a living organism? It is hard to grasp the evolution of the universe and the earth on an intellectual level alone; somehow the awesomeness of the time-space of the universe should be experienced. One way to begin is the "cosmic walk" designed by Miriam. The narrator recites an opening that parallels the prologue to John's gospel: "In the beginning was the dream . . . Through the dream all things came to be . . . " Then the walker lights a personal candle from a candle representing the universe that came into being 15 billion years ago, and slowly begins to walk through a spiral marked by a rope representing the time-line of the universe. Key cosmic events are celebrated: the emergence of the solar system five billion years ago; of oxygen two billion years ago; the first fish, 520 million years ago; the first birds, 180 million years ago; modern homo sapiens, 40,000 years ago; Abraham, the patriarch of three religions, 3,800 years ago; splitting the atom, 50 years ago, and so on. At each, the walker lights a vigil candle. Then others go to the "universe candle" to light their candles and walk the journey.

When we asked Miriam about the institutional church, she shook her head slowly. "If church leaders could look with open eyes at the revelations from seeing with new eyes what God has been up to, all these billion years! They'd realize the images they use to convey the mysteries of their traditions are dysfunctional. That's why I believe the new cosmology is so important!"

As we said goodbye, she gestured toward the gardens, beehives, and farmlands, the tall trees around which people gather for rituals, and the green hills in the distance. For a long moment her eyes rested on the scene, and then she smiled softly. "Reinhabiting this particular place is our way of connecting with the whole earth."

Building a Franciscan Environmental Center in Rome

Since 1990 the Vatican has sponsored the Franciscan Center for Environmental Studies in Rome. Headed by Father Bernard Przewozny, a compatriot of Polish-born Pope John Paul II, it has been a new departure for the Roman Catholic Church. Before we met Father Bernard at the Center headquarters early in 1990, several Italians told us cynically that it had been created for political purposes, as a belated response to public concern for environmental deterioration and to the activities of Protestant churches.

Father Bernard, a compactly built, dark-haired, middle-aged man who exuded nervous energy, insisted that ecology had been an abiding interest of the Vatican. "Ever since Lynn White wrote that *erroneous* paper blaming Christianity for the crisis, we Franciscans have wanted to do something!" he declared fiercely, leaning toward us from behind his book-stacked desk. "We don't even agree with his proposing St. Francis as patron saint of ecology. Respect for nature runs *all* through our Scriptures. Besides, the widespread notion that St. Francis was a 'mystic of nature' in the sense of pantheism is highly misleading. His view was Christ-centered. The praise is to God, not to Brother Sun and Sister Moon and so forth. Because Christ has suffered, nature has suffered. God created and redeemed all creatures, *therefore* they are our brothers and sisters.

"Of course St. Francis and the Franciscans are important," he added quickly. "In 1982 Italian environmentalists organized a meeting and invited both scientists and Franciscans. It was held in Gubbio, the site of Francis' encounter with *il gubbio*, the wolf—a most fitting symbol of reconciliation with nature. The document they produced was enthusiastically received, even by the European Parliament. In 1986 the World Wildlife Fund held a conference on ecology and religion—in Assisi,

Francis' birthplace. In 1987 there was another conference at Gubbio, with representatives of other religions, and many there pressed the Franciscans to establish a center.

"Finally, in 1988 we got a go-ahead. However, it won't actually open till later this year. Throughout these years we've worked on other projects—the International St. Francis Prize for environmental projects, and at Assisi, a 'Green Altar,' a beautiful garden of plants and trees that possess a special meaning in the world's great religions. Last year Franciscans and the International Ecological Association co-sponsored the first Latin American congress on ecology. We're also preparing a volume of papal pronouncements on the environment."

When Father Bernard excused himself for a few minutes, he left us with two of his writings: an article called "Il Problema Ecologico" in the Vatican's *L'Osservatore Romano*, and a booklet entitled *Ecologia Francescana*, of which he was the principal author.[2] Designed to "list some of the elements which seem essential to a Catholic understanding of humankind's role in the biosphere," it included biblical references and Church pronouncements to make it clear that Christianity, especially Roman Catholicism, was permeated with respect for nature. It also included strong criticism of those who pointed to the Judeo-Christian value system as a cause of the environmental crisis. One passage declared that "naive believers were initially manipulated by conservationists—for example, the European Green movements, in favor of non-religious ideologies." Another referred approvingly to the criticism by Joseph Ratzinger (the arch-conservative cardinal who has headed the Congregation for the Doctrine of the Faith, and has been considered the most powerful Vatican figure, outside the Pope) of the "liberal and Marxist ideologies which inspire certain European 'Green' movements." Others warned that hasty interreligious dialogue on the environmental disaster may expose itself to the danger of syncretism. A long section in "Il Problema Ecologico" was devoted to a vehement attack on the "systematic campaigns" to blame environmental deterioration on "the demographic problem" (which the document did concede to be a problem "in certain parts of the world"), and asserted that such campaigns were conducted "without any respect for the cultural and religious identity of the people."

Upon Father Bernard's return, he began talking of plans for the environmental center. They were impressive: a three-year interdisciplinary program, leading to an advanced Master's degree, which included sciences, cultural anthropology, cosmology, ethics, global strategies, and the contribution of monastic orders. Considering the elaborate preparations, and the magnitude of the ecological disaster, we were somewhat surprised to learn that while they expected to have a faculty of 30, only 15 students would be allowed to enroll, five graduating each year.

When we asked his opinion of Berry's ideas, Father Bernard's lips tightened. From "a Catholic point of view," they were "probably too organicist" and verged on pantheism. He had no problem with evolution, added Father Bernard, but he did with "evolutionism." Humans should not be treated reductionistically; they were unique, endowed with unique self-consciousness and responsibilities. To our comment that Berry would not dispute that humans had those special qualities, he responded that he had not read Berry's writings, but only reviews.

Reflections

The two women portrayed in this section certainly do not fit the conventional image of nun, and the priest, although domiciled in the citadel of Roman Catholic power, seems to be on the defensive. They are part of the ferment that is agitating the Western church today.

It is a quiet revolution. Like a great many other Christians, Sister Pat and Sister Miriam are not satisfied with the state of the organized Church. But neither are they rebelling against the fundamental tenets of the faith—namely, the belief in one God who is yet a trinity: Father, Son, and Holy Ghost. A theistic God—one who reigns over the cosmos and humans, listens to prayer, and intervenes in human affairs. A God who is not only all powerful, but just, and grants life everlasting in Paradise to those who fully accept Jesus Christ and repent of their sins.

Many other beliefs—such as original sin, the historical truth of the Bible, and the existence of Satan, Hell, and Purgatory—are more subject to theological dispute. Furthermore, Protestants are divided into more than 2,000 sects.

The concept of a God the Father who intervenes in human affairs does not accurately represent Pat's or Miriam's belief. Pat, for example, experiences God as "the Life Spirit, the energy of love that permeates the universe." Still, they are not nailing new theses upon the church door. They are spending their energies elsewhere—on expanding the boundaries of the faith.

Miriam and Pat do sense that Christianity is changing. They know that centrifugal forces are growing. Christianity has always been a missionary religion, ever seeking converts to the "one true faith." It has succeeded so well that today nearly two-thirds of all Christian believers live in the so-called Third World. Ironically, their cultures, once considered to be on the "periphery," are reshaping Western Christianity. In the belief that the broken alienated peoples of the First World are those who most need to hear the true message of Christ, some are even sending their own missionaries to the very peoples who evangelized them. To many dignitaries, such as Father Bernard, all this is somewhat threatening.

Moreover, these converts come from cultures where religious dance, song, and story have been closely linked to the natural world. The syncretistic rituals that many of them perform in Christian temples today often provoke cries of "pagan!" from the hierarchy. But Sister Pat, Sister Miriam, and growing numbers of other Catholics and Protestants who have sung and danced with them find in these rituals an exciting opportunity to continue experiencing new dimensions of their faith. They find joy, too, in opening themselves to revelations of other traditions.

Like a great many other people today—particularly women—they have been discovering an Earth-based spirituality missing in the religion they were taught. And they want to share it.

Yet Earth-based spirituality has always been an underground stream in the Roman Catholic and Protestant traditions. As we shall see, today it has emerged from its subterranean recesses and become a focal point of controversy.

Western Christianity and Ecology

To suggest, as Berry does, that the earth is the primary sacred community and the maternal source of our being has been tantamount to heresy in mainstream Christianity. Except among those drawn to mysticism, it has been assumed that God, humans, and nature are separate and stand in hierarchical order.

Many other faiths do not share this assumption. In traditional Oriental religions, says mythologist Joseph Campbell, "the ultimate ground of being transcends thought, imaging, and definition . . . Hence to argue that God, Man, or Nature is good, just, merciful, or benign is to fall short of the question. . . . "[3] In Christianity God's identity is manifest when He actualizes Himself in the human historical process. Moreover, "revelation," supposing direct communication between God and His human prophet, clearly implies privilege for those beings created in God's image.

Is this human-centered view directly linked with an exploitative attitude toward the natural world?

Yes, says historian Lynn White, Jr. "Especially in its Western form," he asserts, "Christianity is the most anthropocentric religion the world has ever seen."[4] This provocative thesis, voiced in 1967, is based on God's commandment in Genesis 1:28 to be fruitful and multiply, replenish the earth and subdue it, and have dominion over fish and everything that moves on the earth.

The finer points of White's contention are often overlooked by those who attack it. A practicing Christian (who proposed Francis of Assisi as patron saint of ecology), he was not making a wholesale condemnation of the faith and, as we have seen, this criticism is applicable to Judaism (and, by inference, Islam) as well. Our daily habits of action are dominated by an implicit faith in perpetual progress, which is rooted in Judeo-Christian theology, he says. It also permeates Marxism—which is Judeo-Christian heresy.[5]

The Judeo-Christian tradition is based on "a striking story of creation," he says. God first created the universe, then Adam, then Eve (as an afterthought to keep man from being lonely)—all for man's benefit. Thus "man shares in great measure God's transcendence of nature. Christianity, in absolute contrast to ancient paganism and Asia's religions (except Zoroastrianism), not only established a dualism of man and nature but also insisted that it is God's will that man exploit nature for his proper ends. . . . In antiquity every tree, every spring, every hill, had its own *genus loci*, its guardian spirit. . . . By destroying paganism, Christianity made it possible to exploit nature in a mood of indifference to the feelings of natural objects."[6]

Modern technology is at least partly explained as a Western realization of the Christian dogma of man's rightful mastery over the natural world, White argues. In the world of Eastern Christianity, the emphasis was somewhat different. In the early church and always in the Greek East, nature was primarily a symbolic system through which God speaks to humans.

In the West, however, this endeavor to decode God's communication gradually changed to an effort to comprehend God's mind by discovering how his Creation operates. From the thirteenth century on, all major scientists explained their motivation in religious terms. It was not until the late eighteenth century that the hypothesis of God seemed unnecessary.

Thus modern science can be viewed as an extrapolation of the Western form of natural theology, and modern technology as a Western consummation of belief in transcendence over nature. For centuries science and technology remained separate, but in the nineteenth century they joined to give humankind powers that seem to have gotten out of control. For this, he says, Christianity (especially in its Western form) bears a huge burden of guilt.[7]

The debate sparked by White's thesis has continued, in diverse parts of the world.

An International Chorus of Criticisms

British historian Arnold Toynbee also argues that monotheistic religions have removed constraints on humans' greed and overthrown the

traditional balance between them and nature. Thus the present environmental crisis could be linked to the rise of monotheism.[8]

German theologian Jürgen Moltman declares that when "the world
immanence of God the spirit is surrendered in favor of the world transcendence of God the ruler, the result is a view of nature which is dead,
and spiritless as well as godless."[9]

Native American social critic Vine Deloria, Jr. attacks Christianity
for forsaking nature. In *God Is Red*, he insists that we would do better to
search out Native American traditions for the spiritual foundations to
define an ecological age.[10]

In India, Anand Veeraraj, a Protestant minister strongly influenced
by his Hindu culture, argues that the implications of the Christian cosmology that superseded the Middle Ages' more organic worldview were
that the universe is composed of "neatly arranged three-decker stairs
made up of heaven, earth, and hell." He even declares that "Classical
Christian theology does not recognize any interdependence or interrelationship between different beings and elements."[11]

While most ecologically minded Christians would strongly dispute
this last contention, many are also disturbed by Christianity's emphases.
Their criticisms seem to form four clusters.

Charge Number One: Like Berry, many critics say mainstream Christianity has promoted a split between spirit and matter. Influenced by
Jewish theology and the spiritual/material dichotomy in Greek philosophy, mainstream Christianity developed the idea that the spirit is good,
the body evil. St. Antony is even said to have blushed whenever he performed a bodily function.

This separation is linked with subjugation of women, say many feminists. Some church fathers described the split between body and soul in
terms of differentiation between female and male, observes Rosemary
Radford Ruether. The female was identified with the body, therefore with
sin. The Virgin Mary became the symbol for idealized spiritual motherhood untainted by real sexual acts; real women remained the embodiment
of carnal passions. Thus "the love of the Virgin Mary does not correct
but presupposes the hatred of real women."[12]

Feminists point to witch hunts that scorched England and America
from the fifteenth to the seventeenth centuries, in which perhaps a million women met brutal deaths. Most were women who dealt directly with
nature, or young girls who rebelled against male structures.[13]

Although some scholars believe that patriarchal dominance is inherent in religion, others insist that it is a cultural construction. In the beginning, some say, a great many peoples worshipped the mother-goddess
as the central deity, giver of life. Evelyn Reed, among others, maintains
that the maternal clan system was the original form of social organization.

Its transformation into patriarchy appears to have been caused principally by the introduction of private property.[14]

After fixing the paternal line of descent by law, some cultures even declared that women were incidental to the child-bearing process; it was only the father who created the child. Thus we get the interesting phenomenon of "reverse creation" echoed in the Old Testament account of man giving birth to woman with the assistance of a father God.[15]

Carolyn Merchant suggests that while the earth was traditionally imaged as nurturing mother, it has also been recognized as the arena for violence. If the earth was female, then women must have the same kind of wildness. This image of nature as disorder aroused the modern idea of power over nature.[16] Francis Bacon (who frequently described matter as a "common harlot") declared in *The Masculine Birth of Time*, "I am come in very truth leading to you nature with all her children to bind her to your service and make her your slave."[17] Hence natural philosophers must wrest nature's secrets from her.

Despite Jesus' practice of treating women equally, and their importance in the early church period (murals and sepulchers suggest that some were even bishops), gradually the influence of post-biblical Judaism and the dualistic spiritualism of Hellenism reversed this liberating direction, says Ruether. And when Constantine established the Christian ministry as a social caste with exclusive male privileges, female subordination was institutionalized.[18]

Charge Number Two: Christianity presents a hierarchical picture of the world. In Genesis, creation resembles a pyramid: God supreme, then angels, humankind (with man above woman, and women over children), animals, plants, inanimate substance, down to Satan. Other monotheistic faiths also picture a hierarchical cosmos, and see God as male, autonomous, exclusive, armed with unilateral power over the universe, and opposed to feeling and femininity.

Charge Number Three: Christianity is allied with modern science and technology. In *The Protestant Ethic and the Spirit of Capitalism*, Max Weber tried to demonstrate the compatibility of the two doctrines. As in capitalism, Protestantism, particularly in its Calvinist form, perceived the natural world through a utilitarian lens. Although salvation was considered God's gift, one who was among the elect manifested in his behavior signs of grace—like hard work, self-control, and stewardship of worldly goods. Such values, fostering ascetic dedication to profit-making, were earmarks of early capitalism. Many Calvinists believed that financial success was a sign of being "elect"—thus abetting the desire for dominion over the earth.[19]

As they braved forth into "Darkest" Africa, Christian missionaries preached that salvation could be obtained only through adopting the white-skinned man's god; and "a better way of life" only through adopting Western ideas of agriculture, medicine, housing, monogamous marriage, and proper dress. Some ideas brought material improvement, but cyclical time patterns in traditional faiths of the East and nature religions are saner to live by, says Veeraraj. People with the linear space/time consciousness of classical Christian thought dwell under a "perpetual historical psychosis." Guided by a sense of destiny, they cause immense damage to the environment and their neighbors.[20]

It was missionaries who introduced the idea of technological progress. Ironically, the success of Christianity among the elite in China helped pave the way for communism, likewise cast in a paradigm of progress. Today the blessings of both capitalism and communism are visible in the deforested hills, polluted rivers, and plastic-strewn heaps that grace the landscapes of countries on which the developed nations depend for raw materials.

Charge Number Four: Mainstream Christianity is overly oriented toward human redemption, rather than the totality of the divine.

Christianity is replete with what Paul Santmire calls "metaphors of ascent." Jacob climbs the ladder to heaven, Moses goes up the mountain, medieval cathedrals soar toward celestial spheres. From the early thought of St. Augustine to that of twentieth-century Karl Barth, the emphasis has been on preparing for the next world. Protestant reformers, particularly, tended to take the Genesis motif of the divine curse on nature quite literally.[21]

In its most extreme form, stress on salvation from this ephemeral world results in "dispensational millenarianism": after Christ's Second Coming, He will set up a Kingdom lasting a thousand years. We can *expect* the environment to become progressively devastated; this is a sign that Christ's coming is closer at hand. Thus dispensationalists manage to turn on its head the idea that we must tend and mend the Creation. Blessed are those who care not, for they shall inherit paradise.

Differences in Emphasis Among Christian Traditions

Protestantism is perhaps furthest removed from viewing the natural world as sacred community. Originating about the same time as the scientific revolution, it affirmed one's own self and faith, and the independence of the local community vis-à-vis either the political or ecclesiastical empire. The dynamic organic relationship between God, humankind, and the world in medieval Christianity gave way to a perception of the human self as separate.

To some degree, the organic worldview of the Middle Ages does survive in many Catholic communities. There is a joyous quality in the

Catholic festivals that follow the annual cycles of nature. Flowers, fruits, water, wine, and other bounty of the earth are integral to the celebration. They are intended as symbols of God's communication with humans, but in the festivals one can also sense a simpler, earthy enjoyment of this bounty. Many fêtes incorporate pagan festivals and indigenous customs. One homely example: bicycling through Beaujolais, once the dominion of Roman legions, we the authors found a small chapel, Our Lady of the Grape, where local winemakers make an annual pilgrimage to ask for protection. The Christian rite is always followed a week later by a Bacchic pilgrimage uniting all the friends of Brouilly. And in a small church (now transformed into a wine cellar) in neighboring Juliénas, centuries-old stained glass windows depict vinous festivals, and Bacchus makes merry with several brightly clad damsels.

Many believe that the worldview of the Eastern Orthodox church expresses a more integrated approach to nature than does Western Christianity. It will be treated in a later chapter.

Responding to Charges of Ecological Bankruptcy

Is it unjust to place so much blame for our environmental predicament on Christianity? Bacteriologist René Dubos has argued that other societies also created ecological disasters, hence Christianity should not be held responsible.[22] Social critic/theologian Jacques Ellul maintains that the roots of the crisis do not lie in the Western spiritual tradition; the man-centeredness of Renaissance humanism was more important in furthering the dominance of the scientific perspective.[23] Other thinkers search for new insights within the traditions.

Defenders point to Psalm 104 as the richest biblical expression of what Paul Santmire calls "the fecundity theme," the revelation of a vision of the natural world charged with wonder and awe.[24] We glean from its 25 verses:

> Thou makest springs to gush in the valleys;
> they flow between the hills,
> they give drink to every beast of the field. . . .
> by them the birds of the air have habitation;
> they sing from the branches.
> From thy lofty abode thou waterest the mountains;
> the earth is satisfied with the fruit of thy work. . . .

Many Old Testament passages express Yahweh's love for all His creatures. Among them is Psalm 50:11, in which He proclaims "I know all the fowls of the mountains; and the wild beasts of the field are mine," and Genesis 6:19, where He commands Noah to take into the Ark "every living thing of all flesh."

The New Testament, too, reveals God's concern for the Creation. In Matthew 6:28-29 Jesus admonishes his followers: "Consider the lilies of the field, how they grow; they toil not, neither do they spin; And yet I say unto you, That even Solomon in all his glory was not arrayed like one of these." In the Sermon on the Mount, he speaks of "the fowls of the air," reminding the faithful that "your heavenly father feeds them."

The Continuing Concern for Creation

Throughout Christianity's history, a vital Creation tradition has endured as a substratum. Santmire, for example, emphasizes that Augustine's theology moves to the point where he shows how all things, creatures of nature as well as human creatures, have their own value.[25]

Although never so strong as in Eastern Christianity, mysticism has persisted in the West. For example, St. Francis is known for his loving communion with birds and animals. Paul Wiegand stresses that communion for St. Francis also signified a democracy of all God's creatures. He also linked ecological with social justice by moving the church outside the monastic walls, and calling on all to practice simplicity.[26]

The feminine aspect of Christianity has never been extinguished. In the Middle Ages the cult of the Virgin began in earnest and great cathedrals were built honoring her name. Three of the four medieval mystics whose work creation-theologian Matthew Fox revived were women: Hildegard of Bingen, Julian of Norwich, and Mechtild of Magdeburg— while the fourth, Meister Eckhart, was spiritual director of the Beguines, the women's movement of his day. The four celebrated themes of the Motherhood of God, the goodness of Creation, human earthiness as a blessing, seeing human beings as microcosms, panentheism ("all is in God and God is in all"), compassion understood as interdependence, and the human vocation to make justice and co-create the cosmos.[27]

In the sixth century, when Europe was overgrazed, deforested, and unable to support its population, the Benedictines introduced a practical stewardship ethic. They farmed abbey lands, cleared forests, drained swamps, developed wind and water power, and devised other ways of living with the land in a harmonious relationship.[28] On the other hand, Benedictine monasteries gradually gained power, land, and wealth, becoming despoilers of the earth. The Benedictine experience, then, also represents a contemporary lesson in the ecological deterioration that tends to follow the acquisition of power.

Celtic spirituality revered nature as a divine theophany and applied that vision to everyday life. Celtic monasteries were like small villages, and the religious lived in harmony with their environment. Many admitted women and men, married laypersons as well as celibates; many abbots were married. Celtic poetry, both religious and bardic, rhapsodized on nature, and Celtic saints often attracted animal friends. This may represent continuation of pre-Christian nature worship.[29]

In the Middle Ages most people lived in small communities where individual needs were subordinated to those of the community and they enjoyed intimate contact with nature. The church touched all facets of life, and the material and the spiritual, this world and the world to come, were seen as integral parts of one reality, the Body of Christ. By the late nineteenth century this organic view had largely disappeared under the impact of modern science, anthropology, and Darwinian evolutionary thought. But a respectful exchange of ideas between religions and between science and religion had begun. Priest/paleontologist Teilhard de Chardin's view was limited in several respects, as Berry points out, and he saw nature as good because it elicits the spiritual, not because it is good in itself. Yet many Christians continue to be fascinated by his ideas linking cosmogenesis and Christogenesis.

The Ferment Today

In ecotheology these themes predominate:

- We must rediscover our kinship with other earthlings. Thomas Merton, for example, sees the natural world not as object, but sustaining *friend*—friend who is Other, friend who is Intimate.

- We can no longer compartmentalize the sacred and secular; this is to undo the integrity of Creation. In the idea of the incarnated Christ, we can find the great unifying principle joining body and spirit, the divine and this world.

- Hence the new theology must be less anthropocentric. Many Christians, such as Protestant theologian Wesley Granberg-Michaelson, stress a triangular relationship of God, humanity, and the rest of Creation.[30]

- Our role must be that of wise caretaker for the earth and all the creatures upon it.

- We must emphasize a covenantal relationship between nature and humans. The Noah's Ark story demonstrates that God made His covenant not only with Noah, but with all living things.

- We need to see Creation not as one primary event "back then," but ongoing, here and now. Christians can join hands with this God of Creation to share in recreating the universe.

- There is a rich potential for expressing both biblical and ecological views of the world in process theology, which John Cobb describes as the view that all entities have both mental and physical aspects; their lives are linked through the great web of life. In this panentheistic vision (all is in God), process theologians picture a loving deity, and divine protection consists in being totally open, perfectly responsive.[31]

- Total openness means actively seeking opportunities to listen to the insights of contemporary science and philosophy, seen as partners in the pursuit of truth.

An undercurrent in all these themes is reaction against the paradigm of dominion and the anthropocentrism implied. At the same time, these themes suggest a lingering implication: humans are uniquely endowed with intelligence and wisdom, hence should exercise good stewardship.

The recurring emphasis upon listening to the insights of scientists and working with them is significant, but represents a task fraught with difficulties. For example, while the so-called "Big Bang" theory represents majority thinking in the scientific community today, scientists by no means agree on it. Some religious leaders seize on it as scientific "proof" of their view of God. Pope Pius XII, for one, told the Pontifical Academy of Sciences in 1951 that it meant that "Creation took place in time. Therefore, there is a Creator. Therefore, God exists."[32]

Moreover, some of the most visionary tabloids also respond handsomely to human eagerness for corroboration of what Bible stories have told us since childhood. After NASA astronauts repaired the Hubble telescope in late 1993, *Weekly World News* announced that "the giant lens focused on a star cluster at the edge of the universe—and photographed Heaven!" and that "the pictures clearly showed a vast white city floating eerily in the blackness of space," quoting a "scientist" as saying "We found where God lives."[33]

The questions among both scientists and theologians concerned with finding significance in the cosmic process are many. For example: Does one assume a God whose main attribute is providing purpose and structure? Can one also assume a personal God? Such a God is repudiated by some theologians as incompatible with the post-modern view of reality, and by even more scientists; in general, they can tolerate the possibility of a divine force as creator of the universe, but not the idea of a personal god who continues to intervene in the world.[34] Still, some scientists *are* devout believers. Physicist and theologian Ian Barbour, for example, has spent most of his life seeking an integrated vision of theology, science, and technology, and concluded that process thought is consonant with an ecological understanding of nature as a dynamic and open system.[35]

Such issues are very complex. They are touched on only to indicate the enormity of the questions with which sensitive theologians are wrestling in the search for a functional cosmology.

To suggest that Christianity (with its sibling religions) has been the prime cause of the rift between humans and the natural world is highly debatable. But there can be little doubt that it has contributed to a view that desacralizes the natural world and encourages humans to consider themselves superior to other creatures, endowed with the right to exploit them. It is an attitude far more widespread in Western theistic faiths than in other religions.

Today we are coming to see traditions as evolving. That view does not simply happen; today more than ever before, people at the grass roots can participate in that process. Sometimes they are well ahead of theologians in the spiritual beliefs and intuitions they act on. Their convictions may not show up in any formal belief system for a long time. Religions help shape a living ethic, but science, economics, politics, and the sheer struggle for survival and for making sense of the world also shape religion. Nor is it only a question of how we humans are changing the face of the earth. We tend to forget that in this cosmos of connections, Earth itself acts on how we image and experience it.

At least four important visions of a new paradigm emerge:

(1) Broadening liberation theology to include liberation of all humans oppressed by our present exploitative practices. A new theology of Creation could use similar approaches to help people become aware of how they are impoverished, materially and spiritually, by the ravishment of the natural world, and could stimulate their creativity in preserving the earth.

(2) Consciously subordinating the spiritual motif of Western theology to an ecological one, and using this new motif, shaped by a metaphor of migration to a good land, as a framework.[36]

(3) Developing an organic model of Christianity that speaks to a broad range of contemporary concerns and particularly to the ecological crisis. Theologian Sallie McFague points out that in one form or another the organic model has been accepted throughout human culture—in native and Goddess traditions, for example, and to some degree within the

Christian tradition. She attempts to look at everything through one lens, the universe as God's body.[37] It is only one model and does not say everything, she says, but it unites human beings to everything else on the planet in relationships of interdependence. The Christian paradigm is extended to oppressed nature, since humans have caused nature to be the "new poor." The model of the world as God's body is consonant with the view of reality in contemporary science. At the same time, she affirms a belief in the personal god of the Abrahamic traditions.[38]

(4) Working toward an inclusive universal paradigm by stressing the features that Christianity shares with other faiths. It would be grounded in the common Creation story recounted by scientists: everything that exists has, at some level, a common beginning and a common history. This understanding can generate many images of the future. For Veeraraj, it is the dream of a "Green Religion," as the only force that can effectively confront dominant worldviews. Chances that the Green Movement will actually emerge as a brand new religion are remote, he admits. Instead, it will have to borrow myths, rituals, and symbolism from existing faiths. In the end, a unique eco-religious-social paradigm will emerge—the most ecumenical that the world has ever seen.[39]

What role would Christianity play? That is hard to predict. But despite its many rigidities, Christianity has proved to be one of the most syncretistic of all faiths, he claims. If it is open to the unity theme as fundamental tenet of its cosmology, Christianity will play a significant part.[40]

As we are seeing, today growing numbers of women and men are quietly turning new visions of creation into reality. By their very lives, they are helping shape religious traditions.

Responses in the Catholic Church to the New Vision

The ecospiritual movement, by its very nature, is ecumenical. This poses problems for the Catholic hierarchy, always ambivalent toward ecumenism. Many Catholic individuals and groups have figured prominently in the movement, but virtually without leadership from Rome.

True, in the 1960s and 1970s Vatican statements included references—vaguely worded—on the deteriorating relations between humankind and the environment, and humans' "ill-considered exploitation of nature." John Paul II's 1987 *Sollicitudo Rei Socialis* was widely hailed as his "ecology encyclical," but disappointed some Catholics. Jane Blewett, Director of Earth Community Center in Laurel Maryland, applauded its call to change the spiritual attitudes defining each individual's relationship with self, neighbor, and nature. Nevertheless, the life systems of all living creatures were somehow passed over, she noted: people in the lifeboat, yes; the lifeboat itself, no! While proclaiming "limits" on the dominion of human beings over the earth, it fell short of declaring deeper identity with other beings.

On January 1, 1990, John Paul II finally issued a more strongly worded statement; the gist was that the ecological crisis is a moral problem, to which the solution is a new life-style.

Theological alienation from the earth also inhibits Vatican movement toward a comprehensive environmental ethic. If the body and our intimate connection with the physical world came to be fully accepted, it could open up nightmarish questions over sensuality, sin, and control.

A more encouraging sign is that ecumenism does flourish on the local level in many places around the world. Moreover, sometimes groundbreaking work by Catholic groups and individuals becomes so admired that bishops applaud it. Occasionally, bishops become leading voices. For example, the bishops in the Philippines who authored "What Is Happening to Our Beautiful Land?"[41]; and in the U.S., Cleveland Bishop Anthony Pilla's "Christian Faith and the Environment: Reverence and Responsibility,"[42] which speaks in plain language of the illusions and denial we harbor, and is unusually specific about ways our consumption-oriented life-style leads to disaster.

Communities of sisters—and to a lesser degree, communities of monks—have been in the forefront. Many emerge from traditions of tilling the land. The Sisters of the Humility of Mary, for example, still tend orchards and fields at the 800-acre motherhouse in Villa Maria, Pennsylvania. The Franciscan Sisters of Oldenburg, Indiana, use organic methods for growing crops at their 300-acre Michaela Farm, support an environmental education center, and hold national conferences on bioregionalism. Indeed, Catholic sisters and laywomen have been more prominent than their male counterparts in the movement; the women seem to lend it a certain passion.

Justice for human beings has long been a concern among Catholics. For some, the idea of human rights has extended to include the rights of all the earth's citizens. Ecojustice is beginning to be considered in many Catholic seminaries. In Canada the Holy Cross Centre at Port Burwell, Ontario, has founded an institution for spirituality and ecology, and has produced offshoots like the Earth Community Center run by Jane Blewett, formerly on the Holy Cross staff.

Growing numbers of essays on humans' responsibility for the Creation have appeared in the *National Catholic Reporter*, *Commonweal*, *America*, *Maryknoll*, and other magazines, as well as some scholarly journals such as *Cross Currents*. Roman Catholics took a leading part in organizing the World Wildlife Fund (WWF)'s celebration of an inter-national, interdisciplinary "pilgrimage of life" at Assisi in 1986, and in the conferences of the Global Forum of Spiritual and Parliamentary Leaders on Human Survival. Many Catholics helped organize the founding meeting of the North American Conference on Christianity and Ecology (NACCE) in 1987, and its first president was Eleanor Rae, a Catholic. Former Catholic priest Don Conroy founded the North American Conference on Religion and Ecology (NACRE), a 1989 off-shoot of NACCE.

These "movers and doers" are not representative of what is happening at parish level. Partly because there has been so little interest at the top, priests are only slowly beginning to consider that care of the Creation might be a fit topic for a homily, and that church practices could be part of the problem. Today, however, some churches are finding ways of conserving energy, and converting their flower gardens to "edible land-scaping" of lettuce, tomatoes, peppers, and peas.

Roman Catholics have also joined with other faiths in the National Religious Partnership for the Environment (NRPE). The four member groups include the U.S. Catholic Conference, the National Council of Churches of Christ, the Consultation on the Environment and Jewish Life, and the Evangelical Environment Network. Funded by generous grants from major foundations, its multi-faceted program includes clergy and lay leadership training, legislative updates, environmental curricula for seminaries, a Green Congregation Hotline, and sending education and action kits to 53,000 congregations, including every Roman Catholic parish.

As one American Catholic puts it, "Those of us who *commit* our-selves to building an ecological community are still seen as aberrations." Such activists are not necessarily regarded as a political (Marxist) threat, like base communities in Latin America, the Philippines, and Africa, but they do embody a threat: grassroots power that ultimately cannot be con-trolled from above. Indeed, it is likely to be Roman Catholics who rebel, at least inwardly, against what they see as the rigidity of Rome who are attracted to the ecospiritual movement—precisely because it draws out creative, individual, untamed yearnings of the heart, and yet unites them in communal action.

Responses Within the Protestant Churches

Protestants have written many books and called many conferences on the topic of ecotheology, but it is trickling down only slowly into the thought and action of congregations.

In 1997, in the midwestern town (pop. 11,000) where we the authors now live, we made an informal survey of 10 Protestant churches—five mainline and five fundamentalist or evangelical. Only mainline ministers expressed interest in the topic. In the previous 12 months, three had devoted parts of one sermon to "preserving the Creation" themes, usually on the Sunday nearest Earth Day. Five had inserted the county's "Soil and Conservation Week" flyer into weekly church bulletins. Four churches had placed some emphasis on such themes in children's sermons or children's Sunday School. Two had instituted recycling activities on church premises; one had launched a short tree-planting program on the grounds. Two had installed energy-efficient windows, but none had thought of doing a complete energy audit. Only two had received materials sponsored by NRPE; one had made use of them. None had engaged in community ecological projects or pushed the community to become more active.

In general, the evangelical and fundamentalist ministers felt that "the Lord wants us to keep the environment clean," recycling (by the town) was a good idea, and "we ought to be proud of the place where we worship." Two such churches had planted trees, but not with an ecological purpose in mind. All these pastors listened politely, but their response was some elaboration of the idea "We focus on the Creator, not Creation," or "Our task is to save human souls." With great emotion, one fundamentalist lumped earth-worshippers, Buddhists, socialism, and "feminists like Jane Fonda" together. All emphasized that God created the world for humans. Yet several ended with "Thanks for calling—it's got me to thinking."

However, in a similar survey we made in 1990, only two mainline ministers had expressed any interest at all in incorporating ecotheology into their work. There has been movement.

Although as far back as 1933, the much-revered Lutheran theologian/missionary/physician/music scholar/philosopher Albert Schweitzer observed that "the great fault of ethics hitherto has been to deal only with man's relationship to man,"[43] ecology as a spiritual issue has been slow in developing among Protestants. In the 1960s concern began to spread. The World Council of Churches, or WCC (which is made up of many Orthodox and Protestant churches, the latter in the majority) began to focus more attention on the environment. In 1966 the National Council of Churches of Christ (NCC) published *Human Values on Spaceship Earth*,[44] and Lynn White, Jr., a Protestant, came out with his landmark speech, "The Historical Roots of the Ecologic Crisis."

Still, few Protestant churches paid attention to the first Earth Day in 1970. The programs during the late 1960s and 1970s in San Francisco's Grace Cathedral and New York's Cathedral of St. John the Divine were very much the exception.

Since the early 1970s, the WCC has published a series on a wide range of scientific and environmental issues, its *International Review of Mission* has included articles on ecojustice, and it has instituted the section known as Justice, Peace, and Creation. As Dr. Freda Rajotte of the Church and Society Division put it during our visit to WCC headquarters in Geneva, Switzerland: "Today the World Council's primary concern is the integrity of Creation. You can't talk peace without justice. And you can't have justice if you destroy the climate, allow flooding, permit ruin of tropical forests, ignore sustainability. This becomes a question of poverty—of oppression."

In the 1970s a few liberal Protestant journals, such as *Christian Century* and *Christianity and Crisis*, were publishing articles on environmental stewardship. By the 1980s some evangelical magazines like *Christianity Today* and *Moody's Monthly* were following suit. At the same time, Protestant-based magazines that focused on building an environmental ethic were forming—for example, the Society of Friends' (Quakers') *Befriending Creation* and *Earthlight*, the Christian Environmental Association's *Target Earth*, the Evangelical Environmental Network's *Green Cross*, and in Canada, the Christian Farmers' Federation of Ontario's *Earthkeeping*. Protestants contribute regularly to ecumenical newsletters like NACRE's *Eco-Letter* and NACCE's *Earthkeeping News*.

Creationists (who take literally the biblical account of Creation) and dispensationalists (Christians with an end-time worldview) have shown little interest. A statement in *End-Times News Digest* in spring 1990 links Earth Day to a socialist-communist plot, and declares that "environmentalists are often like watermelons, green on the outside, but red on the inside."[45] Yet even among creationists and dispensationalists, a few writers stress that stewardly care for creation has a certain importance, for—who knows?—it may be thousands of years before Jesus returns.

Several Protestant colleges link environmental and peace studies. The Church of the Brethren's Manchester College, for example, emphasizes a "green peace" that will require replacing our obsessive consumerism with a more responsible life-style. Some Protestant seminaries feature courses in Creation theology, and six (Union Theological, Claremont School of Theology, Lutheran School of Theology, Meadville-Lombard Theological Seminary, Hendrix College, McCormick Theological Seminary) have been designated by TEMEC (Theological Education to Meet the Environmental Challenge) as lead institutions.

Protestants were instrumental in organizing a coalition called The Joint Appeal of Religion and Science for the Environment. It was followed by a number of grassroots programs sponsored by Christian and Jewish congregations, culminating in the founding of NRPE.

"Protestants have begun to foster a new theological focal point—Creation theology," says David Hawley, a Presbyterian minister who serves a local church and also teaches at United Theological Seminary in Dayton, Ohio. "Today there are other big issues to struggle with, like abortion and questions of sexuality. But Creation theology is in there. Because it is so biblically oriented, it offers a doctrinal center. Protestants tend to need something doctrinal to hang onto."

Three Protestants in Action

An Environmental Scientist's Efforts to Put His Faith into Practice

Calvin De Witt is director of the Au Sable Institute of Environmental Studies, Professor of Environmental Studies at the University of Wisconsin-Madison, and a prolific author of articles for scientific and Christian publications. He is also a man of action. Among other things, he has organized successful campaigns to preserve forests in Michigan and led a Wisconsin town to develop a model stewardship plan for its wetlands, woodlands, and agricultural lands.

In his own modest words, De Witt is "a student of the Scriptures," inspired by his "gratitude to God" to "open up the university of Creation to students so they can receive a life-long education." An ecumenical Christian, he attends a Reformed church during the academic year and a Mennonite Church in the summers. "Environmental responsibility is at the heart of Christian faith and life," he insists. "There must be a conversion among Christians—mainline, evangelical, fundamentalist—to acknowledge God anew as Creator, not only in word, but in deed. People of *all* faiths, and the whole of society, must do an about-face."

De Witt was brought up in the Reformed Church, which stands on the borderline between evangelical and mainline churches and holds that no part of one's life should be separate from Christian faith. Thus, one should learn to know God through two great books: Creation itself and the Bible. While not "fundamentalist," it takes the scriptures very seriously. But it also fosters a love for science, art, and civic life.

A VISIT TO DE WITT'S "NATURAL CLASSROOM"

The Au Sable Institute, serving students from kindergarten through college, is the first American environmental education center to incorporate Christian teaching and practices. Its mission is "to bring healing

and wholeness to the biosphere and the whole of Creation." Its very
setting, the northwoods country of Michigan's Lower Peninsula, illustrates De Witt's belief that nature itself is a university, once accessible
to everyone but today barely existing in the consciousness of many people. To this natural classroom come students from Christian colleges for
courses in environmental stewardship, some of which lead to vocational
certificates, such as water resources analyst. The Institute also serves
7,000 school children with programs in basic ecological principles, and
offers college and church groups a site for retreats and environmental
conferences.

One August morning we made our way down a path graced by trees
and plants, all marked by name, to Earth Hall, where assistant director
Bob Barr offered a tour. "Cal," whom Barr described as "terribly over-
worked, always in demand," would join us later. For the next hour we
walked the paths, observed a class in insect ecology, and visited parts of
a "walk through early American times" (a living museum depicting, in
chronological succession, Indians, fur traders, settlers in covered wag-
ons, and Michigan loggers). "It has real impact on youngsters," said Barr.
"And our school program is growing fast." Even the youngest children
did field work; college students engaged in more sophisticated field studies, such as groundwater analyses.

We passed an earth-sheltered laboratory that De Witt had designed
and arrived at the simple dining room. Like the faculty members, we sat
with the students. The young faces around us looked intensely serious,
yet from time to time quiet laughter rippled through the room. Just before
dessert, a young instructor stood up and talked about the relevance of the
Jonah story to the relationship between humans, God, and the earth.
There was nothing preachy in his tone, and the examples he used were all
drawn from contemporary everyday life. The students listened intently,
some with heads bowed, others gazing meditatively into the distance.

"Yes, you can talk easily about God here," said Bonnie Stout, a shy-
looking girl from Grand Rapids Baptist College. Particularly interested
in birds, she liked the holistic approach here. "Usually ornithology is
taught so that you learn to identify a bird, but not what kind of tree it's
in or what kind of water it's drinking. Here we see how all these depend
on each other.

"We get to know our teachers and their families personally," she went
on. "We do a lot of fun things, like sailing and swimming. But we also
have discussions—any time—about repairing the environment. There's
fellowship in being with others who feel the same way—it gives you a
foundation. That makes it easier to talk later with people who aren't so
aware of sewage problems and lawn chemicals and water quality and how

these relate to human life."

As the others were leaving, De Witt entered the dining room with a quick stride, puffed his apologies for being late, shook hands with us warmly, and insisted that we call him "Cal." Motioning us to one of the tables, he fetched a sandwich and faced us squarely.

He was of medium height, with graying hair, a slightly plump but athletic build, round face, pink cheeks, and bright brown eyes. Considering the rapid pace of his day, he seemed remarkably relaxed; his voice, gestures, and laugh conveyed a deep enjoyment of life.

From reading his work, we already knew that he sees "Seven Degradations of Creation's Integrity" as the chief environmental problems today: alteration of planetary energy exchanges; global warming and ozone layer destruction; loss of land to urbanization, soil erosion, desertification, and salinization; deforestation and loss of habitat; species extinction; water quality degradation; and human and cultural degradation.

To Cal, the last problem is perhaps the most severe. Cultures that developed ways to live at peace with the land are being violently displaced by destruction that produces a windfall of merely momentary riches.

Could he tell us more about his philosophy?

He looked out the long wall of windows to the forest beyond and then began slowly. "I try to *see* things whole. That includes science and religion. Most often if we take science seriously, we don't take religion seriously, and vice versa. I try—to use the words of early scientists—'to think the thoughts of the Creator after him.' To me this is the best way to understand the Creation and our place in it. You come to see a world without dualism."

"As you see it, when did the split between religion and science develop?"

"With the objectification of the world, during the Enlightenment. Today many scientific texts do little to convey a sense of awe and wonder for the natural world. Nor do they give us a moral compass to navigate through the world described in science. Without that we're prone to press nature into our own self-service. With my own students I make my first goal the instilling of awe and wonder for the biosphere, for the universe. From such wonder action springs.

"Many scientists know this awe. It comes from realizing the immense order and integrity of the universe. Even chaos theory discloses order in what seems disorder. Chaos has consistent patterns. This is what much of the excitement is about in the new physics!" He leaned forward intently. "For me, it is most reasonable to believe that this order is derived from a single source, a just and ordered mind. The mind of God, whose testimony is so convincing throughout our universe that everyone must

know something of His everlasting power. Not the warring gods of poly-
theism, nor the gods of pantheism in every rock and tree. Instead, one
God who is orderly and steadfastly just. Who transcends all things, ind-
wells all things, sustains all things."

"How does your thought differ from Thomas Berry's?"

He rubbed his chin thoughtfully. "Berry. Well, Thomas has been with
us here at the Institute and we have great admiration for each other. He
and I and his brother Jim have had numerous discussions. Thomas and I both
try to remain true to the best information from the sciences, and we both
come to the conclusion that Earth is being degraded and needs love and
care. But we have different beginning points. My cosmology begins with
the Creator, whose mind and Law pre-exist everything that has been
made, and proceeds to what we currently call the Big Bang and on
through the creation of matter and life over the earth's history. The Big
Bang and all Creation derive from the Creator—the one mind by whom
all things have their integrity. Thomas—if I understand his cosmology
correctly—begins with the Big Bang and goes through the creation of
matter and life. He also remains true to the findings of modern science.
But having begun with the Big Bang, he moves from the development of
sentient and human beings to a kind of collective mind that he sees as
what we have come to call God. God is the hydrogen atom becoming
aware of itself, God is the mind that transcends individual minds, God is
a product of the universe in its course of natural history."

We were puzzled. "That is not our understanding of Berry's thought.
In our reading and talks with him, he has not spoken of the hydrogen
atom reflecting on itself. The *human* is the being in whom the universe
reflects on itself, in a special mode of conscious self-awareness. And the
concept of collective mind has never come up in our talks or reading his
works."

"Well—well, that is what I get out of it. A collective mind. The basic
thinking is that God is an emergent property of the universe. It still brings
one to a point of recognizing God, but owes its origin to human and other
sentient beings. Of course, this has consequences."

"Such as?"

"For one thing, it makes prayer a difficult exercise. To me, it tends
to elevate ourselves to gods, or collective gods. This is temptingly attractive, but it confers divinity upon human beings. Honesty requires that we
see ourselves as the causative agent of environmental destruction.
Berry's view leads us to a certain divinization of humankind. Instead of
addressing the desecration of the biosphere, ultimately it feeds the arrogance that got us into the situation."

"Berry himself decries such arrogance."

"Well, to me his thinking implies moving from the teaching that people are made 'a little lower than angels' to the idea that we are 'a little lower than God,' even gods ourselves. My belief is that the human being—and its collective mind operating today—are at the heart of the problem. It's not that we don't really know better. We invent a compass that gets *us* where *we* want to go. 'The good that we would, we do not; the evil that we would not, that we do,' says Paul.

"Also, seeing the divine as emerging from a collective human mind or as ultimate product of Earth's development does little to help us explain the order permeating the world, or satisfy our wonder about why it is so integrated and why it exists at all. In monotheism the world is ordered because it has a single source in a wise, just, and sustaining God."

We recalled Berry emphasizing his view that the knowledge of God emerges in the human mind, not directly but through the manifestation of God "in the things that are made." We remembered how he stressed that the universe is not a puppet world without an inner power; rather, God enables beings to be themselves and act in a manner that brings themselves into being. This seemed far from the divinization of humans or the concept of human "collective mind." But to argue De Witt's reading of Berry's ideas seemed inappropriate at this time. Still, we had gained another insight into the depth of the controversy surrounding Berry's new ideas, the depth of emotions surrounding longstanding theological assumptions. It was particularly saddening that this should occur in a domain where not only the ultimate goals, but many of the perceptions were basically the same.

And we had come there to listen. "Today scientists understand that sub-atomic particles must have certain properties to form atoms," Cal continued. "Atoms need certain properties to form molecules, and water molecules must be so ordered as to provide for water freezing from the top down, and so on, up to making it possible to form the genetic blueprint for a frog's eye and a galaxy's structure. Although various theories are still being discussed, what we now know is consistent with an order-producing law which pre-exists the universe—or at least is created at the very beginning. For bacteria, rocks, dragonflies, people, and galaxies to flourish, the universe must have had that potential from the beginning. Otherwise, it would have remained a kind of sub-atomic soup—ordered, perhaps, but with less development and differentiation."

Privately, we reflected that some of these ideas were not very different from Berry's, although the implications that De Witt perceived were different.

"Do you believe in evolution?" we asked.

"Well, evolution is a theoretical construct explaining some aspects of what we see. It's not something that calls for 'belief' as monotheism does. To the extent that what we call evolution is substantiated by what is happening, we should incorporate it. What I learn from the natural world I believe has the same author as the Scriptures, so the testimony in both is reliable.

"Unfortunately, the debate over how God made the earth is not even informed by *modern* evolutionary theory, which emphasizes cooperative as well as competitive relationships. Social Darwinism was extracted from early evolutionary theory and made the centerpiece of economic theory and social life—'looking out for Number One.' Many things in nature can be explained only by cooperation, altruism, community. Some bird song is just for joy! And it's not merely territorial announcement, it can be altruistic.

"Many," he continued, "see legal and technical measures as solution. But alone, they don't work. Lawyers can always get around laws. The only answer is to get to people's hearts."

"And the way to do that?"

"Explore the religions we have. Way back, I saw that here is a book, the Bible, that has survived 3,000 years. Is it reasonable to say a book this sustaining should be set aside at a time of crisis?"

"But isn't Berry suggesting we set aside the Bible *temporarily* and only because it's a barrier that prevents us from clearly seeing and feeling what we should be experiencing? In essence, that we should become as a little child again?"

He looked at us for a long moment. "Well, yes. And I, too, think we should become as children—as the Bible says. But not set aside writings that may help us. We should see what the Bible says for our time, rereading it with our ecological glasses on. Many people suffer the arrogance of believing that we can invent in a decade what has taken centuries to develop."

"How do you relate this to the biblical verses citing human dominion over the earth?"

"Genesis 1:28? We can't extract one verse from its context and pretend it gives the whole story. Human beings are special creatures only in the sense that we can conceptualize how the earth is ordered and respond in a caring way. In the Scriptures dominion means humble *service*. And in Job the hippo is described as a creature of God whom God ranks first among his works. In the zoo we see the hippo lying on a slab of concrete, his body flowing across it, looking as if he should enroll in an exercise program. But God isn't singing of a hippo imprisoned in concrete, but one lying under the lotus, hidden in the marsh. He swirls his tail like an eggbeater, spreading his dung in a watery cloud, and grazes on nearby grass like an ox. And God says, 'Look at that!' It's not just those animals that are friendly and cuddly that are beautiful. The Creation is a kind of symphony. Waiting for people who will harmonize with it."

The Bible was *full* of principles for ecological action, he continued. With astonishing ease he recounted many scriptural teachings, including that in Genesis 2:15 to keep the earth; in the Sermon on the Mount, to realize that the meek shall inherit the earth; in Luke 6, to put what we believe into practice; and in many parts of the New Testament, to seek contentment as our gain.

"But the problem is that these teachings are rarely put into practice?"

"Yes. My suggestion to students is, 'Don't pay as much attention to what they say, as what they *do!*' We don't find biblical principles put into practice in many places. But still, the meek people of Amish communities, for example, work directly out of biblical teaching. It's time not to think of such folks as 'quaint,' but explore the biblical basis of their caring for the land."

"So how would you describe the most fruitful approach for scientists?"

"Well, scientists have three choices—agnosticism, atheism, or believing in God. Scientists want to see things whole, so an atheist would have to build an entire cosmology based on the material. This requires developing a kind of evolutionism. Agnosticism leads in the same direction, but has the advantage of not cutting us off from non-material options. Starting with the belief that God exists allows us to stay within any theoretical constructs our data will support, and doesn't drive us to fill the gaps with weaker theory or speculative materialism. If that belief is accompanied by confidence that the whole world is ordered, it will actually expedite our scientific work. Such a God-believing scientist is free to discover the beauty of death in the way it returns material substance to the various biogeochemical cycles that sustain all life. And this can inform his or her theological perspective on life and death."

Cal stood up and suggested more coffee. He had been talking a long time, but looked animated and eager to continue. Sipping his coffee, he commented that by working from what little part of the universe each of us sees, we could come to believe that all the universe is ordered.

"The Scriptures help develop an answer to 'What is right?' and science, to 'How does the world work?' We need answers to both. Take some of the cottagers here in the wilds. Many are what I call 'Recreational Mowers.'" He grinned. "They mow lawns once or twice a week, practically down to stubble. Most are urban types who 'escape' to the north woods. They come up for the weekend—and spend it mowing." As De Witt spoke, we looked across the forest floor with its vegetation; there were no lawns at Au Sable, we realized.

"They even act as if this were some kind of religious duty! But professing to make things orderly, they bring disorder. Not understanding how the world works, they poison the earth and the lake with chemicals. They are people with a new kind of poverty; their knowledge of how the world works is impoverished. Knowing what is 'right,' but not knowing how the world works, they destroy the very world that attracts them. All of us are something like that. Knowing what is 'right' and not how the world works, we destroy the world; knowing how the world works but not caring about what is right, we defile the earth."

"So environmental laws and techniques are necessary but not sufficient?"

"Exactly. We need education that helps get our moral compass in place, and education that gives us an ecological understanding of our own yards and the planet. Then we can act. There are three questions: How does the world work? What is right? and Then what must we do? If we fail in any one of these, we have failed in *everything*."

All over the world there were enough examples of failure for an environmentalist to despair, we reflected. But in Cal's voice we could detect only resonant hope. "Perhaps you could tell us more about your life?" we asked.

He leaned back, closed his eyes for a moment, and then began slowly. "Religion has always been very important to me and my family. The sermons at our Christian Reformed Church were probing, intellectual. Today while I'm working I can recall them—vividly.

"When I was three, I cared for my first turtle. Soon I was keeping lizards, snakes, alligators, frogs, and various mammals in the backyard, a cockatiel in the kitchen, and 39 parakeets and a tropical fish in our basement. The snakes and lizards hibernated in a cage next to my mother's washing machine. She just shrugged and smiled. We were a loving family.

"After Sunday night church, my father would take guests down to the cellar to show off my animals. As I grew older, some asked, 'Shouldn't Cal be studying practical things?' and my dad would answer, 'No, he's doing just fine.' Later he told me 'Do what you love to do. Eventually, you'll do it very well, and eventually someone will even pay you for it.' And you know, I've never applied for any job I've had. They've found *me*."

De Witt taught natural history and biology at Calvin College, then returned to the University of Michigan to complete his doctoral studies in zoology. Following his marriage to Ruth Wiersma, who has worked in biology and natural history most of her life, the couple conducted research together on the desert iguana in the California desert.

Three weeks after beginning his first teaching job at a major university (the University of Michigan-Dearborn), he learned that the "brush" in a campus woods was to be cleared to "make things look neater." That "brush" just happened to be a diverse assemblage of plants that was providing cover for local animals, whose value he planned to discuss and show in his teaching. De Witt was a new professor—clearly vulnerable. Should he object, or go about business as usual? Humbly, he objected, and eventually got faculty and administrative support. The "brush" was saved. It was his first major "choice for obedience"—obedience to his calling.

"A couple of years later, I learned that the powerful Wayne County Road Commission was planning a divided highway through the forest at the west edge of campus. After taking the local Women's Garden Club there to view the spring flowers, I was able to enlist them and others to help stop the project. That was a second major choice for obedience to my calling."

In 1972 he moved to the University of Wisconsin-Madison to take a position in its newly formed Institute for Environmental Studies. Concerned that his work on computer modeling of land-use dynamics would mean losing their connection with the natural world, Cal and Ruth sought an area with the most wetlands. Today they live in Dunn, on a thousand-acre wetlands preserve which they helped establish with their neighbors.

"Sometimes when I look out at the marsh I almost think I see a mastodon in the mist. The bottom layers of the peat under the marsh were laid down 6,500 years ago! Once Lake Waubesa was far larger, too. The area has become a classroom. My students study its history and its possible future—a future depending on what its human inhabitants do.

"We've done other things in the community," he went on. "Ruth and I really believe we should 'think globally and act locally.' For instance, I was Town Supervisor of Dunn, then Town Chairman. We declared a moratorium on land division, then applied the stewardship concept. A committee inventoried the farms, forests, and wetlands, including the types of soils, plants, trees, amphibians, fish, and mammals. The result is a scheme for deciding which land should be allotted to agriculture, which land preserved for historical sites, which left alone."

In 1980, when Cal became director of Au Sable, it had only three cooperating colleges. Now 35 Christian colleges participate, and students from 55 other Christian schools enroll. "In the early 1980s," he recalls, "conservative Christians were doing virtually nothing about the environment. So I felt we should first serve them. Au Sable is defined not by a boundary, but a focus—learning about Christian environmental stewardship."

Cal offered to show us the building that serves as chapel and meeting hall. Walking along the mossy path he told us that every summer they

De Witt demonstrating to his Environmental Sciences class at Waubesa
Marsh. (Photo by Jeff Miller)

hold the Au Sable Forum to explore some aspect of the relationship between religion and ecology. Represented over the years have been the
evangelical traditions, as well as Amish, Mennonites, Roman Catholics,
Eastern Orthodox, Jews, Buddhists, Native Americans, and scientists
from around the world. The purpose is to stimulate discussion, research,
and publication of environmental stewardship materials.

We entered the chapel. Like the surrounding woods, it was of pine.
An enormous fireplace stretched along one side, a large piano occupied
a corner opposite, and before us stood a pulpit. What drew our eyes was
the huge window behind it. Running the length and height of the wall,
the window disclosed a wide porch with a tree growing through it, and
overlooked a pond, aspen, birches, and tall red and white pines. The
scene reminded us of a Shinto temple we had visited in Japan, a shrine
open on all sides to the surrounding forest, and like this chapel in the

Michigan northwoods, propelling us outward into the natural world.

We moved back to the woods. The rain was falling, sounding a hush on the pine needles, moss, and leaves, the mushrooms pushing through glistening ferns. The earth smelled fresh.

Creating a Green Cathedral in New York

"At our first meeting, Berry's ideas hit me right in the stomach," said James Parks Morton, dean of New York's Cathedral of St. John the Divine, as we settled into easy chairs in his office. "They turned me upside down. 'Where have I been?' I asked myself.

"We met in 1975 at the Riverdale Center, where I'd gone with some other people from the cathedral. Almost immediately I asked him to preach during Advent that year. He did, but that first time most people probably didn't understand him. He pulls the rug out from under you."

"But he's spoken here several times since?"

"Many times. For example, one year when the Lenten theme was 'Vinegar for my Drink: the Waters of Pollution and Purification,' Tom spoke on 'Water Symbolism.' Other authorities spoke on the ecology of water, the politics of water, and so on. In 1981 Tom gave one of the sermons at an ecumenical celebration of the 800th birthday of St. Francis, with the theme 'Spirituality and Ecology.' Catholic and Anglican priests, women religious, ecologists, and biologists were speakers, and there was an all-day ecological festival of workshops, music, drama, and 'Duke Ellington's Third Sacred Concert.' Another year he gave the first talk on an Easter series called 'Inhabiting Green City: New Yorkers in Nature.' That's just a sampling."

A sampling—yes, we could believe that. This Episcopal house of worship, often known as the "Green Cathedral," had become famous—and controversial—throughout the world for the extraordinary variety of programs under its roof. To critics Morton retorted that it is intended to be the first medieval cathedral of a post-modern age—a center for the whole community, a place where worship, work and play, art and dance, old and new ideas can all find expression. There were social programs for the homeless, shut-ins, juvenile offenders, and poor families who put in their own "sweat labor" to rehab abandoned apartments. There were also classes for apprentices learning to restore tapestries, and training for the jobless in the almost forgotten art of cathedral stonecutting, taught by master craftsmen from England. In fact, the cathedral housed its own companies of artisans, musicians, and liturgical dancers. Homeless people, atheists, and political leaders sometimes addressed congregations from the pulpit. Some 30 percent of the regular visitors to the cathedral were Jews, who sensed here an expansive community. Worship might be led by Jewish rabbis, Muslim imams, Buddhist monks, Sikh gurus, or include the liturgical chanting of Tibetan monks or Eastern Orthodox choirs, Native American dances of praise, or the mystic whirling of Sufi dervishes. Sometimes Paul Winter's "Earth Mass" blended human harmonies with the cries of endangered species into a new kind of hymn to Creation.

We looked around Morton's colorful office—the old fireplace, the books and papers heaped on tables, the posters on racial discrimination, the photos of Shinto priests in white robes and lacquered black hats chanting a *norito*, the pictures of Sufi dervishes dancing their exaltation of the Almighty, the Taoist calligraphy, the Native American paintings, and the half-finished watercolor on an easel, still in a state of Becoming. Everything seemed to speak of movement, exuberance, joy in the things God has made. "Celebration" was a word made flesh at St. John's.

The Dean himself seemed to reflect that ebullient quality. He was a big, bushy-browed man, with a shock of wavy gray hair hanging over his forehead and a powerful, resonant voice. We knew he had been brought up in a musical and theatrical family, and had studied architecture at Harvard and theology at Cambridge in England, then worked in Chicago's inner city. In 1972 he was called to this massive cathedral (the largest Gothic structure in the world), perched on a hill at the edge of Harlem. In that year his ecological awareness began to unfold.

"We've had a wide range of ecological thinkers here, from John and Nancy Todd of the New Alchemy Institute, to microbiologist René Dubos and bioregionalist Kirkpatrick Sale. But Berry had the greatest impact on me. My teaching had told me 'man sits on top.' His new vision opened up—all of life! Now we even have a Blessing of the Animals every October!"

"Complete with elephants, pythons, and llamas, we've heard."

"Also several billion microbes!" He chuckled. "How could we have life without them?"

"We've been particularly impressed by the René Dubos Consortium for Sacred Ecology. It has so many programs—the Gaia Institute to link ecological theory and practice, environmental training, programs with native peoples, a recycling center, 'green' sacred architecture, an ecological think-tank. And a joint appeal by religion and science for the environment!"

"I'm really enthusiastic about that," Morton responded. "It was heartening to see religious leaders with such diverse beliefs united on this. Out of that came the National Religious Partnership for the Environment. As you know, the cathedral is NRPE's headquarters. And we're aiming for ongoing dialogue among scientists, religious communities, and political leaders."

"All this represents your conviction that ecology is the way to understand life in our time?"

"It is the way to do theology," he replied firmly. "Berry helped me to see that. He helped me to see I'm not sitting *on* the earth, I'm a *part of* the earth! If this shimmering reality we call the earth comes from an exploded star, it is made of stardust, and *I* am stardust, too!"

An African-American's Vision of Ecojustice

When we first met Prathia L. Hall in the mid-1960s for a book we were writing on young social revolutionaries, she was already a veteran of the civil rights struggle. In 1960 she had headed south from Philadelphia, where she was a pre-law student at Temple University, to join the Student Nonviolent Coordinating Committee (SNCC). She still remembers being scratched and spat on and kicked and clubbed and thrown into jail. She remembers a white trooper who fired a gun toward her legs—a half-circle of shots rat-tat-tat around her feet. She recalls struggling with the rage that engulfed her. SNCC militants had been trained to the almost impossible task of not fighting back. Somehow she did manage to discipline her rage throughout the long "reign of terror," for she always held before her that ultimate goal: social justice.

When we met Prathia again, nearly 30 years later, at a conference on Ecology and Christianity at United Theological Seminary in Dayton, Ohio, she was still fighting for justice, but for her that concept had broadened to embrace ecojustice. In the intervening years, she had become a Baptist cleric like her father and, like him, a "fighting minister." It had always been "a vital part of African-American religion to draw no distinction between life and politics," she told us. "That kind of separation—life and politics, mind and body, sacred and secular—is wrong! It means taking the ethical out of religion and leaving a kind of useless piety that is devoid of power. You see, my whole life has been shaped by my religious convictions."

Despite deep personal suffering—she had recently lost her only daughter to a massive stroke—Prathia was still a handsome woman, tall and grave, with a proud carriage and large calm eyes. She was pursuing a doctorate in divinity at Princeton Theological Seminary, "in order to have a part in shaping the next generation of church leaders," and also teaching at United Theological and preaching, mostly in Baptist churches. Feminism had become more important to her; her doctoral thesis was on the roles of women in the Black Baptist church between 1920 and 1960 as they tried to work through the triangular oppression of race, gender, and class.

In the mid-1980s, Prathia told us, she began to experience a deep-

Prathia L. Hall, fighter for social and ecojustice.

ening concern for the environment. "It grew out of my understanding of justice as right relationship—with God, with self, with others. And 'others' includes the whole of Creation. The earth, its products, its people, all belong to God. This means you don't squander, you don't withhold grain from hungry nations through price manipulation, and you don't rape the earth."

She paused, then added slowly, "My only reservation is that some environmentalists place nature over human justice. I'm concerned not just about African-Americans, but indigenous people, and *all* who are poor and oppressed. For instance, I'd like to see Native American fishing rights take precedence over the attitudes of certain environmentalists. For another thing, there are *big* ethical issues in the practice of disposing of toxic wastes in regions where poor people live."

At the workshop that Prathia led on "Liturgical Resources for Environment and Creation," her deep empathy with the oppressed surfaced again and again. "We Western Christians have a great deal to learn from the ignored people in the so-called Third World," she said. "I had the great privilege of being able to attend the 1991 meeting of the World Council of Churches in Canberra. For me the high point was talking with people from Pacific Rim countries and the aborigines who have been living in Australia for 40,000 years. Hearing their cry for ecojustice— that was a stirring experience! They have a real understanding of stewardship. But they also have a *spiritual* relationship with the earth. They're not so much 'close to,' as *of* the land. They say, 'We are *owned by* the land.' This is so very different from feeling separate from the land and then working through to a concept of stewardship!"

Most of the people at the workshop were white, male, middle-class ministers—the image of the church as it used to be. But they were listening intently to this impassioned black woman, asking eager questions about approaches, as they groped their way into the strange green pastures of ecotheology. All those we talked with said the topic was fairly new to them; they were happy that United Theological had begun focusing on it through courses, workshops, and public lectures.

When we asked Prathia whether she often talked about caring for the environment in her sermons, she nodded. "Yes. But that is difficult. African-American people living in inner-city neighborhoods are involved in day-to-day survival. The long-term issue of slow death by pollution is not as important to them as short-term death—say, from crack. Still, I find that when I present the environment as a justice issue, they begin to see it. Education can raise their awareness. When we explain environmental issues clearly, they understand."

Conclusion

In 1999 the people portrayed here were still pursuing their visions of an earth community, but in many cases they have moved on to a new phase. Sister Pat is now teaching fourth, fifth, and sixth grades at Mount Vernon's Traphagen School, where she integrates the new story of the universe into "geography, science—everything I teach. Take history. They don't learn just *human* history; we look at cosmic time." At Traphagen, Pat also began another Kids for the Earth club, which has become so popular that first-graders frequently ask to join in.

Sister Miriam has stepped down as administrator of Genesis Farm, in order to explore new possibilities for community-supported agriculture, focus on land preservation, and continue her work with religious communities. Genesis Farm (where Sister Maureen Wild now serves as administrator) remains the base of Miriam's travels.

Father Bernard carries on as director of the Franciscan Environmental Center in Rome, which has been expanding slowly.

Calvin De Witt continues his activities at the Au Sable Institute and the University of Wisconsin, addresses politicians and religious groups, and works with the National Religious Partnership for the Environment as a concerned scientist to educate the public about the precarious condition of the global environment.

James Parks Morton has moved on to a new challenge. He has created the Interfaith Religious Center in New York, at East 51st Street and Lexington Avenue, in the heart of the city.

Prathia Hall has retired from United Theological, and is Visiting

Scholar at the Womanist Scholars Program of the Interdenominational
Theological Center in Atlanta.

As we have seen, by the mid-1990s the Roman Catholic and Protestant churches, taken as a whole, were showing far more interest in the
fate of the planet than two decades earlier. Every year there are more
conferences, more groups concerned with the ecological responsibility of
the religious community. In action, too, Western Christianity has continued to lead other religious traditions. Action still lags far behind broad
affirmations of principles, however.

These trends stand out:

(1) More Christians have come to believe that Christianity itself is
part of the problem. On the philosophical level, more question the idea
that human beings are supreme in the divine hierarchy of Creation—an
idea that can lead to the implicit assumption that humans are endowed
with all the wisdom to make decisions about the fate of other beings. On
the parish level, recognition that Christianity has been part of the problem involves acknowledging that many churches have themselves been
ecologically irresponsible in waste of energy, in use of church grounds,
in making investments. A few writings have appeared on the subject,
notably the *Eco-Church in Action Manual*,[46] which ranges from Earth
celebrations in worship services to action in the wider community.

(2) Those churches that do become involved in ecological activity
have been using more scientific evidence to supplement or support scriptural teachings.

(3) There is rising concern with environmental justice for the oppressed. As studies such as those by the United Church of Christ have
shown, hazardous waste incinerators and landfills, for example, are often
placed near elderly, poor, or minority populations.

(4) Ecumenism is expanding. On the national level the most evident
sign is the National Religious Partnership for the Environment. Locally,
it is particularly evident among grassroots organizations that have no
formal affiliation with a church. For example, in Cincinnati, a conservative city in middle America, several religiously oriented groups are
quietly working together for a healthier relationship between humans
and the earth. At one, Grailville, members are building an ecofeminist
community on a farm that uses organic agricultural methods. Grailville
also features retreats, workshops in the arts, discussions of racial relations, Zen meditation, and programs of liturgical dance that center on
Earth-based rituals of renewal. Not far from Grailville, Sister of Charity
Paula Gonzalez and many friends have built Earth Connection: two sun-
powered homes that use twenty-first century efficiencies and what
Thomas Berry calls "the technologies of nature." Paula, often described

as a "dynamo," also holds workshops on topics ranging from "Greening the Christian Community" to ways that homeowners can reduce energy bills by 50 percent or more.

A few miles away, members of IMAGO search for more spiritually satisfying and sustainable ways of living on Earth. With their own sweat labor, IMAGO members have transformed an old house in its low-income neighborhood into an Eco-House. The group offers—among other things—gatherings for meditation and Earth-centered rituals led by a former Benedictine nun, an annual Festival for the Earth, and workshops (in conjunction with local churches) on the ecological outlook of various spiritual traditions. In 1998 it held a large regional conference called "Earth Spirit Rising!" attended by over 600 people. Later IMAGO received a $500,000 grant to develop a model Eco-Village.

These groups publicize each other's events, and often co-sponsor a program. In the words of one IMAGO member, "We're working toward similar goals."

Still, overall change in Western churches is slow. What lies behind this hesitancy?

(1) Varying degrees of outright opposition. In every denomination there are people who piously believe, or find it convenient to believe, insidious messages in the media that the environmental crisis is a "non-problem" or a "hoax."

(2) Reluctance to overcome denominational lines and cooperate. For example, one minister told us that even though his denomination belonged to the National Council of Churches, which had joined the NRPE, the kit of basic materials might take a year to reach him, because they would have to filter through the approval process at his denomination's regional and district offices. In one year, more than 30,000 species can die out—forever.

(3) Feelings among many traditional Christians that the growing power of women is a threat. Ecofeminists' efforts to demonstrate connections between oppression of women and oppression of the natural world seem particularly menacing. Some leaders denounce as "paganism" all attempts to discover the feminine face of God. Some go further, identifying reverence for Mother Earth as worship of an Earth Goddess.

(4) A nagging fear of losing religious identity. "Syncretism!" has become a warning of surreptitious activity. Yet from an historical point of view, all religions, even those based on direct revelation, are to some degree syncretistic, absorbing elements of other faiths, and evolving over time. What seems relatively new is that today sizeable numbers of people are consciously striving to create a syncretistic whole that embraces meaning for them.

(5) Deep down, there is denial. How could the dire happenings predicted happen to *us*?

(6) In an age when mainline churches are declining in membership, pastors' fear of preaching ideas that logically suggest radical changes in life-style.

The conference, "Theology for Earth Community," called by Theological Education to Meet the Environmental Challenge (TEMEC) at Union Theological Seminary in October 1994, wrestled with some of these issues and many others as it grappled with the challenge of developing curricula linking religious and ecological concerns.

There were sessions on topics ranging from "Feminist Liberation Theology for the Eco-Justice Crisis" to "The Church and the Environmental Justice Movement," and workshops focusing on liturgy, institutional greening, population-consumption issues, sustainable urban community, spiritual formation, teaching/learning models, patterns in ecojustice literature, Jewish philosophy of nature, and other subjects. All the participants were conscious of difficulties in balancing the deep-seated tendency to associate God with the individual human soul, and the ancient awareness of God's primary relationship to the world.

There was general agreement that theological education must include ecological concepts and Earth ethics. It must embrace direct *experience* of ecological principles in nature, feature practicums with environmental organizations, educate the public, provide outreach services to assist the wider community, and assume a wide variety of other roles.

The many obstacles to such a radical effort were recognized as formidable. There were few signs of optimism. Yet there were also no signs of hopelessness. Indeed, several theology schools were cited as already-successful examples of "institutional greening."

Among the speakers were Christian Japanese-Americans, Chinese-Americans, African-Americans, and Native Americans, with widely varying views of the faith they held in common. A Jewish theologian and a Muslim leader also spoke. One of the most hopeful themes was that listening to a spectrum of stories about the place of the human species in the great cosmic design can enrich our own experience and our ability to serve the earth community. Throughout the conference there was a tangible sense of groping toward a globally oriented, locally grounded, prismatic view that would be responsive to the perspectives of other religions.

4

EASTERN CHRISTIANITY

Introduction

Entering an early Orthodox church is like coming into a vision of cosmic harmony. Through the dim light of candles you see columns, ceilings, and walls glowing with mosaic figures. Saints move in stately procession across the walls in the company of sheep, stags, peacocks, fish, vines, palm trees, and other symbols drawn from the natural world. As symbols they form a language, an abstraction, yet one related to the everyday life of the faithful.

The colored marbles and frescoes, the Byzantine gold work and the elaborately decorated iconostasis, the priest's richly colored vestments and the inspiring a cappella song of the choir, all convey a transcendent otherworldliness. And indeed, the intent of Byzantine art is "to render visible the mysteries of the supra-natural world." You sense that the sacred space you have entered belongs more to the Orient than to the Western branches of Christianity.

The Eastern church stands apart from the Western in several important ways. Here we should like to touch briefly on a few of the differences, since they have a direct bearing on ecological thought and action. In a broad sense they are all theological differences, but it is worth emphasizing that theology, even when it claims to be based on immutable doctrine, can never be isolated from its history or the cultures that adopted and nourished it.

Theological divisions permeate Eastern churches, and make Eastern Christianity particularly confusing to people rooted in the West. Although the two terms are often used interchangeably, Eastern Christianity and Eastern Orthodoxy are not synonymous. The latter is generally referred to—somewhat misleadingly—as Greek Orthodoxy. There are also the "separated" Eastern churches—the Oriental (or non-Chalcedonian) Orthodox and the Nestorians—which split from the original church for doctrinal reasons too complex to go into here. There are further subdivisions: patriarchates, autocephalous (self-governing) churches, and autonomous (not yet fully self-governing) churches, all of which are generally characterized by national origins (Russian, Ukrainian, Polish, Syrian, Cypriot, and so forth). The Eastern Orthodox acknowledge the primacy of the Ecumenical Patriarch in Constantinople (Istanbul); he is the "first among equals," but does not claim universal jurisdiction as does the Pope, and his authority is more loose.

Eastern Christianity does share with the Western tradition the basic Christian beliefs such as monotheism and the afterlife of the soul. There are important doctrinal differences, however. For example, the Orthodox accept the dogma established by the Church Fathers in the early centuries, but not the later doctrines of the Roman Catholic church (from which it separated in the year 1054) about the Immaculate Conception, the Bodily Assumption of the Virgin Mary, and the infallibility of the Pope. Moreover, the Orthodox continue to recite the original Nicene-Constantinopolitan Creed (established in 381) affirming that the "Holy Spirit" proceeds from the Father, while the Western has expanded it to read "proceeds from the Father and the Son."

These differences—and there are many more—may seem of trivial importance to people who are not theologically-minded and especially to those who are concerned about the future of life on the planet. Yet they have been a major contributing cause of "religious" wars (which are largely concerned with politics in the widest sense of the term). There are other sources of subtle friction. Adherents say that Orthodoxy means "right worship," and also "right belief," seen as residing in the writings of the early Church Fathers and the uninterrupted life of the liturgy. Its theologians declare that they do not hesitate to make new interpretations if they maintain continuity with Scripture and tradition. In practice, new interpretations have been rare.

What does this mean for the ecospiritual movement? It means a resistance to the idea of ongoing revelation. It also means a great ambivalence toward an ecumenical relationship with Roman Catholicism and Protestantism; in general, the Orthodox have seen them less as dialogue partners than schismatics who, they hope, will return some day to the true church.

The liturgical sacramentalism of the Eastern church holds out great promise for Christians seeking a cosmological and ethical approach to the ecological crisis. As Larry Rasmussen puts it, "Orthodox Christianity from the earliest stages has consistently understood the sacraments as dramatizations of nature's transfiguration. Humans, as 'priests of Creation, refer the Creation back to the Creator in acts of liturgical doxology."[1] Thus unlike Western Christianity, the Eastern church has never assumed a dichotomy between humanity and nature.

Orthodox theologian Paulos Mar Gregorios adds that Christ "has chosen to have a larger body, partly in heaven (i.e., beyond the horizon of our senses) and partly here on the earth."[2]

The Orthodox in Action

In 1989 September 1 was proclaimed a special conservation Feast Day by the Eastern Orthodox church—the first major church in Christendom to celebrate such a day. It was a landmark event. By 1990 it was planning Project Ormylia, an organic farm to demonstrate Christian teachings on preservation of the Creation, at the Holy Monastery of the Annunciation, a nunnery in northern Greece. It would teach organic farming, gather conservationists and church members to plan recycling activities and campaigns against pesticides, and serve as a model for similar projects on nearby Mount Athos.

In the proclamation, Dimitrios I, then Ecumenical Patriarch, declared, "This Ecumenical Throne of Orthodoxy, keeper and proclaimer of the centuries-long spirit of the patristic tradition, and faithful interpreter of the eucharist and liturgical experience of the Orthodox church, watches with great anxiety the merciless trampling down and destruction of the natural environment. The abuse by contemporary man of his privileged position in Creation and of the Creator's order to him 'to have dominion over the earth' (Genesis 1:28), has already led the world to the edge of apocalyptic self-destruction. . . ."[3]

An accompanying booklet, "Orthodoxy and the Ecological Crisis," speaks of the need to live more simply. " . . . Just as a shepherd will in times of greatest hazard lay down his life for his flock, so human beings may need to forego part of their wants in order that the survival of the natural world can be assured. This is a new situation—a new challenge. It calls for humanity to bear some of the pain of Creation as well as to enjoy and celebrate it."[4]

The very emphasis on the "newness" of the challenge is unusual for the Orthodox church, with its stress on immutable truth and its traditional attitude that social responsibility is a private concern arising out of personal spiritual experience of God. But the central issue remains: how much *active* concern are the Orthodox evidencing in the task that Ecumenical Patriarch Dimitrios called "the preservation of natural creation"?

Constantinople: The Ecumenical Patriarchate and Stewardship of Creation

For us, the first question was: How had Dimitrios' proclamation come about?

In 1990, in Constantinople (Istanbul), Metropolitan Bartholomaios welcomed us into his elegant office and recounted that story. We could not anticipate then that upon the death of Dimitrios in 1991, Bartholomaios would be named His Holiness the Ecumenical Patriarch. In a few years he became famous as the "Green Patriarch."

With his penetrating gray-blue eyes, gray beard, maroon cassock tied with a sash, and purposeful stride, then-Metropolitan Bartholomaios struck an imposing figure. In excellent English, occasionally interspersed with French, he told us that it had all started with an environmental symposium on the Greek island of Patmos in 1988, which had gathered ecologists from all over the world, as well as Greek government officials; spokesmen for the Christian, Buddhist, and Hindu traditions; and representatives of the World Wildlife Fund (WWF) and its affiliate, the International Consultancy on Religion, Education, and Culture (ICOREC).

"We see all of Creation as the creation of God," Bartholomaios continued. "Every day we witness the negative results of the destruction of the environment by modern technology. So the patriarchate wanted to contribute its help to avoid continuation of such catastrophic evolution. After Patmos we began thinking of a special conservation feast day. The first of September was chosen because it is the beginning of the ecclesiastical year and we sing hymns to the Father of Creation. So we combined a traditional feast with a new fête for the protection of nature.

"Our Patriarch had entered into correspondence with Prince Philip of Britain, who is president of the World Wildlife Fund. The Prince was enthusiastic about the idea."

Ecology had been a concern of the Orthodox for several years, Bartholomaios emphasized. The Eastern Orthodox had sent representatives to the 1986 Assisi gathering of world religions to discuss the environmental crisis, and to the second meeting of the Global Forum of Parliamentary and Spiritual Leaders on Human Survival, held in Moscow in 1990. At the first Global Forum, in Oxford in 1988, the Oriental (non-Chalcedonian) Orthodox had been represented. Indeed, the Creation had been an abiding theme in all Orthodox churches.

The Ecumenical Patriarch Bartholomaios, known as the "Green Patriarch."
(Photo by Dimitri Panagos)

India: Power, Privilege, and Creation Theology

In Delhi we talked with Father M.S. Skariah of the North Syrian
Orthodox Church of India (one of the non-Chalcedonian churches). A
dark, intense-looking young man with an elegant beard that comple-
mented his long white robes, Father Skariah described his work with the
poor, his activities with ecumenical groups, and his growing realization
of the importance of saving the Creation. It was essential, he said, that

we visit Paulos Mar Gregorios, a world-famous figure in Creation theology. While his title was Metropolitan of Delhi, he was then working in Kerala, a state in southern India where St. Thomas had introduced Christianity in the first century CE and was headquarters for this jurisdiction of the church. We knew that as WCC's associate general secretary and director of its Ecumenical Action division, Gregorios had been extraordinarily active in interfaith conferences on peace and preserving the earth, and were eager to meet him.

Fate intervened. Plans to take the three-day train trip to Kerala collapsed when one of us was hospitalized. It was not until 1993, at the Parliament of the World's Religions in Chicago, that we finally met Mar Gregorios. Nevertheless, we managed to follow his work through reading and correspondence.

In a religious tradition not noted for expression of political views, Gregorios is an unusually outspoken critic of the establishment. In an informal interview at the first Global Forum, he declared that privilege was part of the ecological problem. He recognized that he himself—born in one of the most poverty-stricken countries in the world—had become a member of a privileged class. We need to see how dependent we are on structures that promote injustice, he insisted. Nor did he have much faith in the perceptions of most religious leaders. What they needed was a conference that would examine the rules of the game of politics, the game of industrial production, the game of injustice, and the integral role that the mass media played in these games. Then it should set up a strategy to deal with these concentrations of power.[5]

At the WCC Assembly in February 1991, when American planes were carpet-bombing Iraq, Gregorios was virtually the only Orthodox delegate to openly "speak truth to power" as he pointed to the human and ecological destruction wrought by George Bush's "just war."

At the 1993 Parliament of the World Religions, where Mar Gregorios was featured as a plenary speaker, he focused more on traditional humanistic concerns than on the fate of the earth. However, he did mention it when he presented his grand vision of a New Enlightenment that would transform civilization "away from the focus on commodities and closer to the right relations of humans among themselves, to the environment, and to the Transcendent."

Gregorios was still recovering from a heart attack when we met at the Parliament, so our talk could focus only on his lifelong concern with wholeness. When we recalled that at the 1988 Global Forum he had observed that "God is not interested only in Christians, but in the whole; once you get at the center of Christian concern, then Christians can be concerned not just with Christians, but about all human beings, all animals, everything," he nodded. "Anything that can help us think about the whole is good. This is why ecological concern is a priority now."

Greece: Orthodoxy and the "Green Philosophy"

Greece, where the Greek Orthodox is the official church (although freedom of religion is guaranteed by the constitution) presents a study in contrasts. Ecological reflection among theologians has been going on since the 1960s. The works of George Mantzarides, Euthymios Stylios, and Elias Economou, for example, propose thoughtful spiritual, ethical, and ascetic solutions to the ecological crisis, and include practical approaches.[6] Moreover, we found far more ecological activity inspired by the Orthodox church than in any other country. On the other hand, cynicism about the church and its motives was widespread.

At the Church of Greece radio station, press director John Chazitodis and engineer Grigoris Maltezos enthusiastically described their two-hour program on ecology, the round-table discussion following it, and other programs offered occasionally. "We tell what some church groups are doing, and how ecology practices are rooted in Scriptures," said Chazitodis. "God created the earth, so we must love it. We must love the fishes, the birds, the animals. We must love them *gently*."

"We are not owners of the earth," interpolated Maltezos. "We must turn it over to our children in a sustainable condition. I talk about renewable energy in a way to help people see that we must be stewards."

The Greek church had begun celebrating the first of September as the Day for Protection of the Environment, we learned. The Ecumenical Patriarch's message had stimulated a similar message from the head of the Church of Greece, Archbishop Seraphim, which in turn had stimulated church publications on ecology and these radio programs. In the future they also expected to expand environmental coverage on the weekly one-hour program on state radio, and to launch a television channel that would include environmental teachings.

"Look at the monks on Mount Athos!" said Maltezos. "They keep the environment beautiful with flowers and trees, and live side by side with God's other creatures. They eat only fish and vegetables. And some live past 100 years!"

"What this means is, to protect the environment, we should reduce our needs," Chazitodis added. As for specific projects, the one at Ormylia was still in the planning stage. But at Katrina, Bishop Agathonikos was speaking out against an electric company that used polluting coal. In Zankinthos Bishop Panteleimon was leading a movement to save the tortoise. In Crete Bishop Ireneos of Hania had begun a campaign on various environmental issues. Elsewhere, local priests were planning demonstrations about the air and water, and warning against the "consumption mentality."

Talks with other Greeks provided insight into the challenges faced by the church. Some felt it lacked the will to take a strong stand. Others said that even when the clergy do speak out, they are not heard, because average Greeks believe ecclesiastics should stick to church matters.

"In Greece, to talk of 'religion' means the established church," said Christiana Prezekis, who had a master's in environmental studies from Boston University, and worked for the non-governmental Hellenic Marine Environment Protection Association, to educate seafarers about the hazards of discharging waste from ships. "Almost everyone belongs to that church. Meaning you go for Christmas, Easter, baptisms, marriages, and funerals. People know it has a lot of money and power. How much faith can they have in it? People have become essentially secular.

"As for the Patmos statement, it's good to have it. But few hierarchs are really progressive. They saw it as a response to a hot issue. I have little hope that action will come."

The secular approach of her educational work gave her more hope. "Most seafarers do want to keep the sea clean. It's difficult. Our member vessels collect garbage, but there are very few land facilities for dumping stuff, in spite of laws mandating cities to create them."

Christiana's activities with children brought her even more fulfillment. All her work was based on the philosophy that there is something that *everyone* can do, and youngsters grasped this idea quickly. They were interested in almost all the big problems in Greece, from forest fires and the decreasing bird population, to the air pollution that continued to plague Athens despite rules that limited driving. "We encourage these children to develop their own ideas, like environmental posters. One poster—showing a fish protesting the pollution it had to swallow—is being used by UNEP (United Nations Environmental Programme) all over Europe."

Many adults were slower than the children to grasp the interconnectedness of things. Many environmental groups focused on only one issue, hence often failed to see the global link. Then, too, the prevailing mentality was to dwell on day-to-day survival, and think of environmental problems in terms of technological solutions. "Still, these groups do make some progress," she added. "More than the church, as far as I can see. The new ethic takes a geocentric view."

Anna Harrisson, a blond, vivacious woman who was married to an Englishman and spoke English faster than we, had found a third way, neither completely secular nor conventionally religious. As a spokesperson for the Green Party (the Federation of Greek Ecology Groups), she was concerned with the twin goals of a more just society and protection of the ecosystem.

"The federation is made up of ecological and minority protection groups. 'Think globally, *act* locally'—that's our motto. We have international links, too—with Greenpeace, for instance." She paused, as if to catch her breath. "Last year our membership *doubled* to 60,000, and we won a parliament seat in the elections! She'll serve a year, then the seat will rotate among three others. We have no paid staff. That's hard. But they're dedicated. There's an esprit."

"You're mostly young people?"

"Well, mostly. The organization is young. We were born 10 years ago, after several groups lobbied against a nuclear plant on the Karistos island—and won. Our poster shows Botticelli's newborn Venus rising from the sea, and the slogan, 'A New Politics is Born!'

"Some of us are veterans. Last Sunday I was in a demonstration sponsored by one of our groups, the Hellenic Society for the Protection of Nature. And who was in there leading the action? Byron Antipas, a 75-year-old mountain climber who heads the society."

"And you—how did you come to your view of the world?"

She laughed. "I've *always* loved nature. Especially birds. I adore birds of prey! I write articles against embalming them, and belong to the National Geographic Society. Well, gradually I saw how birds *and* other wildlife *and* human beings have all been threatened by pollution. I saw how Greece has suffered from tourism. Today there are hardly any beautiful places left untouched. Gradually, I began to see you can't be ecological without being a pacifist. And I came to feel that God is nature, and nature is God."

"Although you say you are Greek Orthodox!"

"Yes, yes. Like all Greeks." She shrugged. "And the church is beginning to do good things for ecology. A few young priests are making themselves heard. We are happy to have any cooperation we can get."

But to many coming into the movement, the "Green philosophy" was like a new religion, she observed. "Awareness of the planet—this is a new way of educating people. The best way to avoid hooliganism is to take the young outdoors and make them aware of the beauty and mystery around them. Coming closer to nature, feeling the network of life—it's the best way to escape the anguish of our time. Ecology brings people together. To me, all this *is* a new religion."

Russia: Tensions Between Old and New

THE RUSSIANS AND MOTHER EARTH

A Russian Orthodox service seems to move between heaven and earth. The fragrance of incense rises like the mist of the fields, the light of candles plays on the priest's brocaded vestments and the tears of the penitents, the faithful touch the gilded icons with their lips. This is a liturgy that reaches out to the senses, raising worshippers into *experience* of the Divine.

But it is the music, above all, that spins glory into the sacred space; music is the heart of the Russian celebration. The voices of the a cappella choir soar upward, then descend swiftly toward Earth, soar and descend again and again. The cantor chants the verses, the choir responds with the refrain, the celebrant intones praises to God, and the antiphonal song moves back and forth, evoking vast distances across wide steppes and up toward the unknown.

Many myths across the world claim a common origin of music and religion, and music is central to many spiritual traditions. Yet Christianity has been particularly ambivalent toward music—one has only to recall the warnings against its sensual seductions among some puritanical sects. To the Orthodox, however, tonal chant has always been a core expression of reverence for the Almighty. Particularly among the Russian Orthodox, it is sung with a quality of brooding, but ultimately of joy. It is song not so much of the individual tormented soul as of the community.

With all its transcendent aura, the Russian service has an informal, terrestrial quality. Worshippers touch the earth as they enter, stand through the hours-long service, occasionally whisper with their neighbors, and move about the church, venerating the icons by prayerfully kissing them and lighting votive candles.

Traditionally, almost every Russian was baptized, every home adorned with holy icons, which often included animals and depicted peasant life. The average village priest tilled a small farm, sharing the labors of the peasants in his flock. Although a monk was required to be celibate, a priest was expected to marry and have many children. The Orthodox church never adopted Latin traditions, and Old Slavonic continues in liturgical usage to this day. Nor did the Russians follow the Greek interest in systematic theology. Instead, they focused on the constancy of prayer, the splendor of the sacraments as doors to mystical experience, and the veneration of icons.

Other branches of Orthodoxy speak of the sanctification of nature. But Russia imparted to Byzantine cosmology a warmth, spontaneity, and even poignancy.

To be sure, in the Russian religious psyche there is a polarity between the earth-loving and the world-denying, a constant theme in Dostoyevsky. In *The Brothers Karamazov*, Father Zossima represents the white, shining, earth-loving stream, and Father Ferapont, the black, world-denying, fear-stricken religion. It is a theme familiar in other traditions, but in the Russian it acquires particular intensity. The passionate Russian soul is ever-striving, ever in search of redemption.[7]

But "redemption" reaches beyond the individual soul. The cosmic Christianity in Dostoyevsky's novels was often regarded as heresy. His work is replete with earth themes. James Billington suggests that in *The Brothers Karamazov*, for instance, the name of the spontaneous, exuberant Dmitry is related to Demeter, the Greek goddess of the earth. As he gladly goes into exile for a crime he did not commit, Dmitry recognizes that "we are all responsible for all," and exclaims, "If they drive God from the earth, then we shall shelter him underneath the earth: . . . singing from the bowels of the earth, our tragic hymn to God in whom there is joy!" Dostoyevsky seems to be saying that even if man cannot believe in God, he must rejoice in the created universe.[8]

Father Zossima, the village priest, expresses the yearning of the simple people for spiritual intimacy with the natural world. "Love all God's Creation, the whole and every grain of sand in it. Love every leaf, every ray of God's light. Love the animals, love the plants, love everything. If you love everything, you will perceive the divine mystery in things."[9]

Pre-Christian animist elements, maintains Fedotov, blended with Orthodox rituals, and in the nineteenth century were still deeply rooted.[10] Billington adds that Easter sermons traditionally preached that "the goodness hidden in the hearts of the holy shall be revealed in their risen bodies," just as trees long veiled in the snow "put out their leaves in the spring."[11] And in the rural life of pre-industrial Russia, he says, "God came to man not just through the icons and holy men of the church but also through the spirit-hosts of mountains, rivers, and above all, the forests. Each animal, each tree had religious significance like the details in a religious painting." An oft-recurring Russian theme is that of the ravished forest eventually triumphing over the axes of men.[12]

The characteristics of trees and birds were associated with events in Christ's life and death, and if an icon failed to revive a dying person, the ancient intermediaries of the gods of nature—swans or mountain birds—were often called in to heal.[13] In folk tales recounted even in the twentieth century, animals often partake in the life of humans.

Like St. Francis of Assisi, the fourteenth-century Saint Sergius of Radonezh left a life of luxury in the city to adopt a monastic way of life in the countryside, and was reputed to calm wild beasts and preach to animals. In the eighteenth century, too, St. Seraphim of Sarov left the monastery for the forest, where he often preached to animals and shared his food with them.[14]

The earth is understood not in a global sense but as life-bearing soil. Indeed, until the advent of industrial civilization, the Russian peasant considered himself or herself less an individual than a transient moment in the life of the *rad*, the eternal kinship community. Like many indigenous peoples, the Russian folk saw themselves as being brought into the *rad* from the sperm and ovule of their parents, just as the seed, buried in the earth's womb, gives new life to the corn procreated through the death of the seed. And then they return into the womb of Mother Earth.

Mircea Eliade tells us that in the Ukraine, young couples used to roll on the furrows on St. George's Day after the priest had blessed the crops, and in Russia the priest himself was rolled on the ground by the women, not only to consecrate the crops but as part of some confused memory of the primeval sacred marriage."[15] In the twentieth century the first Russian folk song ever recorded referred to the River Volga as "dear Mother."[16]

Dostoyevsky was able to grasp the subtle religious intuitions of the folk. In *The Possessed* the crippled Maria asks an old nun endowed with the gift of prophecy: "What is the Mother of God? What do you think?" To which the old nun replies: "The Mother of God is the great Mother, the damp earth, and herein lies great joy for men; and every earthly woe and every earthly tear is a joy for us; and when you water the earth with your tears a foot deep, you will rejoice at everything at once, and your sorrow will be no more, such is the prophecy."[17]

In pre-industrial Russia peasants even took the earth as witness to an oath. Slava Smirnov describes a woman's actions before going to church. She makes peace with her family, then extends it to her neighbors and all of nature, addressing the fair sun, the clear moon, the dark nights, the blowing wind, and the earth. "Moist Mother Earth," she confesses, "I shed my tears upon you. Moist Mother Earth that nourishes me and gives me drink, I am a worthless foolish sinner, for my legs trample you down as they walk." Then she purifies her hands by rubbing them with earth, and resumes: "I wish to touch you with my head to beg your blessing and your pardon. I have torn up your breast, cutting with the iron plough. . . . I have bruised you under the harrow with its rusty teeth of iron. . . . Pardon me in the name of Christ the Savior."[18]

In the Russian tradition a tension has always existed between the simple intuition that one is a child of Mother Earth and theologians' insistence that the human is the summit of the animal and plant world, and represents the most advanced expression of cosmic life.

Today, as in the past, priests call on humans to participate in the divine plan for the ultimate transfiguration of Creation, a transcendental vision often depicted on icons. Then new flowers, grasses, and trees will burst forth upon the earth. Human redemption at the Last Judgment becomes integral with the transformation of Mother Earth to a new level of beauty and cosmic glory.

AN ECORELIGIOUS PILGRIMAGE THROUGH THE RUSSIAN NORTH

In August 1991 we had the extraordinary good fortune to experience a critical moment in history: the attempted overthrow of Soviet President Mikhail Gorbachev, the defeat of the coup by a people's resistance, and the overthrow of the communist regime.

We had joined a "Christianity and Ecology" study tour of the Russian North. Those three weeks became a profound experience of apprehension, joy, and hope—hope that the crises we witnessed might spur regeneration of the land, the church, and the spirit of the people.

Four days before the "August surprise," 70 people from the North American Conference on Christianity and Ecology (NACCE) and 210 from the Soviet "Save Peace and Nature," or SPAN (a Soviet NGO of environmental, peacemaking, and educational groups), gathered on the cruise ship *SS Fyodor Dostoyevsky* on the Moscow River.

Of the 70 Americans, 29 were Orthodox, most of them adherents of the Russian tradition. To them this was an opportunity to gain a more intimate sense of the love for the earth in the Orthodox heritage, and go back to their spiritual roots through visits to ancient churches and monasteries.

Many of the Soviets[*] were actively involved with environmental problems. About 30 percent were already baptized; many others were drawn to Christianity. To the Soviets, however, the idea of an explicit alliance between religion and ecology was somewhat puzzling.

When we woke on August 19 to the rumor that President Gorbachev had been ousted, we were stunned. Nevertheless, some of us visited the Church of the Transfiguration in Podolsk to participate in its reconstruction. When we returned to the ship most of us had seen tanks, watched the visibly fearful Muscovites reading posters in which Russian President Boris Yeltsin called for a general strike, and listened to the American Embassy's warning to stay off the streets. Several of us, however, stayed in the heart of the city to witness the unfolding drama.

One young American woman, an Orthodox convert, stood before

---

[*] We refer to the citizens of the former Soviet Republics collectively as "Soviets" simply because no better term has emerged.

Soviet tanks in Red Square and blessed the astonished soldiers. After
Boris Yeltsin had broadcast a short-wave appeal to Russian Orthodox
Patriarch Aleksy II, the Patriarch responded by calling on Soviet soldiers
not to obey orders that would result in bloodshed. Father Aleksandr
Borisov, an Orthodox priest elected to the Moscow City Council, partici-
pated in talks with the Patriarch, and on his way to the Russian White
House, baptized troops and gave out 4,000 New Testaments.

Despite the exhilarating resistance, the overall mood in the first two
days was one of foreboding. What if this became a bloody counter-revo-
lution?

Yet for some religious leaders in the group, the events had a different
dimension. On Monday evening, while the confrontation around the
Kremlin became more intense, Father Dmitri Melnik of the Church
of the Transfiguration—who was to be with us for the entire trip—
withdrew to pray. Young Father Gerasim, from the St. Herman of
Alaska Monastery in California, told us that he would remember this
day not for the uprising, but as the Orthodox Feast of the Transfiguration. He had visited the church that Father Dmitri was rebuilding.
"The physical events today—" He shrugged. "Just a bunch of in-

Father Dmitri Melnik, Church
of the Transfiguration in Podolsk, near Moscow. (Photo by
James Young)

sects—replacing another group of insects.

"Let's reflect. When we visited the St. Sergius Holy Trinity Monastery in Zagorsk on Sunday we could see the *magnificence* of the icons, jewels, censers, vestments! But is that the true Church? At Father Dmitri's church we saw walls rising from the rubble. Rebuilt by the hands of believers! It was a privilege to work beside them. The volunteers who come regularly are simple people. Some lay stones. Some do artisanry. Some paint icons."

His voice was breathless, his eyes shining. "The congregation is planting flowers and vegetables. Renewing the earth! It is a way to encourage self-sustaining communities—and the *sense* of community. Rebuilding and renewing, from the grassroots, that is the resurrection—and the true primitive church."

The next day, even while Soviet tanks patrolled the streets, we set sail up the Moscow River for the Volga and Lakes Onega and Ladoga. In the opening ceremony, while we stood on the deck in the radiant Moscow sunshine, the voices of the all-male ecclesiastical choir in gold-embroidered maroon robes soaring heavenward, the threat of terrestrial warfare seemed distant. The choir chanted with joyous solemnity, we lit candles in the wind, and the priest blessed bread topped with an egg, then offered us pieces. A folk singer and her accordionist husband entertained us with peasant tunes and dances; clergy and layleaders addressed the throng; and after a lively snake dance around the ship, we adjourned to a communal refection of vodka, wine, and traditional dishes.

On Wednesday, while nature-walking, we heard that the "bad guys" had fled. It seemed incredible. Our Soviet companions appeared subdued, uneasy about the unknown looming before them.

The days became full. There were lectures on Russian culture, talks on each country's political and economic problems, and a series on the "seven environmental degradations"—and the seven biblical injunctions to prevent them—delivered by environmental scientist Calvin De Witt, whom we had known through visiting his Au Sable Institute. Renat Perelet, the Secretary of the Soviet Committee for International Geo-Biospheric Programs, led discussions on threats to the Soviet ecosystem, and together with NACCE director Fred Krueger, coordinated daily programs. Father Dmitri described the efforts of the Russian church to save the environment, and Father Herman, Abbot of St. Herman of Alaska Monastery, outlined the basic features of Orthodoxy and recounted his happy childhood in Latvia before "atheistic communism." There were visits to ancient churches and monasteries, and "ecological walks" with De Witt and other environmentalists. And every night there were concerts by the ecclesiastical choir, classical recitals, or programs of Russian and American folk song and dance in which everyone participated with lusty enthusiasm.

In the American group the 29 Orthodox were the dominant element. In addition to Abbot Herman, there were three young monks from his mission in California, one nun from a nearby convent, and one deacon. The monks lived in the forest, followed the monastic tradition of abstaining from meat entirely and fasting two days a week, gave Earth its sabbath, and grew most of their own food. But except for Father Gerasim, they demonstrated little awareness of the complex interplay of biological, agricultural, economic, and political factors in the ecological crisis. They saw it almost entirely in terms of sin. The monks came only occasionally to the environmental discussions, and the nun spent most of her time praying. To Father Herman, the environment reflected the spiritual state of society, hence needed "cleaning up." It soon became clear that he was chiefly occupied with converting Russian souls to Christianity.

If ever anyone could be called "charismatic"—in the original sense of seeming to have some divinely inspired power—it was Father Herman. A tall, broad-shouldered man with a flowing gray beard, flowing black robes, and bright blue eyes, he strode everywhere he went, yet could stop at any moment and give you his undivided attention. Everything he said seemed uttered with the passionate emphasis of a Dostoyevskyan personality.

Many of the American Orthodox laypersons had a keen grasp of ecological problems, but their awareness seemed to have been stimulated chiefly by secular movements, not the church. Most of the converts had been attracted by the concept of original church, the emphasis on mystic experience, and the ritual. There was a fervor among them. They often embraced each other, their faces glowed as they touched the earth and kissed the icons in the crumbling churches, and their voices crescendoed in countless al-le-*lu*-i-as as we stood through improvised services.

Father Dmitri's long talk "The Russian Orthodox Perspective on the Environment," sounded like a strange mixture of Creation theology and fundamentalism. The Devil implanted sins into the hearts of man. Man did not want to repent, so the Lord drove him from Paradise. Then nature became ailing, like man. . . . He did not discuss specific environmental problems, or biblical injunctions to prevent degradation, or plans for church action, except Metropolitan Pitirim's statement that ecological concern must become a priority; so far, Dmitri admitted, little had been done.

Yet Dmitri had ventured into the world of action with his grassroots effort to rebuild his church and renew the earth on which it stood, and had initiated an imaginative project to save his community from pollution. We decided to ask him and his wife Tatyana more about it.

He was a slim, earnest-looking young man with intense gray eyes, long dark hair, and a pointed, finely trimmed beard. We had often seen him, clad in a long gray robe with a high collar, walking the deck alone, absorbed in thought. He welcomed us shyly into the cabin and sat down beside his wife. She had straight brown hair, dressed plainly, and wore no make-up. But her quick smile, direct gaze, and expressive gestures radiated warmth. She also spoke better English than he, and her vivaciousness seemed to draw him out of his reserve. As time passed, he occasionally teased her by pushing her shoulder, she pushed back, and they both laughed softly.

With Tatyana's help, he told us that he was born in the Ukraine 33 years ago, had been a priest for nine years, and had met her when he was studying theology at Zagorsk, where she was a librarian. They had married 10 years ago, and had no children.

He had been interested in "the problem of ecology" since last year when he was given the Church of the Transfiguration as his parish. "The lake on our church property was dirty!" he said with a grimace. "Then SPAN asked us to join a peace walk of Russians and Americans to make protests about nuclear testing at the island of Novaya Zemlya in the White Sea. Later authorities did stop it! On that walk we also saw what had happened to nature. We saw that peace and repairing the Creation go together. And also, repairing the economy."

"We made friends with Americans," interpolated Tatyana. "We all slept in tents, we sang together, and at night we'd come together and talk about politics, religion, the alcohol problem, the position of women, all kinds of things! We also talked with people in villages about what we were doing. They were glad. It seemed to give them courage to speak to authorities."

"So when you got back, you thought about taking action?"

"That's right. Factories were dumping polluted water into our lake. We complained to the Podolsk town council. They listened politely, and did nothing. So we made a canal that returned the water to the factories. Fish had died in it. We took a dead, smelling fish on a platter to the council. 'If you give us bad water,' we said, 'we give you bad fish.'" She laughed merrily. "Well, the plants stopped polluting! And a swan returned to the lake—a sign of good water!"

"What about your sermons?" we asked Father Dmitri. "Do you urge people to protest to the central government about ecological problems?"

He sighed quietly. "Well—when I talk about them, it is what *we* can do to improve things here in the village. Our people have so many problems, especially money problems."

Later we talked with Tatyana alone to learn more about her role as a woman in the Orthodox church. Yes, women were subordinate, she said—they were not even allowed into the sanctuary behind the iconostasis. But this did not trouble her. "My work is devoted to the church and my home. I sing in the choir, I write letters for the church. I help Dmitri with people who have problems." Women have always played an important if somewhat invisible role in the church, she insisted. And today, unlike the old days, women could sing in church choirs.

"Would you like to see women priests?" we asked.

"Oh, no!" Her eyes widened. "That would change the church. It must keep tradition."

The Soviets quickly comprehended Calvin De Witt's "seven degradations of Creation," and in environmental workshops described vivid examples of each. Land conversion, for example, had caused loss of Siberian forests vital to the oxygen supply of the world. Water had been drained from the Aral Sea to irrigate cotton; today the half-drained shore was laden with salt dust, which poisoned humans and blew destruction on the very cotton the water was to nourish.

Land degradation had touched Soviet lives through topsoil loss; fields had become chemicalized. As for conversion of resources, transformation of petroleum into plastics and some pesticides resulted in poisoned ground water and rivers. "Just look out the window at the Volga, the great artery of our history—polluted!" several exclaimed. Often with great emotion, they described toxic runoff and the way dams severed fish migrations. The flood control gates at St. Petersburg (which environmental groups were opposing) could bring disaster.

Engineers from the Chernobyl nuclear plant described their experiences of the explosion, and Natasha, a young Ukrainian, spoke about her work with leukemic children, victims of Chernobyl. Yet few could envision any solution but a technological one—new devices, from America.

They were painfully aware that burning coal, oil, and wood resulted in unhealthy air. Polluted air, water, food—these were their primary worries. Sometimes they felt powerless. Then they reminded themselves that even though it had little money, the environmental movement had seen significant victories, such as forcing authorities to cease nuclear testing in Kazakhstan, and halting the lowering of the Aral Sea water level.

Although they had little acquaintance with the Bible and none with De Witt's approach, many Soviets did respond to his paradigm of seven biblical injunctions to prevent environmental degradation: keep the Creation as God keeps us; be disciples of the last Adam, Christ, not the first; provide the Creation with a Sabbath rest; enjoy, not destroy, God's Creation; seek first the Kingdom, not self-interest; seek contentment as your greatest gain; do not fail to act on what you know is right. Some responses seemed pent up for years. Is man descended from the ape? asked Alexei, a young physicist. Can man live without culture? asked Irina, a middle-aged nuclear scientist. What is culture? asked others. Whereupon Father Dmitri equated it with religion and gave a long lecture.

Irina went further, pouring out a long anguished catharsis of suffering under "Godless Communism." The nuclear disaster of Chernobyl was the "work of devils, the red hour of evil." The Communists pulled down holy churches. Now, however, Bibles were arriving from America. The fate of Mother Volga was the fate of the people and culture. Before the revolution thousands of clear streams fed it with trout, and it gave people a communal togetherness. The church owned much of this land and contributed to the sense of community. But the Soviets built huge hydropower stations, uprooting millions. And she went on, for over an hour.

It seemed useless to comment that over the centuries the church had also been a feudal landlord, with vast wealth and many serfs, and although sometimes at odds with the czars, on the whole a willing partner in power. A few Americans pointed out that the problem was not communism per se, but industrialism and its handmaiden, materialism, and added that the Communists' exploitation of resources could be explained by their perceived need to catch up with the West. In the United States, too, hydroelectric projects had uprooted powerless people. Irina and other Soviets nodded, but it was clearly difficult to comprehend that this could occur in America.

The common nature of our problems became palpable, however, when the Russians, with assistance from Americans, staged a skit depicting a town meeting to protest a chemical spill in a Russian river. The company director (Russian) assured the meeting that the guilty would be punished and the situation was under control, while the Greens (Russian) declared that they had campaigned vainly for safer technology when the plant was approved. The director repeated that the water was not badly contaminated, but still, the guilty would be punished, etc. Local protesters (Russians and Americans in the audience, acting spontaneously) leaped in. An American insisted that Greenpeace be admitted. Russians applauded. A Russian pointed out that the plant was important to the military, and urged workers to strike. An American demanded that the director live with the people if he was so sure the water was pure; and the local priest (Father Dmitri) presented officials with poisoned fish and asked them to eat it. Finally, a dying woman (American) was carried in by two doctors (Russian), and amid huzzas and laughter, the town council chair admitted it was time to close the plant. It all happened in the Soviet Union, and to Americans it all felt like home.

Only a few Americans had been in the Soviet Union before, and even fewer Soviets had seen the United States. Gregory Temkin, international vice-president of SPAN and chief organizer of the trip, had traveled extensively in both countries.

He was a dark, balding man with small tired eyes and a reserved manner. As he talked, however, he began to smile, somewhat gravely, and to become more expansive. In excellent English, acquired at Moscow State University's famous language school, he told us that he had been born in Moscow in 1950, and that his wife and son were with him.

While working as an English-language interpreter in Syria and Iraq, he had written a book on the culture of Syria—"a meeting place of the three world monotheistic religions"—and become fascinated by Islamic art. Returning to Russia in 1985, he realized he could no longer endure a conventional life. "I traveled. I went kayaking, canoeing, getting more interested in wildlife. As I saw what was happening to our environment, I began to plan SPAN. An NGO like this would have been impossible before Gorbachev."

SPAN's first trip was a sail in an old renovated fishing boat on the White Sea to protest nuclear testing on Novaya Zemlya. "Our only means of determining direction and weather was a transistor radio and a map. We called on villages and talked about nuclear testing. Later we demonstrated against nuclear testing or environmental destruction on the Volga, the Black Sea, Lake Baikal, and also the River Vuoksa where it crosses the border between Finland and Russia. Because pollution from Finnish paper mills crosses into Russia and Russian pollution into Finland, there really *is* no border. Along with American groups, we also co-sponsored three peace walks last year—to the Ukraine, the Semipalatinsk nuclear testing ground in Kazakhstan, and the Archangelsk-White Sea testing ground. Forty-eight people on that trip were baptized in the Sea at Solovetsky Monastery—the first baptisms there since 1917.

"We need more people-based NGOs if we are going to save the planet. And saving it could draw us together. The interests of the planet *must* come before interests of independent sovereignty. That kind of recognition is an historic leap in our civilization."

"And the church—where does it fit in?" we asked.

He pondered a moment. "It is—part of the total picture. In the Soviet Union the ideology of the Communist Party is dead. There is no ideology at all, no ethic. There is a void."

"Many in the rest of the world feel a void, too."

He nodded. "I've seen that. Here, it is more clear. But there is great opportunity, too, because society is being reorganized. The church is the visible center where this can happen."

"Is the church doing enough?"

"No. For the planet, especially, the church could do more. But there is a beginning. Alexei II endorsed and blessed this trip, for instance."

"The church seems hampered by the past," we observed.

"True. And by its memories of power. And in Communist times there was collaboration. And it is still very hierarchical. But today it is looking forward—renovating buildings, and setting up hospices, soup kitchens, orphanages. Many Russians are turning to Christianity. The church has *survived*. It is one part of our heritage that goes on."

He looked out the window at the birches and pines, the sturdy wooden farmhouses and onion-domed churches lining the Volga. "We need a planetary vision," he said slowly. "But we also need roots. Last year I was baptized in the White Sea. It was a way of merging with my roots. In a kind of Dostoyevskyan sense, I feel—well, my Russianness more today."

The young Ukrainian woman who taught Russian classes on ship and worked with Chernobyl's children was also thinking about being baptized, but was not sure she was "ready."

Natasha Shablya had long straight blond hair and carefully made-up bright blue eyes, and she dressed somewhat provocatively to enhance her slim figure. To see her in the dining-room exchanging flirtatious glances with men, one might not have guessed how important it was to her to find some meaning in life during this era of upheaval and confusion.

As she sat in her cabin, twisting her handkerchief, the words came haltingly at first. "Nature was always important to me. Religion, not so much. My mother and father were baptized, but they did not go to church often. It was permitted by the government, but not encouraged. In these last years, I feel, inside, I am a believer. And at the same time, the environment seems more important. Especially since Chernobyl."

When the Chernobyl explosion occurred, Natasha was studying foreign languages in the Ukraine. She was horrified. "Then I became a close friend of a woman whose child was born with cerebral palsy. It was torture for me. At least a thousand children just in my town, Vinnitsa, were affected by the radiation. One day a woman phoned—she needed a volunteer translator for a children's fund. I agreed, and one project there led to another, and last summer they sent me with a group of victims to Sweden for three weeks.

"They were not the worst victims—for them it was too hard to travel. But all the children on the trip had lost their families, and some were in rags. None of them could smile."

The Swedes were "wonderful," Natasha went on. Their philosophy focused on teaching youngsters how to be as self-reliant as possible, because as orphans, essentially they would have to deal with their problems alone. "They learned to collect logs, tie them, burn them for cooking, and make log tables and chairs without nails. It was almost like the Stone Age. They ate fresh vegetables, and milk, and learned to cook and gather berries and other food from the earth.

"They learned a lot from the Swedes, who care very much about the earth. Every day there were lessons from nature. Like how to make a sundial and canoe. Once we followed a road with hunters' traps, and saw how cruel it could be for an animal to suffer for days and then die of starvation. The children collected waste paper in brigades, competing to get the highest pile. By the end, most of them could smile a little. And they had learned very much. I did, too."

Since then, her life had become more complicated, Natasha continued with a sigh. She volunteered even more time to the Vinnitsa Children's Fund. But she also had to earn a living as English teacher and translator. She had almost no time to herself.

She was groping to put it all together. "Before this trip, I was a believer. But not so much as now, after going to all the churches we've seen. Before, I never thought of a connection between religion and saving the earth for the children, and their children, and their children. Now I am thinking about all these things."

A silent participant in the dialogues was the earth itself. It seemed to unite us through some invisible power. In places the Volga was sullied, but in others it was almost clean, its flow a blessing upon life itself. In cities the sky was sullen with smoke from the icons of progress, but in the countryside there was rich green forest and the living, brooding, wondering land.

In the discussion groups Russians and Americans found more common ground, on topics ranging from education to human economy vis-à-vis God's economy. Among the guidelines that emerged was recognizing the uniqueness of humans in God's Creation, while affirming the primal goodness of nature; teaching Christian ecological principles; and acknowledging that market forces, while dynamic, lack social, spiritual, and environmental responsibility.

Interspersed with discussions were visits to churches and monasteries. From a distance, the gilded onion-shaped domes in the sunlight seemed to flicker like flames and, inside the churches, the voices, too, seemed to spire upwards like flames. As the choir intoned the hymns, the voices of ordinary folk often sang a refrain, if not more than a resonant sound from the depths of their bodies. Sometimes believers would stand before an icon, transfixed for long minutes, tears washing their

Father Dmitri Melnik and Father Herman (right) in baptism service on Kizhi Island at the Pokrovsky Church of the Intercession. (Photo by James Young)

cheeks. And we recalled a service at the Leningrad Cathedral in 1967, where we watched a young man making the rounds of each icon in the vast interior, kissing each as if to embrace it, then repeating his circular pilgrimage again and again, all the while weeping tears of communion.

The church and setting of Kizhi Island were the high point of the trip. There 15 Russians from our ship were baptized into the Christian faith.

After being submerged thrice in the cold waters of Lake Onega, then rubbed down and kissed by Father Herman, they walked up the hill to the old wooden Pokrovsky Church of the Intercession. From there one could see little but birch forests; no motor sounds broke the stillness. Inside, the four-tiered iconostasis was replete with gold, but there was no electricity and the walls were of logs joined with mud and moss. We could glimpse the primitive church.

For three hours we stood through a service welcoming the new believers. Candles were given to the converts. Behind the iconostasis, "the screen beyond which the heavenly mysteries are enacted," the priests changed their black garb for richly hued church vestments. From a large spoon dipped into the chalice, Father Dmitri and Father Herman administered to each communicant the intinctured bread and wine, as the priests chanted "This is my body, this is my blood." Through it all the congregation sang their embrace: "Receive the fountain of immortality."

Periodically, priests emerged from the sanctuary to read a prayer, sing, or perform altar rites. Standing near a door of the iconostasis, we could see into the sacred space; it was strewn with planks and icons waiting for restoration, and priests were talking informally.

Worshippers wandered in and out. Several peasants touched the earth as they came in, crossed themselves, and watched these unusual visitors, their eyes big with wonder.

Tatyana sang alone, joined in congregant singing, read part of the divine liturgy, walked up to the priests to discuss urgent matters, and adjusted Dimitri's vestments—but never went behind the iconostasis.

Our fascination stimulated one Orthodox woman to invite us to join in the gift of the blessed bread offered to any who wish to receive it. (The bread intinctured with wine is only for full members of the Orthodox community.) We did eat of the loaf, good peasant bread, and it brought images of loaves shared beside another lake, millennia ago.

Father Herman took confession by pressing a Bible onto each penitent's head, placing his stole over it and his own head, leaning down cheek-by-cheek to listen intently and converse, and finally, over the stole, making the sign of the cross. During Natasha's confession, sounds of weeping emerged from the stole. For long afterwards her body trembled with sobs, until at last a deep calm seemed to come over her.

Not far from us stood Sasha, a slender Radio Moscow journalist with lively black eyes. His face was glowing in the light of the candles. Afterwards he approached us. "I can hardly describe it. The quiet inside me! The joy!"

The farewell celebration was a festive affair. There were speeches and dancing and singing, hugging and toasts. Together we had lived through the beginning of a second Russian Revolution. And we knew in our bones as well as our heads that all creatures share one earth.

Gregory was so encouraged by the trip's success that he planned to go ahead with a cherished dream—leading a trip to Islamic sites in Kazakhstan and Azerbaijan. That dream was a reflection of his continuing search. Over the years he had talked with Muslims and Buddhists, studied yoga, and become attracted to the idea of a universal karma.

"Early this century, Vladimir Vernadsky, a great Russian geochemist, helped found the Cosmist movement. He spoke about the *biosphere*, which produced man, and the *technosphere*, which was produced by man and has interfered with the biosphere, and the *noosphere*, which would be a merging of the two. A oneness of the Creation and conscious development."

"Sounds like Teilhard de Chardin, who influenced Thomas Berry," we observed.

"Teilhard's work I know, but just a little. Berry's not at all."

Gregory listened with great interest as we told of Berry's writing. Then he seized on an article we had brought about Berry's work, and said he would try to meet him. "It sounds as if Berry speaks in a concrete way about regaining the wholeness of primitive man. But this wholeness, I think, we must *create*, so it will be more conscious."

REFLECTIONS ON THE "SECOND RUSSIAN REVOLUTION"

As we ponder the happenings in the former Soviet Union since August 1991, it is hard to imagine anything but ultimate disaster to "moist Mother Earth" if present trends continue. Within a few months of the revolution that was to bring freedom from Communist oppression of people and land, American, French, Japanese, and Korean firms began to shop for nuclear technology at bargain prices, log Siberia's forests, mine its coal, export its natural gas, and use its land for reprocessing nuclear waste. Today industrialized countries and transnationals continue to exploit such resources. Environmental groups have protested, but today they have less money and power. Across the globe, the World Bank has generally placed market forces above long-term survival of the planet, the welfare of people, and the endurance of cultures.

Meanwhile, the economic "shock therapy" promoted by the United States and the IMF has brought unemployment, general deterioration of dwellings, and degeneration of the universal health care system. Yet for many years, the Russians in power felt they had no future if they failed to join the world market as defined by the West.

The results? One is a "consumerism boom." Many of the goodies of a system "just like America" are not only imported (causing depletion of Russian rubles) but are what people need least—Coca-cola, Western cigarettes, pornography, designer clothes, and luxury cars.

Thus a few people have done well, and the new Russian Mafia, very well indeed. What about the others?

A few grim statistics on health are revealing. Between 1990 and 1994, the lifespan of Russian men dropped from 64 to 58[19] . . . The number of young women suffering from chronic disorders has increased from 43.9 in the 1980s to 75 percent today. Since they are carriers of the gene pool, this level of health represents a grave threat to the nation's future . . . More than two-thirds of the people live in areas suffering from ecological problems—resulting in increases of digestive, circulatory, respiratory, heart, and nervous disorders . . . Only ten percent of school children can be considered healthy . . . Many children are just plain hungry, for jobless parents cannot afford to feed them . . . The calorie content of school meals comes to about 25-30 percent of recommended norms . . . Almost two million children have ended up on the streets.[20]

In 1967, 1982, 1985, and 1991, we visited many parts of the Soviet Union and visited many schools, known as offering the world's best system of mass education. Everywhere we saw rosy-cheeked, boisterous, laughing youngsters. The children were always referred to as "our treasure." Today many pupils are too weak to learn. In many cities and villages, there is only one textbook for every four children. Many teachers have not been paid for half a year or more. In January 1998 nearly half a million teachers went on strike—something virtually unheard of in a country that traditionally honored professional duty in teaching.[21] One of the world's richest states, in terms of natural resources and education of the people, is being reduced to pauperism.

For decades, environmental abuse has been a thorny problem in Russia and her sister republics. Under the centrally planned Communist economy, pollution control, energy efficiency, and pesticide regulation were poor in comparison to the United States. But in the long run, an economy oriented to consumerism and profit-making, and tied to the West's expectation that it act as supplier of primary raw materials, is likely to wreak more devastation upon the ecosystem.

In 1990 Soviet authorities and all Soviet faith communities, notably the Russian Orthodox church, co-hosted the Global Form of Parliamentary and Spiritual Leaders. It was an unprecedented partnership. Both President Gorbachev and Evgeni Velikov of the Soviet Academy of Sciences spoke of the spiritual element of the environmental crisis, while Metropolitan Pitirim described "the innumerable disasters that we have caused the earth" and a plan to use the Volokolamsk monastery for teaching ecological principles. Nearly a decade later it was still "in the planning stage."

Renat Perelet, the Russian geophysicist who helped lead our trip, described the situation in a letter to us: "In my conversations with Russian churchmen I could not ignite any real interest in taking the environment as an urgent issue for the Russian Orthodox church. They usually saw it as a non-issue, being firmly certain that the Bible has everything about the environment and there is nothing to discuss or no sense to dig into the Bible to better understand its environmental dimensions, as well as to learn how other religions treat it."

The church seems preoccupied with other issues, especially the threat posed by new "free market" competition with Roman Catholics and evangelical Protestants.

There have been some bright spots. While we could never get news of Father Dmitri and Tatyana, we managed to communicate with others.

Natasha phoned to tell us that she had received a fellowship to study English as a second language at Kent State University and, masters in hand, was returning to the Ukraine. Through a friend we learned that Gregory had expanded SPAN, called it Global Span, set up offices in ecotourism groups to Siberia and Muslim regions of the former Soviet Union. He also founded a 100-page monthly devoted to ecology.

After Father Herman suffered two strokes in 1992, Father Gerasim took over, broadened the monastery's educational and pastoral work, and continued organic gardening with monks and neighbors. Yet Father Herman miraculously recovered and proceeded to found new monastaries in California and Indiana.

In Moscow, we learned in a letter from Renat Perelet, a university has been founded, stressing ecology and its interrelatedness with other disciplines, a concept congenial with Thomas Berry's ideas about education in the ecological age. Called the International Independent (meaning private) University of Ecology and Politology, it opened in 1992 with 1,600 students enrolled in departments of ecology, economy, law, journalism, political sciences, linguistics, and business.

This was the picture in 1996. Since then, as Russia has moved closer to disintegration, we have had no news of our friends.

There have been signs of a spiritual renewal in Russia and her sister republics. Thousands of churches have re-opened, hundreds of monasteries and convents restored, and television runs programs on the cultural heritage of the Orthodox church. Catholics, Protestants, Jews, and Muslims have also experienced a revival. According to one survey, 30 percent of Russians under 25 have converted from atheism to a belief in God. Nevertheless, another study shows that many people want to exhibit their involvement in the faith, but few really believe.[22]

Thus some are drawn to the immutable quality of the Orthodox tradition in a fast-changing world. Others find it conflicts with "rational" views. In the words of one young Soviet from Kazakhstan: "My heart *wants* to believe, but my head cannot." People like him are looking for a way that encourages personal evolution, "makes sense," and is less religious (in the sense of adherence to doctrine and ritual) than spiritual. *Dukhovnost*, which can be roughly translated as "spirituality" and has meaning to both believers and non-believers, is a word heard increasingly among Russians, including some political leaders.[23]

In the face of growing societal breakdown, could the more liberal wing of the church form an alliance with ecological forces and groups committed to social justice? It could not provide the whole key to renewal of religion at the grassroots. But it would offer a unique opportunity for the Orthodox church to attract the young and become a more vital actor in a changing society. It could animate a greening of the old faith.

We often remember our feelings at the old wooden Pokrovsky Church of the Intercession as we looked out at Lake Onega, and thought of another lake in Galilee, and the miracle of the loaves and fishes. In the primitive church lies a model of communal participation and the commitment to simplicity that are essential for "moist Mother Earth" to survive.

Developments in Eastern Christianity

The Ecumenical Patriarchate's 1989 "Orthodoxy and the Ecological Crisis" has been so widely praised that it was one of two documents recommended to all the World Council member churches after the 1991 Assembly. What action has emerged since the original message?

Each year the Ecumenical Patriarchate has issued a similar encyclical on September 1. There have also been several conferences in Europe. While including some discussion of possible action, the emphasis has been on religious alienation and the need to develop an *agāpe* kind of spirituality before nature.

The fact that concrete problems and action steps are included at these conferences seems largely due to the ongoing support of the World Wildlife Fund (WWF) and its affiliate, the International Consultancy of Religion, Education, and Culture (ICOREC). Largely because of that influence, scientists and environmentalists are present. Particularly notable was the first-ever gathering of all the Patriarchs of the Orthodox Church in 1993. Among other things, it was agreed that each jurisdiction make September 1 a day for prayer and action on ecology, and incorporate environmental theology into seminaries. Notable, too, was the 1992 seminar on the island of Chalki, at which Greek-born Prince Philip of Great Britain, WWF International President, issued a subtle challenge: "There can be no honest theology unless actual processes of nature—animal, vegetable, and mineral—that Christians believe were created by God are accepted and become part of that theology. Humanity may be a 'special creation,' but the natural system is interdependent."[24]

The church in Greece, particularly, has been responsive to such continuous prodding. The Ormylia project has been functioning since 1991, and the monastery (a nunnery) runs training sessions for local farmers and village officials in organic farming. Several monasteries on Mount Athos are working with WWF on environmental programs, such as preserving the last major tract of wild forest in Greece, and ecumenical programs on theology and ecology have been established on Chalki. Many monasteries on the Greek islands are working with WWF in monitoring wildlife or providing nesting sites for migratory birds—an important function in the Mediterranean, known for the many hunters who derive ego-satisfaction from killing birds.

Romania hosted a World Fellowship of Orthodox Youth seminar on "Man and Creation" that included training in practical skills, and there are other projects in Romania, Bulgaria, Ethiopia, and elsewhere.

How much activity will emerge on the parish level in these countries remains to be seen.

Challenges Before the Church

Despite the U.S. reputation for being progressive, Orthodox institutions here have generally lagged behind their European counterparts in recognizing the partnership of religion and ecology. One reason is that the Orthodox are splintered into up to 50 churches (depending on how one counts them), reflecting their ethnic origins and sectarian splits. The ongoing conflicts are less theological than jurisdictional. Moreover, Orthodox participation in religion and ecology conferences has been weaker than in the case of Protestant and Roman Catholics.

In the 1990s the number of conferences did begin to grow. A major spur was Ecumenical Patriarch Bartholomaios' visit to the U.S. in late 1997. The Orthodox have yet to match this progress with more attention to the subject in their periodicals and seminaries. The *Orthodox Observer*, *Orthodox Word*, *Orthodox Church*, and *Epiphany* occasionally refer to the "ecological problem." *Epiphany* even devoted an entire issue to "The Transfiguration of Nature." All these periodicals contain some concrete ideas, but in general the conclusions are variants on the proposition that "the real answer to the ecological problem is to recover a sense of our true identity as immortal beings." Despite the 1993 agreement that all Orthodox seminaries incorporate environmental theology, in mid-1999 neither of the two leading seminaries (St. Vladimir's and Holy Cross) offered a single course in the subject.

Some individual priests and lay persons have kept the proposals in the Ecumenical Patriarch's message alive by writing about them, or—more rarely—involving their congregations. Minnesotan John Munter, a member of our 1991 "Christianity and Ecology" group in Russia, has written ecological commentary for the *Orthodox Church* and pursues his own environmental projects, such as raising alpaca, that will be useful for people uprooted by the growing world climate changes. Elizabeth Theokritoff of Holy Trinity Church in Randolph, New Jersey, has published articles outlining proposals on Christian environmental education, parish action, and mobilization of young people to initiate local projects (ideas drawn directly from *Orthodoxy and the Ecological Crisis*, pub-

lished by the Ecumenical Patriarchate and WWF). Neither Munter nor
Theokritoff is involved in any activities at parish level, however.

Behind the Orthodox inertia lie several impediments to movement:

- The age-old reluctance of Orthodoxy, a more contemplative tradition than its Western counterparts, to promote social action. As we
  have seen, there are times when it does meet challenges with organized activity. There is nothing prohibiting it.

    In the U.S. Orthodox clergy agree that preserving the Crea-
  tion is a legitimate concern. But at the diocesan level, you are
  told that an appropriate response to the Ecumenical Patriarch's
  Message is up to the local parish. At the parish level, most
  priests are only vaguely aware of the Message, and they are too
  involved in "more demanding" immediate concerns.

- Preoccupation with other problems. Among them, ongoing debate over membership in the NCC and WCC, concern over the
  splintering of the church, the departure of many young people,
  and growing insistence among laypersons on more participation
  in church governance.

- As in Roman Catholicism, ambivalence toward the "feminine element." It is strong in the liturgy, art, and music, and Mary the
  Mother is revered—yet real women are subordinate. Most Orthodox women appear content, and often find places where they can
  contribute their gifts—through pastoral duties or sitting on church
  councils, for example. Nevertheless, unrest has been fermenting
  for many years. The three conferences that WCC convened on the
  role of women in the Orthodox church arrived at few conclusions,
  but revealed the growing diversity of viewpoints.

    In the U.S. Eva Catafygioutu Topping has become a leading
  spokeswoman for a small but growing number of Orthodox
  women. Her hardly radical proposal is that a commission of hierarchs, priests, laywomen, and laymen study all aspects of women's
  status, ranging from their "uncleanliness" to the thorniest issue of
  all—ordaining them. Today hierarchs talk of reviving the role of
  deaconess (serving only women), but refuse to discuss ordaining
  women. As one priest told us, "Women are *morally* equal to men,
  but we need to work according to the categories of Creation."
  How, then, could women fully share in the task of restoring the
  battered web of Creation?

- The strong inclination toward anthropocentrism, or one of its variants, theanthropocentrism (everything revolves around God and humanity.)

- A wide gulf between the ways of the cloister and the ways of the world. On the other hand, it is precisely in this area that some of the most promising change in thinking and acting has begun. The Orthodox 1989 Message on protection of the environment emphasized that in an age of consumerism a certain asceticism—asceticism for all—is needed, and pointed to the monastic tradition as offering important insights. It develops sensitivity to the suffering of all Creation, and emphasizes community rather than individual life as central to a balanced understanding of our needs. As we have seen, Project Ormylia is one monastery where "community" has taken on a new meaning. Thus far there are only a few such places in the Orthodox world where monks, nuns, priests, and laypersons work together to demonstrate creative ways of living simply and joyfully with the forces of Creation. But such meeting places are growing, leading the way for others to follow.

Moreover, as we shall see in the Conclusion of this book, in 1995 the Eastern Orthodox church, traditionally wedded to the past, gathered together an international array of religious, scientific, and environmental leaders. At an inspiring meeting place, the Mediterranean island of Patmos, they discussed their visions of a new millennium. A similar conference followed in 1997, and later that year, Ecumenical Patriarch Bartholomaios made a whirlwind trip around the United States, becoming known as the "Green Patriarch."

Ecumenism, Eternal Truths, and Earth

As we have seen, sacramentalism (recognizing the divine in, with, and under all nature) permeates Orthodox thinking. Rasmussen declares that it is strong in the ceremonies of native peoples as well.[25]

Orthodox theologians and clergy (as distinguished from ordinary believers, especially peasants) do tend to see objects and beings in the natural world as symbols, opening on to the greater reality beyond. God's "transfiguration of Nature" on Judgment Day is a prominent theological theme. It is worth emphasizing, however, that while some indigenous peoples share such a vision, a great many—perhaps most—of them perceive air, wind, birds, animals, serpents, rocks, as in themselves manifestations of the divine. (See Chapter 6, "The Way of Native Americans.")

At the 1991 WCC Assembly—where the theological theme was "Come Holy Spirit, Renew the Whole Creation"—dramatically different kinds of sacramentalism came into conflict.

The keynote address was delivered by Dr. Chung Hyun Kyung, a Presbyterian theologian who was young, from a Third World country (Korea)—and a woman. The event began with the vibrating, haunting sound of the Australian aborigines' primary instrument of worship, the *digeridoo*, a horn that seems to vibrate from the earth. Two powerfully built aboriginal men moved about the stage, sounding their horns, playing clapsticks, and dancing a silent propitiation to the gods. Sixteen white-robed second-generation Australian Koreans, male and female, filed down the aisles, playing drums and gongs, and carrying candles, flags, and incense. Slowly, they began a reverent ancestral dance. Dr. Chung entered in white robes, and summoned the 4,000 participants: "My dear sisters and brothers, welcome to this land of the Spirit!" In the way of many Asian and Pacific peoples—and Moses before the Burning Bush—she took off her shoes as an act of humbling herself to enter holy ground. Then she invited everyone to do the same, "while we are dancing to prepare the way of the Spirit!" Her invocation continued with a long call upon a series of spirits—among them, the spirit of Jews killed in gas chambers; the spirit of "jelly babies" in the Pacific nuclear testing zone; the spirit of the rainforest, being murdered every day; the spirit of the earth, air, and water, raped and tortured by human greed.

After speaking passionately of First World domination, genocide of indigenous peoples, and "the ecocide of our earth," she called for genuine repentance, and named three urgent changes for survival. The first, from anthropocentrism to life-centrism, would bring traditional Christian thinking into greater harmony with that of many Asian and indigenous peoples, for whom the earth is the source of life and nature is sacred.

The second change, from the habit of dualism to the habit of interconnection, might be intuited from the Asian concept of energy, *Ki* (or *Chi*), the breath of life, thriving in the harmonious interconnections among the sky, earth, and people.

The third change would be from the patriarchal culture of death to the culture of life. Women's powerful tears have been the redemptive energy. Only when we have an ability to suffer with others can we transform the culture of death to one of life.

For this young Presbyterian theologian, the image of the Holy Spirit came from the image of Kwan-In, goddess of compassion. As *bodhisattva*, enlightened being, she can enter Nirvana any time she wishes, but she waits until *all* beings in the universe—people, trees, birds, mountains, air, water—become enlightened; then they can go into Nirvana together. This, she suggested, might also be a feminine image of the

Christ, one who goes before and brings others with her.

At the end, Dr. Chung called on the assembled to build communities for Justice, Peace, and the Integrity of Creation. "Wild wind of the Holy Spirit, blow to us! Come Holy Spirit! Renew the Whole Creation! Amen!" The aborigines, the dancers, and Dr. Chung herself joined in a wild, solemn, joyous dance, exulting in a vision of the Creation renewed and made whole.

Her presentation created a furor. While it was greeted with a standing ovation, some delegates—particularly the Orthodox—were incensed. The Orthodox declared, "We must guard against a tendency to substitute a 'private' spirit, the spirit of the world or other spirits, for the Holy Spirit who proceeds from the Father and rests in the Son."

It became clear that to the Orthodox, Dr. Chung was brash, irreverent, disdainful of a way of perceiving and honoring the Almighty that had proved its truth over the centuries. At later workshops they declared that she turned her back on genuine dialogue. She said the same of the Orthodox, adding, "I think all this talk of syncretism, paganism, and other name-calling is an exercise of power: white, male, academic power of those privileged persons who want to own the church—and even nature. We non-colonials and women of the world have been listening to the West, to men, to dominant theologians for 2,000 years. We are the new wine and we will not be intimidated. The criteria of our faith and practice come from simple people, not from power!"[26]

There they stood, politely but firmly locked in confrontation: representatives of a time-honored sacramentalism, passed down from the early church fathers, and a new sacramentalism—new, yet rooted in ancient traditions—inspired by a feminist vision of liberation.

Tears

Perhaps there is a parallel between this passionate young woman from the Third World and the aging Dostoyevsky, that spiritual seeker who never left Orthodoxy, but remained peculiarly sensitive to the polarity between the institutional church and the faith of simple people. Perhaps *The Brothers Karamazov* holds a parable in the novice Alyosha's conversion to a wider way of serving God. After the death of his beloved Father Zossima, Alyosha's grief is compounded by the shock of realizing that the monk's body is decomposing prematurely. The saintly monk, after all, was subject to earthly decay. As a smell of corruption fills the air, "scandal" grows. One learned father points out that incorruptibility of the bodies of the just is not an Orthodox dogma. But his words provoke mocking retorts, particularly from jealous monks who cling to order.

After an anguished evening in which Alyosha transforms the bitter heart of a young woman of ill repute through compassion, and in turn is transformed by her sisterly love, he returns to the monastery. Joy begins to fill his heart as he prays over the body. He dreams that Father Zossima tells him to begin his work now. And he steps out into the night.

"The mystery of the earth" is "one with the mystery of the stars." Alyosha stands, gazes, and suddenly throws himself on the earth, sobbing. He does not know why he embraces it. But he kisses it weeping, vowing passionately to love it forever. "Water the earth with the tears of your joy and love those tears," echoes in his soul. He weeps even over the stars shining to him from the abyss of space, and there seem to be "threads from all those innumerable worlds of God linking his soul to them."

Within three days Alyosha leaves the monastery, following the counsel of his elder who bade him "sojourn in the world."[27]

5

ISLAM

Introduction

In the Al-Azhar Mosque in Cairo, the faithful are offering optional prayers. Unlike the soaring space of a Gothic cathedral, the rectangular interior of the prayer hall is wide and spacious, suggesting the horizon of Earth. Rich red prayer rugs woven in elaborate patterns cover the floor, the prayer niche indicating the direction of Mecca is ornamented with blue stones, and softly burning red lamps set in crenulated brass hang from the ceiling. Almost everywhere the eye meets arabesques, interlacing patterns with motifs that suggest, but do not imitate, the world of plant life. The overall atmosphere is one of simplicity. There is no organ, no choir, no stained glass window, no altar, no pew. On Friday, the day for communal prayers, an imam will speak from the pulpit. But today believers have come individually, to reflect and to pray.

Outside the air is thick with noise, dust, and acrid fumes. But inside, a reverential quiet pervades the hall. Several men are prostrating themselves in the direction of Mecca. One is offering homage to the All-Merciful One before the prayer niche. An elderly man sits on the floor reading a newspaper. A group of students from Al-Azhar University, the oldest continuous university in the world, squats on the floor listening attentively to a teacher. A few yards away two young men, each with a Qur'an, sit reading intently to one another. Near one corner two boys, who could hardly be more than 10 years of age and seem to have come here alone, squat reading back and forth from their Qur'ans, occasionally stopping to discuss a passage in subdued tones. A little girl runs merrily up and down an aisle of the carpet.

Some distance away small circles of women sit on the floor, apparently chatting. But as one of us wanders near, a young woman wearing a white scarf concealing her hair, but no part of her face, approaches with a smile. "Come join us!" The women, she says, are studying the Qur'an, under the leadership of one who knows it well. She herself is a student at Cairo University, and would like to meet and talk with American women. She cannot understand why so many believe that Muslim women suffer from inequality. Her delicate oval face, framed in white and adorned with no make-up, seems to glow as she says firmly: "We are equal in the sight of God. At prayer gatherings, we pray equally with men—they are in the front of the hall, we behind them. And in Muslim society, men respect us."

Muslims pray in many places—mosques, homes, deserts, a stairwell in a factory. We have visited mosques in 11 countries ranging from China to England, and belonged to a Christian-Muslim dialogue group in the United States that included Muslims from the Middle East, northern Africa, Bangladesh, and Malaysia. Islam is the fastest-growing religion in the United States; by the year 2000, its following is expected to be second only to Christianity. It is also the fastest-growing religion in the world, already embracing more than one billion people. Today, as all faiths begin to sense that they play a critical role in determining the fate of the earth, the role of Islam will be crucial.

Basic Themes in Muslim Belief

The Islamic concept of knowledge is based on the two fundamental axes of unity and hierarchy, says Seyyed Hossein Nasr, a scholar of comparative religions. Islamic science, art, and ethics are all affirmations of the *tawhid*, the Divine Unity.

Hence the key to understanding Islam is "order." This helps explain the profound appeal of the faith to converts, its remarkable endurance over the centuries, and its fear of Western values. As we shall see, it also casts light upon its views on ecology.

Islam means submission to the will of God, called Allah in Arabic. (Christian Arabs also say "Allah.") The broader meaning of Islam is "to surrender to God's law and thus to be an integral whole." From the same root, *slm*, comes *Muslim*, a person who surrenders by accepting God's law. The Qur'an declares the entire universe to be Muslim, endowed with order through obedience to God's law. But there is a fundamental distinction: while nature obeys God's law automatically, human beings should obey it by choice.

The duties of worship, the five "pillars" of Islam, are: (1) the confession of faith ("I witness that there is no deity except God, and Muhammad is the messenger of God"); (2) prayer; (3) contribution to charity; (4) fasting during the month of Ramadan; and (5) pilgrimage to Mecca.[1]

The *ummah*, the universal community of the faithful, transcends ethnic and national boundaries and is a powerful reality to believers. It confers identity, continuity with the past, and a shared belief in an ideal society. Despite many signs of disunity, most Muslims feel that the Islamic world is an entity. Yet it is not an international institution with centralized authority, like the Roman Catholic church. Nor is there a formal priesthood. In theory any learned and respected male believer can lead a congregation as its imam/sheikh.

Largely because of the fervency of Muslim belief and the fact that it is an ideology as well as a religion, no faith has provoked so much hostility, fear, and controversy in the West. Covert racist attitudes also play a part. Ironically, Islam belongs to the same lineage as Judaism and Christianity, the Abrahamic tradition. Many biblical figures, including Adam, Abraham, Moses, and Jesus, are accepted as prophets, even though Muhammad is regarded as the final prophet.

Like Judaism and Christianity, Islam is theistic. God is seen as Creator of the universe and as a personal deity. He is both immanent and transcendent, dwelling in all things, yet ultimately a power above, beyond human comprehension. The emphasis is on the transcendent dimension.

Like Jews and Christians, Muslims believe that humans have a special place in God's Creation. Like Judaism, Islam stresses religious law. Like Christianity, it is universalistic, and while placing importance on living an ethical life here and now, emphasizes the next world.

Ideally, Islam is a way of life. In principle, there should be no separation of church and state, for this would deny the unity of all life; God is the true ruler.[2] In the real world today, however, many Muslims have come to believe that the two institutions should be separated.

Muslims hold that the Qur'an, revealed through the Prophet Muhammad, is the final revelation from God and contains absolute commandments valid for all times and places. It is believed to remain exactly as it was when it was set down by the Prophet's Companions, in Arabic, nearly 1,400 years ago. Muslims have no authority to make changes in the commandments.

The two main branches, Sunnism and Shi'ism, are more or less in basic agreement in doctrine and practice. The organization of Shi'a clergy is more hierarchical and centralized; the basic variance is over authoritative leadership—an issue too complicated to delineate here.[3]

There are four foundations regulating the believer's behavior. The most basic is the Qur'an itself, which is considered an absolute "decisive proof" and could be called "the constitution of Islam." The second is the *hadith*, the sayings of the Prophet, which constitute commentary on the Qur'an. The third is the *shari'ah*, which is largely based on the Qur'an and the *hadith*, and forms a comprehensive code on Islam as a way of life. A fourth foundation is *ijma*, literally "agreeing upon" by every scholar; in practice it tends to be not consensus, but majority opinion.[4]

Explication of the *shari'ah* devolves upon the religious leadership, the *ulama*, which includes various schools of jurisprudence. Particularly in new cases for which no "clear text" is available, the scholar/jurist seeks the *hadith* that seem relevant. There is no final judge of the content and meaning of the *shari'ah*. While it is generally considered adequate, the external conditions to which it is applied are changing, and specific modes of application change. Hence in the absence of a centralized church, definition of what is orthodox is a problem, especially today.[5]

Although Muslims often refer to the *shari'ah* as the universal basis for law, today its authority is largely confined to questions of personal status: marriage, divorce, child custody, inheritance, adoption, public dress, and behavior. However, conservative Muslims have been pressing for a full-fledged *shari'ah* court system.

Dismissing Westerners' distinction between "fundamentalist" and "liberal," Muslims tend to simply assert "The Qur'an says—," while leaving it to the scholar/jurist to make correct interpretations when there are questions. As we shall see, however, interpretations vary today even more than in the past. Islam is evolving, albeit slowly and somewhat imperceptibly.

Nowhere, perhaps, is this more true than in the "woman question." The status and activities of women are changing, although this is often hard for outsiders to recognize. The subject is so complex that in this book we can deal with it directly only in the later section of this chapter, entitled "Karachi: Empowering Women, Reinterpreting the Qu'ran." At this point, we shall offer only a few observations, to help counteract misunderstandings so widespread in the West:

- The status of women is a topic of passionate controversy within the Islamic world, as the growing literature by Muslim feminists attests.

- Veiling is not a divine commandment, and the Qur'an is somewhat ambiguous on the subject.

- Most Muslim women look upon the Prophet Muhammad as a liberator of women, at least for his time (seventh century CE). Customs and practices vary greatly from culture to culture.

• The issue is entwined with internal politics, and with fears of Western threats to Islamic culture.

To this we add our own conviction that while their roles need not fit Western conceptions, the full, free participation of women is essential to the task of preserving the ecosystem.[6]

Nature, Music, and the Mystic Quest

Every world religion includes a tradition of communing with God through contemplation and love, without the instrument of human reason. Even Islam, with its stern emphasis on law, orthodoxy, knowledge, and order, embraces a mystic tradition: Sufism. In reaction to the emphasis on sobriety and practical ethics, less than two centuries after the death of Muhammad some Muslims began expressing a longing for an emotional, individual relationship with God. For similar reasons, some Westerners today have turned to Sufism. Much of its appeal lies in its celebration of the sacred aspect of nature.

Sufis tend to follow the universal observances of Islam, and at the same time pursue their mystical way to truth. Not only religious scholars, but outstanding scientists and even political leaders have been Sufis. Some orders are devoted to curing the ill, some stress mystic experience, and some even retain a certain political function. Many revitalization and reform movements within Islam have originated from Sufis. While the number of adherents appears to be in decline, it still flourishes in many parts of the world, especially Africa, India, Indonesia, and Central Asia.

Expressing hidden archetypes in concrete symbols, Sufi themes image the descending arc of Creation, the formation of the human soul, and its return through the ascending arc of the Quest.[7] They are remarkably parallel to themes uncovered in other religions by psychoanalyst Carl Jung and mythologist Joseph Campbell.

Each seeker can create his or her own spiritual path within the general pattern of self-discipline, fasting, and spiritual detachment from material concerns. Often the sense of being reborn is expressed in symbols, such as the moth casting itself into the candle's flame.

Although ascetic movements already existed in the eighth century, the spiritual wisdom of a woman, Rabi'ah al-Adawiyah (d.801 CE), sparked the actual transition from asceticism to true love mysticism. An Iraqi slave, eventually freed because of the depth of her piety, she created a vision that has endured in poems and prayers. The prevalent concern with fear of hell and desire for paradise was wrong, she insisted; love of God must be a loss of self in mystical union with the Beloved. From time to time she withdrew to live as a vegetarian hermit in the desert and contemplate Divinity with pure devotion:

> But in that love which seeks Thee worthily
> The veil is raised that I may look on Thee.

Thus unlike mainstream Islam, which cites the guide for behavior in the Qur'an, *hadith*, and *shari'ah*, Sufism stresses a higher law: the love relationship. In the poetry of Jalal al-Din Rumi, called Mawlana (d.1273 CE), it is expressed in particularly poignant, symbolic terms.

Born in Balkh (now in Afghanistan), Rumi lived in Persia, Syria, and finally Anatolia, a region of present-day Turkey. There he married, fathered two sons, and began writing poetry in Persian. His long *Mathnavi* has been called "the Qur'an in the Persian tongue."

For Rumi, it was an intense, mystical love relationship with the wandering dervish Shams-al-dinh, "Sun of Religion," that provided a microcosm for ecstatic identification with God. It was while experiencing the pangs of a temporary separation from Shams that Rumi was suddenly transformed into a poet who sang of his love and longing for the Beloved while whirling around to the sound of music. After Shams' mysterious death (the relationship had become a source of jealousy and scandal), Rumi experienced a spiritual crisis. Eventually, however, Rumi "found him in himself, radiant as the moon," in the words of Rumi's elder son Sultan Walad. He built up a circle of disciples that included craftsmen, small shopkeepers, powerful ministers of state, and a number of women. Christians and Jews were counted among his friends.[8]

As in Hinduism and Buddhism, the novice is guided in the path to God by personal teachers. Women may take part, although they do not dance with the men, usually have their own groups, and are barred from singing or reciting the mystic verses in the presence of men.

The order of Mevlevis (the "Whirling Dervishes") traces its lineage to Rumi and his son Sultan Walad. "Listening parties" listen to music, often by singing poetry intended to ignite a mystical experience. If that comes, to the accompaniment of mantra-like chanting of "*La*—il-la-*ha*—il-la—al-*lah*" ("There is no God but God"), they rise up in long white robes, their arms outstretched, their faces immobile, to whirl counterclockwise with the music, which crescendos to a peak of enraptured abandon and union with Ultimate Reality.

Mainstream Muslims have tended to be hostile to Sufism, especially the music and dance that are the lifeblood of its practice. Like certain Christians, they see music as seductive, dance as immoral (sexual), and theater as subversive. The rationale is that they are frivolous distractions from contemplating the wisdom of the Prophet. The deeper fear, perhaps, is the implicit threat to order.

Is no religious music, then, permissible in mainstream Islam? In principle, "religious music" is a contradiction in terms, for even hymn singing and the mellifluous chanting of the Qur'an are referred to with special designations, in order to avoid secular implications. For centuries, how to differentiate between admissible and inadmissible music has been a topic of controversy. One Syrian-American lover of music concluded—after discussing it with his imam—that "if a certain music does not lead you to thinking anything bad, it's okay."

Even strict interpreters of Qur'anic tradition accept the simple chanting of the Qur'an and the call to prayer. The latter can take several forms; in Indonesia, for example, the call is often by drumbeats, which carry into the jungle much farther than the muezzin's voice. However, these admissible forms have also influenced folk music and become part of secular art music. All over the Islamic world the Prophet's birthday, the end of Ramadan, and departures for Mecca are occasions for festivals. Hence it becomes extremely difficult to draw firm distinctions among religious, folk, and art music.

In virtually all Muslim cultures, as in others, dance, theater, and music are too deeply rooted to be eradicated by doctrine. Millions of Muslims from all walks of life have discovered in them a path to recollection of their celestial home. Apparently, no strictures can make people forego these primal forms of expressing their relationship to other human beings, the earth, and the Mystery.

To listen to the Sufi message is to empty your mind and then open it to whatever images, whatever feelings unfold in your being. For each listener, glimpsing the path is a unique experience, but almost always it unfolds under the spell of poetry, art, dance. For some it can mean—as it has for the two of us—journeying out of the either-or, categorical thought of the Western world to the Orient. To a world where religion or spirituality lie at the center of public and personal experience, where the quest for what is "really real" is a real part of everyday lives. To us it has evoked memories of Delhi: of Sikhs gathered in the Golden Temple to pay clamorous homage to Wah Guru on harmoniums, sitars, and drums, their faces glowing with the fiery light in the temple . . . of Kathmandu: Buddhist monks in a semi-circle, chanting and striking their cymbals and horns in deafening harmony with the Source of all being . . . of Jerusalem: walking the walls, amid stark silence, on a sabbath evening and glimpsing Hasidim, their faces lit by flickering candles, come together in a circle to sing and dance their praises to G–D. In each, the sounds seem to move in gyrating circles, vibrating from the earth itself, and reflecting the great curve of the universe.

Within the multi-faceted tradition of Islam, Sufism seems to harmonize best with an ecological ethic. Trees, animals, fish, and birds figure prominently in Sufi literature and painting, as reflections of paradise. A few Sufi schools border on pantheism. Dancing and music, with all their "earthiness," are seen as crucial forms of religious expression. Sufism is more open, more responsive to change, than mainstream Islam. Women are more likely to be included on a quasi-equal basis. Homosexuals are more likely to be accepted; many Sufis have even seen homosexual relations as an expression of the spiritual link between man and God.[9]

Sufism is so universal in its appeal that—together with the Bhakti movement—it inspired the split from Hinduism that came to be known as Sikhism. It has influenced Judaism and Christianity. Some passages of Rabi'ah al-Adawiyah seem to presage the verse of Teresa of Avila, and the eleventh-century physician and Sufi scholar Ibn Sina Avicenna had a profound effect on Christian thought. Within Judaism a tradition developed that could be called Jewish Sufism. In thirteenth-century Egypt, some upper-class Jews formed pietistic brotherhoods similar to Sufi orders there, and called themselves *Hasidim*, the Talmudic word for "pious." Abraham, son of the renowned Jewish philosopher Moses Maimonides, emerged as spiritual leader of this circle. He attempted to introduce the kneeling position of Islamic prayer, imitated mosque patterns by requiring standing in straight rows during the Eighteen Benedictions, and inaugurated other pietistic reforms. Later some Egyptian Jews imitated the patterns of life in the Sufi convents in the hills around Cairo. Some Hasidic singing and dance seem remarkably similar to their counterparts in Sufism.

Sufism realizes the "connectedness of things." It speaks to the simplicity that is essential to any ecological ethic. Muslim Sufism also tells us that we need not follow asceticism only within cloistered walls; it is possible, even better, to do so as we take part in the hurly-burly of the outside world, where difficult decisions must be made and lived out in practice.

Islam and Ecology

Consider Creation as pure and crystalline water
In which is reflected the Beauty of the Possessor of Majesty
Although the water of this stream continues to flow
The image of the moon and stars remains reflected in it.
                                                    —Jalal al-Din Rumi

While this verse comes from the pen of a Sufi,mainstream Islam, too, is rich in affirmations of the Almighty's perfect design for the heavens and the earth. Proverbs and precepts in the Qur'an and *hadith* remind the faithful of the balance in God's plan for Creation, and of human responsibility for preserving it. For a great many Muslims, these sayings are enough to prove that Islam has always embraced a complete environmental ethic. Others are more critical. They, too, insist that the guidelines are all there in Islamic doctrine. *Tawhid* (unity), *khilafa* (trusteeship), and *akhirah* (accountability or, literally, the hereafter), three central concepts of Islam, are also the pillars of Islam's environmental ethic. They add, however, that Muslims have strayed from this nexus of values and need to return to it.

Many of the Qur'anic verses they cite bear a striking resemblance to passages in the Bible. Q.6:1 proclaims "Praise be to God, who created the heavens and the earth and the Darkness and the Light." Q.17:44 reads in part: "The seven heavens and the earth and all beings therein declare His glory: there is not a thing but celebrates His praise . . ."[10]

To man is given the role of *khalifa* (trustee): "Behold, the Lord said to the angels: 'I will create a vicegerent on earth . . . '" (Q.2:30). But it is a role to perform wisely, fully aware of one's accountability to the Almighty. "Do no mischief on the earth after it hath been set in order, but call on Him with fear and longing in your hearts . . . " (Q.7:56). Other parts of the Qur'an tell us that all nature declares God's bounties; the variety in Creation points to the unity in His plan; and God gave man spiritual insight so that he should understand nature. Moreover, the principle of balance is fundamental: "And the earth We have spread out like a carpet; set thereon mountains firm and immobile; and produced therein all kinds of things in due balance" (Q.15:19).

The Qur'anic message is also full of moral lessons based on the workings of nature. Q.16:68-9, for example, relates that "thy Lord taught the Bee to build its cells in hills, on trees, and in men's habitations; then to eat of all produce of the earth, and find with skill the spacious paths of its Lord: there issues from within their bodies a drink of varying colors, wherein is healing for men: Verily in this is a Sign for those who give thought." Q.2:205 condemns destroying the natural world and spreading corruption, as it describes a type of man whose "aim everywhere is to spread mischief through earth and destroy crops and cattle." Living simply is enjoined. In the *hadith*, one of the Prophet's companions, Abdullah bin Omar, relates that once the Apostle of God grasped his shoulders and exclaimed. "Live in the world as if you were a stranger or wayfarer!" And the classical Muslim jurist Izz ad-din ibn Abd as-Salam formulated a bill of rights for animals in the thirteenth century CE.

A number of devout Muslim men and women have become leaders of international environmental organizations, ranging from the United Nations Environmental Programme to the United Nations Population Fund. On the other hand, most Muslims seem only vaguely aware of the depth of the ecological crisis, and perceive only a few of the problems.

Moreover, a common argument is that "when we catch up with the technological superiority of the West, *then* we can begin to focus on this issue." Some Muslims even see environmentalism as still another form of Western control, intended to keep the Muslim world from developing and the Muslim population from expanding to a point of strength.

Hence it is hardly surprising that, generally speaking, there has been little discussion about actually applying Islamic principles to environmental practice. A few scholars and grassroots leaders, however, have begun to grapple with this challenge.

Three Scholars View a Threatened Planet

ISLAM AND NATURE CONSERVATION

Among the many reasons that theologians like Iraqi-born Mawil Y. Izzi Dien offer for protecting the environment are: (1) humankind is not the only community to live in this world; (2) the balance in the universe created by God must be preserved; (3) the environment is not in the service of the present generation alone; and (4) only the human can carry out the trust of dominion over the earth, for the burden of viceregency is so great that no other creature would accept it when it was offered by God.[11]

Indeed, the word "earth" occurs 485 times in the Qur'an, Izzi Dien tells us. The Holy Book emphasizes that Allah created humans from dust and water, and ritual cleansing with water is prescribed for the Muslim preparing for prayer. Next to water in purity is earth. If no water is available, one should rub the hands on clean earth and wipe the face and arms.

The concept of the human as God's viceregent/vicegerent is similar to the Judaic and Christian idea of steward. Since the human's role is to benefit from the earth and its creatures, but also protect them, waste or unnecessary destruction are forbidden.

He also cites the traditions of *hima* and *harim*. *Hima* refers to protection of certain areas, which may not be cultivated or developed in any way, except for the welfare of the people, for example, for grazing by animals of the poor (a custom remarkably similar to the old English tradition of the village commons). Today the government of Saudi Arabia practices *hima* to protect wildlife. The *harim* is an inviolable zone which cannot be used except with state permission, and is usually associated with wells, natural springs, rivers, and trees planted on barren land. These two concepts—reminiscent of the ancient Jewish custom of the *migrash*, a "green belt" reserved for animals and public amenities—persist in many Muslim countries today. He also cites current conservation in-itiatives, such as Saudi Arabia's efforts to save the Arabian oryx from extinction, its commissioning of a basic paper on Islamic conservation propositions, and pan-Arab conferences on the environmental aspects of development. His hope is that all conservation education will be science-based, but also identify environmental policies with Islamic teachings.

It is worth noting that although he discusses "the comprehensive nature of Islamic ethics," he does not speak of the comprehensive nature of the ecological crisis. He also focuses largely on nature conservation, never mentioning such complex and politically sensitive issues as over-population, ozone depletion, climate change, or air pollution from fossil fuels such as oil, the major export of Saudi Arabia and many other Middle Eastern countries.

DEFENDING THE RIGHTS OF ANIMALS

The work of Al-Hafiz B.A. Masri has focused on a passionate de-fense of animal rights. Until his death in 1993, at 79, he was traveling the globe almost constantly on behalf of the World Society for the Pro-tection of Animals.[10]

Unlike the vast majority of Muslims, Masri was a vegetarian. Born into a meat-eating family in India, he studied at the University of Punjab and the renowned al-Azhar University in Cairo, became headmaster of the largest secondary school in East Africa, and eventually settled in England, serving as imam of the Shah Jahan Mosque in Woking, then the European center for Islam. Increasingly, he became troubled by the lack of Muslim sermons on caring for nature—a lack rendered more lamenta-ble by the fact that "Islamic instruction and guidance on animal rights and man's obligations concerning them are so comprehensive that we need not go elsewhere."[12] Masri does not enjoin all Muslims to adhere to vegetarianism, but does call on them to become aware of animals and our interdependence with them, then act according to what appears to be right.

He discovers facets in the tradition that are rarely emphasized, and while his interpretations are acceptable to Islamic orthodoxy, they border on the radical. Pointing out that Q.6:38 reads: "There is not an animal that lives on earth nor a being that flies on its wings but forms part of communities like you," Masri concludes that each creature has a share in all natural resources. Moreover, animals do communicate with each other and with human beings; there are many Muslim legends about holy men who could talk to animals. Even inanimate elements worship God without articulate speech. Water is sent not only to satisfy humans, but to "give life to dead land, and slake the thirst of things we have created—cattle and men in great numbers" (Q.25:49).

Far more than most other Muslims, Masri is intensely aware of the need for Islamic law and practice to adapt to the modern era. Issues like hunting for sport and experiments on animals did not exist when the Qur'an was sent down, he says. Hence when there are no clear laws in the Qur'an or *hadith*, general principles have to be translated into juristic rules through using inferences by analogy. For example, the Prophet halted barbaric treatment of animals in his time; through reasoning by analogy, humans can see that today it is wrong to kill animals by the millions for furs, tusks, oils, and other commodities. All Islamic laws have been left open to exception, and actions are to be judged according to intention. Thus hunting for sport is wrong, and hunting for food should be limited to that which is absolutely necessary.

The Qur'an is specific about what animals are lawful (*halal*) or un-lawful (*haram*) to eat, and jurists have elaborated on those injunctions. For example, cud-chewing animals and animals living in water (such as fish) are *halal*, while pigs, frogs, cats, dogs, and animals zoologically human in form (like monkeys) are *haram*. One *hadith* enjoins: "If you must kill, kill without torture." There are specific proscriptions against vivisection, breaking animals' backs, skinning a body before it is dead cold, blood sports, and using animal skins as floor coverings.

Taking issue with the belief that since pre-slaughter stunning does not allow all the blood (considered unhygienic) to drain from the carcass, it is unacceptable, Masri says modern scientific work shows stunning does not affect the flow of blood. If killing be done, rendering the animal unconscious before cutting its throat is most consonant with broad Is-lamic principles. Nor does Islam approve of imprisoning birds, or useless cutting of trees and bushes. Citing Islamic authorities, Masri condemns overworking animals and slaughtering any in the presence of other ani-mals. (Many of the principles cited are strikingly parallel to those cited by Jews from their Scriptures.)

Even his courageous criticism of pilgrims' ritual sacrifice of animals at Mecca is supported by Qur'anic quotations. However, he goes further, including a discussion of factory farming and the use of herbicides and pesticides. Comparing them with the "good husbanding" that once reigned in both Islamic and European countries, he not only demonstrates a sophisticated knowledge of ecologically sound methods of farming, but clearly condemns chemicalized agriculture.

What alarms him is that so many Muslims, theologians and lay persons alike, are uninformed about animal welfare and environmental problems. Muslims, he laments, have begun to follow the West in the name of commerce—thus permitting selfish and short-sighted interests to make havoc of ecological balance.

Both these writers retain the traditional view that man's role is that of vicegerent, but they differ significantly in their emphases. Izzi Dien upholds the idea of humans' hierarchical superiority to other creatures; it is no accident that he is enthusiastic about the promise of modern technology and "sustainable development." By contrast, Masri emphasizes that man is inferior to animals in many respects, that his only superiority lies in his spiritual power to differentiate between good and bad, and that we should learn to treat all life on earth homogeneously. He is also more concerned with a sustainable *society*, one recognizing earth's life-systems.

NATURE AS SYMBOLIC OF A TRANSCENDENTAL REALITY

While few Muslims consider the study of comparative religion important, since Islam represents the "final revelation," Seyyed Hossein Nasr takes the whole spectrum of religion into his field of vision. A scholar of philosophy, art, and science, he is one of the few Muslim men of letters who have concerned themselves with the relationship between humans and nature in the light of the ecological crisis. Born in Iran, he studied physics and math at the Massachusetts Institute of Technology and obtained a doctorate in science and philosophy at Harvard, then returned to Iran. After the Khomeini revolution in 1979, he began teaching Islamic studies in the U.S. Although most of his works (more than 20 books) focus on Islamic civilization, some deal with the spiritual crisis facing humanity today, and all evidence a formidable knowledge of Western and Eastern scientific and religious traditions. We were fortunate to be able to meet him in his office at George Washington University.

A dark, slender man with a neat, graying beard and magisterial bearing, he spoke gravely, in impeccable English. We asked him to comment on the impact of the movement to ally religion and ecology.

"Well, in the West, it has made some compelling statements. But one has to ask, 'What power does it have over the political domain?' The politicians may nod and even agree—but the developers go right ahead, cutting down woods, uprooting endangered species. That's a result of the Western dogma of separating science from the sacred, religion from the secular. In Islamic countries religion is a stronger force. In a *true* Islamic society, political leadership could act in accordance with the *shari'ah* as set out by doctors of the law. If they declared polluting industries and certain kinds of development in violation of Islamic principles, political leaders would have to take strong measures. Remember, I am talking about what would happen in a *true* Islamic society. Unfortunately, today the West dominates the world economy, so Islam reacts to the West both economically and politically. The West sets the agenda."

"From reading your work, we've seen how destructive you feel the separation between religion and the secular domain to be."

He nodded. "That is rooted in Western modern science and its domination of our view of nature, which separates nature from the sacred. Renaissance humanism gave rise to a world centered on man instead of God. Before, all civilizations looked beyond themselves to God—to revelation. I'm not hostile to Western science, but to its claim to be the only valid science of the natural world. There are other ways of 'knowing.' Western science *has* become illegitimate, because scientists and the rest of society fail to see the need for a higher knowledge into which it could be integrated. The spiritual value of nature is destroyed. We can't save the natural world except by rediscovering the sacred in nature."

"That is what Thomas Berry is talking about," we observed.

"Yes. Yes, Berry speaks to the heart of the matter. But his 'geologian' concept of religion is limited to the earth, without remembrance of transcendence. The traditional perspective of the Muslim—and Christian—is that man comes from a sacred heaven to an earth which is also divine creation. Even American Indians have a sky father. What I am saying is, the whole of nature is descended from higher spiritual realms. There can be no sacredness of the earth without the sacredness of heaven. Man is that special creature who transcends the earth. A theology is not valid unless we remember where the sacred comes from."

"What are some other ways your thought differs from Berry's?"

"I would say you cannot hold a true ecological philosophy and a belief in Darwinism at the same time. Darwinism eradicated the sense of the sacred. 'Survival of the fittest' runs counter to the harmony, the cooperation so basic in nature."

It seemed to us he was not doing justice to Darwin's observation in *The Descent of Man* that in many animal societies, the struggle between individuals for the means of existence is replaced by cooperation, which develops faculties assuring the best conditions for survival. But it seemed best that the short time together be focused on asking him to elaborate on his views.

"You suggest we need to reestablish a metaphysical tradition in Christianity, to provide a criterion for regulating the sciences. And for evaluating evolutionary theory, too?"

"Yes, we would no longer rely on evolution as dogma. It gives rise to pseudo-philosophies like the survival of the fittest, picturing man as the inevitable winner of the long struggle, with the right to dominate all things. This destroys the spiritual significance of nature—which depends on the fact that it reflects a permanent reality beyond itself."

"And this sense of the sacred pervaded the world of Islam and the rest of the East until the onslaught of Western science and technology?"

"Yes. And missionaries brought modern medicine and technology, working hand-in-hand with Western governments for what they called 'progress.' The very idea of progress disoriented the East. As pressure grew, even the Arabs and Persians, who had once created the glories of Islamic science—the very foundations of European mathematics, astronomy, chemistry, physics—proceeded to learn Western science. And to be corrupted by its mechanistic and materialist worldview."

He sighed heavily. "In the West today, they want to remove problems brought on by destroying the balance between man and nature through further domination of nature. The problem is not underdevelopment in the Third World, but *overdevelopment* pressed by the West."

"Yet to some degree Islamic societies *have* resisted Western modes of thought?"

He nodded. "They are the only ones where significant segments of the population, from jurists to villagers, refuse to consider any form of knowledge as secular. Where religion can still function as the foundation of a wholistic approach. It's true, certain countries try to copy the West, mostly because they have to recycle petrodollars and so are forced into this game. Their pretense of being completely Islamic societies is not completely true, especially as far as the environment is concerned. Still, throughout the world there are many Muslims trying to rediscover traditional Islam. Traditional as distinguished from neo-fundamentalist Islam."

"Could you tell us a little more about how you see that distinction?"

"Certainly." He looked at us appreciatively. "There is little understanding of this in the West. Today there are basically three types of Islam: traditionalism, modernism, and various forms of revivalism usually brought together as 'fundamentalism.' Until 200 years ago, in spite of the many schools and interpretations, all Muslims lived within the tradition, with its roots in the Qur'an, *hadith*, and the *shari'ah*. It was a living tradition, emphasizing the harmony of law, art, and all forms of knowledge. In the eighteenth century, modernism, with its roots in secular humanism, entered the world, in all fields, and traditional Islam began to weaken.

"Most so-called fundamentalists are pseudo-traditional, as can be seen in their attitude toward the environment. Like Christian fundamentalists, many pull a verse from the Scriptures and give it a meaning contrary to its traditional commentary. Also, even while denouncing modernism as the 'Great Satan,' many 'fundamentalists' accept its foundations, especially science and technology. For traditionalists, there is beauty in nature and beauty in every aspect of traditional life, from chanting the Qur'an to the artisan's fashioning an everyday pot. But both fundamentalists and modernists could produce mosques that look like factories. Many 'fundamentalists' even seek a Qur'anic basis for modern man's destruction of nature by referring to the injunction to 'dominate the earth'—misconstruing the basic idea of vicegerency."

"To turn to a tangible problem, overpopulation—what would traditionalists say?"

"It is a problem, a major one," he said slowly. "But it is not soluble as an entity unto itself; it is connected with other issues. Because of the imbalances in the political situation, many Muslims feel that power lies in numbers. In the end, overpopulation *is* too great a burden. Now there are new interpretations among scholars who try to interpret the Prophet's teachings to enable planning for one's family in accordance with one's possibility of supporting them."

"Good. But isn't the real question 'How many can the *earth* support?' And doesn't a just and workable solution involve allowing more women to become Islamic scholars and jurists?"

He looked at his watch and stood up quickly. "I would like to be able to discuss these matters with you, but regrettably, I have an appointment. Women do have more power in Islam than most Westerners realize. I regret I must end our conversation now."

Dr. Nasr's writings spell out many of these ideas in detail.[13]

A running theme is "Man's total disharmony with his environment": the crisis is the externalization of an inner malaise that cannot be solved without "the spiritual rebirth of Western man." Man's destiny calls on him to fulfill his role as God's vicegerent on earth and protector of the natural order, thus bearing witness to the truth that the whole of nature speaks of God.

The Renaissance led to the separation of philosophy from theology, reason from faith, and mysticism from gnosis, illuminated knowledge.[14] In medieval times Christianity, like Islam, was steeped in tradition. But as the rigid logic of Aristotelian thinking came to be emphasized, the sense of the sacred diminished. By the seventeenth century the science of the cosmos was secularized. This mechanized the view of the world, and eventually led to examining man and society as elements that could be measured with the aim of manipulation and predictability.

In attacking what he calls the "hypothesis" of evolution, Nasr uses the term to mean not modifications within a particular species (which do occur, he says, in the process of adapting to changed natural conditions), but the belief that through natural processes one species is actually transformed into another. Nasr passionately criticizes this on a wide variety of grounds—metaphysical, cosmological, religious, logical, mathematical, physical, biological, and paleontological—with arguments too complex to recapitulate here. His central concern is that what he calls "the deification of historical process" has become so powerful that in many souls it has taken the place of religion and veils the archetypal realities.

Hinduism, Jainism, Buddhism, Islam, and many other traditions do demonstrate awareness that other creatures have preceded man on the earth and that its geological configuration has changed. For example, over a thousand years ago Muslim scientists knew this to be true. But in all sacred Scriptures there is not a single indication that higher life forms evolved from lower ones. Contrary to Darwinian theory, each new species entered life very suddenly, over an extended region, and with all its essential characteristics. A truly scientific statement would be that nature produces species that are unchanging, but occasionally disappear.

Underlying this secularization of the science of the cosmos was the absence of a higher form of knowledge encompassing all learning and phenomena: metaphysics. In the East this "sacred science" endures to this day. Moreover, Islam's elaborate hierarchy of knowledge is integrated by the principle of unity (*tawhid*), running as an axis through every mode of knowledge and being. There are juridical, social, theological, gnostic, and metaphysical sciences, their principles all derived from the source of revelation, the Qur'an. Within Islamic civilization there developed philosophical, natural, and mathematical sciences integrated with the worldview of Islam. On each level of knowledge, nature is seen in a particular way. For jurists, it is the background for human action, a domain to be analyzed, and for the metaphysician, the object of contemplation, reflecting suprasensible realities. All Islamic sciences affirm the Divine Unity.

Nasr finds throughout Islam's history an intimate connection between the metaphysical and the study of nature. Many Muslim scientists were Sufis. In Islamic, as in Chinese civilization, observation of nature and even experimentation generally stood on the gnostic and mystic side of tradition. "Islam has preserved an integral view of the Universe and sees in the arteries of the cosmic and natural world order the flow of divine grace, or *barakah* . . . . Man can learn to contemplate it, not as an independent domain but as a mirror reflecting a higher reality."[15]

Across the centuries, the same principles of the Divine Unity have guided Islamic science, art, and law. Islamic cosmology and cosmography have served as matrix for the sciences, from geography to alchemy. Maps were based on actual observation and remain amazingly accurate, yet are also works of art. Islamic medicine produced detailed, accurate anatomical studies, even while following the ancient injunction against dissection. Founded on the doctrines of unity and balance, Islamic medicine is practiced with great success in places like the Hamdard Institutes to this day.[16] The plant world was studied with minute care, and with the goal of gleaning spiritual lessons. Muslim scientists always recognized that nature is, above all, a reflection of the paradise whose memories we still bear in the depths of our souls.

This symbolic approach can be linked to the Orthodox Christian view that icons image the divine world. Indeed, Nasr observes that Islamic science is in the most profound sense art, enabling the human to contemplate the visible cosmos as an icon revealing the spiritual world beyond.

Thus in Islam, man's goal has been to study animals not only for their own sake, but also to know better his own inner reality. This reality is the total reflection of the Divine Names and Qualities, just as animals are the partial, but often more direct reflections. Man, as central being in the terrestrial environment, is better able to exercise responsibility for it. But "man cannot gain an awareness of the sacred aspects of nature without discovering the sacred within himself or herself," he once told an interfaith conference on "Spirit and Nature" at Middlebury College that was video-taped for a program of Bill Moyers.[17]

The perfect expression of the microcosm opening to the macrocosm lies in Sufism, says Nasr. The author of several books on Rumi and other Sufis, he frequently quotes from their works, as in these lines of the Persian poet Hafiz:

> There is no veil between the lover and the Beloved;
> Thou art thine own veil, O Hafiz remove thyself.

Trees are not only a necessity for maintaining life but a recurring symbol. The Qur'an compares the cosmos to a tree whose roots are firm in the heavens and whose branches spread to the whole of the universe, symbolizing the cosmos in prayer. In Attar's *Conference of the Birds*, the flight of 30 birds to their original homes symbolizes the human's journey toward God. The literary masterpiece *Tales of Bidpai* reveals the concern not only to study animals, but to learn from them and see them as creatures who share in man's ultimate destiny. He has the right to dominate them only on condition that he remain aware of his limits. Islamic science, too, sees limits on humans' power to destroy the earth, reminding them that their end is to journey to a world beyond.

Ranging through a spectrum of wisdom traditions, Nasr pays homage not only to the other Abrahamic faiths, but also the spiritual traditions of Native Americans and Shintoists, for whom revelation is directly related to natural forms. Thus we have many traditions, yet one, the Primordial Tradition, which *is*. This does not lessen the originality of each, which emanates as a direct message from heaven and conforms to a particular archetype. From interfaith dialogues one should expect only understanding of another world of sacred form—while preserving one's own.

The geometric patterns in Islamic art reflect the archetypal world. Traditional Islamic architecture and city planning never sought to convey a sense of defiant human power over nature. Where there were hot deserts, streets were narrow to prevent the sun from dissipating the cool night air. Slatted wind towers on housetops caught the breezes that ventilated homes. Even religious architecture reflected harmony with nature. Light and air entered easily into the mosque, and birds often flew around during the most solemn moments of a ceremony. Use was made of the sun to heat buildings, of wind to turn mills, of water to provide energy for small technologies. In the Middle East the Muslims perfected the ancient system of *qa'nats*, elaborate underground channels that stored water and carried it long distances without danger of evaporation. Many are used today.

Like all traditional civilizations, the Islamic aimed at local self-sufficiency, and sought not maximum production, but the maximum happiness possible within the limited conditions of Earth. Many of the technologies suggested by Ivan Illich, Theodore Roszak, and E.F. Schumacher are found in the Islamic past and continue in the present.

In the traditional Islamic pattern of life, even today work reflects natural rhythms. An artisan's workday, for example, may last from dawn until long after sunset, but his work is done in the bazaar, the bosom of the community, and is interrupted by coffee-drinking with his fellows, dining at home with his family, prayers at the mosque, or meditation.

Today concern for a greater reality in the contemporary world can be seen in the growing interest in ecology, says Nasr. Awareness of the interrelationship among all living beings is stressed even by agnostic scientists, and carries within it an urge to rediscover the sacred.

Thus if the limitations imposed by a desacralized mode of knowing were removed, the sacred would manifest itself of its own accord. "The light has not ceased to exist in itself. The cosmos seems to have become dark, spiritually speaking, only because of the veil of opacity surrounding that particular humanity called modern."[18]

Although not all their ideas are mutually exclusive, Nasr's perspective stands in sharp contrast to Berry's. Among the many ways they differ are the following.

The starting point for Berry is the natural world, while Nasr begins with the divine world. For Berry "revelation" is the awakening of the sense of ultimate mystery, and he speaks of the "revelatory import of the natural world." For Nasr, "nature" is a symbol of a transcendental reality, a symbol that teaches human beings about God; he perceives reality through the lens of archetypes. For Berry, nature's creatures are not simply windows to some transcendent reality, but manifestations of divinity; that which is communicated thus participates in the divine.

These contrasts seem related to a fundamental difference between the religions that nurtured these men. Although each faith includes elements of both, Christianity tends to be a way of love, Islam a way of knowing through illumination. Metaphysics is a realm that Berry seldom discusses; for Nasr, it is the *scientia sacra*.[19]

To Nasr, the concept of "evolution" is a vain attempt to prove that higher biological forms emerge out of lower ones; it violates the principle of hierarchy, and is wrong in its influence on other modes of thought. Berry finds excitement in the idea that earlier life forms were simpler than later ones, that the earth is in a state of continuing transformation. Berry focuses on cosmogenesis, understanding the universe as always in the process of becoming. We humans also evolve. We are truly *of* the earth; our sense of the divine reflects the outer world, and can alter as that world is altered. Such views transgress the principle of the unchanging nature of sacred realities that is fundamental to Nasr's thought. For him, the Way is the way back, through the revival of great traditions. Only thus can we rediscover the sacred, and dissipate the loneliness of a world from which the spirit has been banished.

Each way—Nasr's and Berry's—contains wisdom. Although their perspectives differ radically, both philosophers suggest that we humble ourselves before the mystery, the awesome forces of Creation—and simplify our lives accordingly. Both remind us of the peril of hubris, that forgetfulness of human limits.

Four centuries ago the Persian Sufi poet Abd al-Rahman Jami foresaw with uncanny prescience the predicament of power-driven humanity today:

> I lost my intellect, soul, religion, and heart
> In order to know an atom in perfection.
> But no one can know the essence of the atom perfectly.
> How often must I repeat that no one shall know it;
> then farewell!

Islam in Action

Nairobi: Population, Poverty, and Energy

In Nairobi a few men and many women crowded into Dr. Yusuf Ali Eraj's office, a clinic established by the Muslim Welfare Society of Kenya but open to people of any faith. A few miles away, local imams/sheikhs were speaking of the duty of good Muslims to refuse contraceptives, because children were God's gift and it was a flagrant attack on His wisdom not to accept it. Yet most of these women had come for instruction in birth control, for Dr. Eraj was widely known as the founder of the Family Planning Society of Kenya.

Dr. Eraj welcomed us into his tiny examining room. A short, genial, vigorous man who seemed unhurried although he moved under great pressure, Dr. Eraj worried about the fate of the earth, particularly that part of it called Kenya. His concerns ranged from introducing alternative forms of energy to halting desertification and enacting stringent recycling laws, and he had addressed the World Muslim League and the United Nations Environmental Programme (UNEP) on such issues. One of his greatest sources of anxiety was the loss of trees throughout Africa.

"Ninety percent of the African population depends on firewood for fuel. Yet our government permits cutting trees to make charcoal—a business. At the same time, there are too many people. Energy, population, poverty—these problems go together."

Population was a problem that not many Muslims talked about, he conceded. But that was changing. "Many clergy cling to old customs. But Kenya's population doubled between 1970 and 1990! Using birth control does not mean following the West. Tourists come here, impregnating women, spreading AIDS. Muslims can practice family planning, following Islamic principles. It is a *myth* that Islamic doctrine opposes it! All methods are approved, even sterilization. Abortion is different. It is not contraception, but taking life that already exists. And even abortion is permitted in certain cases, like when the mother's life is endangered. I lectured at Mecca about this. Religious leaders must speak out.

"But if societies are poor and illiterate," he added, "the women are treated badly. They are not educated about what they can do for themselves. Their status keeps family planning down. If contraception is not explained, it is not used—and illegal abortions go up. Our hospitals are full of women suffering from complications after illegal abortions."

Jerusalem: Persevering Toward Peace

The place was a hotel room in East Jerusalem, the time was 1990, the subject was the ecological problems facing Palestinians, and the person with whom we were talking was Nafez Assaily, a Muslim who succeeded Mubarak Awad as head of the Palestinian Center for the Study of Nonviolence.

"Water!" he exclaimed passionately. "It is very big problem here. Economic problem. Social problem. War problem. And water—we Sufis say it is *sacred*."

"You are Sufi? You never told us that."

"I didn't? Well—well, you are surprised?" His plump, placid face broke into a broad smile. "Because there are not many Sufis in Palestine? Because I wear ordinary clothes?"

We did know that many Sufis work in business, political, and other worldly fields. But we still felt unprepared for this disclosure from a non-violent activist for human rights, one who had endured harassment and threats of imprisonment, and stood with villagers before settlers' bulldozers to stop the building of roads and the clearing of confiscated Palestinian land.

Nafez was rushing on. "The latest Intifada leaflet urges us to plant trees!" He waved the leaflet above his head. "It says nothing about guns—which is what outsiders always think we are thinking about. The vast majority of Intifada actions have been strikes, demonstrations, boycotts of Israeli products, refusing to pay taxes, praying, fasting—27 kinds of non-violent protest! What we think about is the future. And trees, they represent the future. They are sacred."

"Trees have a special meaning to you?"

"Yes! But we Sufis believe everything on earth, in the sky, and under water is sacred. From seed up to grown tree, from green grass up to flesh. The miracle of man is his senses. The nose how it can smell, the tongue how it can taste, the stomach how it can digest meat but not itself, although the stomach is also meat. We ascend to heaven to think about it. Heaven has no pillars. It stands by itself. We see the sun, and stars, and it doesn't hang, it is a miracle. Eventually, we see that *God* has power!"

We groped for some kind of response. But Nafez was plunging ahead. "If we want to make our life miserable, it is in our hands. If we want to make a good life, it is in our hands also. God gives us choices. And we Sufis see people, birds, and animals on the land as children of God. But life under water, it is even more sacred than life on the land. There are more species. The miracle of water makes up two-thirds of the planet." He paused, breathless.

"Muhammad said to us, 'Even if you have an ocean, don't spend too much.' Our Sufi practice is to save water, and also not use too much money or food. We pray—" He stood up, and with his hands gestured to show Sufis praying in rows. "We pray, we submit to God, gradually, gradually, we speak with God as the beloved. We begin with Adam. Adam was created by God. Adam never sleeps. Abraham, the friend of God, never sleeps. There are special prophets like Noah, and Moses the speaker to God, and they also never sleep. Jesus, the spirit of God, never sleeps, and Muhammad, the Prophet of God, never sleeps. The water, plant, trees, sun, stones—the universe never sleeps. It is a circle of life, always in motion!" He raised his hands, closed his eyes, swayed back and forth, and whirled a little to the right and the left.

A long moment of silence followed. Awkwardly, we ventured to return to practical issues. "There are also the political problems of water."

"Yes, yes." Nafez nodded. "Very difficult. I have seen Israelis digging artesian wells beside ordinary Palestinian wells, so the water table goes down and Palestinian wells dry up. I have seen Israelis cut off water to Palestinian villages. But they will see we have one land, one source of our water. We must share." He moved to the window and looked out at the sky. "The Sufi way is also the Jewish Kabbalah. In the Sufi way there is more submission, but the thinking, it is the same. Rabbi Steinsaltz is into Kabbalah. He is the most admired rabbi in Israel."

"Were you born Sufi ?"

"No. My parents were traditional Muslim. In 1974 I met Yacoub Karish. He is Palestinian, jailed here, then deported to Jordan. There, he is in Parliament and is sheikh. He opened my eyes. At our services, we repeat God's 99 names, every name 10, 50, 100 times over and over, that is the *zikr*, for purification. Sometimes alone, sometimes in circle. Then we stand and dance. This is the Sufi way. I would like that all Muslims become Sufi."

"And at the same time you, who have traveled in England and studied in France to become a French teacher, you seem so open to other faiths."

"Of course, of course!" He smiled. "Once at a meeting of Presbyterians in England they said, 'Tell us about you.' And I said, 'I am Nafez. I went to Roman Catholic and Coptic Orthodox schools. I am of Muslim religion. I practice the Sufi way. I am a non-violent Palestinian resister. And I love Quakers!' At Cambridge Friends Meeting in England as soon as I entered I felt something—something close—" He pressed a hand to his heart.

"The Quakers say there is that of God in every one."

"Yes! And *I* say—" Like Hindus, he pressed his palms together, and bowed slightly. "I kiss the hand of God in you, and you kiss the hand of God in me. I kiss the sacred in you!"

We talked for nearly two hours. Nafez moved easily from the spiritual to the political and economic planes; for him they were naturally interconnected. He had studied water issues thoroughly, and concluded that they could never be resolved unless the Jordan Basin powers (Jordan, Syria, Lebanon, and Israel/Palestine) came up with a water-sharing regional plan. He talked of the perseverance of Center volunteers who continued to plant trees in the face of hostile actions from the many Israeli settlers who uprooted them. He described the Center's Library on Wheels, which rotated more than 5,000 children's books in Arabic to Palestinians in some 100 villages and refugee camps.

Finally, he shared his ideas about the future of Palestine. It would be a demilitarized state. Unarmed civilian guards would do the police work. "If we had guns, they would bring only trouble—more excuse for Israelis to use guns. And without army, we have money for industry, agriculture, education. Our real strength, it will be economic. Trade with Israel, Jordan, other countries. There will be tourism. This is Holy Land for three faiths. We Palestinians know this land, we will not spoil it. When peace will come, all faiths will come here."

Nine years later, Nafez and the Palestinian Center for the Study of Nonviolence were still persevering. Israel and the Palestine Liberation Organization had signed peace agreements, but true peace seemed more remote than ever. Still, the Library on Wheels, supplemented with a children's puppet show and cassette books for blind children, was continuing, and the Center was conducting seminars to educate Palestinians in nonviolent strategies. Nafez was even more convinced that violent "solutions" only engendered more violence—and that "peace" could have no meaning unless it included peace with the earth.

Cairo: Egypt's Green Party

Egypt has been called a "hopeless case." Cairo's air is so foul that many traffic policemen are in a coma-like state at the end of the day. Less than 4 percent of the country is cultivable, yet urbanization is devouring much of the good agricultural land. In spring desert winds add even more dust to the pollution-clogged air. The Nile is increasingly contaminated with human waste and industrial effluents. In the Pharaohs' tombs, carbonic acid is eating away the stones—an indirect product of the tourist industry that the government continues to promote.

The population (more than 65 million in 1999) continues to grow at a rate of nearly a million a year. The inhabitants of greater Cairo (12 million) are so crowded that hundreds of thousands live in cardboard boxes on apartment roofs; at least half a million dwell in mausoleums. Although Islam, the religion of over 90 percent of the people, has no precept against contraception, as in other Islamic countries a great many Muslim clergy in Egypt preach that it does.

Here one would hardly expect to find a Green Party—the first in the Arab world. But in 1990, after three years of bitter struggling for official recognition, it was granted party status.

The first chairman was Hassan Ragab, famous for reviving the art of papyrus-making, founding the Dr. Ragab Papyrus Institute and building a "green oasis" on an island in the polluted Nile within the boundaries of Cairo. Built entirely in the style of pharaonic Egypt, it lodges some 300 Egyptians who live in the ancient atmosphere and practice agricultural and industrial activities with ancient implements, using methods that harmonize with the environment.

Across from the island is a large houseboat, home of the Papyrus Institute and the Green Party. It was there, in 1990, that we first met Dr. Ragab. He was jauntily dressed in a checked sports coat, maroon sweater, and visored *képi*. Compactly built, with a small moustache, lively black eyes, and sharp features, he radiated energy. It was hard to believe that he was 79 years old. After offering us coffee, he responded easily, in excellent English, to our questions.

"As a party, what can the Greens do that is different? Professors at Cairo University have told us the government *is* trying to control pollution."

He smiled wryly. "The government is one of the biggest destroyers of our environment. When it wants to build a drainage plant, it looks for land—like a public park. Its army has built barracks on land of some of the most precious gardens in the city, uprooting people and trees. It allows cement and steel factories near Cairo. Their pollution kills trees—and children."

"What *should* the government be doing?"

"Encouraging people to plant trees and grow gardens. Imposing strict rules on new factories. Encouraging renewable energy." He drew out a map showing how solar and wind power could be used. "It should limit the number of cars. But gasoline is too cheap. The government should impose international standards on exhausts. New laws *have* been introduced, but not enforced—our police are underpaid.

"Tankers dump oil in the Suez and Mediterranean when they're being cleaned! Adding to the sewage already there. So more parasitic diseases come from the dirty overloaded drains.

"But the root of the problem," he added, "is the Western countries, with their big plants, big cars, big arms industries, big everything. Basically, they are destroying themselves. The best help for Egypt would

Dr. Hassan Ragab, founder of Egypt's Green Party.

be for the big powers to help themselves."

As for the widespread belief that a good Muslim should be fruitful and multiply, leaders were now finding scriptures declaring that humans should not throw themselves to destruction. "That opens the way to limitation. We cannot survive unless we limit our families. Human beings are the big source of pollution."

During our second talk, we learned more about his life.

He grew up in Alexandria, on a farm with wetlands that attracted enormous numbers of migrating birds. As time passed, he saw that many were disappearing, and that this corresponded with the growing use of agrichemicals. "I felt sad. Those birds were my friends. I began to see that fish were disappearing, the bananas we grew were catching diseases, new roads were being built, and children were getting diseases from swimming. I was thinking about cause and effect."

After studying engineering in Cairo and Paris, Ragab worked as electrical engineer, then held successive posts as military attaché at the Egyptian Embassy in Washington, head of research for the Egyptian Armed Forces, and ambassador to China, Yugoslavia, and Italy.

Back in Egypt in the late 1960s, he spent years searching out the lost art of papyrus-making. "Today I use papyrus as a symbol. The ancient Egyptians used the hieroglyphic sign representing papyrus for things green and fresh. Also, in our campaigns we feature environmental teachings in the Qur'an, and even some from the ancient *Book of the Dead*."

The goals in the Green's platform are far-reaching. They include:

- informing the people about their right to an equal share of natural resources and environmental services;

- creating a new ecological value system;

- stimulating community participation;

- incorporating sustainable development concepts in all develop-ment plans; and

- promoting Middle East peace and condemning efforts to introduce nuclear, chemical, or biological weapons.

These goals are similar to those of Greens in the West, which have always seen environmental, political, social, and economic issues as in-tertwined. But questions pursued us as we remembered the many moder-ate, well-educated Egyptians who declared despairingly: "There is no democracy here. And American aid goes only to the rich and powerful." How could Green goals be put into practice in a society that was expe-riencing worsening poverty, and becoming polarized between secularists and Islamic fundamentalists seeking to channel resentment of the West into new solutions? A meeting with eight Green Party members provided some insights.

Most were university-educated and generally secular in outlook. One man was a Coptic Christian. Neither of the two women wore the tradi-tional headcover. The eight agreed that the worst problems were the population explosion, overcrowding in the Delta, and pollution of the Nile. Their chief solution was education, through universities, public meetings, and television debates.

A chemist said he often talked about the growth of "biological ecol-ogy." An economist described his conception of economics as "dealing with culture, industry, agriculture, everything." A farmer spoke of the need for agricultural cooperatives like Sweden's. Several members de-clared that Sweden's democratic socialism offered the best all-around model for Egypt.

Women numbered about 10 percent of the Green Party. One of the women present, who worked at the Ministry of Information and as a volunteer with an NGO called "Protection of the Environment," observed that women offered a special strength; they could demonstrate that a clean environment begins at home, and urge teachers to include environmental lessons at school.

Qur'anic precepts about the environment were sometimes brought out in religious classes at school, she told us; the Greens encouraged this. "Also, we try to get the sheikh, or the Coptic priest, to announce when there will be environmental meetings. The Copts even have an environmental project—reclamation of the desert at Wadi Natroun."

What chance do the Greens have to make a real impact on Egyptian society? The U.S. continues to pour in foreign (mostly military) aid to avoid "subversive threats" once labeled "Communist," but now "Islamic fundamentalist"—threats that become sufficient grounds for keeping the U.S. military establishment alive and well. It serves to remind the entire Middle East who has the ultimate power. The U.S. corporate-government partnership would hardly favor what the Greens call "a new value system," with reduced arms expenditures, individual rights to an equal share of natural resources, and less dependence on oil.

Yet even when they feel virtually hopeless, Egyptians, heirs of a great river civilization, seem to retain an abiding awareness, flowing somewhere in the subconscious, that their destiny and that of the earth are intertwined. As the Greens reach out, they sometimes remind their listeners that the 5,000-year-old *Book of the Dead* relates that the newly deceased were asked whether they had polluted the Nile, or cut down a fruitful tree. The answer determined their fate.

Karachi: Empowering Women, Reinterpreting the Qur'an

In the office of World Wildlife Fund (WWF)-Pakistan, we were talking with half a dozen grassroots activists. All were working for organizations concerned with environmental protection, health, community development, or human rights. All were women. It was yet another surprise in this paradoxical country.

Pakistan was still a stronghold of conservatism. Yet a woman, Benazir Bhutto, had managed to become prime minister, the first female head of government in the Muslim world. There were women's rights centers in the main cities, women's studies programs at some universities, and an array of small but determined women's organizations.

Still, even in cities it was somewhat rare to see an unaccompanied woman on the streets. The literacy rate for women was estimated at 50 percent in the cities, 14 in rural areas. It was no coincidence that Pakistan had a very high population growth rate, more than 3 percent.

Like most other Muslim countries, Pakistan generally followed principles consonant with Western ideas in matters of civil law, but *shari'ah* dominated personal and family law. Moreover, the secular lower courts were supervised by the *shari'ah* courts, which could overturn "non-Islamic" laws and judgments. Interpreting its complex rules in present-day society evoked passionate debate. Most controversial here was the Hudood Ordinance, passed in 1979 as a political move to "Islamicize" Pakistani family and criminal law. While dealing with various offenses, the ordinance was particularly harsh in relation to *zinah* (extra-marital sex) and *zinah-bil-jabr* (rape). Men and women accused of *zinah* were to be dealt equally severe punishment—after conviction established by self-confession or the testimony of four Muslim males of known moral repute. But by applying the same principles to cases of adultery and rape, the Ordinance effectively blurred any distinction. Unless the rapist confessed, he could be found guilty only through such witness. (How four moral Muslim males could have allowed the act to take place is never explained.) Thus if a woman was raped and could not offer this proof, it was generally assumed that she seduced the man; she could be convicted of adultery or fornication.

Court decisions were extremely important, for they could vary a great deal; penalties on the books were often more severe than actual sentences. For example, the Ordinance called for stoning to death or rigorous imprisonment, plus up to 100 lashes (canings), but in recent years stoning was extremely rare, while the number of lashes varied, and sometimes was reduced by the *shari'ah* court. The penalties on the books, however, served as a threat.

Moreover, traditionally a woman raped was unmarriageable. Her own brothers would feel so dishonored that in some cases they might even kill her, or themselves. Bhutto had not dared to counter the religious right by repealing Hudood, despite her party's promise to do so.

This was only one example of the way men held the power and the mechanisms to perpetuate it indefinitely. Yet the vibrant young women in this room radiated the quiet confidence that comes from commitment to a long battle with no easy victories.

Nor was it long before the "woman question" surfaced as an inseparable aspect of the struggle for human rights and a healthier ecosystem. When WWF began here in 1972, its activities centered on pushing legislation for parks and wetlands preservation, we were told. Then they began to realize that they must work with women's groups like those in this building and plunge into education, particularly through field-based, grassroots work, to deal with such problems as widespread disposal of solid waste in open pits and predominance of waterborne diseases.

In Pakistan health was inextricably entwined with birth control. But many religious leaders opposed family planning. Hence concerned organizations used the words "health" or "family welfare planning." They could listen to what people perceived as their problems; eventually, many women would complain that they had too many children.

"Do you talk with religious leaders about preaching on *other* environmental problems?"

"*Religious* leaders?" they echoed. "A death knell! It would be seen as attaching ourselves to a religious group. Most religious leaders are attached to some party—it can be useful for both religious and political figures. To survive, we stay away from politics—hence from religion."

"But an international network, based in France, called Women Living Under Muslim Laws, has a research group working on a fresh interpretation of the way the Qur'an sets out the position of women," observed a member of Shirkat Gah who had been sitting quietly in the circle. "Eventually, success will influence our work with women on issues that affect the environment. As you can see, in this country we must often work indirectly."

Her name was Farhat Naz Rahman. She was a slim, dark-eyed, graceful young woman with a classic Eastern beauty. Her bright flowered pantaloons and matching tunic (the national dress) accented her vivacious manner; she seemed completely caught up in her subject. We were drawn by Farhat's enthusiasm, and spent the rest of the morning with her.

"We want to change only certain *interpretations* of Islam. The chapters in the Qur'an concerning women. My particular goal, it is to become an Islamic scholar whose interpretations would be accepted. In this country, up to now all the scholars with authority are men, and not one is progressive. First, I will need a Ph.D. in Islamic Studies. But so far, whenever I apply for the program, I am denied by the admissions committee—all men."

"Could you get your Ph.D. abroad?"

"Yes. Like a few other Pakistani women. But if I can become the first who has done all her studies here, then it's hard for the obscurantists' lobby—some call them fundamentalists—to label me a 'Western-oriented woman.' My hope is, some day I will sit as judge on a *shari'ah* court. There are four court levels: lower, high, *shari'ah*, and supreme. It is all very complicated, but I'll try to put it simply. All these types of cases— civil, family, Hudood—go first to the lower court. But if there's an appeal, you go on to a district judge, or high court, or *shari'ah* court, depending on the type of case and other circumstances. Generally, the cases that get to *shari'ah* court are adultery, rape, serious theft, divorce, all the matters related to Islamic provisions. If you wanted to challenge a law as un-Islamic, you would go directly to the *shari'ah* court. It is very powerful. No woman has ever held office at that level."

"The problem is the way men have *interpreted* the Qur'an?"

"Yes. The Qur'an gives women their rights, but Muslim women do not have consciousness of them. I have been doing research on Islamic social laws. The condition of Muslim women has *not* been the same in different periods of history or different countries. Also, a *true* Islamic society has never existed, it is only an ideal. Today even in countries such as Pakistan, which are Muslim but where Arabic is not the spoken language, the Islamic legal system still shows the print of the Arab mind of the seventh century."

"But if the Qur'an is seen as eternal and unchanging?"

"The *spirit* of the Qur'an is unchanging and infallible. But most Muslims have not understood that Islam is wholly future-oriented. It is very elastic. All the *principles* are given in the Qur'an and *hadith* to be applied in forms dictated by the situation. If traditional interpretations frustrate the spirit of Islam as dynamic force, we need liberal ones."

"And you say the laws in traditional Muslim jurisprudence are not divine, but based on interpretations by fallible beings?"

She nodded. "The Prophet's Companions listened to him and learned the Qur'an by heart. Then they started putting it together under his guidance. But the *hadith*—*that* was started after his death. There have been many schools. So what does this mean? Women must study the Qur'an and the *hadith* and Qur'anic laws *themselves*. They can see how obscurantists use Surah 4, the famous chapter on women, by saying the passages describing men as guardians of women mean the female is subordinate. But in the Arabic language there is no such word as 'subordinate.' You see, study of Arabic linguistics is part of my strategy. Also, verse one of that chapter says God created the human being from a single soul, and created, of like nature, her mate."

"*Her* mate?"

"That is the way I read it, because here the gender used in the Arabic language is feminine. Also, the verse goes on to speak of 'fear of the wombs from which you have been created.' It is not the biblical idea of Eve being created from Adam's rib. I need to do more research on the Qur'an and the *hadith* along these lines. It will be a long work." She sighed.

"How did you arrive at your present thinking?"

"It's a long story. My father died when I was 17, so my mother, sisters, and I lived alone. My brother was away at engineering school. I learned how hard it is in this society for women without men, at least if you don't come from a rich family. I don't. I began to think about all this. Eventually, I became a radical feminist, when I went to Switzerland, France, and Somalia on an exchange sponsored by Women Living Under Muslim Laws. What I found is that women are oppressed everywhere. And religion is always used to oppress them."

"So if you get your Ph.D. in Islamic Studies, how will you use it?"

Her body stiffened, as if she were imagining the long fight ahead. "I would work on family law, especially Hudood. Now some brave women lawyers sometimes obtain release of women from prison. Partly because civil law inherited from Britain also operates here. But think, if there were women judges on the *shari'ah* court! The federal *shari'ah* court once ruled that women *can* be such judges. But it hasn't happened. I'd also continue community organizing with poor women, who are victimized most. My aim is to help them see that the negative ideas about women in the Muslim world are rooted in theology. Unless the misogynistic tendencies in Islamic tradition are abolished, they will continue to be victimized. No matter how much improvement occurs in educational, economic, social, political, and environmental rights."

That night Farhat took us to a meeting of a group called War Against Rape at the All-Pakistan Women's Association, where a film from India about distorted images of women was shown. The next day we accompanied her on a visit to a poor neighborhood to observe an outreach program. The most frequent problems presented by the patients—most of them women and children—were respiratory ailments, malnutrition, dysentery, skin diseases, and "too many children."

"Most of these are essentially environmental problems," Farhat observed. "Women are much closer to nature than men are, they must work for a healthy environment. That is happening a little, but it will happen more when they win more freedom."

Since our visit, Farhat has left Shirkat Gah and taken a new job as coordinator at the Center for Social Science Research providing legal aid and basic legal information to women at the grassroots level. In 1990 she helped Shirkat Gah and the "Women Living Under Muslim Laws" network to organize a meeting in Pakistan on "Qur'anic Interpretation by Women." Throughout the 1990s, she regularly applied for admission to Karachi University's doctoral program in Islamic studies, and stubbornly went on with her research under a progressive female doctor in Islamic Studies. As part of her plan, she obtained a law degree in 1992.

The Pakistani government has expanded its support of family planning programs, but they have not been publicized as such, and the message is lost on poorly educated people. As for the Hudood Ordinance, it is still in force. During the Bhutto regime, Farhat became increasingly disillusioned. "In my personal view," Farhat wrote, "Benazir Bhutto is more politician and feudal than woman. . . . She compromises on women issues to retain the power, and a compromising woman leader cannot bring any change in the situation of the common women. So in a way

Feminist activist Farhat Naz Rahman of Karachi, Pakistan.

she is from the right gender but wrong class."

In a phone conversation, we asked Farhat why her mother was so supportive to a daughter who had stepped outside traditional roles. "My mother says I am 'exceptional case,'" Farhat answered with a little laugh. "Also, in her heart, she has been liberal from the beginning! My mother is very inspiring figure, the one who has always stood beside me."

In 1995 she greeted us on the phone with great excitement. "I've been accepted into the doctoral program of Islamic studies!"

We discussed with her the challenges she would face. They were almost forbidding. One was "educating the men, as in a patriarchal society females are inclined to think through the brain of their male family members." Another was dealing with "forces desperately looking forward to introducing secularism in the country, although they fail, as religion is deep-rooted among the masses." Still another challenge lay in handling attacks from the other side: the "obscurantists" or so-called fundamentalists. Although in 1994, for the first time ever, two women were named to Pakistan's high court, no woman had yet been appointed on the *shari'ah* or supreme court level, positions that carried more "Islamic" weight.

By 1998 there were significant changes in Farhat's situation. She had finally found a man with whom she could "share everything." Her new husband was a journalist, and they were working together against the Hudood Laws.

Farhat was still pursuing her doctorate in Islamic studies and had begun writing her dissertation on the social laws of Islam, she told us. But for the time being, at least, she had given up her dream of becoming the first woman to sit on Pakistan's *shari'ah* court. The corruption and intricate politics on the three important court levels—high, supreme, and *shari'ah*—had become so notorious that judges no longer commanded respect and real authority.

She placed more faith in Rahm, a new organization of Pakistani women working on interpretation of the Qur'an. The group was growing, had been allowed to register with the government, and seemed destined to wield some power.

What makes Farhat's approach a promising one is that she is pursuing several tracks at one time: obtaining a doctorate in Islamic Studies, lecturing, writing a book on feminism, and reaching out to poor women with legal aid and information that can help them, among other things, to fight rape successfully, choose the number of children they wish, and take the initiative to form grassroots environmental action groups. Finally, she is working in concert with small but growing sisterhoods in both the national and the international spheres.

From such strategies a liberation theology can emerge. New beliefs—or rather, new perspectives—influence action, and action nudges belief.

Conclusion: Fixed Truth, Change, and a Deteriorating Earth

It is impossible to consider the possibilities for a full-fledged Islamic environmental ethic without considering the political, economic, and historical aspects of Islam as a living community. This is true of all religions—but particularly true of Islam, which is seen as a way of life.

Today there are some promising signs of Islam-inspired ecological activity, notably an organization arising from the WWF Network called the Islamic Foundation for the Environment and Environmental Sciences. Dedicated to creating projects and education worldwide, it is beginning with community-based initiatives in Pakistan, Jordan, Sri Lanka, and the United Kingdom.

The potential is enormous. If the disparate forces of Islam, the world's fastest growing religion, were to get together and take off, it could become a leader in the ecospiritual movement. Moreover, the fact that in principle, at least, it does not separate the secular and the sacred domains means it embodies the latent energy to transform vision into reality. The Qur'an and *hadith* are rich in ecological precepts that are valid today. Moreover, the very emphasis on law implicitly sets boundaries around individualism and recognizes the rights of the community. Indeed, the Qur'an's affirmation that "there is not an animal . . . nor a being that flies on its wings but forms part of communities like you" prepares the way for the wider vision of an earth community encompassing all creatures.

Of all the Declarations of Assisi, says WWF advisor Martin Palmer, the Muslim Declaration, drawn up by the Muslim World League, is remarkable for its honesty: the failure of Muslims to live out true Islamic law in relation to the rest of Creation. "The notions of unity, trusteeship, and accountability . . . must guide all aspects of our life and work," it asserts. "We must imbibe these values into our very being. . . ."[20]

Unfortunately, the openness of this self-criticism does not seem typical of Islam today. Nevertheless, the Declaration does represent the thinking of a small but growing group.

Thus, Fazlun Khalid's entry for Islam in the *Encyclopedia of the Environment* recognizes that all decisions made by a community (including the *ummah*) are in the final analysis political—and that all political decisions sooner or later affect the finite resources of Creation: the environment.[21] Some Muslims have been talking about establishing a *"shari'ah* of the environment." If this comes to pass, all devout Muslims will feel obliged to follow its dictates.

One of Islam's great strengths, then, lies in its recognition that everything is interconnected. The other side of that strength is the danger implicit in its "total worldview." If the belief that there is no dichotomy between the secular and spiritual domains leads to a wedding of church and state, the age-old peril looms: power begets lust for power. While there are dangers in a small secular group making environmental decisions, it could be as dangerous for a select group of religious leaders to do so. Many Muslims are committed to democracy. But it is not at all clear what form "Islamic democracy" would take.

There are other deep-seated problems. One is the steadfast belief at the very heart of the faith: the eternal, unchanging truth of the Qur'an. For many Muslims, that conviction extends to almost all the *hadith* and even to the *shari'ah*. Thus the difficulty in even recognizing that the ecological crisis is an unprecedented situation, calling for new responses. The notion of fixed truth also poses a barrier to a genuinely open exchange with non-Muslims and becomes an obstacle to accepting the study of comparative religion.

Nor is the Divine Feminine integral to the faith, as it is in the reverence for the Virgin Mary; for the *bodhisattva* of mercy Kwan-Yin; or for Mother Earth in almost all indigenous religions. Most of the 99 (some say 1,001) names of Allah are those associated with maleness. This is not the same as saying that the faith discourages equal roles for women in the mosque and public life—although it clearly does. But there is a link: if patriarchy were to diminish in the actual practice of Islam—a possibility over which rank-and-file Muslims have some control—a feminine element, essential to the vitality of any religious tradition, could slowly begin to influence its very ethos. (Whether an ecofeminist movement specifically relating mistreatment of women with mistreatment of the earth could ever emerge is another question.)

At the same time, relaxing the mainstream disapproval of music and dance as expressions of the sacred could open the way to celebrating humans' kinship with other elements of the universe. These are threatening questions that go to the heart of Islam.

The human-centered nature of Islam also poses a problem. Like many Jews and Christians, Muslims tend to call their theology not anthropocentric, but theocentric. When the human being remains as God's vicegerent/viceregent, the distinction becomes fragile, however.

Can a basic tenet of Islam be changed at will? Obviously not. However, the late Fazlur Rahman has underscored the need for reinterpretation of Islam. A wider sociohistoric approach, grounded in more systematic scholarship, is the only adequate method to understand the Qur'an's social values. Scientific knowledge must also answer the question, "Does it point to a higher will and purpose?"[22]

Thus the Qur'an must be left textually intact, he says. But there is considerable latitude for reinterpretation, bearing in mind that "the basic impulse of the Qur'an is dynamic and action-oriented, seeking to direct history on a spiritual value pattern and attempting to create a world order." To reform Islamic law yet prevent its secularization, he proposes that an international committee of Muslim jurists and scholars undertake major works on the history of law.[23]

Although Rahman advocates democracy, he does not address the question of whether, or how, ordinary people might influence Islamic law. Nor does this prominent scholar mention the relation of human beings to the earth in light of the environmental crisis. This is but another sign that thus far ecological thinking has not penetrated far into Islam, even its progressive circles.

As our exploration of Islam-in-practice suggests, certain aspects are more subject to change than others. Some are linked to the global political situation. As Nasr puts it, Islam is reacting to the West, economically and politically; the West sets the agenda. Thus population growth can be traced not only to religious factors, but to poverty, poor education and health services (particularly for women), and a desire to overcome Western domination and find power in numbers. Consumerism, the root cause of global warming, ozone depletion, and extinction of species, is stoked by multinational enterprises based in the West. The gulf between rich and poor is widening everywhere, and most countries with Muslim majorities are poor.

Exacerbating all these causes for resentment is the widespread lack of dialogue among different faiths on how to meet these problems together. In the United States, Christians and Jews seldom think of including Muslims in ecumenical events. Whatever dialogue has occurred generally takes place in the halls of academia or at conferences of leaders meeting in five-star hotels. Particularly in the United States, with its claim to multiculturalism, it is time for exchange among ordinary citizens at churches, mosques, synagogues, homes, and civic meeting halls. Indeed, traditionally mosques are places to exchange political and social ideas.

Some aspects of Islam-in-practice are less subject to Western influence. Within Islamic society today there are passionate debates on how Muslims can find their own way to revitalization of Islamic values, yet meet challenges of the modern world. Outsiders are only vaguely aware of the precise nature of the debates. It is worth noting that at the same time, rank-and-file Muslims have generally tended to accept co-existence in a secular state. Witness Nigeria, Malaysia, Pakistan, Egypt, Jordan, and Tunisia. While the Islamists, the so-called fundamentalists, take advantage of discontent there, they do not represent the majority.

In reflecting on the potential contributions of Islam to dealing with the ecological crisis, the basic perplexity revolves around the question: What is immutable in Islam, and what lies in the gray area of possible change?

6

THE WAY OF NATIVE AMERICANS

Keeping an Ear to the Earth

"It seems the canoe of the indigenous people still sits in the shadows of the great religious ships of state, rocking gently on the great sea of life . . . as they search for spiritual reality and salvation," declared Iroquois Chief Joagquisho (Oren Lyons), faithkeeper of the Turtle Clan of the Onondaga Nation, at the 1988 Global Forum of Spiritual and Parliamentary Leaders on Human Survival. "Our canoe sits close," added the chief. "Perhaps we may know a direction that may help in this search. Please note our humble offer, for indeed have we not guided the strangers on our shores through the mysteries and rhythms of our lands down through the ages . . . "

Thomas Berry observes that "the Indian peoples of America have their own special form of nature mysticism. Awareness of a numinous presence throughout the entire cosmic order establishes among these peoples one of the most integral forms of spirituality known to us. . . . This numinous mode of consciousness has significance for the entire human community."[1]

Everywhere there are signs that many have come to look to Native Americans for guidance as the ecological crisis darkens and deepens. Increasing numbers of environmental conferences include representatives from the American Indian community. There is a surge of interest in Native American writers who can articulate their ancient traditions. Chief Seattle's famous speech warning the white man

190

that "All things connect. Whatever befalls the Earth befalls also the children of the Earth"[2] is cited in churches, in schools, and in public forums.

Some Westerners attracted to these traditions romanticize the shamans, vision quests, and Sun Dances, as if observation or even participation in ceremonies could confer instant salvation. Some, upon realizing the difficulty of following through on a new orientation to the world, abandon the attempt. But the lives of some seekers are changed forever. Although they may go back to a daily round of computering, commuting, and consuming, their vision of the earth beneath the pavements is altered. They see, feel, hear different elements of the natural world as they walk through parks. This, more than the reaching for some exotic experience in a peyote-induced trance, is perhaps the true meaning of "vision quest."

For Native Americans, too, the quest can be difficult, even forgotten. Today many are alienated from the land and their traditions. Others may find their way back after years of wandering. Still others find that as their commitment to their own people grows, so does their commitment to other indigenous people—and to the other creatures with whom they share this planet.[*]

Nature as Manifestation of the Sacred

The traditional Indian lives in a universe pregnant with power. Oglala Sioux Chief Luther Standing Bear once put it thus: "From Wakan Tanka, the Great Spirit, there came a great unifying life force that flowed in and through all things—the flowers of the plains, blowing winds, rocks, trees, birds, animals—and was the same force that had been breathed into the first man. Thus all things were brought together by the same Great Mystery."[3]

It is a universe not so much observed as experienced. The "sacred" does not *denote* something consecrated, says Sioux-Laguna Pueblo poet Paula Gunn Allen. The symbolism in American Indian ceremonial literature, for example, is not symbolic in the usual sense; the four sacred mountains do not stand for something else—they *are* those mountains perceived psychologically or spiritually. She adds that the sacred, ritual ways of American Indians are similar in many ways to other sacred cultures on the planet, including the Melanesian and Polynesian.[4]

Even the Abrahamic religions employ some nature symbolism. In

---

[*] "Native American" is used by some native people, but is more often employed by whites anxious to show respect for the continent's first inhabitants. "American Indian" is the usage among most of the native people we have known, hence we shall use the two terms interchangeably but "American Indian" more often.

Christianity—as in many other faiths—water is seen as a holy agent, standing for life and purity. Indeed, Christianity is replete with nature symbols: the light of the world, the wind of the spirit, the sun of righteousness, the tree of life, the dove of peace. However, here the sun stands for righteousness, the dove for peace; all these phenomena in the natural world become symbols of something beyond themselves. This is not the Indian experience. Thomas Berry, who was strongly influenced by Native American world views, understands this difference well. To Berry, the manifestation *participates* in the divine. It is a distinction, not a separation. All creatures participate in this experience of intimacy, for they are expressions of a reality that is divine in itself. The human becomes religious by sharing in the religious experience of the universe.

Most human beings have some need to personify the divine. Incan nobles, Egyptian pharaohs, and rulers in some other cultures saw the sun not only as the supreme source of power and life, but as their own progenitor. Often the earth embodies the female principle, and is seen as the object of the sky's desire. The moon is frequently imaged as female. Indeed, "menstrual," coming from the Latin *menses*, month, and still denoting "monthly" in astronomy, is associated with the moon's cycles. Millennia ago, people noted that the ebb and flow of seas were linked with its rhythmic phases. Hence the frequent connection of moon deities with the waters of the earth.

Around the world, birds, reptiles, plants, rivers, and many other modes of being may become foci of religious adoration. They may be glorified as gods or lesser deities or heavenly helpers. Llama herders in the Andes, for example, have traditionally called on birds as messengers of the gods. Sometimes identification with other creatures has gone deeper, as in these lines from a song preserved from the time of the Incas:

> Oh, perhaps my mother was the vicuña of the pampas
> or my father was the mountain stag,
> to be wandering
> to walk without rest
> through the mountains and the pampas. . . .[5]

Most American Indian tribes believe that other creatures possess the same essential qualities as humans—including personality, volition, and feelings like love, anger, jealousy, and sympathy. When a Sioux took the calumet, he would hold it up so that the sun could take the first puff. The Kutchin of the Upper Yukon believe that every man carries within himself a piece of caribou heart, and every caribou, a portion of human heart. Thus each knows and feels what the other feels. Many traditional Indians speak to the game they kill in familial terms, to make an apology, and after slaying mourn its death, sometimes with an elaborate ritual. They believe that every animal form has a spirit-protector to whom the soul of the slain animal returns, perhaps to lodge complaints about bad treatment which could deprive the hunter of game in the future. It is sacrilege to take life except to support one's self and family.

The sense of a sacralized cosmos does not exclude speaking of God. More often, however, it is of the Great Spirit or the Creator or the All Spirit. The fundamental way is to speak of a "power" presence. As John Grim, an anthropologist who has lived with several Indian groups, points out, their focal point is not *theos*, God, but cosmos, the universe. Theology has less relevance than cosmology. Among the indigenous peoples of the Americas, it is a functional cosmology, which Grim defines as "a story of the world, which informs all aspects of life among a people, giving subsistence practices, artistic creation, ritual play, and military endeavor a significant context often discussed as 'religion.'"[6]

Thus the Pueblo people see the four sacred mountains defining their tribal territory as the pillars that hold up the sky and divide the world into quarters, and the Apaches believe that mountains are always alive, the homes of supernaturals called mountain people. The act of smoking the sacred pipe, observes Blackfeet/Cherokee scholar Jamake Highwater, "is a ritual of communion with *everything* in Creation, with every possibility of being—what lies before us and what lies beyond our understanding and knowledge."[7]

Native Americans feel that all movement is related to all other movement; all of life is living, contributing to the continuing life of the Great Mystery, says Allen. In their art and ritual dance, their song and sacred stories, tribes seek to share the primal reality, to bring the private self into balance with the reality, to verbalize the sense of the reverent mystery of all things. Moreover, all ceremonies support the sense of community—a community not only of the tribe's members, but of all beings inhabiting the tribe's universe. While Indians speak of many spirit-presences in the landscape, and their names vary, they are but diverse manifestations of one mysterious power.[8]

Every member of the tribe can sense this power, but there is generally some special sacred person, often called medicine man or woman, healer, or, increasingly, shaman—who has an extraordinary gift. It is the ability to make contact with the spirits, who confer healing and vitalizing power. The shaman experiences that power, and then brings it as sustaining energy to the community. "The shaman," says Grim, "is the person, male or female, who experiences, absorbs, and communicates a special mode of sustaining, healing power."[9]

He or she is summoned by a call from beyond the visible world. There the spirits, which often take the aspect of a wolf, bear, bird, or other creature, become the shaman's personal helpers. Upon returning from the journey, the shaman typically engages in healing by means of a trance state, divination, prognostication, interpreting dreams and visions, guiding the souls of the dead, offering sacrifices to appease offended spirits, and conducting initiation of new shamans. Sometimes the shaman also aids tribal members who undertake a vision quest by guiding the seeker to a certain secluded spot to await the vision, and later interpreting it. The guardian of tribal traditions, the shaman journeys through distant spaces, meeting the spirits and receiving their instructions. The natural and supernatural worlds are forever merging.

This consciousness endures as the natural heritage not only of shamans, but of all American Indians who still listen to the earth.

Some Comparisons Between Native American and Western Religions

Since Native Americans speak of a power presence, in a sense there are many deities, emerging from the many places and beings that the people experience as holy. In *God Is Red*, Vine Deloria, Jr., a Yankton Sioux with legal and theological training (having once studied for the Christian ministry), claims that when a religion is based on experience, it seems to be of a polytheistic or pantheon-oriented nature. In seeking an ultimate answer to the meaning of existence, he adds, modern man has foreclosed the possibility of experiencing life in favor of explaining it.[10]

Thus Christians think of revelation as original revelation from God; this extraordinary event becomes more important than one's immediate experience, he says. For spatial peoples, revelation is a particular experience at a particular place, such as a river or mountain. In it they do not find a "universal truth," but an awareness that certain places have a holiness above others. Most world religions also have particularly holy places, but to native peoples "place" is absolutely central.

Tribal religions do not insist that their own view of Creation is an unequivocal historical recording of that event, Deloria adds.[11] Many have somewhat similar Creation stories, such as the great deluge into which creatures from on high plunged to get a portion of mud, which then expanded to become Earth. While differing considerably, all origin myths reflect an ecosystem centered in a certain place.

While Old Testament events were regarded as actual happenings, American Indians' view of history is more a recognition of the cyclical nature of life. Chief Seattle put it thus: "But why should I mourn at the untimely fate of my people? Tribe follows tribe, nation follows nation, like the waves of the sea. It is the order of nature, and regret is useless."[12]

Since God is more like an undefinable presence, even when Native Americans use a term like "father" and "grandmother," it does not become the basis for establishing a set of relationships. According to the Pawnees, for example, Tirawa, the One Above, did not speak to humans, but instead sent certain animals to tell them that He showed himself through the beasts and that humans should learn from them, and from the stars, the sun, and moon.

While many native people speak of "instructions," these are not commandments, but usually general principles of peace, equity, and justice. Since deity is experienced as an all-pervasive numinous presence, worshippers are less inclined than followers of Semitic religions to have a strong expectation of divine intervention on behalf of the individual. True, the vision quest, a search for a sign of the presence of one's guardian spirits, is in some sense a prayer for help; many have mortified the flesh so that the All Spirit might cure individuals and the group. But the dominant mode is relationship between the great power and a particular community.

The Indian, says Stan Steiner, is proudly, defiantly, individualistic—and at the same time, committed to something greater. "He lives within himself, but not for himself. The distinction is vital. Everything in tribal life is based on the community's protection of the individual . . . [Communality] protects him socially and thus frees him individually."[13] Visions are experienced by the individual, but ultimately acquire meaning in the message they carry to the community.

Some Christian theologians have held that nature, like humans, has fallen from grace. This idea is puzzling to most indigenous peoples. For many tribal religions, humans and other parts of Creation cooperate. Allen says that even the All Spirit has limited power. He needed help from the four things he had created—water, light, sky/air, and the peoples of the water (birds) to make a dry solid place. The ability of *all* creatures to share in ongoing Creation makes all things sacred.[14] It is interesting that "humanity as co-creator" has recently become an emphasis in Christian Creation theology.

If all living things share a Creator, isn't it logical to assume that all have the capacity to relate to all other parts of Creation? asks the "primitive" Indian. "Did you know that trees talk?" asks Walking Buffalo. "Well, they do. They talk to each other, and they'll talk to you if you listen. Trouble is, white people don't listen. They never learned to listen to the Indians, so I don't suppose they'll listen to the voices of nature. But I have learned a lot from trees; sometimes about the weather, sometimes about animals, sometimes about the Great Spirit."[15]

Indians tend to be less concerned than Christians about death, observes Deloria. Some tribes do speak of a westward journey through prairie country until the soul arrives in the land of spirits, a beautiful country interspersed with clear lakes and streams. But except for the Handsome Lake religion, which showed some influence of Christianity, native images of life after death do not involve elaborate theories of heaven, hell, final judgment, or other apocalyptic happenings. Creation is seen as an orderly process, death as a passage from one form of experience to another. Most Indians simply assume some sort of survival after death. One's body becomes dust once again, contributing to the ongoing cycle of Creation. As Chief Seattle put it, death is merely a changing of worlds. It is a mystery no human can fathom. Yet in one sense, it is simple and perceptible, for in the words of Crow Chief Curley: "the soil you see is not ordinary soil—it is the dust of the blood, the flesh, and the bones of our ancestors."[16]

Many ways of conceiving the divine co-exist—for each is rooted in place. Absent is the urge to compete with other denominations. The great Seneca orator, Red Jacket, once said in a retort to a missionary: "You say there is one way to worship and serve the Great Spirit. If there is but one religion, why do you white people differ so much about it?"

Traditional native people also draw no firm line between what is material and what is spiritual. They are expressions of the same reality. The closest Western analogy is Einstein's idea that matter is a special condition of energy. Yet to him, energy is unintelligent. To the Indian, energy is intelligence manifested in yet another way.

Traditional Practices Under Assault

Today many Native Americans are in conflict—with the U.S. government, with other tribal groups, and with themselves. They are experiencing a conflict of values. One place that conflict reveals itself is the land. Today the soil where they live can be perceived as sites for casinos, malls, or toxic waste dumps.

Another arena of conflict—inner conflict—is religion. It has become increasingly important to Indians to recover or maintain their sense of cultural identity, an identity that cannot be separated from traditional beliefs and practices. Yet many were born into families that converted to Christianity under the powerful influence of missionaries determined to conquer "paganism." Few missionaries tried to understand the indigenous faiths. Many mistook the Indian's reverence for her or his ancestors as "ancestor-worship." With few exceptions they simply assumed the superiority of the education and religion they brought.

Over time many Indians did convert, if only because they saw they needed the white man's schooling in order to survive in a changed world. In reservations today stand schools and churches built by Christians, and many Indians seem to be devout adherents of the white man's faith.

Does this mean they have severed their connections with the traditional ways? No, many reply; one can still smoke the sacred pipe, or attend to the sacred duties of the Sun Dance, the vision quest, the healing rituals. Some anthropologists explain that the indigenous religion maintains beliefs and rituals sanctioned by beings beyond observation, while Christianity serves political, social, and economic purposes.

On the other hand, the occasional appearance in visions and prayers of Jesus and angels suggests that for many Indians, an integrated view comes naturally.

Nonetheless, there can be confusion and pain. Stan Steiner tells of meeting many such Indians—among them, an Episcopalian archdeacon who was also father of Vine Deloria, Jr. The archdeacon believed it was easy for his people, the Sioux, to accept Christianity, since they already had their own kind of Christianity. But he was angry with white men who insisted that they possessed the only path to the Great Spirit. He feared their violence, their arrogance, their hate for themselves. Sometimes he despaired of their ever becoming true Christians. Sometimes he went down to his cellar, where he kept his drum, and beat on it quietly, "so the Lord will not hear me, so that the Lord will not be offended . . . I feel better then. I feel Indian."[17]

Moreover, today the federal government decides tribal membership on the basis of property interests of descendants of the original enrollees. Tribes can no longer form and reform on the basis of religion, culture, or whether the member now appears in an active role in the tribal community. Among some groups, no special qualities are needed for leadership, except the ability to win votes, hence corruption is rife. Some Indians forget the well-being of the community and the land in favor of deals that bring profits from selling resources or running casinos.

Since the 1960s, however, there has been a growing movement among Native Americans not only to understand their own history and develop political power, but also to return to traditional religions, the crux of their identity. The Iroquois have been in the forefront.

The Iroquois and Their Religion

Iroquois-speaking Native Americans include some 15 groups. Six form the Haudenosaunee, or Iroquois Confederacy: the Onondaga, Seneca, Cayuga, Mohawk, Oneida, and Tuscarora. Their reservations lie in Canada, upper New York State, and a sliver of Pennsylvania; offshoots exist elsewhere.

Traditionally, they have been a matrilineal people (tracing their ancestry through the mother) and also matrilocal, meaning that the husband lives with his wife's people. In the past they lived in communal longhouses constructed of poles covered with sheets of bark. Among some Iroquois, the longhouse was intended to be a micro-cosmos: the floor symbolized the earth, the ceiling represented the sky, the east door was seen as the place where the sun rose, and the west door, the place where the sun set. Today most Iroquois live in single or extended family dwellings but gather for both communal meetings and ceremonies in the longhouse.

Awareness of the cosmos permeates the life of traditional Iroquois. It is told that the cosmos was created by two spirit-forces who were twins. The good twin brought forth flora and fauna and is associated with order, warmth, and life. His evil brother was cold and associated with darkness, disease, and death. Each left behind a number of major and minor spirit forces, including wind, thunder, sun, moon, and stars. Power is present everywhere, but is most clearly experienced in the earth, the cycles of nature, and the visions and deeds of spirits, ancestors, and living people.

There is no clear distinction between the sacred and the profane; at special times, ordinary objects can become invested with holiness. Moreover, in practice religious beliefs are fluid. Leon Shenandoah, the Thadodaho (or head speaker in the Longhouse) and the "chief-of-chiefs" of the six-nation Iroquois Confederacy, told us that the Indians' way of life was given by "the Father Creator—the man up there." Then he added, "We don't call him God." Maisie Shenandoah, clan mother for the Shenandoah clan of the Oneida Nation, asserted that the sex of the Great Creator is "unknown." Chief Thundercloud, who is Cherokee (the southern language group of the Iroquois), told us that "the Creator is time, the beginning of the world. He is a little old man. I saw him once, in a vision. I also saw Jesus. It was in a kingdom. There was an altar, and in back of it the Creator, sitting there, and he told me I must return and teach about the earth and his true way."

The Iroquois faith is primarily concerned with affirming and intensifying life; the basic attitude toward spirit-forces is thanksgiving. Audrey Shenandoah, an Onondaga clan mother and elder, puts it simply: "We don't *praise* a tree. We don't *worship* nature. We thank it." All ceremonies begin and end with thanks to the forces of earth and sky that create and support life.

The Seneca-Cayuga of Oklahoma begin the spring ceremonials with the Sun Dance and the Blessing of the Seeds. All ceremonials begin with a prayer and an Indian whoop, then offer thanksgiving: "Our Father or

Our Creator in Heaven, who created the heavens and the Earth, that knows no evil; Our Father of many voices, since He understands all nationalities of the World. You created the Earth that knows no evil. We thank thee that you have given the beginning of time, the sunlight to all the world by day. We give our thanks for the moonlight also . . . for the rain, lightning, and thunder. . . . We are thankful for the angels who guide us day by day. . . . "

Among the Iroquois, "medicine societies" maintain the ancient shamanic traditions. Unlike the communal ceremonies, their rituals evoke power rather than offer thanksgiving, and invoke the guardian spirit of that society. The largest, the Society of Medicine Men, is dedicated to medicine animals who have promised to heal humans in exchange for ceremonies and feasts.

When traditional Iroquois cut trees, gather plants, or take minerals, they present a gift of sacred tobacco and make an apology for disturbing the web of life. While this ethic of incurring as little damage as possible reflects their cosmology, it has also served a conservation function. In the past, each band had a recognized area, took a continuous game census, and would hunt in only one section a year. The groups migrated periodically within a well-defined territory, thus relieving pressure on game and fish stocks and allowing cultivated soil to renew itself by returning to forest land. Many of the intertribal wars were caused by another tribe's overhunting in one's territory. Thus an ecological change that often stemmed from excessive growth of the offending tribe's population.

In 1799 a Seneca known as Geneodiyo, or Handsome Lake, was overcome by devastating illness exacerbated by drink. As he lay dying, he was visited by a series of dream-visions, in which the Four Messengers from the Creator announced His instructions, guided Geneodiyo on a sky-journey, and promised him shamanic powers. He recovered and began to preach the "good word."[18]

The Iroquois had experienced losses of land and power, and many had fallen into apathy, alcoholism, and moral disintegration. In his journeys among them, the new prophet condemned alcohol, witchcraft, abortion, adultery, undisclosed multi-marriages, wife-beating, youngsters' disobedience, child abuse, boastfulness, malicious jokes, refusing food offered as hospitality, and interference in marriages—activities reflecting a breakdown in the traditional way of life.

His precepts were influenced by Christians, especially Quakers, who tended to take a less lofty approach than other missionaries. They taught that while outward forms of religion are made by men, the Great Spirit himself puts the Inner Light in every man, and even counseled Indians to learn to read and write so that they might see for themselves whether or not the white man's book was true. Christianity's influence is clearly suggested in Handsome Lake's principles that no person who truly repents can be damned and that "it is better to be poor on earth and rich in the sky world than to have earth riches and no heaven." Sin and repentance, heaven and hell (although not damnation that lasts forever) play a more important role than in other Indian traditions. Yet the heaven envisioned was a paradise of succulent fruits—where no white man entered. In Handsome Lake's visions, Jesus appears, the two discuss common difficulties in reaching unbelievers, and the crucified prophet from the Holy Land ends by admonishing the prophet from Indian land to "tell your people that they will become lost when they follow the ways of the white man."

Reforms would enable the people to be strong enough to preserve their traditions, yet survive in the conquerors' world. A few children should be educated in whites' schools to be able to deal with them on legal and political issues, single family houses should be built on the Quaker model, and the men should take up farming, even though it was seen as primarily the domain of women. Abstention from vices, especially alcohol, was emphasized. (Before the whites' arrival, the Indians had had no experience of alcohol, hence a people to whom self-control was a cardinal virtue—captured warriors were expected to endure excruciating tortures without flinching—had no technique for resisting it.)

Since the 1950s, there has been a growing revival of the traditionalist Longhouse religion: a synthesis of Handsome Lake's revelations, ancient shamanic practices and agricultural ceremonies, and organizational meetings of the confederacy. No accurate count of its adherents is possible, for most Indians have a distaste for census-takers, anthropologists, and tax-collectors.

In *Apologies to the Iroquois*, Edmund Wilson describes the week-long Midwinter, or New Year festival, which includes partial recitations of the "good word." Ordinarily, it is closed to visitors, but Wilson had the exceptional good fortune of receiving an invitation to Seneca ceremonies through William Fenton, an unusual anthropologist who had been made an honorary member of the Hawk Clan. Here we can only distill from Wilson's account a few glimpses of the festivities, which offer some insight into the Indians' intimacy with the natural world.[19]

In the Bear Society's Bear Dance, the dancers uttered grunts and growls, pawed at a saucepan of strawberry syrup, and sometimes became possessed by the bear. In the Fish Dance, men and women first took a few steps to the right, then to the left, like the movement of salmon swimming upstream. Then, facing each other, they danced forward or backwards, reversing at the end of each song to face a different partner. In the corn dances, the women sang the message that the ears were supposed to be saying ("We are happy to be home"—that is, hung to be dried for the winter). There was the Great Feather Dance and a dance called Shaking the Bush, a dream-guessing ceremony and a child-naming rite, a Buffalo Dance, and a Dark Dance. The latter, almost an oratorio, was a set of song-sequences sung in the dark, which seemed to embody some projection of the human spirit that had survived through the centuries.

In an elaborate drama, two supernatural heralds of the Huskfaces— each wearing a round mask made of cornhusks fringed, like the sun, with an irradiation of fine corn-leaves—burst into the Longhouse and charged through the room with long staves, announcing that they were going to the other side of the world to till the crops. This was followed by dancing, then the appearance of masked clowns, some with Falsefaces (red masks with distorted features, other masks with original designs) for a perform- ance in which young and old disguised their ages and the sexes ex- changed clothes. Suddenly the merrymaking stopped, the actors were seized by panic, and the heralds dashed through again with a swiftness that made them seem apparitions from another world. Throughout these festive rites (which, incidentally, barred alcohol) all ages, from small children to oldsters, took part in some way, onlookers entered into the celebration with laughter and shouts, and performers sometimes seized partners from the audience.

The last day was devoted to solemn ceremonies, as the elders offered the tobacco invocation, a rite of thanks that also supplicates the spirit- forces to bless the people during the coming year. Wilson could not at- tend this ceremony or the recitation of the Handsome Lake "good word," the final element in the synthesis that has evolved over the centuries.

Meeting the Iroquois

As you drive south on I-81, about 10 miles from Syracuse a highway sign points to the "Onondaga Nation." Symbolically, it is also a sign that the U.S. government recognizes—in principle—the sovereign status of the Onondaga people and their fellow Haudenosaunee. No flags, no uniformed officers, no customs barriers mark the approach to this 6,100- acre nation. Instead, a diner and a somewhat forlorn-looking store deal- ing in beer, cigarettes, Indian souvenirs, and sundries stand near the beginning of the road through the territory. As you near the village, on either side of the road lie dumps and cannibalized cars. Most of the dwellings are aging trailers. Here and there, however, stand neat, new- looking log cabins, and a few ranch-style houses. In the cluttered yards, some families are gathered in circles, eating, smoking, talking quietly, and staring at visitors' cars. Beside the road stand several "Onondaga Mission" churches with well-kept cemeteries. And in the hazy distance rise low round hills, still thickly wooded with tall trees and nurtured by streams, a reminder of the distant past and a fading way of life.

THE CHIEF-OF-CHIEFS

Leon Shenandoah, the chief-of-chiefs of the six Iroquois nations and the uncle of Oren Lyons, greeted us with a certain reserve. A white-haired man in his 70s, still slender and vigorous-looking, he motioned us to a seat in his smoky living room, and regarded us with intent, watchful eyes. Although a new-looking television set stood against one wall, most of the furniture was worn, and the only heat came from an electric heater. We remembered that it was a tradition among families from which chiefs were chosen that they should not be ostentatious: indifference to money and belongings was a sign of superiority. In the next room an infant grandson played on the floor under a calendar with a photo of an Indian chief astride a horse, in full regalia.

The chief listened somewhat impassively as we explained our interest in American Indians, particularly the Iroquois. After a moment of reflection, he nodded.

"Our way of life is what our religion is all about. It was given to us by the Father Creator. We do not even use the word 'religion,' except to help the white man understand. It is more like giving thanks. The way we think, Mother Earth is your mother. We get nourishment from her. It is a duty to work in harmony with her. All our ceremonies are related to Mother Earth."

"Can you tell us more about them?"

"Well, a little," he said slowly. "We do not allow visitors at the ceremonies. Some Indians do, but we don't. Our children, though, they come. You can't deny them their rights. That's how they learn. All of us, we carry on from what we learn from the elders. It's continuous. We have a ceremony for every season, and two others between seasons. We can tell you about them, but you cannot attend if you are not an Iroquois." He paused, as if to be certain that we understood the full import of his message.

"This is a *nation*," he went on. "We Iroquois insist on that."

"Other Indian tribes seem to refer to themselves as nations, too."

"That's true," he said, a little impatiently. "But we insist on being *treated* that way. Like we have our own passports, saying 'Onondaga Nation' or 'Mohawk' or whatever. The Iroquois and the Hopi are the only ones with their own passports. We tell the United States we never have been American citizens, and never will be. The others, they're supposed to have that right to their own passports, but they don't fight for it. We've had to go through a lot to get them. Another thing, our disputes—well,

most of them—are settled by the elders, and the police are not supposed to come in here. They keep trying, sure. And we have fights.
But we win."

The phone rang, and he moved to the dining room. "Yes, you can
come tomorrow," we could hear him reply. "I'll be here all morning."

He sat down again. "The whites, they come to us now to learn," he
continued. "They've already learned a lot. Their constitution was copied
from the Iroquois Confederacy, they learned democracy from *us*, they
knew only kings until then. Right here in Onondaga stood the Tree of the
Great Peace, the white pine that was uprooted so our nations could throw
their weapons into the pit before putting the tree back. That's where white
people get the phrase 'burying the hatchet.' They never got to practicing
it, though."

We remembered that according to oral history, the Iroquois Confederacy was founded perhaps a thousand years ago, by a Mohawk named
Deganwidah. Many U.S. founding fathers—especially Benjamin Franklin
and Thomas Jefferson—admired its constitution, the Great Law of Peace,
and saw in it a model for their new nation. Representatives of the Con-
tinental Congress met privately with ambassadors from the Confederacy
and the Lenni Lenape, known as the Delaware Indians. Some features of
the Confederacy government—debate and compromise, two houses of
legislature, and uniting several sovereign units into one government—
were adopted, but many other ideas, such as agreement through consensus, were never included. Friedrich Engels lauded the Iroquois as
exemplars of primitive communism who lived without social class or
private property (beyond some personal effects). We had come to see that
in traditional Iroquois society, status depended more on moral qualities
and leadership skills than on lineage or wealth.

"Can you tell us more about how you choose leaders?" we asked.

"Okay. Every Iroquois nation has several clans with names like bea-
ver or wolf or turtle, and every clan has two leaders and a clan mother
working together for the people. And it's the women, the clan mothers,
who choose the men. They've seen the children growing up, so they
can study the person to see if he has the right qualities, like truthful-
ness with the people. So the clan mother talks it over with the other
women and then chooses the clan chief. All the clan mothers together
choose the Chief Statesman for their Nation. Those chiefs approve the
Thadodaho, the chief-of-chiefs for the Confederacy. He comes from
the Onondaga Nation, because the first Thadodaho was an Onondaga.
The Thadodaho is supposed to keep the Council Fire, because the
Onondagas are the Firekeepers of the Haudenosaunee. So he shares
that trust with his cousins, the other 13 Onondaga chiefs. I started out
as a subchief, a faithkeeper.

"Today I'm chief-of-chiefs. But what I learned, I learned from the heart. Not from the book. Today it's different. The children all go to school here. It's run by the state. They get brainwashed." He sighed.

We told him we had visited the school. With its classrooms adorned with Indian craftwork, poetry, and student paintings, it had seemed a bright, cheerful place. The principal—who spoke with great admiration for Indian culture—was white, but most of the teachers were Indian.

"Yes, there are Indian teachers, but they're brainwashed, too," he said impatiently. "The children can learn the Indian culture and language up to the eighth grade, but then they go out to the high school, and there are no Indian teachers. That's what the government wants, that we lose our traditions." His lips tightened.

"Did you have much formal schooling?"

"A little. I went to a Quaker school a few years. It was all right. But when I was 16, I went into the longhouse and I said to myself, 'This is where I belong. This is our way of life.' So I worked on the land. All day we ploughed with a horse. We worked hard, but we were close to the land. It was natural. Then things got harder and harder, and I had to go out to work. I went into construction. White people look for Indians to work on bridges and other kinds of high steel, because they're agile and they aren't afraid of high places. So a lot of our people live in cities a long time. Then they come back. Some of them do."

No, he didn't regret not getting a modern education. It took away from common sense, he told us bitterly. Take water—if it was polluted, it only made sense not to drink it, then do everything possible to prevent pollution. But the white man made everything complicated.

"The Christian God doesn't believe in Mother Earth." He shook his head. "We were given Christianity by the Europeans. Before the white man came, we could drink from any stream. Pretty soon we won't be able to drink *any* place. But these white ministers say their way is better than mine. They also say the man put on the cross is the son of the Creator. I say, 'Oh, you have two Gods!' Well, *we* look up to God, and they look up to Jesus."

The infant grandson crawled into the living room, and up to his grandfather. Stroking the child's head, Chief Shenandoah spoke slowly. "I have a heavy heart. Children like Michael—what is their future? Bad air, bad water, bad earth. . . . " His voice trailed off.

"I think about our young people," he went on. "Some get into drunkenness, because they're all mixed up and haven't had good education. Some, they even want casino gambling. But we don't allow it here. We go by the Creator. Later a lot of them begin to think about that, and then go into deeper thought, and then think more about people. They need to come back home to find themselves. Only the ones who are ready for that can survive. Those who are sucked into the almighty dollar, they're beyond saving.

"It's hard to get away from the dollar, even here. They approach us to let industry in, because we have no taxes. We just say 'no.' We get calls from Nevada, Ohio, all over, from companies that want to dump wastes—even nuclear—on our land. Nobody wants it, they think of us, the poor Indian. We could make two million dollars easy. But you are selling the children's life away if you give in. You know our saying: 'We have a responsibility unto the seventh generation.'"

The phone rang again. The chief moved to the other room, and began a long quiet conversation in Onondagan. He returned, sat down, and faced us gravely. He had said he had only a little time, but we had been there over two hours, and he showed no signs of impatience.

He spoke first. "Oil, it's part of Mother Earth's intestines. The whites are drawing the oil out of her. Then they burn it up into poisons, and put them back in the ground and the air. Mother Earth, now, she's nothing but webs of roads around her body and they're strangling her to death." He sighed. "I'm afraid it's done, it's too late. I know what's coming."

"A wasteland?"

"Yeah. Still, some white people *are* concerned. I do what I can. Like I talked in Kentucky at a high school a month ago and had them in tears. I just got back from Mexico. We talked with the Maya Indians about how their traditions are disappearing. I've been to England three times, Switzerland two times, Holland once. Over there they're really interested in the Indians. I spoke about human rights at the UN in Geneva, and next month I'm going to Australia to a conference about the environment and I'll meet the aboriginal people and hear what's happening to their human rights. I'm going with my nephew, Oren Lyons. He is an educated professor. I'm a traditional professor. He goes to the ceremonies, too, but we're different. He doesn't see what I see."

"Yet you do seem to have a bit of hope."

"Well, some. As things get tougher, more of our young people begin seeking and then come back to the old way. They will get their strength back if they continue in this direction. Some white people are seeking, too."

"If you could sum it up all in a few words, what would you say is the answer?"

For the first time he smiled a little. "Live in a simple way."

IROQUOIS WOMEN

From our research, we already had some idea of the importance of women in this culture. So strong was the woman's position that a wife

whose husband engaged in reprehensible behavior might have him publicly reprimanded, then put out of the house. Centuries ago, some even
believed the earth would not bear fruit unless it was cultivated by women.
Some Iroquois say their women have enjoyed so much power because it
was noted that among animals maintenance of the family depends almost
entirely on the mother. What interested us now was to learn more about
present-day activities of women. Leon Shenandoah had suggested we talk
with Maisie Shenandoah, clan mother for the Wolf Clan of the Oneida
Nation, and her sister Gloria Halbritter.

Maisie Shenandoah worked in an "Iroquois trading post and museum" near the entrance to the Oneida Territory. We met nearby, in the
neat frame house of Gloria, a registered nurse who was also the clerk
for the Oneida Nation. Although we had called only a few hours earlier,
they welcomed us graciously. "It's Indian tradition to be hospitable," said
Gloria.

Both women wore simple suits. The modest house was furnished with
the most up-to-date conveniences and was meticulously ordered. Both
women, too, were decidedly articulate.

In the past clan mothers were almost always senior members of the
clan, explained Maisie, a tall, quiet, dignified woman. Today more depended on their honesty, knowledge, and willingness to work for the
benefit of people. She herself had been chosen for this lifetime position
in 1975, at the age of 43, by other women of the clan.

"I married an Onondaga, and he moved here; my children are
Oneida," she explained. "You can't marry someone from the same clan,
but outside your clan it's all right to marry someone of the same nation.
Iroquois people inherit land through the clan mother. Most other Indian
groups are not like that today, but the Navajo are."

"The clan mothers are the heirs of the title?"

"Yes, because the Peacemaker arranged families into the clans and
then set up the clan leaders, 50 in all. The clan mothers' choices for clan
chiefs have to be ratified by the whole clan and the nation, but the people
have great respect for our judgment. A clan mother is supposed to correct
a chief who is disorderly or not doing right, and if he neglects his duties,
or refuses to attend Council, the other chiefs ask the female sponsor to
demand that he come. After three warnings, she can depose him. That's
not just a threat. It happens."

"It's like impeachment, then."

"Yes. The whites copied a lot of their constitution from the Iroquois
Confederacy, too. But they left out one thing—the women. And Indians
and black people. Our constitution has always given rights to all clans
and all clan members. Also, full rights to anyone who joined the Iroquois,
as some white men did. Just think! If you'd had women in there from the

beginning, voting and exercising their rights, you'd have seen a big difference in the U.S. today."

Another function of clan mothers was to mediate quarrels, she told us. "We go to each party privately, and usually settle things before the chiefs do."

Maisie described herself as "traditional." Christianity had no appeal to her. Although Christians in the confederacy could attend ceremonies, they could not become clan mothers.

In other respects she had departed from traditional ways. "In the last 10, 20 years, our women, especially, are going more for education. When Indian rights are violated, we have to know how to fight back—like how to take these matters to court. One of my daughters is in social work, and one of Gloria's is studying for her doctorate in education at Harvard. One of her sons is studying law at Harvard, and his goal is defending Indian rights."

Gloria, a short, energetic-looking woman who had sat quietly listening, told us she was a Seventh Day Adventist. "There's no contradiction," she said with tranquil conviction. "Christianity is like Indian religion, except for Christ. We pray to the same Creator." She believed in millenarianism, and believed that Christ would return to earth in visible form at the end of the age. Yet she also felt certain that good Hindus and other non-Christians could go to heaven.

On several other issues, the two women were firmly united. One was the importance of educating white people about the Indians' view of the world. To this end, Iroquois women often spoke about their culture at local schools. Another issue was preserving Mother Earth.

It was the women of the Confederacy who had taken the lead on many such questions. "Look at disposable diapers, for instance. They don't disintegrate—they interfere with nature!" said Maisie passionately. "This is so serious. Why not *ban* Pampers? We Indians have a great council to decide such things. After discussion, all the women did stop using Pampers. But the whites, they have scientists, they know, and *still* all they say is, 'Give us time.'"

"Pollution is killing Indian people, especially," said Gloria. "The Mohawks up on the St. Lawrence used to have good cattle, but now they're small, unhealthy-looking. People have died from cancer. Why? Reynolds Aluminum dumps toxic wastes into the river. We protest, and they go right on doing it. It's like they think Indians aren't people. And up the hill, just outside our own territory, they come and dump in the night. We know something's going on; we ask, but the government denies it. And this is near the place where my mother used to take us children sometimes to sleep all night in the woods under the stars."

Maisie nodded. "Our mothers taught us the ways of nature. We cut bark just a certain width, so it will grow back. Plants, too—we always leave a bit, so it won't die. If we don't use them, we don't cut them at all. Our mothers taught us how to tell the difference between female and male plants. And today we talk in the longhouse about what plants we can survive on."

We had read that among the Tukano of the Northwest Amazon, birth control is widely practiced. A principal method—in addition to abstention—is use of plants that cause temporary sterility. For the Tukano, any growth in human population means eventual increase in the numbers of animals and fish that have to be killed, hence decrease in the resources on which members of the tribe depend. Did the Iroquois also use plants to help control population? we asked.

Both women nodded. "And many do, even today. Our mothers taught us about birth control, using bark from certain trees," said Gloria. "Today people are born at such a rate the earth can't hold them. But what do the wise white men *do*? Nothing. Even centuries ago the Iroquois knew what to do, and they did it. They understood not to abuse Mother Earth."

Keeping the Sacred Fire: Chief Oren Lyons

Oren Lyons holds the honored position of Faithkeeper of the Turtle Clan of the Onondaga Nation. He is also director of Native American Studies at the State University of New York/Buffalo; a distinguished artist; a champion lacrosse player; founder of *Daybreak*, an American Indian quarterly; an activist for Indian rights; and a prime force in the growing worldwide movement of indigenous peoples.

We first met in a friend's home in Onondaga, a well-furnished brick ranch home, modest but perhaps one of the most modern in the village. In the living room, colorful Indian rugs covered the chairs and the floor, and lacrosse trophies, a row of mugs, and husks of corn adorned the mantel. The walls were decorated with paintings: a clown, an Indian chief in ceremonial headdress, and a landscape portraying the earth womb, as well as a mystical work picturing four human beings—and the wolf, bear, deer, and buffalo—gazing at each other from each corner. It was clearly the work of Lyons himself; as faithkeeper, one of his mandates was to keep alive the stories of his people's traditions.

He was a rugged-looking man with broad shoulders, high cheekbones, and bushy eyebrows. In his pink trousers, black-and-white striped shirt, and sneakers, he was dressed like many white Americans, but the long hair combed back in a ponytail and the leather-thong necklace with an Indian pendant suggested an insistence on his heritage. His broad smile was genial, and came often, yet there seemed to be in him the same watchfulness we had sensed in his uncle.

Chief Oren Lyons of the Onondaga Nation addressing a Fall 1998 conference, "Religion and Ecology," at the United Nations.

Lyons listened closely as we explained our mission, then shook his head. "Even though I was known as a spokesperson for the American Indians at the Global Forum, I am *not* a spiritual leader. I'm a faithkeeper—a position that does combine certain spiritual and political functions. But 'spiritual leader'—few people understand what it takes. In one of our ceremonies there are over 100 songs. There are no shortcuts a spiritual leader would know. These things are being lost, because most Indians are just struggling to survive."

"Can you give us some examples of what happens in that struggle?"

"Well—" He leaned back, legs propped on a stool. "What's important to understand is, the basic Indian philosophy is involved with tradition. But the aim of the Bureau of Indian Affairs (BIA) is assimilation. The worst of it is, today it's all-Indian. These guys give lip service to our culture, but no real support. Even a few Iroquois, like Louis Bruce, a well-intentioned man, have been co-opted into the bureaucracy.

"America tries to Americanize the Indian." His voice was even, but edged with anger. "That's the function of the BIA. Our way of life, our values, are a threat to the capitalist system. The process used to seduce people by means of materialism is very insidious, very powerful. Today we've come to the apex with presidents who sell off ancient forests and open nature to industry. Americans are very successful in exporting their economic colonialism. We Indians always knew this. And I see what it does to people in the Third World."

Only gradually did Lyons come to his involvement in politics, we learned. In the eighth grade, after quitting school because the white children were loud and picked fights with the Indian pupils, he was taken to the truant officer. "I just listened while he said, 'Indians are all alike, dumb.' Then he said I should go to school. I was measuring the distance between me and him. I didn't jump him, but I told myself, 'I'll learn my way, so some day I can shove it down his throat!' I don't carry that anger now, but I did for a long time."

He quit school for good, and spent his time hunting and fishing and playing lacrosse. "It's our national game, the Iroquois played it before Columbus arrived. It's fast, you have to be very agile, so it can be used as training for your overall development. But first of all, it's a medicine game for the welfare of the community—the Creator's game, a gift to humanity. You've got to be a real *team* player. The emphasis is on cooperation and fairness. My father, my grandfather, my daughter Lonnie played it. My son Rex was named Most Valuable Player in the Canadian National Lacrosse Championships. My grandsons play it. It's part of our long tradition, a continuation of community. Today just about everyone in the Iroquois community will turn out for a game."

Lyons took equivalency tests, got an athletic scholarship to Syracuse University, excelled in art, and was given the Orange Key for athletic and academic achievement. He also married. After graduation he moved to New York City, with his wife and by then two children, to design cards for the Norcross Greeting Card Company; he soon became planning director.

Yet he found himself returning more and more to Onondaga for the ceremonies. During the political turmoil of the 1960s, many American Indians had experienced a renaissance of pride in their culture and an urge for Red Power—the power to run their own lives in their own way. In the 1950s and 1960s growing militancy took hold. In 1968 the American Indian Movement (AIM) was born, thrust into being by an alliance of older traditionalists and younger people.

"By 1967 life took a new turn. I was asked to be Firekeeper, one who keeps the faith. Until 1972 I was involved in a Unity Caravan of the Hopi and other Indians, moving around the country talking to Indians about our traditions. Today we operate in the U.S. and Canada as the Traditional Circle of Elders and Youth; any elder or youth is welcome in the circle as it travels."

A young man entered the room quietly, and bent down to whisper something in Lyons' ear. With a brief nod to us, Lyons got up and left with him. During the nearly three hours we spent there, the front door opened frequently, and figures passed in the hallway to the kitchen. We sensed that this house was a center of community.

He returned, sat down, and regarded us intently, smiling with his eyes. "Where were we? Oh yes. By 1970 I was ready. The year I was divorced. I returned home in time to join the battle when the state tried to widen I-81 into *our* territory. We battled for six months—it was an issue of jurisdiction. At one confrontation, there were troopers with blood in their eyes. Suddenly they were pulled out and sent—with the same riot gear—to stop the uprising at Attica prison.

"When the court found that we were a sovereign nation, we won." He grinned broadly. "Meanwhile, AIM was gravitating toward us Iroquois because of our tradition of stubborn resistance. In 1972 some of us went down to BIA headquarters in Washington with Russell Means and Dennis Banks and others. The government hadn't kept its promises— again—and there had been some nasty incidents. So a lot of us organized the Trail of Broken Treaties—automobile caravans that went all over the country and then converged on Washington."

The U.S. Parks Department reneged on its promise of providing camping ground. Then BIA director Louis Bruce opened his building to the caravan. When some guards began to shove caravaners around, fear of violence spread. In self-defense the Indians blocked all entrances. With all BIA personnel off for the weekend, the building was occupied more by circumstances than anything else. Negotiations proceeded, but continuing police threats to attack kept the occupiers in a state of panic, and they reacted by damaging the building. Bruce reentered the building to try to settle the conflict, but was ordered by his superiors (whites) in the Interior Department to withdraw. Later they dismissed him.

The damage was indisputable, said Lyons, but later evidence clearly suggested that there had been government agents-provocateurs among the protestors. The resentment bred by this revelation and other events in the bitter history of Indian-white relations stimulated Lyons and others to join the demonstrations at Wounded Knee, South Dakota, in 1973. Basically it was a conflict between tribal politicians promoting the sale of the Black Hills, and the Lakota people who felt helpless to challenge them. AIM activists led by Dennis Banks and Russell Means were called by Lakotas to help defend the people.

"What you've got to understand for perspective is, traditional peoples are quite conservative," said Lyons. "But when our youth really understood the situation, they realized their heritage was not the pinstriped suit. So they rebelled. A lot of leadership came out of that era."

During the 1970s he helped Dennis Banks organize "the longest protest walk ever," a nationwide trek to educate people about the ways the federal government was still violating Indian treaties. Lyons also began taking part in Cathedral of St. John the Divine services featuring a spectrum of speakers concerned about the fate of the earth. It was there he met Thomas Berry—"a great man." In 1977 he was part of the

Haudenosaunee delegation to the First International Conference on Racism, and in 1980 was invited to the Bertrand Russell Tribunal, which focused on the rights of indigenous peoples in the Americas.

"Racism is entwined with imperialism, so much that Americans aren't even aware of their own behavior," he went on. "In every small country that Americans invade, the generals say, 'It's Indian country.' Vietnam was 'Indian Country,' Iraq was 'Indian Country.' Even though many American Indians took part in the action. Everywhere," he added, "the world capitalist system is the biggest cause of racism."

"You go to the annual conferences of the World Council of Indigenous Peoples, where they discuss combatting racism and genocide, right? And ways to preserve their land and its wildlife and resources?"

He nodded. "At first I wanted to defend the Iroquois. Then my sights broadened to other Indians around the country. Then I saw this had to include defense of the indigenous peoples all over the world. Recently, I've come to look even further, to what some call the family of man, and to me includes animals, birds, trees, mountains—the family of all beings."

During our second visit with Lyons, he talked more about his experiences with first peoples. "One of the most important was a meeting with the Australian aboriginal people after an environmental conference near Sydney. They were far less developed politically than we. And kind of suspicious. But they warmed up after a while, and we talked about organizing. There are 228,000 of them and their roots are even more ancient than ours. But they're experiencing the same stress, especially loss of land and the relationship to it. And yet, what's remarkable is that they still have intimate knowledge of the earth—and it's even rubbed off on the whites. Also, Australians are close to the Antarctic ozone problem, and many are getting skin cancers. That makes people think. We need to work more closely with the aboriginals, and Australians in general."

"How do you intend to do that?"

"Supporting what aboriginals are doing. Bringing them to conferences. Exchanging experiences. Building coalitions. Encouraging white people to listen."

"You've also come to know the Saamis—the so-called Lapps—who live in the northern zones of Finland, Norway, Sweden, and Russia."

"Right. They're going through the same struggle we're into—the state trying to assimilate them. Traditionally, they've been accustomed to moving across the northern region following the reindeer and fishing. But now those countries are imposing borders, trying to force nationalistic concepts. What's worse, the land and the reindeer were devastated by the Chernobyl disaster. In Sweden the law says if you stop herding in one generation—which the Saamis may have to do because of Cher-

nobyl—you can't start up again in the next. So the assimilationists' policies will be strengthened. Every time I attend meetings of the Nordic
Saami Council, Saami land and lifestyle look more and more like the
mainstream. They're likely to live in houses in towns, not in tents. Like
other indigenous people, their kids see TV and begin to leave the old life.
And the government and economic pressures are intense. So today there
are more Saami fishermen than reindeer herders. It's a change in their
whole way of life."

"What about the Indians in Central America and South America?"

"It's even worse than here because you have a long, long, history of
overt brutality and systematic oppression. What's happened to Brazilian
Indians who've fought the developers is happening all over Central and
South America, and to the Maya in Mexico. Some tribes are dying off,
taking with them, forever, secrets of traditional medicine. More than that,
knowledge of living with your natural habitat. I'm active in rainforest
action groups. We have to fight together."

"What do you think first people have to offer us in our predicament
today?"

"Well—" He leaned back in his chair, pressed his fingers together,
and pondered a moment. "Perspective. Knowledge of the land. If you've
lived from the land and been there a long time—that's what 'aboriginal'
means, from the beginning or earliest days—you know about where the
sun rises and how the water flows and what wastes the land. You have
the long-term perspective that's needed these days. Indigenous people
demonstrate knowledge of how to live with the world as it is, and they
show respect and thanksgiving. The children see their parents go to the
ceremonies and give thanks. The Iroquois to the maple tree and the corn
and the colorful squashes, and the Saamis to the bear and the reindeer.
Respect for trees, animals, and all forms of life is learned from your
elders, and it's learned through ceremony, which is passed on to the next
generation. Thanksgiving comes naturally, because it's something you do
all the time. Indigenous people all have a spiritual quality in the way they
live. That's what is missing in capitalism."

We nodded. "A whole dimension of life. We understand there are
some 200 million indigenous people in the world. If their land and cultures are destroyed, and languages disappear—"

"You've lost a long, long body of knowledge. About adaptation,
about survival."

"The kind of knowledge we need today."

"Exactly. It's frightening. Still, some creative thinking is going on.
The Global Forum is one thing I really believe in. The people who participate—scientists like Carl Sagan, England's James Lovelock and Russia's Evgeni Velikov, spiritual leaders like the Dalai Lama, political

leaders like Al Gore and India's Karen Singh—the caliber is extraordinary. Now if the U.S. could just open up to these ideas!

"But no—" He shook his head slowly. "The power structures of the Pentagon and the multinationals go on. We will die, the earth will die, if power and profits continue to be so important. These power structures forget the natural law. They think they have real power. The reality is, we are all governed by the natural law."

"And that is?"

"Quite simply, the law tells us if you poison the air, the water, the earth, you will die. Your children will die. It tells us no single entity can grow unchecked without damaging itself and the environment. We eat too much. We breed too much."

"So you see overpopulation as a real problem?"

"The biggest problem in the world," he said emphatically. "Humans cannot grow unchecked. It goes back to the natural law. Which is also spiritual law."

"And it's violated almost everywhere today."

"Yes, and that could go on a while longer. But not much. If we continue to break the law, there will be a sudden crash—and then the deterioration will go fast. There is no forgiveness under the law of nature. Americans are used to buying their way out. But that won't happen this time. AIDS, for instance, is a democratic disease. And a breakdown in the immune system."

We did not meet again until 1992, for lunch in a diner near SUNY-Buffalo. As he bit into his sandwich with relish—this was his "breakfast," for he had risen at 5 A.M. in Onondaga to take a 6 o'clock bus to Buffalo—Lyons described with boyish enthusiasm the Parade for Indigenous People organized as a counter to the annual Macy's Thanksgiving Day Parade, signaling the start of the New York Christmas buying season. "Seven hundred people—Indians from the U.S., Canada, South America, plus a lot of supporters—gathered at the Museum of Natural History. After traditional dances, Cree drummers and I led the parade. It was a chance to focus. On Thanksgiving we ought to think about the earth—that's where our food comes from."

"It must be hard not to think of the white man's first Thanksgiving without bitterness."

"Yeah, 90 percent of the aboriginal people were wiped out by wars and disease."

Recently Lyons had also been a featured speaker before a number of international groups, including the Inuit Circumpolar Conference, which represents 115,000 Inuit of Canada, Alaska, and northeastern Siberia. At the Moscow Conference of the Global Forum, Lyons had been instrumental in promoting invitations to traditional elders of indigenous peoples—who became the second largest among the religious delegations, after Christians. "They came from all over," he said. "Native people from Hawaii, central Brazil, the Philippines, Kenya, Saamiland, and Nigeria. And, of course, North America—people like our old friend, Hopi elder Thomas Banyaca, and members of the Santa Clara Pueblo and the Haida Nation of British Columbia, and Onondagan elder Audrey Shenandoah. In fact, Audrey gave the spiritual keynote address to the delegates— 1,000 of them, from 83 countries. She got a tremendous response, particularly when she said 'There is no word for "nature" in my language. "Nature" in English seems to refer to that which is separate from human beings. It is a distinction we don't recognize.'

"The indigenous leaders were one delegation, because we have some common cultural and environmental traditions. In Moscow some of us began planning a Global Circle of Traditional Elders of Indigenous People along the lines of our Traditional Circle. And we recently had our first meeting in Onondaga. They came from all over the earth."

"What are some of the goals of the circle?"

"Sharing ceremonies and problems. Then moving on to action, like preserving our languages so that the people can know who they are. Legal status is the bottom line. The reason we've managed to win some battles with the U.S. is that it signed treaties with us, at least theoretically recognizing us as nations, and this country is supposed to be founded on law."

"Secular law. Would you say indigenous peoples always have a sense of the law of nature?"

"Yes. The law of nature is at least implicit. For us, the Iroquois, the idea came to crystallize under the Great Peacemaker."

"Deganwidah?"

"Well, that's the word the whites use. We are instructed to use his name only at the Condolence (raising chiefs) ceremonies. So we simply say 'the Great Peacemaker.' He came amongst the Iroquois a long time ago, no one knows how long, but we know it was a time of crisis. The Mohawk and Oneida and Onondaga and others were warring. It wasted the land and the blood of our finest young people. The Peacemaker was from the north—some say Huron—but it doesn't matter because he was really a spiritual being, a messenger with the message of the Great Peace. He went among the Iroquois nations, laying down rules, but when he came to Onondaga, the Thadodaho, the great chief, gave him a hard time—he was fierce and wasn't about to share power. But eventually, when the Peacemaker, along with Hīyǎwatá and leaders of the Mohawk and four other nations approached him, singing the sound of a bird who was singing of peace, they convinced the Thadodaho to change his ways. They said if he would join them, the Onondaga would be Fire-keepers of the Haudenosaunee. The leaders saw it was better to use their minds together than use force. So the Peacemaker uprooted the Tree of Peace, the white pine, and commanded them to throw their weapons into the pit, and after planting the tree again, proclaimed, 'We've planted the Great Peace and the Council of Good Minds, who will counsel for the welfare of the people.'"

"So it's really a spiritual tree?"

"Yes, a spiritual center. A spiritual law. People ask us where it is, but it's nothing you can see. You feel it, you know the root is here. Well, the Great Peacemaker took five arrows for what were then five nations and bound them together and said, 'This is your unity, this is your strength!' And then he gave us our laws. Of course, we've elaborated on them over time. They set out how we should choose our chief statesmen, clan mothers, and faithkeepers, and arrive at our decisions. The laws have endured—and *we* have endured."

"For a people who have suffered so much, that's remarkable."

"Yes. That's why some indigenous people want to learn from us. Still, the troubles go on. Sometimes reaching a crisis. Like the time of Geneodiyo, whom some people call Handsome Lake. He was shown the future and given instructions on how to live better and deal with white people. He saw the future—deterioration of life as we know it. He was shown a field, but nothing was growing. He cupped water in his hands to drink, but then he saw it was dirty."

"As we are seeing today."

"True. But the vision he received had hope—destruction *could* come in every generation, but each was to see it didn't happen now and plan so it didn't happen in future, at least for seven generations to come. That was also the instruction given by the Great Peacemaker."

"Yet even many of your own people don't seem to be following it today."

"That's right." He stared into his coffee and stirred it slowly. When he looked up, his eyes appeared tired. "Sometimes I feel powerless. But people look to me. I've never liked publicity, but it comes to me. Because I'm active, speak English well, have education, and travel. But it's hard to transmit what I've experienced and learned to my people because most have little education, and pretty limited lives. Many have known little but frustration. That's why some get into drugs—the fastest growing enterprise in the world."

"That makes your task extremely difficult."

He nodded. "I want to re-educate my own people. The need isn't to *return* to old ways, but to reflect ancient tribal values in new ways, so as to transfer knowledge to future generations. For instance, following the law of nature as a spiritual guide. For thousands of years our way of life was based on the laws of peace, harmony with nature, and community in our villages, together with the ethic of sharing. You can't really follow the ancient instruction of thinking about the seventh generation even before yourself, unless you think of sharing today.

"When our people capitulate and fall into the greedy hands of our white brothers, I tell them it's fool's gold. Like selling rights over our lands to multinationals that mine uranium and leave radioactive wastes. Or opening Indian country to gambling casinos serving white visitors by the busload. Some operations are controlled by organized crime. Many Indians argue that it reduces unemployment and brings a chance to get something back from the white man, beating him at his own game. There's *some* truth in this, especially considering that many reservations depend on federal grants for essential services. But most of the money goes no further than these entrepreneurs' pockets. It's the same old gold fever that seized whites and destroyed our hold on these lands. Many Indians *are* resisting this subtle corruption. But those who do succumb to greed, they're betraying our children's future."

"That's a message for white people, too," we observed.

"And the betrayal is happening now. You can tell by the quality of our children's lives, things are almost *bound* to get worse. That we have so many homeless youngsters tells us something about our society. We were instructed that one way to gauge the deterioration of the environment and well-being of the world was to observe how societies treat their children."

"It's interesting that the end of the Great Law of Peace, your Constitution, says specifically, 'Everyone has a responsibility to protect and preserve the earth, Our Mother, for the benefit of her children seven generations to come.' If we could put that into *our* Constitution!"

He smiled. "You need a spiritual center. But we're not missionaries, we don't impose our ideas. If asked, we'll impart our experience and values. *If* the white people want to listen."

"But you seem to find that many whites are turning to you now."

"That's right. It was foretold a long time ago, in a Hopi prophecy, that the children of the white people who thought they had conquered us—that their children would come to *us* some day. It's happening. We'll work with whites wherever we can find common ground. The environment is common ground because it's the reality of everything."

"So you seem to alternate between pessimism and hope."

"Um—m, yes. On one hand, I sometimes think the ecological crisis will be a catalyst to make more people aware of what's wrong with our values. On the other hand, you can witness a shift from racism to dangerous classism. That kind of fight is shaping up. This is the reason

unions are having so much trouble, and one reason Indians are responding to the greed element. There are going to be more resource wars,
inside the country and in the world. It's going to get nasty. Very nasty.
The wars will be over water, food, shelter, productive lands. It will be
brutal, as people migrate to these life-giving resources.

"And yet—" He stroked his chin. "I *am* kind of optimistic about
people. They are so unpredictable. Sometimes they rise to the occasion.
The damage to the land, the whole ecosystem, is terrible, but there's still
a good chance we'll take action. What we really have to learn is to share.
We humans are part of the ecosystem. We're part of the natural cycle,
being born, coming to maturity, dropping back into earth again, the way
trees and birds do. We're all of the same land."

We remembered his painting of the four animals—wolf, bear, deer,
and buffalo—that had arrested our attention when we met the first day.
Could they represent the four corners of the earth? we asked.

He nodded. "And the four men in the corners are spiritual beings who
work for the Creator. So they are also the four protectors of all life,
including human beings."

Connection with the Land: The Mohawks, the Lummi, and the Traditional Circle

"We're all of the land . . . "

In our encounters with Native Americans, we have heard echoes of
that refrain many times, although they are people with diverse educational, family, and cultural backgrounds, widely different goals and ongoing contact with their traditions.

On an Akwesasne (Mohawk) reservation, for example, we talked
with Indians deeply involved in the Akwesasne Freedom School created
by the traditional Mohawk Nation Council of Chiefs and Clanmothers.
All instruction was conducted in the native language. In the words of
Tom Porter of the Bear Clan, "We were afraid that in two or three decades
there would be no more Iroquois language in the entire world. There
would be Iroquois, but they'd be Iroquois only biologically. Anthropologists say over 60 percent of your culture comes from your language. So
we'd be like dinosaurs. What we try to do here is decolonize the children.
We don't want them to look at the world as dollar signs."

Jake Swamp, a Mohawk working for the American Friends Service
Committee to publicize the project, straddling the U.S.-Canadian border
on the St. Lawrence, showed us the reservation and described their
problems. Parents, poor though they were, had to raise money through

fund-raising activities. But their greatest obstacle was the discovery that a mile from the school a General Motors factory had been dumping toxic chemicals, including massive quantities of polychlorinated biphenols (PCBs). The school had been forced to move, at great expense. Forced to move—an old refrain for Indians. But this time the threat came from poisons injected into the earth that Indians had been reared to view as their mother.

At a gathering of the North American Conference on Religion and Ecology (NACRE), we met Jewell ("Praying Wolf") James of the Lummi Nation. A direct descendant of Chief Seattle, and head of both the Lummi Protection Force and Moon's Prayer Foundation (which offers the image of the "Indian in the Moon" as a source of spiritual guidance), James lived in the world of visions and the world of action. All his visions related in some way to the land. "My sister knew dreams, my mother knew dreams," he confided. "My father was a medicine man, one grandmother had extra-terrestrial powers, and even when I was a child I had visions."

In a figurative sense, too, James' work was based on a vision. It had taken him to South Africa to give presentations on conflict resolution, to Amazonia to demonstrate support for rainforest defense, to Europe to talk about alliances among indigenous peoples. and to meetings with Native Hawaiians fighting to save their rainforests and religious shrines, threatened by giant geothermal development. Several Lummi have gone to Hawaii to plan ways of working together.

James spoke passionately of violations of Indians' religious freedom, especially the right to preserve sacred burial grounds. He took special pride in his role as catalyst for the "Bishops' Apology," signed by 10 bishops and church leaders in Greater Seattle, and later read aloud in 1,800 parishes. Confessing to the church's complicity in destruction of native spiritual practices, it asserted: "We ask your forgiveness and blessing." It affirmed the right of native peoples to practice traditional ceremonies, have access to sacred sites, and use religious symbols, such as feathers, tobacco, and sweet grass, and declared: "The spiritual power of the land and the ancient wisdom of your indigenous religions can be, we believe, great gifts to the Christian churches."[20]

Pollution of the land, pollution of water, the "epidemic" of environmental diseases: these were the concerns we heard over and over. All linked with the violation of treaties and the right to hold their own religious ceremonies in their own way—on their own ancestral lands.

"Our diverse cultures get their *identities* from the land," says the Traditional Circle of Indian Elders and Youth. That sense of connection with the land also binds tribal cultures together.

"We need a coalition of indigenous nations and environmental

groups to work more cooperatively to save Mother Earth," declares the
Circle. "Together, we can end the Holocaust against the environment.
Mother Earth needs all of us to pay attention to the Natural Laws."

Contradictions and Conflicts

Yet visitors to many native communities are shocked to see rubbish
scattered in front yards, plastic lining the roads, graveyards of abandoned
cars. It seems an insult to the land that Indians have reverenced. There
seems to be contradiction, too, between their traditional belief in controlling human population and the fact that between 1980 and 1990 their
numbers leaped by 37.9 percent, according to Census Bureau figures
(always open to question, for many reasons).[21]

There is no single explanation. Many Indians deplore such threats to
the earth, but are wary of discussing them with outsiders. What seems
clear is that to most Indians these problems do not appear as serious as
others: poor health, joblessness, poor housing. Indeed, many impoverished Indian women, like their African-American counterparts in inner-
city "reservations," gain a sense of fulfillment through bringing many
children into their lives. In this domain they have power.

American Indians still represent less than 1 percent of the U.S. population. Hence many believe *their* population is not a problem. If the populations of all the world's peoples were to increase 37.9 percent in a
decade, Mother Earth would be devastated. But at this point in their
history, most Indians are too impoverished to think of the planet's survival before their own. They also know that at this point, the size of the
group is one important ingredient of political power. And power, in its
many forms, is a question permeating American Indian life.

The trash problem is very real. To many Native Americans, the most
tangible threat is *other* people's trash: the megatons of rubbish that "corporate garbage men," the nuclear industry, and the federal government
have been seeking to bury on Indian soil.

The trash that "corporate garbage men" offer is described as "non-
toxic," but generally includes high levels of lead, cadmium, mercury, and
similar ingredients of the consumer culture. Waste industry officials, arguing that they are helping native people, offer the tribal group money,
jobs, and often the right to dispose of its own trash at the new dump, free
of charge.

Some tribal councils—citing poverty or arguing that the new dump
will offer protection in contrast to the old ad hoc dumps with no linings—
do approve such a project. Usually, the decision is reached through majority vote, imposed by the federal government to replace the
traditional way of consensus, a way that avoids subsequent dissension.

Majority voting generates power politics and a long legacy of bitterness, often directed more at the other tribal faction than at the federal government or the merchants of waste. "The Establishment knows what it's doing," say many Indians. "It's the old divide-and-rule tactic."

Even more alarming to them is federal pressure to use their lands for storing nuclear waste, with tempting offers of up to $100,000 for permission to "study the potential" for putting nuclear dumps on their land, and several million more to follow if they decide to go on. A few tribes have accepted, but the fury and humiliation roused by the offer are summarized well by Suzan Shown Harjo, president of Morningstar Foundation, an Indian rights group: "Five hundred years of colonization has done a real job on us. It makes us targets of cash and poverty politics."[22]

Grassroots groups have been offering spirited resistance to dumping in its many forms. It is hard work to research the facts and organize community meetings, sometimes braving threats to their lives. Yet there have been many successes. For example, the Navajo of Dilkon, Arizona, the Kaw in Oklahoma, the Mississippi Choctaw, the Mohawk of Canada and New York State, and the Lakota at the Pine Ridge and Rosebud reservations have turned down proposals for incinerators and dumps. Other tribes have successfully opposed multinational mining and lumber companies. It is the work of small persistent groups—many of them headed by women—with names like Native Action, Good Road Coalition, Citizens Against Ruining Our Environment, Kaibab Earthkeepers, and Native Americans for a Clean Environment, as well as the Indigenous Environmental Network, a coalition of approximately 50 groups. Despite their impoverishment, they say "No!"

It is a never-ending struggle. As the waste industry grows more and more desperate in the face of "Not In My Backyard" refusals elsewhere, the pressures to unload the hazards on America's traditional wasteland will only increase. But will this resolve the problem? Leaks of toxic waste do not conveniently halt at the borders of "Indian land."

Resurgence and Hope—and a Restoration of Balance

The land is being assaulted by uranium mining, toxic waste dumping, and the encroachment of real estate development. Yet today ancient ceremonies are being revived or held on to fiercely. They are ceremonies expressing the sense that the destiny of the people and the destiny of the land are one. The Navajo, for example, continue the cosmological ceremony variously called Chant, Sing, or Way. They believe that the balance of a sick or mentally ill person is restored only in relationship to the Navajo *universe*. The medicine woman or man returns the ailing one to the Navajo Creation and Emergence, recreating time and place.

The Holy Beings who live on the sacred mountains connect the patient to the power source, which is the land. When the patient returns, a rebirth has occurred and balance is restored. In the Blessing Way ceremony, "Earth's feet have become my feet. By means of these, I shall live on. . . ."

The arts continue to reflect what Berry calls the "primary scripture of the natural world." Navajo sand paintings continue to tell the stories of the Holy People and personages such as Big Fly and Corn Beetle, as well as sacred plants and other forces of the universe. Some native peoples continue to see their basket-making—from gathering grasses and vegetable dyes to the weaving itself—as a ritual recapitulation of the total process of Creation; the complete basket is the universe in an image. The ritual dances and chants singing of visible and invisible sacred presences are being revitalized after long banishment under the influence of missionaries.

The ancient stories are being revived and passed on to other Indians and to white people. N. Scott Momaday, for example, has retold the Kiowa myths he learned from his grandmother. From many tribal nations, Joseph Bruchac and Michael Caduto have gathered tales that tell of Creation, fire, earth, water, seasons, and other aspects of the Indians' cosmology.

Many of the Native American writers who have emerged in recent decades continue this oral tradition. The fiction of Leslie Marmon Silko, N. Scott Momaday, Louise Erdrich, Paula Gunn Allen, Gerald Vizenor, Simon Ortiz, and Duane Niatum, for instance, rings with a story-telling quality. Sometimes, too, one can recognize archetypal characters and conflicts that parallel those from age-old tribal narratives. Indian writing of today frequently portrays a world inhabited by natural and supernatural forces, by people leading bitter and turbulent lives. Moreover, many of these writers are being published by mainstream houses.

Frequent themes in contemporary American Indian novels are white invasion and colonization, and the despair, the loss of self that goes with loss of the land. Permeating almost all the work of these writers is conflict between two cultures.

How does one achieve wholeness—accepting traditional practices and at the same time assimilating attitudes required by living in the mainstream society? The characters in these novels respond to this knot in a complex of ways, for the authors have not tried to reverse the old stereotypes by portraying Indians as heroes, whites as villains. The protagonist of James Welch's *The Indian Lawyer*, for example, is not just the victim of a blackmail scheme to thwart his rising career as a lawyer and his plan to run for U.S. Congress. In some respects he brings his fate on himself. He also finds his own salvation. Always concerned about environmental issues, he turns to real commitment, by moving back to a simpler life, nearer his people, and fighting for their rights to the water that farmers and hydropower concerns were diverting from the reservation reservoir. He rediscovers the peace—and the power—in the land.[23]

Silko's panoramic *Almanac of the Dead*, which has been called "a kind of moral history of the Americas," depicts a vast array of people, all struggling to find some kind of equilibrium among the many forces that connect them to their history and to each other. The clash supersedes ethnic divisions. Ancient legends awaken in the lives of contemporary characters. The Barefoot Hopi presents the ancient prophecy, and spirit beings appear, shadowing the desecration of the earth. The giant stone snake does not care if people are believers or not; the work of the spirit beings and prophecies goes on regardless.[24]

Many Indian authors write not only novels and stories, but essays and poems as well. Their work is both harsh and lyrical. The poetry of Paula Gunn Allen, Roberta Hill, Linda Hogan, Gerald Vizenor, and Ray A. Young Bear, for example, confronts the ugly, violent reality of today. Yet it also speaks of the persistent voices of Coyote and Raven and Grandmother Spider, the insistent presence of earth, water, sky.

Filled with long-simmering anger at being defined by whites, these writers are asserting their own experience, their own sense of what it means to be Indian today.

The characters in Indian fiction tend to be remarkably resilient—like their ancestors, people who refuse to die. Their connection with the earth helps them endure, even with hope. However weakened it becomes under the pummeling of industrial civilization, that bond endures.

In the words of poet Philip Yellowhawk Minthorn: ". . . we cannot fail / this earth, / this arduous earth."[25]

Another sign of cultural renewal is the emergence of "learning circles" in various parts of the U.S. Most of the members are Indians who have never lived on a reservation and have little knowledge of their traditions. Most are working-class people who have grown up in crowded urban settings, often with parents who were ashamed to call themselves Indian. Few have enough "Indian blood" to enroll in a tribe. (Sufficiency is defined by the BIA as one-quarter or more.) In fact, the "Indian Arts and Crafts Act" forbids anyone not federally recognized as Native American to sell any good which suggests it is Indian produced. Considering that intermarriage over the centuries means that only a third of all Indians could meet the BIA "blood quantum" today, and the proportion continues to decline, many natives would call this tantamount to "arithmetical genocide."[26]

Yet today they are looking for their roots. They meet regularly with other Indians from a wide variety of tribal backgrounds, to begin learning—through story-telling, chant, flute music, dance, painting, and native technologies—what it means to be Indian. They sleep in tepees; enter, sometimes awkwardly, into sweat lodges to find healing; and listen to leaders tell about their history, the significance of story, the importance of circles in ceremonial life. Only when the expenses for a leader living some distance away must be paid do they charge a fee, a nominal one. Occasionally, they discuss BIA or Indian internal politics, but only rarely do they talk about the subtle modes of exploitation prevalent today, or the broader impact of industrial civilization. Still, they sense how these forces affect their struggle for clearer identity.

An offshoot of one learning circle we know is planning to purchase a 300-acre tract in southern Ohio, where they will form a land trust, live as a community, and cultivate the soil using both traditional native and modern organic methods. (Such communities have already been created elsewhere in the country.) The Indians do not use the word that many environmentalists use—"bioregionalism"—but the vision is the same: to live on a functional community basis in regions with mutually supporting life-systems that are generally self-sustaining.

One electrician put it simply: "We *need* the land."

Extending the Vision

Even many rank-and-file Indians who have to grub for bare existence feel some solidarity with other indigenous peoples and their struggles. Some native leaders, and even whites who have lived for a time among Indians, feel this solidarity with particular force.

When the Maya in the Chiapas region of Mexico rose up on January 1, 1994, to protest their oppression, anthropologist John Grim called it a "cry of despair from a people reduced to violence so as to be heard." The Iroquois, who periodically gather tribal groups from around the U.S. and other parts of the world, experienced a particularly strong bond of anger and affinity. "The Maya I visited were living near the rainforest," Chief Shenandoah recalled. "Developers were cutting mahogany. Others were burning woods to make pastures for cattle. For American beefburger chains. We could see the fires at night. Since then, the Maya have come to visit us here."

In Chiapas the issues are complicated, but they are all interrelated. Twenty families have monopolized the best land, while *indigenas* possessed less than a hectare (two and one half acres) per person. Corn is more than a food; it is national identity. In the Mayan creation myth, humankind was born the child of corn. Yet Indian communal ownership of land (which traditionally concentrated on corn farming), was effectively sabotaged by Mexico's President Carlos Salinas de Gortari while in office. Led by multinationals eager to replace corn cultivation with more "efficient" farming, such as beef ranching, the foreign invasion was climaxed in 1993 by the signing of the North American Free Trade Agreement (NAFTA).

It is no accident that the Maya broke into open rebellion on the day NAFTA was to go into effect. NAFTA was final proof that elites had launched an all-out push to wrest the land from the *indigenas'* hands. Since then even more Indian farmers have had no choice but to head for the city slums. But that sacred abstraction, "the market," has become free.

"The core issue revolves around NAFTA," asserts Lyons. "The new surge in the multinationals' quest for more development will focus on 'Indian lands'—they're the most vulnerable. A revolution has begun. It will go on for years."

In his observations on "the great religious ships of state rocking gently on the great sea of life as they search for spiritual reality and salvation" at the 1988 Global Forum, Oren Lyons suggested that "perhaps we may know a direction that may help in the search."

They do indeed know a direction. We who live in mainstream Western culture can never be Indian; it is absurd to imagine that we can fully experience what the Indians have experienced over the centuries and still feel in their sinews today. But they know a direction for humankind—a way of listening, a way of seeing.

In rare moments of illumination, we who live in mainstream Western culture give thanks, like the Indians, to the sun, moon, birds, animals, trees. We may even talk with them. When a man in Austin, Texas, who had been forsaken by a woman he loved took revenge by pouring a powerful herbicide around a 500-year-old oak cherished by the community, citizens and experts rallied to save it. And a man who loved trees came daily to offer apologies to the stricken oak.

In moments of liberation, we listen to the earth as Native Americans have done since time immemorial. Scott Momaday, a Kiowa, writes of "a wind like music in the land." He remembers ancient ceremonies and recalls dancers at a wedding, "their feet shaking the hard earth . . . unaccountable and unaccountably the same thing. They described every impulse, the whole rhythm of the turning of the earth, the returning of time upon it forever."27

Momaday's identity is still rooted in the land: "The events of one's life take place, *take place* . . . they have meaning in relation to the things around them . . . I existed in that landscape, and then my existence was indivisible with it. I placed my shadow there in the hills, my voice in the wind that ran there, in those old mornings and afternoons and even-ings."[28]

As a youth riding his horse into a new life in the white man's world, he carried within him a wellspring of harmony: "I sang in the sunshine and heard the birds call out on either side . . . I could feel my horse under me, rocking at my legs, the bobbing of the reins to my hand; I could feel the sun on my face and the stirring of a little wind at my hair. And through the hard hooves, the slender limbs, the supple shoulders, the fluent back of my horse, I felt the earth under me. Everything was under me, buoying me up; I rode across the top of the world."[29]

We may never reach the heights that Momaday rode, but all of us who keep an ear to the earth can share, in some way, in these experiences. It is no accident that so many white poets, musicians, and artists have been touched by the Indians. But we need not be poets. We know whereof the Indians speak.

To many non-Indians, the prime gift from the native peoples is their spirituality. But what is "spirituality"? As Dennis Banks once told us, "If you've never experienced it, spirituality is hard to understand. But it's not about being Indian or non-Indian. You don't have to follow the medicine man. Look into yourself. Walk in the woods. There's a whole clinic out there."

For the two of us, walking in the woods, together or alone, has become an ever-revealing experience. Listening to the trees, we have come to sense that a tree is not only a tree, but the sun and the soil that nourish it, the sound of the birds, wind, leaves, and insects that make it their home. And it speaks—to all our senses.

Almost everywhere in America one can find "Indian land." It lies beneath our footsteps, our plows, our highways. It is the same soil that Indians trod: their bones, and the bones of the creatures with whom they sensed kinship. The bones of the wolves and buffalo, snakes and larks, ants and beetles, trees and rocks—the other beings in the great web of Creation. The vibrant life in that soil has changed, yet not changed. It is not easy to sense Judaism around you if you are Christian, or Islam around you if you are Jewish. But we all have some of the Indians' spiritual heritage around us and within us, if only we look, and touch, and listen. It is part of our flesh and bones and being, because we, too, have sprung from this soil.

The lessons from Native Americans are not new; they are reminders of truths we have kept alive somewhere in our hearts. They remind us that, ultimately, there can be no separation between spirituality and the rest of our lives. That social, economic, and ecological justice go hand in hand. That the earth on which we walk is our common origin and our common destiny.

The relationship to the natural world cherished in American Indian tradition is more than a mystical communion. The essence of the relationship is also simple and realistic, as tough-minded as it is tender-hearted. At its heart is the abiding awareness that we are all subject to the laws of nature. For the Indian, nature can be as cruel as she is kind, but ultimately she metes out justice.

7

BEYOND THE WESTERN HORIZON

Introduction

To many Westerners seeking a spiritual vision to live by, the Semitic faiths seem to pale beside Earth-based traditions like Hinduism, Buddhism, Shinto, Taoism, and indigenous religions. Throughout much of North America and Europe, small but growing numbers of people are looking to these traditions for insights into the great mystery of being.

How do these faiths view the relationship between human beings and the earth? How do their followers *experience* that relationship today? What are they doing in response to the challenge of preserving the planet?

These were some of our questions during visits to Hawaii, Japan, Taiwan, Thailand, Nepal, India, and Kenya. Here we offer glimpses of our explorations into some of these faiths.

Traditionally, the spiritual leaders of these societies have enjoyed a level of respect and authority unparalleled in the West since the Middle Ages. Religion has been embedded in the art, music, and literature; in the gorgeous festivals; in the ceremonies used in greeting the day; and in the home altars to honor the ancestors and other spiritual presences. Religions often seem to meld with one another. It can be difficult to discern which tradition is celebrated in the fruit-festooned wayside shrines to some god, goddess, *bodhisattva*, or earth spirit. Even today, the longer one lingers in these cultures, the more one senses a certain animism at the core. To most traditional people, the entire universe pulsates with life and there is no arbitrary distinction as to what they should worship.

On an earlier visit to Kyoto in 1963, one of us, Marjorie, encountered a Zen monk who observed placidly, "A true Asian, even one who calls himself Christian, feels not that he is ruled by God, but that he is part of all Nature."

His words were to come back to us again and again.

Sacred Mountains and Forest: Cultural Revival Among Two Native Peoples

Hawaii: "Pele's Family Is the Land Itself"

Christianity invaded this crescent of islands in 1820, following Captain Cook and a succession of Western traders, and soon became the dominant religion. Its alliance with the Western entrepreneurs who became de facto rulers brought handsome profits, as many missionaries turned from saving "savage" souls to developing the land for lucrative sugar and pineapple exports.

Missionaries could not stamp out the "pagan, sensual" practices of the Native Hawaiian religion completely, however. Today it is enjoying a certain revival, as Native Hawaiians fight what they see as an invasion of their culture, their land, their right to determine their own destiny. The story of their struggle for freedom, in some ways similar to that of Native Americans, is too complex to recount here. But we shall take a look at the "Save Pele" movement.

Pele, the primary deity and daughter of Haumea, Mother Earth, is the fiery goddess who inhabits the Kilauea Volcano on Big Island. She is not the tender goddess of all-encompassing love and forgiveness, but like many deities all over the planet, a divine manifestation of a fierce, powerful force in the natural world. (Some Hawaiian deities are more gentle, and Pele herself has her quiet, joyous, dancing *persona*.) "To us she is not only the volcano itself, but also the lava, the steam, the heat," say many Native Hawaiians. "Pele's family is the land itself. We pray to her daily. Many of our chants and hula are for her. We believe some of us are descended from her. For us it is a sacrilege to drill holes into Pele's body."

That was just what was happening. The Wyoming-based True Geothermal Energy Company had begun exploratory drilling on the slopes

of the volcano for energy to expand industrialization and tourism on Big
Island; surplus geothermal power would be transmitted to the other islands to further their already-booming development.

The consequences would be "colossal," Pele Defense Fund leader Dr.
Emmett Aluli told us. Geothermal production released toxic hydrogen
sulfide, which smelled like sewage, and could sicken children, old people, and pregnant women. The noise from venting geothermal wells could
last eight hours a day. New power lines would criss-cross Big Island.
Development plans there included not only more tourist facilities, but
also a missile-launching facility and a metals-smelting plant, which
would desecrate the quiet countryside and pour toxic waste into the rich
fishing grounds. The island's Wao Kele O Puna rainforest, unique in the
world—98 percent of its wildlife could be found nowhere else—would
be irreparably damaged.

Together with other organizations, the Pele Defense Fund—armed
with data from environmental scientists—had been fighting a determined
campaign with mass demonstrations, sit-downs, publicity, and appeals to
state agencies, state courts, the U.S. Congress, and the U.S. Supreme
Court. "The big problem," explained long-time activist Davianna McGre-
gor, "is that the courts won't recognize this as a religious issue."

After our departure, the movement suffered a long series of defeats.
Exhausted members (almost all volunteered their after-work time), listened to pleas to give up—and plunged on.

In February 1995, the fight culminated in a dramatic victory. Represented by the Sierra Club Legal Defense Fund (in 1997 renamed Earthjustice Legal Defense Fund), a 12-organization coalition settled a
four-year-old lawsuit alleging that Hawaii was promoting the massive
geothermal project without complying with state law requiring full environmental disclosure. The state agreed to stop the master planning process, and cancelled contracts with geothermal consultants. True
Geothermal abandoned activity in the rainforest. Defense Fund spokes-
man Palikapu Dedman exulted: "Finally, the state has gotten wise!"

The native people have another victory to celebrate—this one, as in
the case of many other indigenous peoples, tinged with bittersweetness.
Before World War II, the island of Kaho'olawe, a sacred ritual site close
to Maui, had belonged to the Native Hawaiians. After Pearl Harbor, the
U.S. Navy took it over for target practice, promising to return it at the
end of the war. It reneged on its promise, however. Native activists protested; two were killed. It was only in 1992 that Washington ordered the
bombing stopped. The land *was* returned—but to the state of Hawaii, not
the native people, says Kekuni Blaisdell.

Partly as a result of these victories, more than 60 native rights and
environmental groups joined into an action alliance, which today strives

to preserve the land, rainforest, natural resources, and cultural heritage of this unique archipelago.

Kenya: "Today All Is Disorder"

In a culture nearly halfway round the world from Hawaii, a parallel struggle to revive earth-based traditions was emerging. The Torch of the Living God was drawing large crowds to open-air sermons in markets and other parts of the city.

"We are *not* a sect or religion. We are a movement to restore traditional values!" declared three Torch elders after seating us, together with a reporter, our translator, on broken-down chairs.

We looked around the office, the vine-covered courtyard of a musty shop devoted to acupuncture and herbal remedies. It was a strange contrast to the swank shops for tourists that made Nairobi appear an extension of Europe or America. The ultimate symbol of its gleaming affluence was the 60-story, Times-Media complex that the World Bank and entrepreneurs like Robert Maxwell were planning to finance. That project, pushed by Kenyan President Daniel arap Moi and vigorously opposed by Wangari Maathai, the outspoken founder of a women's environmental movement known as the Green Belt, stood for the influences these three men were fighting.

Dr. Ngonya Wa Gakonya, an elder with a short bushy beard and long plaited hair, eyed us severely. With the *Nation* reporter acting as interpreter, he went on, "In the past there were set systems, set moral values. Your children respected you. Each man was given respect according to his age. You could find 28-year old virgins, female or male. People were led by the fear of God. Today all is disorder."

"What has happened?"

"We were removed from the God we knew, and introduced to a god we didn't know. New gods, new ideas. It is confusing. Now we don't know whether we are doing right or wrong."

"The colonialists came over 100 years ago," added an elder with quick black eyes, short gray braids, and a round white knitted cap. "The new ways have led us into darkness. The only thing we have learned is social dishonor and disrespect for the earth."

"You cannot separate capitalism and the Christianity of the missionaries," asserted the third leader, a tall angular man, likewise wearing a white knitted cap.

As the three men talked on amid the hubbub of visitors who kept streaming in and out of the smoke-filled courtyard, their anxiety about what was happening to the earth kept surfacing again and again. Before the white man came, there were forests all over Kenya. Forests were central to all life. There were animals in abundance, there were shrubs, there were medicinal plants, increasingly difficult to find today. In that society it was taboo to cut firewood in some forests. Now there was cutting everywhere. The leaders also blamed the Mau-mau, who had won independence for Kenya, yet destroyed many trees. But today, the white man's thinking was *everywhere*! Money. Buy land, clear it, plant cash crops where great trees once grew.

Yes, it would be hard to educate the people. The population was growing fast; unless they found alternative fuel, they would go on cutting trees. But the biggest obstacle was the big men—government men, business men—who bought big tracts of land and lived for today.

"In the past Kenyans considered future generations?"

"Yes!" The three nodded vigorously. "They didn't cultivate on the hills," said Dr. Gakonya, punctuating his statement with sharp, decisive hand gestures. "They cultivated on the banks of the river, they understood watersheds and how trees are needed to hold the soil that holds water. Some parts of the earth can be cultivated, some must be left alone. Our ancestors understood there must be balance. And the mountains were *sacred*. God's blessings came through the mountains."

Unlike Pele Defense Fund leaders, we reflected, Torch of the Living God elders had no clear program. These men lacked formal schooling in the areas of science, agriculture, and principles of community organizing. Yet the two movements shared the same purpose: re-awakening consciousness of the wisdom in the old ways, consciousness of the bonds that hold a society together and the bonds that unite people to the earth.

"The mountains are *still* sacred," Dr. Gakonya declared emphatically, as we stood up to leave. "God's blessings still come through the mountains. We pray God while facing Mount Kenya without closing our eyes."

Since leaving Nairobi, we have made repeated attempts to find out what has happened to the Torch of the Living God. In vain. As the government has become increasingly repressive, even groups labeled "devil worshippers" are investigated, and at least one that tried to reintroduce the form of worship of their forefathers has been declared "an illegal assembly." We did hear from our old friend Wangari Maathai (who finally won a victory in the battle against the Times-Media complex despite threats to her life and the bitter enmity of President Moi, who called her "a woman with insects in the head"). She had heard nothing about Torch followers, who seemed to have dissolved or gone underground. Certainly, they would not have been allowed to do traditional worship, she wrote. "The dominant religions here (Christianity and Islam) are very intolerant of other forms of spirituality. I perceive it as a form of cultural colonization. . . ."

Dr. Wangari Maathai, feminist and founder of the Kenyan Green Belt Movement, is shown standing before a Green Belt sign. (Photo by James Young)

New Life in Old Faiths: Taoism and Shinto

Taiwan: Prosperity, Pollution, and the Place of Faith-Based Action

Taiwan is reputed to be the most polluted island in the world. As the country's economy has industrialized, crescendoing with a boom in the late 1980s, Western luxury cars crowd downtown Taipei, enormous electric billboards advertise state-of-the-fad wares, and businessmen display their success with exotic dinners like three thousand dollar meals of bear-paw.

Only the few live on such heights, however. While Taiwan from the 1950s to early 1970s was one of the most egalitarian societies in the world, in 1990 the quality of life for average people was deteriorating. Crime and the cost of housing were soaring, nearly half of the 61 industrial zones had no waste water treatment facilities, air pollution was so bad that the government frequently refused to give out figures, and cancer was the leading cause of death. Behind the drive for industrialization lay Western investors eager to take advantage of cheap labor, who had introduced cement, chemical, and plastic industries. Within a 20-mile radius of Taipei, an area of 6.5 million inhabitants, General Electric and Westinghouse had built two nuclear power plants (each with two reactors).

Buddhism, Confucianism, Taoism, Christianity, and animist faiths co-exist peacefully. But all religions were ill or dying, many people told us. The magnificent Confucian temple in downtown Taipei was nothing but a museum commemorating Taiwanese and Chinese greatness. In theory most Taiwanese were Buddhist, but in practice they worshipped the god of consumerism. Taoism here was, in general, little more than a cult of magical rites. The Christians were doing very little to oppose materialism. Even some of the indigenous people showed only tepid interest in preserving their culture. "They prefer junky tourism," said Taiwanese-born Dr. Lucia Severinghaus, an ornithology professor who had become an environmental activist. "The young sell rare fish so they can play pinball games." As for efforts to save the island's ecosystem, most people we talked with agreed that organized religions fostered the passive belief that "God will provide."

Yet the more closely we looked, the more we realized that despite fears of protesting in public, environmental activity was simmering.

In response to growing public anxiety, environmental groups had grown to more than 20. Some groups focused on preservation of wildlife, others on conservation of the dwindling virgin forest, others on popular education. Women frightened by the health hazards had mobilized into a highly vocal group known as the Homemakers Union. Twenty-seven dams had been stopped, thanks to the cooperation of university professors, other intellectuals, and villagers whose homes would have been destroyed. Local groups had broken into polluting factories, occupied them, and organized boycotts. Fed up with government projects, many communities had organized self-help groups.

Nor was faith-based environmental action absent. Dr. L.K. Chang, a Yale-educated professor of physics at Taiwan National University and the founder of the Taiwan Environmental Protection Union, told us that a number of Catholics and Presbyterians had joined protests. They could speak only as individuals, but the churches did offer facilities for Union activities. Dr. Huinang Yang, a Buddhist nun who taught Buddhist philosophy at the National University, described two lay Buddhist groups that, to some degree, encouraged action. On our visit to one, the Center for Buddhist Studies, we learned that its main channel for promoting action, the magazine *Good News*, regularly ran stories on environmental degradation.

Finally, a few Taoists had begun to manifest active concern about preserving their spiritual heritage, the goal of achieving harmony with the cosmos.

TAOISM: "THE WAY"

The concept of *tao* is not specific to Taoism, for it belongs to all streams of classic Chinese thought. It encompasses many meanings, including: the way to follow, method, rule of conduct, the power of magicians, the natural order, the Cosmic Mother, and the Primal Unity and Source. Ultimately, it is nameless, for it cannot be conveyed by either words or silence. But in the broadest sense *tao* can be interpreted as "the way at the core of all existence." It is the ordering, or balancing, principle of the universe.

Taoism is generally associated with Lao-Tzu, a Chinese philosopher who lived from 604-531 BCE and was a friend of Confucius. However, Lao-Tzu cannot be considered Taoism's founder, for the magical and shamanistic beliefs, the sacrifices to hills, streams, and ancestors belonging to much earlier periods could also be called Taoist in a general sense. Like many other Asian faiths, Taoism is too diffuse to be codified. Moreover, the term applies not only to a religion—with many sects—but also to several schools of philosophy. It was once customary to distinguish between a Taoist philosophy of the great mystics like Lao-Tzu, and a later organized Taoist religion, but in reality Taoists of different backgrounds—philosophers, alchemists, ascetics, and priests of popular cults—have always influenced each other.

Moreover, throughout China's history Taoism has been an important factor in the country's thought and folk faith. Today Taoism functions fairly freely there as a religion, albeit under the watchful eyes of alert authorities. It flourishes in Hong Kong, Singapore, Vietnam, Cambodia, and other countries with overseas Chinese communities. On Taiwan, its center today, temples have been built or restored; there are more than 8,000, and nearly 30,000 priests, who have been able to preserve much of the traditional Chinese music, ritual, and ceremonial dress.

Both Confucianism and Taoism are oriented toward the cosmos. For both, it is essential to live in harmony with nature. However, Confucianism's emphasis is on benevolent government and harmony of humans with one another; it sees the *tao* as representing a general ethical ideal. Taoism, in both its philosophical and religious aspects, focuses on the metaphysical and mystical.

A cardinal concept is that Heaven and Earth emerged from the nameless Way. The universe and human society are in continual interaction. Taoism sees all beings, the universe itself, as a dynamic process of continual transformations, a view not unlike that of Swimme and Berry. Moreover, the human is seen as a microcosm reflecting the macrocosm; one's body reproduces the plan of the cosmos.

Taoism emphasizes the ancient Chinese concepts of *yin* (the shaded, or cold, passive, feminine aspect of the natural order), and *yang* (the sunny, warm, active, masculine aspect)—each balancing the other, for any one thing can be *yin* or *yang* in its relation to the other. Lao-Tzu stressed the superiority of the feminine principle, as representing quiescent and adaptive qualities. While this did not betoken the superiority of women, in Taoism they have traditionally enjoyed higher status than in Confucianism; some groups have had women leaders.

Over time, religious Taoism adopted alchemy and developed a pantheon; Lao-Tzu advanced from sage to god. The focus, however, has always been on the relationship of humans to the cosmos. A supremely important rite for the higher priests is that of cosmic renewal.

In Chinese history Confucian rulers often planned large-scale engineering works and city streets in rectilinear patterns. In contrast, the Taoist ideal—often unrealized in practice—has been that humans should interfere with nature's patterns and processes as little as possible. Hence instead of imposing anthropocentric notions of "order," humans should adapt their architecture to the natural world, emphasizing earth's natural curves (or what Berry and Swimme call the curvature of space throughout the universe). Humans should observe the spirits of the earth, understand the balance in the forces of nature, and adapt themselves to this harmony.

One way to achieve this is to concentrate on *chi* (air, inner essence, breath—ultimately, cosmic energy). Every person receives a portion of this primordial life-force at birth. In *chi* breathing exercises, the goal is to identify one's vital rhythm with that of the natural forces.

Simplicity (but not necessarily self-denial), spontaneity, and detachment are the means to achieve harmony with the natural order. Deep involvement in the political sphere has generally been discouraged. When involvement becomes necessary, it should be in accordance with *wu-wei*, non-egocentric activity. The hermit meditating on the mountain has long been regarded as the ideal.

A MYSTIC IN THE WORLD OF ACTION

The young Taoist priest we met in Taipei was no hermit. Fong Mau Li lived in a small house near Chengchi University, where he taught Chinese literature and tried to instill ecological awareness in students. He had a wife, a son, a daughter, three cats, two dogs, and a bicycle.

But his home was near a mountain. "That is very important to me," he said as he led us into his tiny living room and motioned to us to sit on the bamboo couch. A lace cloth covered a dining table, and one wall was decorated with a bamboo-and-leaf hat and a hanging woven of bright yarn. A small television set stood in a corner, and books lined two walls of the room. After the raucous jangle of downtown Taipei, the quiet here was like a blessing.

"When I look at the mountain, I pray," he said as he curled himself into a lotus position. His navy loose-fitting pants and navy jacket topped with a mandarin collar had a jaunty air, his long hair repeatedly fell over his forehead, and his lively eyes often crinkled with laughter.

"I need Nature, and Nature needs me," he went on, "I like walking in the mountains alone. But also, every Sunday, I go to a temple in the mountains with my students or friends. We sing and bow and chant and do meditation. We feel *chi* in our bodies."

"To have learned those difficult *chi* breathing exercises must have taken a long training."

"Difficult? Yes. But they bring peace. I have learned to teach Tai Chi. Once I went to the mountains with my master. We arrived at a forest and stayed there a week, fasting, praying *chi* under a tree. My master said, 'If you truly practice *chi*, your heart and body are at one with the forces of Nature, you take part in the universe.' And now every year he and I spend at least a week in Nature. Fasting, not even water. When I fast, the body, the mind, and the heart become clear. I hear the birds singing. When I return to Taipei, I lose this feeling. But when I go back to the forest it comes again immediately. Here, I will make you tea." He exited quickly.

He returned, beaming, with a teapot and three simple white porcelain cups. "It is *Taoist* tea! It is always very clean. It grows high in the mountains in small quantity; it is wild."

"It is delicious! Now tell us—you were always Taoist?"

"No. My parents are not, but they lead simple lives. I studied Taoism, then I went to mainland China to study it more, also Zen. Temples are being rebuilt there, but they belong to the nation. Still, the Tao is a living tradition. I ate with the priests. They do not eat too much. The temples where I stayed were simple, pure, and they had not many colors, only brick color, the color of earth. So you feel very calm. The priests, they live in harmony with the earth.

"After I came back, I began practicing as priest, I-Quan sect, it is simple. But—" A frown clouded his serene face. "The little town where I grew up near Taipei, it was changed. The water used to be very clean, but industry and tourists came in. I tell my students how Nature used to be."

"And they understand? They care?"

"Some do. I say, 'The Nature life belongs to us. If we lose it, we cannot find it again.' I tell them to go to the mountain. Then they can find real life. After they try it, some students say, 'You are right!' I talk to city children, too. I say, 'You can create many situations in your life.'

I repeat, and repeat, and repeat: 'You can change what is happening to Nature.'"

"In the West we are told that the Taoist ideal is passivity and non-interference."

"Yes. But also, Taoism is social. From the beginning, non-intervention has not meant *no* action; it has meant respect for the rights of all things. And today the world is changing, Nature is being changed. So I try to speak also with people in industry. I say, 'The rivers are dead. You get much money, but other ways you have lost much.' I make speeches to groups like the Lions Club. I say, 'We have one earth. We must adopt this place. All people must think ahead for their children. We can change our ways with Taiwan and the earth.' You are going to ask if these industry men change. I think, a little. It is not easy to tell."

"But a Taoist priest talking about acting to influence society—that's significant in itself."

"Yes. Yes." His eyes dropped. "And it is not easy," he said slowly. "I talk to people in government also. I say, 'The nation has pollution. You must pay attention to the *earth*, and think about the children.' Also sometimes I publish letters in newspapers. And every year Taoists have a big assembly, and I say to them, 'We must change. We must think about the earth. Our country has richnesses. But we are also rich in our hearts. We must act together.' Yes, they listen. Each time I say it, they listen more. I think some day they will also act."

"We have always thought of Confucianism as more activist than Taoism. You sound a little like a Confucian."

"Of course!" He laughed. "Well, shall we go to supper?"

After dinner in a small neighborhood restaurant, Fong Mau Li took us to visit Chihnan Temple, perched on one side of Houshan (Monkey Mountain). Actually, it was a giant complex of five temples, we learned. Taiwanese folk religion, Buddhism, Taoism, or Confucianism were represented in four of them; the fifth, Chihnan Main Temple, was dedicated to Lu Tung-pin, one of China's Eight Immortals, a powerful, playful, philandering deity.

As the taxi careened up the narrow rocky road, barely missing the precipice of the valley below, we wondered if the talismans around the driver's neck protected him from mundane emotions of terror. As cold rain began falling, we left the taxi and set out, for the rest of the ascent, up several hundred of the thousand stone steps that formed the original path. Along the way stood stalls set up as restaurants, stands for soft drinks and beers, and booths displaying plastic dolls, fruit, cookies, and tinsely objects with no observable religious significance.

The first temple—which Li called "folk with a little bit of Tao," and is commonly known as the Shrine of the Earth God—was small, but we were dazzled by the light, the profusion of red and gold. A long table held offerings of crackers, coffee, and gilt wrapping paper. Before the altar, shining with red light from electric candles, stood other offerings: oranges, pineapples, papaya, powdered milk, cookies. Two women were praying. The older one held a rosary in one hand, and with the other, kept throwing into the air two pieces of gourd, which made a clapping sound as they hit the ground. The younger woman was waving a lighted incense stick before statues of Buddha-like figures glowing with a crimson light from behind.

The Buddhist Chihnan Temple, white-pillared with a curving roof of red and white tiles, was larger and newer, and greater quiet prevailed. In the covered passage approaching it, vendors sold statues of Buddhas and *bodhisattvas* to those who wished to inscribe their names and place them in the temple, thus obtaining "merit" for the next world. Inside, three Buddhas gazed down from the altar. The two plump Buddhas, clearly of Buddhism's Mahayana branch, bore a fiery mien; the third, which Li told us came from Thailand and must have belonged to the Theravada branch, was slender and ascetic-looking. The ceiling was covered with bright squares. As in the Shrine to the Earth God, fruit, cookies, and cans of food lay on an offering table.

The next shrine, Chihnan Main Temple, honoring Lu Tung-pin, was modern and grandiose. Since our chief interest was in the more traditional faiths of Taiwan, we did not linger.

The Taoist temple Lin Hsiao Pao Tien was an imposing five-story structure dedicated to the Jade Emperor. In Taiwan he was regarded as the Supreme God of Taoism and also as the God of Heaven worshipped by many, including some Buddhists. The temple also housed a training school for Taoist priests where Li sometimes lectured. Standing there in the dark silent night we could hear the soft sounds of a waterfall, seeming to surround us with the flow of time.

Several devotees were going from one temple to another with offerings of flowers and fruit. "They believe this makes it more certain, a good afterlife," said Li.

Near the summit stood the Chihnan Confucius Temple. A one-storied building, it was smaller and simpler than other Confucius temples we had seen. This one had a special attraction, we realized as we moved through the front hall, past an image of Confucius flanked by two other immortals, on to the back. On all sides, more than 100 images of Buddhist, Taoist, and folk gods and goddesses gazed back at us. Here they were all worshipped together.

We moved outside and stood quietly, looking at the temples down the holy mountain.

"Confucian, Buddhist, Taoist, folk—could you say all of them are different paths of the Way, the Tao?"

He smiled. "You could say that."

Japan: Shinto, the Indigenous Tradition

Like Taoism, Shinto emerged out of a shadowy matrix of myths, stories, and ancient practices of the people who inhabited the Japanese islands before recorded history began. It refers to "the divine way" of interaction of the Japanese people with each other, and also means "the way of the *kami*." Japan is seen as the land of the *kami* (gods or spirits) who dwell in the natural world.[1]

According to Japan's creation story, Izanagi (a male *kami*) and Izanami (his spouse) produced the islands by thrusting the "jewel spear of heaven" into the waters below. As they raised the spear point up out of the water, the drops solidified into the Japanese islands. The couple descended to the land they had created, and produced other *kami* and other elements of the cosmos. From their daughter, the Sun Goddess Amaterasu, came the imperial line of Japan.

The homeland and Japanese people, then, are seen as unique, even sacred, but the rest of the world is not excluded. Indeed, "*kami*" signifies not only the gods of heaven and earth, but also anything that inspires awe, or expresses some sense of vitality. It is the diffuse sacred power that sustains life—a concept not unlike the belief of many American Indians in Wakan Tanka. For Shinto, human life lies at the center of the universe, but animals, rocks, birds, trees, or seemingly inanimate objects also partake of this force; they are part of a reverential interaction. As in Taoism and many native faiths, certain mountains have special powers and are worshipped as sacred.

Even today, when less than 30 percent of the population lives in agricultural areas, Shinto festivals celebrate rice planting, rice harvesting, and the offering of new rice as thanksgiving. The love of fetes linked to the natural world is also expressed in the star and the chrysanthemum festivals. Like traditional Russian Orthodox peasants, Shinto believers see each human as part of a continuous stream of life that flows through ancestors and on through posterity.

Today few Japanese take the creation story literally, but Shinto is very much a part of daily life. Japanese frequently make pilgrimages to the shrine of Amaterasu at Ise and to other holy places. Shinto shrines can be found on the roofs of department stores, and even hard-nosed industrialists pray for the blessings of the *kami* before launching a new enterprise. It is still customary that a Shinto priest officiate at birth and marriage ceremonies and many families still have a Shinto *kamidana*, a "god-shelf" for daily prayers.

While they are all interrelated, four types can be distinguished: Shinto of the Imperial House (not open to the general public), Shrine Shinto, Sect Shinto, and Folk Shinto. Shrine Shinto revolves around worship of the *kami* at sacred buildings considered to be their dwellings. For nearly a century the combination of Shrine Shinto and Shinto of the Imperial House, a combination known as State Shinto, was the official religion of Japan. The Allied forces disestablished it in 1945. Sect Shinto refers to the movement consisting of 13 major sects—sometimes known as the "Shinto-based new religions"—formed during the nineteenth century. Folk Shinto has no formal organizational structure or doctrine; it centers on ceremonies to foster good harvests and rites to the spirits (not *kami* in the full sense) at roadside and home shrines.

Since World War II, many Japanese, bewildered and disillusioned by defeat and the Emperor's announcement that he was an ordinary mortal, have strayed from Shinto. Some also lost faith in Buddhism or the very institution of religion. Many lapsed into confusion and apathy. Others began searching for fresh sources of security. It was in this atmosphere that the new forms of the "new religions" proliferated, and came to be known as the "new new religions."

Each "new religion" contains features from one (or more) of the already existing religions, generally Shinto and Buddhism, has an identifiable founder, and usually began by establishing itself among the common people. Most do not make exclusive claims to absolute Truth. Significantly, they first appeared in the early nineteenth century during another era of confusion: feudal society was collapsing and poor peasants and city laborers were experiencing impoverishment. Oomoto was one of the "new religions" that came out of a rural setting.

Oomoto: Daughter of Shinto

Its founder was a woman. On the lunar New Year, 1892, at the age of 56, Nao Deguchi, the widow of a poor carpenter, felt possessed by a *kami*. She conceived a faith in the *kami* Konjin, who created paradise out of the wicked world. Later she was joined by Deguchi Onisaburo, a religious practitioner who was born into a destitute family near Kameoka and eventually became her son-in-law. They developed Oomoto (meaning the Great Source), a faith system embracing purification rituals and methods of spiritual healing largely based on shamanistic techniques. More controversial was its political agenda—namely, opposition to capitalists, landlords, and industrialists, who were displacing the peasants; reconstruction of the state, emphasizing a return to agrarian society; and preparation for the fulfillment of Oomoto's apocalyptic prophecies of a restoration of just government by the *kami*.

Oomoto has experienced a turbulent history, because pre-World War II governments mistook its message as a cry for violent overthrow of the regime. Since the end of World War II, it has placed great emphasis on world peace and a new world order, and fervently promoted ecumenical services and the international language Esperanto. It has also participated in international, interfaith conferences, including several devoted to preserving the planet.

A Visit to Oomoto's Teaching Center

At Kameoka, we were welcomed with great warmth by Masamichi Tanaka. A lithe, slender man, who had been on the Oomoto staff for 20 years, he immediately conducted us to a lecture room to receive an overview of the faith. Oomoto's rituals, altars, and vestments are largely derived from Shinto, he explained. Like Shinto families, every Oomoto home has a *kamidana*. But Oomoto is extremely respectful of other world faiths, regarded as so many branches of a single tree. Oomoto drew from the Shingon and Tendai sects of Buddhism, and founder Nao Deguchi urged that followers work to realize the ideal world of the Buddhist savior Miroku. Oomoto priests sometimes hold funerals and other services with their Buddhist counterparts, and Oomoto followers believe in reincarnation and ancestor worship, traditionally Buddhist concepts. Women can become priests. Indeed, the role of spiritual leader always goes to a woman, through a daughter-succession originating with Nao Deguchi. "Women guard the spiritual," we were told; men are "born aggressive." But men can take other roles. The "spiritual advisor" to the spiritual leader is always a man: it is he who travels to conferences and manages affairs.

Among the spiritual leaders who had visited here were the Dalai Lama; Dennis Banks, American Indian Movement leader; and James Parks Morton, dean of New York's Cathedral of St. John the Divine. Morton had participated in services with Oomoto priests; in return, Oomoto priests had visited the cathedral for joint rituals. Thus Oomoto followers lived their belief that all religions are one, issuing from the God of the Beginning and the End, the Creator of the Universe.

Then we were shown a video of an all-night purification ritual. At the beginning, a priest in a flowing white vestment with wide sleeves rubbed sticks to ignite a fire, and from it lit candles. Then he blessed the faithful with cleansing rites, bowed at the altar, and presented an offering of rice, beans, fish, turnips, seaweed, cabbage, lotus leaf, bananas, and oranges. The younger priests, likewise garbed in white robes and plumed black caps tied under their chins, prostrated themselves before the altar, whereupon the chief priest made another low bow, the

Dean James Parks Morton, while dean of St. John the Divine Cathedral, poses in group photo with Mme. Kiyoku Deguchi (right), Spiritual Leader of Oomoto.

congregation joined in prayer, and two girls performed a purification dance. After a procession at dawn to the river, the congregation chanted, jars holding rice paper were thrown into the water, and priests tossed out soybeans for the faithful to take home and plant in their gardens.

Both the rice paper and the unglazed jars disintegrate in the water; they are biodegradable, Tanaka informed us. Moreover, Oomoto conducts several environmental programs. Its grounds here have been designated a wildlife sanctuary. The sect also sponsors "save energy" programs, tree-planting, and a campaign to teach waste prevention. It encourages people to grow their own food, especially with macrobiotic organic methods using waste wood enzymes for manure, and it publishes a magazine that includes articles on environmental problems. Oomoto does not take action as a group to influence government policy—a stance understandable in light of the sect's troubles with earlier regimes—and leaves that decision to individuals.

Neither Tanaka nor the other Oomoto members we met conveyed a sense of believing that the world was undergoing a pervasive environmental crisis. They seemed to understand parts of the crisis, but not the whole picture. It was not surprising. Like middle-class Americans, they were protected from the most glaring realities, for, like Americans, they were living in a rich and exploitative society. Nevertheless, they were making more efforts to heal Earth's wounds than were members of most other religions. And they were reaching out to work with other faith traditions.

While Tanaka prepared to take us to the main shrine, he told us about the Oomoto School of Traditional Arts. People from all over the world come to study Noh drama, Budo (martial arts), calligraphy, flower arrangement, the tea ceremony, weaving, ceramics, and both folk and ceremonial dancing; students contribute some of their artistry to the Moon Festival and other celebrations. Next to the shrine that he was about to show us stood a Noh stage, as well as a house and garden for the tea ceremony. The arts, he believed, have always been closely connected with religious experience. Indeed, Oomoto's co-founder Onisaburo once said, "Art gives rise to religion." Closely connected with this belief was one of Onisaburo's great rules of learning: "Observe the phenomena of Nature and you will be able to glimpse the body of God."

As our host led us up the path toward the shrine, we began to experience a sense of timelessness. We moved through groves of centuries-old trees, past ancient springs and mounds of stones; everywhere there was silence. At last we arrived at a moat, circling the remains of a 400-year-old castle that lay on a hilltop within the grounds. Beyond the bridge, on a forested knoll, stood the main sanctuary. It was a simple rectangular structure of fine lustrous wood, with gracefully curved tile roofs. With its broad porches, large windows, and wide entrance, it was virtually open on three sides to the natural world. The floor of the spacious hall, empty of chairs, was spread with straw mats. In the inner sanctum, flowers, plants, and fruit graced the altar. As we stood there, only the wind, the singing of birds, the rustle of leaves, and the soft sound of distant water broke the stillness. The altar and the natural world seemed to merge.

Reflections

We remembered standing on another sacred slope, the "holy mountain" outside Taipei. . . . Taoism and Shinto, two traditions so far apart, yet so akin, seem to reflect the same core experience: everything in this universe pulses with life. Hence like Native American worldviews, they do not exclude the miraculous or supernatural. And while Taoism is more metaphysical than Shinto's *kami*-centered perspective, both see human life as one aspect of a great cosmic pattern.

Yet the focus is on this world, manifested in the fruits of the earth arrayed on the altar. Individual salvation in the next world plays some part, but it is more important to concentrate human energies on this terrestrial existence, with all its joys and sorrows, its opportunities for dancing, painting, singing—for celebrating the many revelations of the life-force. Powers of renewal lie within ourselves and the world that we know, rather than with some father deity on high.

Both Taoism and Shinto have always been remarkably open to varying perceptions of truth. In both China and Taiwan, some sects have combined Confucianism and Buddhism with Taoist practices, and Taoist priests, like their Oomoto counterparts, sometimes officiate with Buddhist priests. Taoist mysticism has influenced the Chinese Zen schools that became Rinzai and Soto in Japan. In a broader perspective some Taoist beliefs were adopted, at various times, in Japanese courts and among the people.

The ancient Chinese concept of *tao*, basic to Confucianism and Taoism and influential in Buddhism and Shinto, conveys a sense of perpetual motion. To contemplate the *yin-yang* emblem of the *tao* is to see an image of balance, and also an image of Earth, of the cosmos itself. To meditate on it is to experience mutuality, mystery, movement.

Reflecting on Taoism and Shinto, we sensed that today they are moving, evolving. Despite inertia and resistance, they are reaching out, however tentatively, to include action to protect the source of all life.

Buddhism

Although limited in scope, some of the most significant work in the ecospiritual movement is emerging from the Buddhists. Since Buddhism is generally regarded as passive, this might seem surprising. Let us first touch on some highlights of the tradition.

Gautama Buddha, the Enlightened One, was born about 563 BCE under a tree in India, near the present border with Nepal. Today most followers are concentrated in Southeast Asia, East Asia, and the Himalayas. The Theravada Buddhists of Sri Lanka, Thailand/Siam, Myanmar/Burma, Laos, and Cambodia revere the historical Gautama Buddha (Theravada means "Teaching of the Elders") and its holy books, the Pali Canon, are seen as closest to the sayings of the historical Buddha. One is expected to work out one's individual salvation in a gradual process by following faithfully the way that he demonstrated.

In the Mahayana tradition (which began to appear in the second century BCE and eventually came to dominate in China, Japan, Korea, Taiwan, and Vietnam), the faithful also venerate Gautama Buddha, but regard him as one of many Buddhas who have appeared in many universes, all of them manifestations of one primordial Buddha nature. Mahayana seeks the welfare of all, and salvation may be obtained through the aid of *bodhisattvas*, saintly humans who voluntarily refrain from entering the final blessed state of Nirvana in order to act as helpers of humanity. The third form of Buddhism, Vajrayāna, is also known as Mantrayana, Esoteric Buddhism, or Tantrism. Originating in India, it was preserved in only a few places, mainly Japan (where it became known

as Shingon), Nepal, and Tibet. Hence it is sometimes called Tibetan Buddhism, or Lamaism. There are many sects as well, but Buddhists stress
that the differences within the tradition are far less important than the
commonalities.

Buddhism does not hold that it alone holds the "true faith." In Vietnam, for example, many families perform their devotions at Buddhist,
Christian, and Confucian shrines in their homes, seeing no contradiction
in their all-embracing vision of Truth. In its pure form, Buddhism is not
theistic: it does not conceive of God as one and perfect, just and merciful,
endowed with mind and will, and conceivable in images drawn from
human life. Indeed, in its pure form, Buddhism does not speak of God;
the Buddha is, rather, the revered teacher who can show the way. In many
Mahayana sects, it is true, the Buddha has become a deity to whom to
address prayers. In all three branches, the emphasis is on ethical living
and on Enlightenment. And while the Abrahamic faiths are God-centered,
Buddhism is centered more on the cosmos.

The Buddha declared Four Noble Truths: (1) suffering is with us
throughout life; (2) the cause is craving, desire; (3) the way out of suffering is the way beyond desire; and (4) that way is the Eightfold Noble
Path: right views, right intention, right speech, right action, right livelihood, right effort, right mindfulness, and right concentration.

Many of Buddha's teachings focus on *dharma* (in Sanskrit) or
dhamma (in Pali), which means pure Truth, the Way, the teaching, the
actual nature of being, the law of nature. An important aspect of *dhamma*
is *balance*, often manifested as "the middle way."

"Yes, but also—" is a response Westerners are likely to encounter in
any discussions of morality or the-nature-of-things. Yes, the Buddha in
that pagoda is the historical Buddha. But also, there are as many Buddhas
as there are sands in the sea. Yes, in the Scriptures there is a precept
against killing. But also, in certain circumstances, as when the community is in danger, killing by laymen may be permitted. While stressing
faithfulness to the *dharma*, a monk will also tell you, "In Buddhism is
no absolute dogma. All is according to circumstances."

Hence Buddhists are likely to speak of precepts (*silas*) rather than
commandments, of wrong acts that can be rectified rather than any persistent sense of sinfulness. "Everything in the world has relations," says
the monk. "Nothing can be evaluated independently. All is in flux. It is
the law of interdependent causes." This does not mean that "reality" is
entirely a matter of subjectivity; it suggests the absence of metaphysical
absolutes. The categorical either-or thinking so characteristic of Aristo-
telian/Cartesian views of reality is foreign to Buddhist thought.

Moreover, many Buddhist thinkers maintain that Buddhism is more
scientific than other religions, and cite correspondences between Ein-

stein's theory of relativity and the Buddhist doctrine of interdependent co-arising.[2]

Throughout, there is great emphasis on compassion—a feeling that goes beyond pity and becomes feeling *with* others, with both their sufferings and their joys; it is a feeling that can bring a deep sense of oneness with all beings, human and non-human. Indeed, *karuna*, compassion, is seen as a supreme cosmic power. The emphasis on universal compassion is perhaps Buddhism's greatest contribution to humankind's search for meaning today.

Thus the dynamic interdependence central to ecological thinking is fundamental to Buddhism. It is an interdependence that goes beyond conceptual paradigms, and summons experience. Vietnamese monk Thich Nhat Hanh calls it *interbeing*: an intuitive, subtle sense of interacting with every entity in the dynamic cosmos.

To be sure, average people—"the folk"—rarely experience all these fruits of contemplation. While short periods of meditation are often integrated into their daily lives, elements of animism, even magic, also blend into the practice of popular Buddhism.

When one of us, Marjorie, was in Vietnam in 1963-1964, talking with monks and students who had sparked the successful non-violent campaign to bring down French-installed dictator Ngo Dinh Diem, a monastic at Saigon's Xa Loi Pagoda explained: "We monks follow Zen. The religion of the people is Amidism, Pure Land. That means the Western Paradise. For one who is enlightened, however, the place is a matter of indifference, for Pure Land lies within oneself."[3]

Entering the Mahayana pagodas of Vietnam was to witness the people celebrating their faith in an exuberant, earthy way. In the courtyard, cross-legged women sold incense, candy, and fruit; barefoot children played together; young people strolled and watched the world go by. Within the pagoda, the faithful prostrated themselves before an altar festively decorated with green oranges, bananas, and coconuts, while the sounds of cymbals and gongs reverberated through the temple. The pagoda was the center of both spiritual and communal life in those years, before the deepening war virtually demolished the traditional society.

As the present Vietnamese government struggles for power and identity in a world dominated by global capitalism, it perceives the traditional Buddhists as representatives of a rival power. But that is another story. Over the centuries Buddhism has suffered persecution and fought injustice in many countries, and this is still true today. Yet because of its remarkable openness, adaptability, and inclusiveness, Buddhism endures. It continues to evolve today.

A NOTE ON AMERICAN BUDDHISM

Since the late 1950s, Buddhism has witnessed a boom among growing numbers of Americans. By 1999 there were some 100,000 adherents in this country and nearly 1,100 English-language Buddhist teaching centers.

American Buddhism differs from its Asian forebears in several ways. Although there are some monks and nuns, for the most part it has rejected the monastic system. Women exercise more authority. Some groups tend to be more democratic in decision-making. Especially among celebrities who find this faith to be exotic and chic, there are comparatively few devotees who faithfully practice the ideal of renouncing accumulation of wealth and living as simply as possible. The emphasis is on the individual, on one's own enlightenment.

Indeed, says Japanese-Canadian religion professor Victor Sogon Hori, some overturn beliefs basic to most Buddhist traditions by imposing Western ideas of "self-fulfillment" on traditional teachings stressing that the individual exists only in relation to others. For example, after one Zen retreat, Chinese-Americans said the week's meditations had made them more aware of their faults in dealing with others; Anglo-Americans said it helped them in understanding self-realization. Using Buddhist labels for Western concepts, making *dhamma* into a middle-class commodity, says Hori, could eventually co-opt Buddhism and make it incapable of criticizing Western society.[4]

ENGAGED BUDDHISM

Some American Buddhists give the impression of believing that "socially engaged Buddhism" was invented in the West. While it is true that excellent writing on the subject has appeared here, involvement in social and political action has long been one strand in Buddhist faith.

True, the overall emphasis is on renouncing worldly desires and the ego, the small self. But also, this many-faceted tradition embraces what some would call a vision of the Large Self, a vision that can take many forms. In 1963 a Vietnamese monk involved in the resistance to dictator Diem explained, "In the Lotus Flower scriptures, it is written that for monks, burning the self is allowed in the case of forgetting the small self. The Large Self is *there*"—he pointed upwards—"and the small self here—" He pointed to his body.

Later Marjorie came to know two Vietnamese students who had joined in a pact with two other youths: if all other means of non-violent protest failed—and the people, who had lost their morale, failed to become rearoused—the four would immolate themselves, one by one. In the end the monks forbade them to do it. After we had talked many times, one of them, Aí, confided: "The sacrifice would have been *for* life. To help bring freedom and peace to the people. You could call that forgetting the small self for the Large Self."

Lest self-immolation be seen by Westerners as a contradiction of non-violence, it should be emphasized that Vietnamese monks used this form of protest only as a last desperate resort; generally forbade it to lay people; and considered that in circumstances of all-encompassing threat, it was not suicide but sacrifice.[5]

Aí's vow could be called an example of "engaged Buddhism," the practice of compassion with the suffering of others through active involvement in society's problems. In Vietnam it took political expression in the Buddhist-led movement against Diem. Later Thich Nhat Hanh left for the West and became the leading Vietnamese voice for peace. He formed the Buddhist Peace Delegation in Paris, where the two of us met him to learn more about his plans for a Third Way. It was to be a middle way between the extremes of capitalism and communism. Today, as a poet, he continues to spread the message of inner and outer peace. He visits the United States regularly, and three Buddhist centers, all following Nhat Hanh's tradition, have been established in Vermont.

Especially in Southeast Asia, Buddhist history has been witness to many liberation movements led by monks, who felt that an assault on their nation's autonomy was an assault on the culture and Buddhism itself. Most of them left their traditional roles only temporarily, to respond to the need for charismatic, respected leaders. Today "engaged Buddhism" has taken a less revolutionary but more self-conscious and articulate form.

Sarvodaya (the Awakening of All), for example, originated in India under Gandhi but became especially active in Sri Lanka, where the population is two-thirds Buddhist. In the 1970s and early 1980s, it brought middle-class youth from the cities to work with the outcasts and created work camps to serve the people. It brought community renewal to some 6,000 villages before the long-simmering civil war virtually tore the country apart.[6]

The Buddhist Peace Fellowship, founded by Robert Aitken, presently the Roshi and Director of the Diamond Sangha, a Zen community in Honolulu, follows Thich Nhat Hanh's principles and publishes the *Buddhist Peace Fellowship Newsletter*. The International Network of Engaged Buddhists was established in Thailand with three distinguished patrons: the Dalai Lama, Thich Nhat Hanh, and Buddhadasa Bhikku. Today there are some 200 members from 26 countries (including the United States). Its concerns include spiritual training, women's issues, human rights, preserving the planet, alternative development, and the integration of spirituality and activism.

In the United States, Charlene Spretnak, Joanna Macy, Kenneth Kraft, Paula Green, Andrew Getz, Gary Snyder, and Robert Aitken have emerged as some of the notable writers about engaged Buddhism.

It is to Asia, however, that one should turn to see how monks, nuns, and priests are heeding the call from many Buddhist milieus to take a stand for social and environmental justice.

Japan: Rush to Development, Refuge in Tradition

The Japanese live in a world of paradoxes. Their country ranks among the first in gross domestic product, as well as number of years to expect to spend on this planet. Yet many feel the quality of life is declining. Japan is one of the most efficient users of energy in the world, although it remains a major source of global greenhouse emissions. Middle-class Japanese possess more leisure time than in the past, but much of it is spent in the frenetic pursuit of visible possessions in glittering shopping malls. They seek to refresh their weary spirits by making pilgrimages to religious shrines in ancient forests. Yet Japanese enterprise finances depletion of Asian rainforest, the main source of hardwood used as molding for concrete in the construction industry as well as for toothpicks. Shinto and Buddhism revere all life. Yet the degradation of water quality in many lakes has killed a variety of creatures who live there. Most Japanese feel a nostalgia for the land as it was when a rural village truly represented a community of values. Yet their society finances bulldozing of Japanese farmland to build industrial "parks," and in other countries promotes destruction of farmland and forest in order to create golf courses where businessmen regularly fly on long "fun" weekends, an arrangement actually cheaper than paying membership fees in Japanese golf clubs.

Although they try to banish these paradoxes from awareness, a lingering malaise persists. "Is all this perhaps meaningless?" many ask themselves. "Isn't there something more?" A few find meaning in working with secular environmental organizations like Friends of the Earth and World Wildlife Fund (WWF)-Japan. Others grope for a spiritual answer. Some find it in Shinto or Buddhism. But in today's secular Japanese society, the long-established religions have lost strength. On the other hand, there is a surge of interest in the "new religions" and "new new religions" that emerged out of Shinto and Buddhism. Even as millions of Japanese tourists course through the world, they reach back for identity through fierce pride in the Japanese way of doing things, in their indigenous Shinto, and in a Buddhism that bears a distinctively Japanese imprint.

THE WAY OF THE BUDDHA IN JAPAN

In Japanese history Buddhism took its place beside Shinto, religious Taoism (which at one time took the form of a government bureau of religious Taoism), Confucianism (which never created an organization with priests, but served as the basis of Japanese education and social relationships), and Japanese folk-religion, unwritten sets of beliefs and customs that still exert some indirect influence today. Buddhism in practice cannot properly be understood apart from them, for through the centuries all have influenced each other. Moreover, the Japanese tend to be puzzled by Westerners who ask: "What religion do you belong to?" To participate in both Shinto and Buddhism at certain times in one's life is regarded as normal, and enhances rather than detracts from one's sense of unity in viewing the world.

Many Japanese consider the *kami* and *bodhisattvas* to be the same. Many know little about the doctrine or beliefs of the faith with which they have some family affiliation, and do not consider that knowledge to be particularly important. Shinto priests often preside at birth and marriage ceremonies, Buddhist priests at funeral services and periodic memorials. Traditionally, every family has a miniature Shinto shrine, together with a Buddhist altar for offerings to all its family ancestors and recurrent memorials to certain ancestors.

The family, then, is a central social and religious institution. In general the Buddhist temple is not the place for weekly services (although some sects do have regular sermons); the temple is commonly regarded as the site of rites for the dead.

Japanese faiths posit no sharp distinction between humans and deity, humans and Nature. The ideal of harmony among these three elements of life is a foundation of Japanese religion.

Buddhism came to Japan from China and Korea in the sixth century CE, together with other elements of Chinese culture, but over time has acquired distinctive Japanese characteristics. Several important schools have arisen which possess lasting influence. One is Shingon, rooted in the Tantrism of Tibet. The others (belonging to Mahayana) are Tendai, which derives from China and tries to unite differing viewpoints; Pure Land, based on faith in the salvific mercy of Amida (Amitabha) and rebirth in his Pure Land; Zen, which eschews complex rituals and focuses on direct insight and enlightenment through meditation; and Nichiren, which has aimed to restore the "right teaching" of the Lotus Sutra in order to bring virtue and order to troubled society. Some powerful, lay religio-political organizations today, such as the "new religion" Soka Gakkai, are related to Nichiren's teaching that active involvement in social welfare and politics is important.

Has Buddhism lost its importance in the secularized society of to-day's Japan?

One cannot answer so complex a question without looking at what has been happening to organized religion as a whole. The movement of people from country to city erodes traditional family ties to a specific parish temple. Discontinuance of government subsidies to Buddhist temples and Shinto shrines has meant that many priests have had to find part-time jobs to supplement their income. Buddhists are not happy with this development, but it is less difficult to accept than it would be in Theravada countries, where monasticism is the norm; for several centuries Japanese priests have been allowed to marry and live in the community. Finally, in a country where nation, culture, and religion have been as intertwined as in Japan, the globalization of culture has placed great strain on religious life and the sense of cultural identity.

Yet the religious impulse is still vital. Although university students tend to disdain organized religion, they evince great interest in religious activities and new expressions of spirituality. Ancient Shinto shrines and Buddhist temples all over the country remind the people of a glorious heritage, and along roadsides people still pray before *kami* or *bodhisattvas*. Although today's nuclear families perform rites before home altars less frequently, their ancestors remain important. Religious festivals draw enthusiastic crowds. Nature is still celebrated in painting, literature, and music. Many sacred places have become tourist sites. Often set on mountains and in forests, they offer worshippers an opportunity for purification and expressing gratitude to the deities while enjoying the glories of Nature. To most Japanese, these experiences blend together.

The proliferation of cults attests to the fascination with miracles and mystery, seances and spiritual power. Good luck charms obtained at religious centers can be seen all over Japan. Does this mean that the Japanese, apparently an eminently rational people, are superstitious by nature? Not quite. It seems to be not so much a clear belief in the supernatural as a pragmatic unwillingness to rule it out.

One of the cults with the most powerful appeal is Soka Gakkai, which criticizes the reigning materialism in strong terms and offers a religious alternative. Although accused of fascist tendencies because of its zealous conversion activities and participation in politics through its links with Komeito (the only religiously based party in Japanese history), it inspires a spirit of sacrifice that some have compared with early Christianity. Significantly, both Soka Gakkai and the "new new religion" Agonshu speak of nuclear war and environmental depredation, reflecting a widespread anxiety that the Japanese find difficult to repress.

Some Japanese have believed that mainstream Buddhism would reorganize and become a more dynamic force of renewal. If that occurs, will it embrace a strong movement to ally Buddhism and an explicit ecological ethic? Some environmentalists have begun to include Buddhist ideas in their work. Another potential force lies in the religious leaders who attended the 1986 faith and conservation conference at Assisi, or meetings of the Global Forum (one of which was held in Kyoto in 1993). Thus far, these discussions have seldom filtered down to parish level. Yet they suggest new thinking among scientists, intellectuals, and some political and religious leaders.

For example, Masao Ichishima, who attended the 1988 Global Forum and heads the Buddhist instruction faculty at Taisho University, told us he often gives "environmental lectures" at international conferences, on topics such as Indian and Chinese periods of Buddhist history when the faith was "very ecological." Since our visit, he has begun to introduce the issue of "environmental deterioration and the crisis of values" more often into his classes on world religions.

Some priests do preach ecological sermons. Parishioners are interested, but often feel helpless because "power lies with the politicians." A few young priests have been engaged in action to halt nuclear power. Sometimes irate parishioners will paste their cars with "Pay attention to the spiritual!" Yet the priests persist, and the environmental action they provoke has been spreading. Out of Sainenji Temple in Hyogo Prefecture, Keisuke Aoki runs a citizens' group working to reconstruct the natural shoreline along the local section of the Seto Inland Sea. In Kyoto, Kensho Nagao, the priest of Jojakkoji Temple, launched a drive to clean up discarded beverage cans, then went on to fight for a city ordinance to deal with the cans. Since then he and his parishioners have branched out into other concerns.

A Buddhist Dam-Buster

The ancient capital of Kyoto is home to some of the most revered Buddhist temples and Shinto shrines in the country. Today in some parts of the city they are overshadowed by massive hotels, office buildings, and convention centers.

Soon after our arrival, we learned that one symbol of this frantic drive for development was a proposed flood control project on the Kamo River. The plan was being fostered by a de facto coalition of developers, the powerful Ministry of Construction, and wealthy city merchants. It was opposed not only by environmentalists, but by Shincho Tanaka, resident priest of Shimyoin Temple in the beautiful, thickly wooded Kamogahata Valley north of Kyoto.

Tanaka had become the central figure in the movement to stop the dam. His research had convinced him that not only would it fill the Kamo

River with silt, but the new lake created behind it would inundate some 200 acres of forest and become contaminated from an existing industrial waste dump. Pointing out that the prevailing custom in today's Japan was to plan such a project without considering the environmental consequences first, the priest was demanding that an objective environmental assessment be made before going further.

We met Tanaka and his wife Tomoe at their home in the temple itself, set beside a stream which was the source of the Kamo River. Clad in brown baggy pants and a dark green loose jacket crossed over in front, he was a stocky man with short black hair, a broad face, wide lips, and stubby fingers. As we sat on cushions around a low table with a brocaded cover under which we slipped our feet for warmth, he often leaned back and let out a belly laugh. His energy seemed to fill the room. What a contrast with the tense, almost harassed-looking faces of many businessmen we had seen on the streets!

"Japanese love for Nature! Ha!" He shook his head vigorously. "That was long ago. Today, Nature is cash money. And Japanese who say they 'love Nature,' most of them look for something man-made, artificial. But *here* one feels Nature as it really is."

We looked out the windows at the porch overhanging the stream and fish pond. The light on the branches above the waterfall cast the scene in dramatic chiaroscuro, and the ceaseless sound of flowing water seemed a reflection of eternity.

His wife, a fine-featured, oval-faced woman with a gentle manner, insisted that we call her Tomoe, then led us to the porch. "This water we use for cleaning, for cooking, for drinking. It is pure. And those fish you see in the pond, I cannot eat them. They are my family."

"The stream water is purest from midnight till two in the morning," said Tanaka. "Every morning at six we offer this purest water to the principal image of the Buddha. We are Buddhist, but this temple is close to Shinto. There was Shinto here before the Buddhists arrived. Some people pray to calm the spirit of the Kamo River. Water is the life of humans, frogs, all life!

"But now," he added, "the people of Japan forget that. Today government and big business, they work together. So Japan has big money, big power. So it wants to spend big money on big dams, big airports, big hotels. Twenty-eight hundred dams in Japan! All this bigness on very small islands! Japan is sinking, with cash in hand."

"And realizing all this spurred you to take action on the dam?"

"Yes, yes! We gathered friends to plan demonstrations. People down the road formed another group and we work together. The older people here are foresters. Most of the young go to work in Kyoto, they do not like to work in forests, they are drawn to the bright lights. Almost all

Japanese people have low consciousness of environment. They dance rock music. They think of fashion. And every day, *pachinko*—Japanese pinball—games."

"But our sons—they are 16 and 20—they work with us," interjected Tomoe. "Every Sunday we all gather here to plan action. Everyone takes home work. We have a word processor and we make leaflets. Newspapers write about us, and we speak on television, sometimes on the national network. We make petitions. Like, 'Do you care for the river? It brings life water to Kyoto, just as the twin Kamo shrines have always assured Kyoto of the River God's protection. The beautiful Kamogahata Valley would be filled with an artificial lake, and downstream, a historic river would be robbed of life.' Then we pointed out the reasons not to build the dam."

"Tell us more about how you became involved in all this."

"It all began in 1987, when the Kyoto Prefecture established the Kamo River Improvement Council. *Improvement*!" Tanaka grimaced. "We began to do research. By late 1988 we and some scientists had enough information to rouse the people and hold a meeting. Two months later, we formed the Kamo River Dam Opposition Committee. We convinced lawyers from the Bar Association to investigate the issue, and a citizens' committee inspected the area. Then a citizens' group, called the Public Eye, asked the prefecture to release information on the dam to the public. The prefecture did, but Public Eye found the report—how do you say?—full of holes."

"Meanwhile, several Japanese newspapers published stories about the project," continued Tomoe. "The Kyoto Symphony Orchestra played a benefit concert for us, and the Japan Environmental Exchange held a discussion of the project, and led a hike to look at the area. The Exchange is sponsored by Americans. We have become an international issue!"

"And *then*—very important—a *Los Angeles Times* reporter visited here and wrote a long story," said Tanaka. "And the person who introduced him was another American—Rick Davis, who is editor of the *Japan Environment Monitor*.[7] Yes, it is very important that people see this isn't just a Kyoto problem. It is the world's problem. The Kamo, it is a river of the world."

"But the prefecture got more difficult," sighed Tomoe. "It refused to reveal the 20 dam sites being considered. Then an 'independent' commission *chosen* by the prefecture announced there is nothing wrong with keeping them secret."

"Democracy! Ha!" Tanaka snorted.

"But you haven't given up?"

"Never! We are collecting signatures for a big petition drive. And I shall make visits to people who are famous here—philosophers, historians, other scientists—and get their support."

Two months after our departure, the petition drive took off in earnest. Well-known intellectuals submitted requests that dam construction be reconsidered. The Kyoto Bar Association filed a suit demanding annulment of the prefecture's decision to withhold information on the construction plan. At the same time, the Opposition Committee, infuriated but invigorated by the refusal, stepped up its efforts; within three months it gathered 26,000 signatures of people calling for cancellation of the plan. At a prefectural assembly on July 2, 1990, the governor formally declared that the dam project was cancelled. Democracy and the environmental movement had won a significant victory in a country where such activism is still young.

Today Shincho Tanaka, the upstart priest-*provocateur* of these actions, continues to be engaged in activities designed to heighten awareness that the natural world still lingering around Kyoto is a sacred trust to pass on to future generations of humans and other beings. One project is to invite city children to his temple, with its waterfall, stream, and ancient trees. "They can hardly believe that the spring water—delicious!—which flows down from the large rocks behind the temple can be drunk without disinfecting it first!" He laughs, and then sighs. "We have a long way to go."

A GREEN KINDERGARTEN ON TEMPLE GROUNDS

Traditionally, Japanese education fosters conformity. The atmosphere tends to be regimented, and even kindergartners learn to march in kiddie fife-and-drum corps. Children are seldom encouraged to be curious about the natural world.

Yet Eisho Yoshida, resident priest of the Buddhist Eishoji Temple in Kofu, and his wife Takako have confronted tradition by creating a "green kindergarten" within the temple precincts.

It was Rick Davis who introduced us to the couple. Forrest, the son of Rick and his Japanese wife Eiko, was enrolled at the school. Before we entered the temple, he explained that in Japan, kindergartens are private and children generally attend for three years between the ages of three and five. To Reverend Yoshida, and Rick as well, it was the ideal age for acquiring a love for nature that would last for life.

We were met at the door with an effusive handshake from Yoshida himself—a husky figure, clad in gray silk pants and vest, with a powerful voice and wide smile. Mrs. Yoshida, a youthful-looking woman wearing blue jeans and a black sweatshirt, welcomed us into the living room, then disappeared into the kitchen where she and her mother were preparing dinner. Thanks to Rick's skilled translation and Yoshida's smattering of English, the conversation flowed even before the priest uncorked a bottle of local Japanese blush wine.

"How did I get started? In 1971 I became director of the daycare center my father began. It was run in the traditional way. My wife and I had other ideas. She is certified teacher, and interested in green principles, too. From her, I learned very much. We began working together.

"Always my idea of a good group has been that everyone—*everyone*—strong or weak, normal or handicapped, joins hands to *make* it real group." He drew a wide circle in the air. "That is not the way it is in Japanese society. You become hierarchized permanently. The competition to 'make it' brings much backstabbing and corruption. People have to have inside and outside faces. It is even true in religion. This is the way to climb up."

"And you believe this is the result of the traditional educational system?"

"Yes, oh yes! It was different in Buddha's time. He fought against castes. Here we go by his precepts that all living things have equality and life is something that comes from Nature." Smiling expansively, he brought out some of the children's drawings. Many showed the grain and vegetables that the pupils were cultivating in the 400-square-meter garden on the temple land. "See?" He pointed excitedly to a picture of

Green kindergarteners harvest vegetables on grounds of Eisho Yoshida's Buddhist temple in Kofu, Japan. (Photo by Rick Davis)

a beet growing. "Beautiful! Why is the child able to see it so clearly? Because he got to know it. He—or she—has seen the leaves going up, up to the sun to gather its rays, and learned how the roots dig down to get water. The children sow the seeds, they water them and watch over what comes up, they harvest. Afterwards they smell the vegetable and hold it and feel the texture. They thank it. Then they cook and eat it. You see what I mean about getting to know the plant? One principle of Buddhist thought is, learn how to see things correctly!" He spread his hands wide, and grinned at us.

We moved to the dining room and sat down on cushions near a sliding screen decorated with blossoms. The couple's nine-year-old son and 13-year-old daughter, together with their grandmother, joined us. As the two women heated the soup at the table, we nibbled soy nuts and turned to Yoshida. "You are saying, then, that drawing the vegetables teaches the children about the cycle of life?" we asked.

"Exactly! Also, the children develop feelings like a mother's. They talk to the vegetables: 'I hope you grow up big and strong!' And they notice shadings of colors. They analyze how one side of a leaf can be smooth, the other side prickly. They see subtleties. So we are teaching the equality inside differences, we spread Buddhist values. People should not be robots, just following what the corporations tell them to do. Also, handicapped children are a little different but also equal. Here we take the handicapped, so they don't go to special schools.

"It is important that children do things with their hands," he added. "Things people did eons ago. If we go on depending on computers, we won't survive. Here we have no computers, right?" He looked at his wife. She nodded and smiled at us. "Computers," he went on, "all they can teach is what we already know. From Nature, children learn something new. Take a persimmon. In the mouth, it is astringent, but if you put it in the sun, it becomes sweet. Computers couldn't teach this. Television couldn't teach it. They learn through *experiencing* Nature."

"Thomas Berry, an American cultural historian, says, 'Earth is the primary Scripture.'"

"He does?" Yoshida's eyes widened. "That is exactly how I feel! Tell me about him."

After we finished doing so, he exclaimed, "He is Buddhist! Oh, I want to read his work. I must study English!" He knocked his head with his knuckles.

"These children sometimes show in song and dance the growing of plants," Rick interpolated. "And once when I came in, they were acting out a storm. One child was the wind, another a tree, another the rain, and so on, and they beat drums to make the sounds of the storm."

We told Yoshida that our talks with influential Buddhist priests in

Japan had revealed that many thought it was important to preserve the planet, but very few took action.

"They are—what shall I say?—the high priests. There are also those who just want to stay comfortable. I am of the people. Our family lives simply. Our only private property is a car, clothing, a few other things. In the end I am fortunate."

"Could you tell us about the influences in your life?"

"Many, many influences! First of all, my wife. Also Rick Davis, the anti-nuclear power movement, the co-op that offers non-poisoned food. Natural medicine. I listen to these ideas, I say 'Ah! Yes! Great idea!' And in turn we become active in educating people.

"It is not easy, no, to be different. But I say, a real Buddhist must act. Most priests, even in my Nichiren sect, just go along. They just want to chant sutras and see money flowing in.

"The corporations and the big shots in the education bureaucracy criticize me. They see this kindergarten as dissident activity. More and more people agree with my approach, so as my name grows, the Establishment hates me more."

Mrs. Yoshida, who had scarcely spoken, but had closely followed the conversation with her eyes, approached us with a gift. It was a small book that they had published on their own, and included a description of the kindergarten's activities, children's drawings, profiles of individual children, a story on the center that Rick Davis had written for the environmental publication *The New Road*, and letters in response to that story from readers as far away as New Jersey and Czechoslovakia.[8] With a smile, she placed a box of candy beside the book. Her mother followed, with a picture she had painted and two placemats she had embroidered.

Yoshida beamed as we voiced our delighted surprise. "This has been a *beautiful* evening! Religion has brought us together. Too often it divides people. Christianity and Buddhism, they are very much the same. They start with simple teachings of the great teachers, Jesus, Buddha. But then, in time, some followers search for money and power, and true teaching gets lost."

"And meanwhile, the earth deteriorates," we observed.

"Yes." He sighed. "And we move faster and faster toward—progress? Still, some people are learning we should go no faster than we can walk."

The entire family stood at the door as we left. "A beautiful evening!" Yoshida repeated, as he seized our hands in a tight grip. "Beautiful! We have communicated with the heart!"

Since that visit, activities at the kindergarten have continued to expand. A program for children who have left to start school has been initiated. This is highly unusual here, says Rick; most kindergartens become totally dissociated from the pupils afterwards. The temple kindergarten has gatherings several times a year where the children learn new things, join in traditional Japanese seasonal events, and take excursions. Summer programs include a two-day gathering at which pupils cook, make their own chopsticks, practice traditional social manners, work at handcrafts, visit a mountain temple, and spend the intervening night together. "Forrest has been quite influenced by this experience," Rick wrote. "You might say, he grew up a little."

To Rick, the kindergarten's "respect for life" education results in a clear difference with many other children. "Our children's cousins, for example, seem typical; they think nothing of torturing insects or small animals to death. I suppose they think it's interesting. But our children echo Mr. Yoshida in saying, 'We have to be kind to little creatures.' They know that if they catch an insect or small animal, they should treat it kindly, give it food, and return it to the wild. Of course, they sometimes forget, and we detect a twinge of regret when the dead insect is produced. So they say, 'Let's return it to the soil,' and go somewhere to bury it.

"Once we raised a dragonfly nymph until it became a dragonfly. Forrest wanted very much to keep that beautiful steel-green creature, but we said, 'The poor thing has been in the water all this time, and now he has just a few days to fly in the sky. What do you think you should do?' He hesitated just a few moments—it's a hard decision for a little boy— and then said, 'I'll let him go.' And he smiled and waved as the dragonfly disappeared among the trees.

"The Yoshidas teach important things through play. For example, making mudballs can teach an important mathematical principle: proportions. To make a good one, you need to work out the proper proportions of dirt and water. Our daughter Heather, who's at the school now, failed miserably at first, but by watching the older girls she soon caught on and now makes a very good mudball. She explained it to me herself: 'You have to get just the right amounts of dirt and water!' It's a question of balance."

Siam/Thailand

DHAMMA VERSUS DYNAMIC GROWTH

In tourist brochures Siam/Thailand* is portrayed as an exotic land of gilded Buddhist pagodas, religious festivals in unspoiled countryside,

---

* We shall use the terms "Thailand" and "Siam" interchangeably, but the preference is for "Siam" since, as scholar Sulak Sivaraksa points out, that was the country's original name; Thailand is a hybrid, Anglicized word and implies chauvinism.

and monks in orange-yellow robes making their daily rounds with begging bowls. Indeed, traditionally every layman has been expected to spend at least a few months or years as a monk, and those who choose monkhood for life have been held in great reverence.

Yet today, although there are more than a quarter-million monks in robes, there are twice as many prostitutes. Monastics are often seen largely as preservers of ceremonies and providers of magical power. Corruption is widespread, not only in government and business but in the *sangha* (the ecclesiastical community) as well.

The faithful are often exploited. To cite one small example: Siamese Buddhists build up merits for reincarnation in the next life, a custom that ranges from filling a monk's begging bowl or helping the poor, to acts to protect animals and birds. One gains merit for releasing them from cages to the wild. Today some businessmen buy up birds and animals that have been hunted down and caged for that purpose, in order that the pious may buy their release.

Especially since the Vietnam War, when the U.S. used Thailand for airbases and "rest and recreation" centers (as early as 1966, there were over 30,000 GIs based in the country), big business has grown in this once-quiet country. Aided by World Bank and Japanese loans, it became a model of dynamic growth. Although nominally a constitutional monarchy, Thailand—except for a democratic hiatus between 1988 and 1991—has been run since 1946 by autocratic rulers, eager to cooperate with the American government and American entrepreneurs. Temples have been demolished, homes razed, and canals filled to make way for wide thoroughfares in Bangkok. Some American professional associations have elected to go halfway round the world to hold meetings here. Sex tours to refresh weary Western and Asian businessmen have proliferated, becoming an important source of foreign exchange. Even traditional funerals often turn into tourist shows. In the rural areas, tranquil fishing villages, such as Phuket, have been transformed into huge beach resorts, and ancient forests have been bulldozed to accommodate hotels, condominiums, and golf courses.

In Bangkok, we were told, traffic was so congested that according to one study, an average commuter spent 44 days a year traveling to and from work. Lung cancer was three times more prevalent than elsewhere in Thailand. One Bangkok hotel, the Shangri-La, used more electricity than one rural province in the northeast. The country suffered from serious water shortages, yet condos often advertised advantages that included jacuzzi, golf courses, tight security systems, and a private solar-heated, temperature-controlled swimming pool for each two-story unit.

The shortage of water and deterioration in water quality were largely rooted in the shrinkage of the forest, which also resulted in soil erosion and flooding. Moreover, as woodland natural habitats for wildlife disappeared, many species had become endangered. Officially, the government was committed to a ban on logging, but handsome multinational deals in exporting logs and other natural resources clearly continued.

To resist such trends, a distinctively Buddhist movement to link community development, preservation of the natural world, and traditional *dhammic* values has unfolded.

THE BUDDHIST MOVEMENT FOR REFORM AND RENEWAL

Since the 1960s, small but growing numbers of Buddhist religious leaders have become concerned about the "crisis in Buddhist values" and have called for change. They point to the materialism seeping into the monastic community, to the ways that the powerful manipulate Buddhism, and to the reluctance of most monks to change old modes of communicating with the people. Only recently, for example, have they begun to preach in ordinary language, instead of the traditional style, a form of recitation. Some reforms are mild; others, calling on clergy to adopt an activist social ethic, meet considerable resistance.

The Venerable Bhikku Buddhadasa, the guiding spirit of the reform movement, began reflecting on a new Buddhist way of life in the 1930s. Its philosophy has been that true Buddhism must regain leadership in today's rapidly changing society before it is too late. Personal and social development must come before materialistic development. Buddhist agriculture, for example, should be a way of life based on spirituality and a holistic approach that integrates farming with ecology, economic self-reliance, and developing communities of mutual support. The Buddhist goal of selflessness is to be achieved not by self-mortification, but through the Middle Path, whereby the social and personal dimensions become one. It has nothing to do with being neutral or indifferent.

Some monks distribute basic health care information to the public and, especially in rural areas, have become known as "bald-headed doctors." Some work alongside villagers. They dig wells, build houses, study ways to diversify crops, promote cooperatives, and help set up credit unions administered by the members themselves. One distinctive initiative is the renewal of the Siamese communal Pha-pha ceremony, traditionally a way of contributing to support of the monks. Today the community becomes the priority; monks and villagers work together, and the donors—many of them middle-class city people—are conscienticized to the rural situation and the objectives of community development. Contributions in kind, or of money, are made to Rice Pha-pha, Buffalo Pha-pha, Books Pha-pha, Medicine Pha-pha, and so on.

Such initiatives have transformed many lives. For example, in several villages poor farmers, who formerly had to rent water buffaloes to work their land, can now "borrow" them from a bank run by a monk. A contract is signed, stipulating that the first baby buffalo will revert back to the bank, and that the farmer will treat the buffalo well. If he abides by the contract, the buffalo is his for life. These people do not need a World Bank to help them meet their needs. The Pha-phas have always been joyous celebrations, with all sorts of theater in the temple grounds. They also revive solidarity among the villagers, forge ties with urban people, and foster a kind of community development that can harmonize with the ecosystem.

Many monks engaged in this work recognize that ancient beliefs can play an important role. In Siam, as in most other Asian countries, the people have traditionally believed that there is an inherent link between women, earth, and rice—they are seen as sources of biological and spiritual nurturing qualities, embodied in spirit-goddesses. Even in the recent past, spirits were thought to abide everywhere—not only in rice, but in trees, rivers, animals, forest, and the fields; periodic celebrations symbolized the affinity between humans and other beings, indeed, the universe. Although Buddhism represented the ideal goal of life, spirit practices permeated daily life. They persist in subtle ways today, making their way into "Buddhist mythologies" and religious activities. Thus in the Rice Pha-pha of one village, the welcoming ceremony for the donors is the "Su Kwan Khao," the welcoming of the rice spirit by a ceremony in which a lay leader begins by calling for the participation of all spirits in the universe.[9]

RENEWAL EFFORTS LED BY THE LAITY

The driving force behind many of the projects has been Sulak Sivaraksa, a lawyer, devout Buddhist, and co-founder of the International Network of Engaged Buddhists. He has written many books criticizing national and international power structures, and calling for recognition of the creative role Buddhism can play in social development. In 1986 and 1991 he was charged with *lèse majesté* (offense against a ruler's dignity—often construed as treason), but because of his international renown, managed to stay out of prison. In 1995 he was acquitted. Throughout this ordeal, he continued to devote himself to initiatives such as the Interreligious Commission for Development, which works for human rights and preservation of the environment.

Moreover, many secular groups have had a religious underpinning. The Project for Ecological Recovery (PER), for example, has received support from German and Dutch Lutheran religious groups and devel-

oped a close working relationship with Buddhist leaders and representatives of the small Christian and Muslim minorities.

From Witoon Permpongsacharoen, PER's project director, we
learned that its central concept is that Thailand is basically an agricultural country and the lives of rural people depend on the ecosystem; it is
the ecosystem that secures the economy. Hence PER promoted traditional
organic agriculture and alternative energy schemes, as well as community
forest projects using nitrogen-fixing trees to help prevent soil erosion. It
has been particularly interested in strengthening local groups. Some
grassroots movements have been remarkably successful. For example,
the Nam Choan dam (built to supply Bangkok and beach resorts, not local
villagers) was halted by a people's resistance. Doi Suthep, a mountain
near Chiang Mai noted for its monastic retreats, was saved from a cable-
car "hookup" by a campaign initiated by environmentalists and villagers,
joined by monks.

"When we work in a village, we have to work with a monk," said
Permpongsacharoen. "We work from a core of tradition. We go to the
forest, hold a ceremony around a number of trees, and cloak them in the
saffron-colored robes of a monk. They have been 'ordained' and made so
sacred that no Buddhist would dare to cut them down."

Wildlife-Thailand was supporting a project known as "Buddhism and
Nature Conservation." While the basic idea originated with Nancy Nash,
an American who had worked with the Dalai Lama and other Buddhist
leaders to bring a new conservation education approach to Buddhist
countries, here it had been adapted to harmonize with specific Siamese
situations, customs, and legends. The project worked with universities,
but its most important thrust was work with the clergy. *Cry From the
Forest*,[10] edited by Dr. Chatsumarn Kabilsingh, a prominent Buddhist
scholar and feminist, consisted of illustrated nature stories from the classic *Tri-Pitaka* that monks—many of whom were themselves poorly educated about Buddhist teachings on nature—could use in sermons. During
our meeting with Dr. Kabilsingh and her colleagues, she explained that
they planned to hold seminars for monks, then send copies to every temple in the country. (Dr. Kabilsingh reported later that copies went to
12,000 major temples.) Moreover, Siam's best-known conservationist
monk, Ajahn Pongsak, would be leading a large seminar. "He knows his
people—he can teach other monks to reach them!'"

GOING BACK TO THE SOURCE: THE TEACHINGS OF BUDDHADASA

Bhikku Buddhadasa has been called one of the greatest Buddhist
thinkers of all time. When he died in 1993 at age 87, he was still receiving visitors at Wat Suan Mokh (The Garden of Liberation); nearly
100,000 people visited the community every year.

True Buddhism, maintains Buddhadasa, lies not in books and rituals, but in *practice*, through body, speech, and mind, to get rid of defilements. The true goal is transformation of self-attachment and self-love into self-lessness and love of others.

In *Dhammic Socialism* he sets forth a vision of a society neither capitalist nor Marxist, but based on a sense of the equality of all beings.[11] Indeed, *dhammic* socialism is the original natural state of things, he says. All religions, all over the world, are socialistic—that is, founded on love and compassion toward all things. The goal of all religions is finding salvation—what we must do so that we may become One with that which is Highest. God, *dhamma*, Tao, and the laws of Nature are in essence the same. It is that which is highest in every aspect of reality. But the essence of religion is always its practice.

Buddhadasa's concept of *dhammic* socialism includes the natural world. Much of his sharp criticism of contemporary society focuses on its destruction of the earth's raw materials, which "belong to Nature, to God, to whatever one may call it."

Some might think of *dhammic* socialism as social democracy, but Buddhadasa's concept is quite different from individualist liberal democracies, where, he says, people can do what they like. Instead, the needs of society as a whole must come first. It accords with the principle of Nature that we take only what we actually need, thus respecting the rights of all beings.

Hence the essence of true socialism, he says, must lie in the *dhamma* of Nature, for socialism is a system which brings about balance in society. If Nature had acted in the ways of a "free" or liberal democracy, it would have destroyed itself soon after the world began. This limiting aspect of Nature has allowed the plant and animal world to survive. A truly socialistic government would set limits on individualistic freedom, but create well-being in the community. Already there is a precedent in the Buddhist *sangha* community: limits are set on what monks can eat, use, and set aside for themselves, creating a society where there is no want.[12]

The most persistent themes in Buddhadasa's thought, then, center on balance, universality, harmony, limits, and interdependence. Morality (*sila-dhamma*) is that which brings about normalcy or the natural balance of things . . . The spirit of socialism exists in everyone . . . We must recognize the necessity of living together in a harmonious way . . . In the natural world, Nature limits any form of hoarding . . . The universe is a system of mutual interactions, so much so that an atom is a socialist system of interdependent parts . . . The essence of Nature is socialism, in the sense that no things can exist independently; they exist relative to each other.

This last thought, emanating from a Buddhist sage almost unknown in the West, parallels Aquinas' concept of an ultimate universal socialism: "the whole universe together participates in the divine goodness more perfectly, and represents it better than any single creature whatsoever."[13]

For Buddhadasa, *dhammic* socialism includes all living things. When we violate the natural balance in the cosmos, we suffer the consequences. When we act against the Natural Law, inevitably we are punished for our destructiveness. The laws of God are the laws of Nature, or the laws of *dhamma*. When we fully understand the Natural Law, we also comprehend the meaning of *dhamma*, of God, of Tao—in short, of everything.

CRY FROM THE FOREST

This is the story of a monk-disciple of Buddhadasa who has lived his belief that when Nature is no longer in balance, it must be set right. It is a story of the slaughter of forests and transformation of fecund soil into desert, a story of human jealousy, free-entrepreneurship, opium-trafficking, a vilification campaign—and murder.

It is also a story of the building of community.

It begins in northern Thailand in the 1980s. But in a sense, it is rooted in no one place or time, for parallel dramas unfold in California and Nepal, in Kenya and Mexico—whenever and wherever humans destroy forests in vital upland watersheds. Soil loss, flooding, drought, and climactic changes are just some of the results, say Britain's Friends of the Earth former director Jonathon Porritt and a host of other ecologists worldwide.

Phra Ajahn Pongsak has been described as a "problem-solver who by calling attention to the problem is seen as a troublemaker." For many years Ajahn, a forest-dwelling monk and the abbot of Wat Palad Monastery and the Tu Bou Meditation Center, near Chiang Mai, had watched the disappearance of the forest and the creatures who lived there. As the watercourses began to dry up, Ajahn helped the villagers improve the irrigation of their fields.

But this was no long-term solution, he knew. The villagers needed to understand the true importance of the forest to their lives. All of them, especially the landless, also needed more land to grow food and prevent dependence on cutting trees for timber and charcoal. They needed a model of truly sustainable development. To promote a "Right Attitude" toward Nature, Ajahn set up the Dhammanaat Foundation for Conservation and Rural Development in 1985. It has been entirely administered by M.R. Smansnid Svasti, an artist, who has loved forests since her childhood. A second cousin of the king, she could be enjoying a life of privilege in Bangkok. Instead she made the decision to spend most of the year in a simple house on the monastery grounds, and expend her energy and resources on the Mae Soi Valley Project. It has been a decision not without danger.

When we first heard of the project in the late 1980s, we learned that in the *tambon* (subdistrict) Mae Soi, the villagers themselves—in some cases with the help of school children—had already built a 10-mile fence to protect the watershed forests on the ridge; created firebreaks throughout the forest; established a seedling nursery; laid pipe to water the seedlings; maintained a 24-hour patrol against hunting, felling, and starting fires; planted degraded forest with trees that nourish the soil; and begun work on feeder canals. We learned, too, that Ajahn Pongsak was facing determined opposition from many high sources. We had to see for ourselves.

At the Chiang Mai train station, we were met by Mrs. Svasti, a short, dark-haired, energetic woman, apparently in her 40s, who introduced herself as "Nunie" and hustled our bags into a Toyota pickup. Enroute to Wat Palad, she emphasized the multi-pronged nature of the project: to save the remaining watershed; repair as much damage as possible; relieve villagers' dependence on forests by promoting modest and ecologically sound development efforts; and encourage villagers' initiative. Monks were the natural leaders and teachers in rural communities, she went on. Although some had always preferred to follow untroubled lives within the monastery walls, in the past it was customary for all matters—spiritual, medical, educational, social—to be referred to them. The temple was the village center—the school, clinic, library, museum, guesthouse, theater. Ajahn—who spoke of principles like *siladhamma*, with which villagers were familiar—had been remarkably successful in the revival of such Siamese Buddhist customs and values.

Meeting the Trouble-Maker

Wat Palad centered on a communal pavilion, open to the forest, in an awesome setting of towering trees. As sun filtered through the high canopy of foliage, lighting the wings of enormous butterflies, the soft gurgle of a brook and the song of birds warbling back and forth seemed to frame the pervasive quiet.

Not far away stood meditation huts for monastics and guests. Monks in sandals and orange-yellow robes were moving almost noiselessly along the paths, staffs in hand. An old oak grew through the pavilion porch and as we approached, a young novice was sweeping the floor and the ground nearby with a broom of twigs. Kittens frolicked across the porch, ate from the monks' plates of leftover rice, and chased each other up and down the trees.

Nunie led us to Ajahn, who was sitting on a bench, an irregular oval
stone, under a giant 600-year-old mango tree. The traditional saffron robe
draped from his left shoulder could not conceal his strong arms and solid
muscular body. His hands were folded and from behind gold-rimmed
glasses, his powerful eyes surveyed us gravely.

We sat down on three of the dozen flat stones arranged in an irregular
semi-circle before him. Regarding us with a long, lingering smile that
seemed to express both amity and detachment, he waited for us to begin.
With Nunie acting as interpreter, we asked how he had come to the idea
of this project. He began speaking slowly, using his hands in slow, gentle
gestures. "After my ordination, at age 20, my feelings about Nature grew.
I spent many years wandering all over the northern forests. That was
nearly 40 years ago. The forests were still dense and green. As I meditated, I understood that all Nature is one. I was in unity with all living
things. So as time passed and I began to see places where Nature was in
imbalance, I saw it must be set right."

"Because you had come to see the interdependence of things?"

"Yes." He spread his fingers, one palm turned up, the other turned
down, moving the two back and forth to demonstrate balance. "When
you reach firmness of mind, you see things clearly. Criticisms don't
throw you off balance. You see things as they are in the circle of life.

Phra Ajahn Pongsak with author Marjorie Hope (left) and translator Nunie
Svasti under the 600-year-old mango tree at Wat Palad monastery in northern
Thailand. (Photo by James Young)

You don't think of the mango tree as something in itself. You see everything has its place in Nature.

"But you have to go to natural places for contemplation. Then Nature breaks through your train of thought, with excitement and tranquillity. Nature infiltrates the body spontaneously. Your spirit becomes absorbed in the greenness." He cupped one hand, fingers spread like the leaves of a lotus, and circled the other hand above it.

"The forest is pure. In a town everything stimulates 'more, more' consuming. Only when you have been in the forest and felt its coolness in the body and the spirit, then you understand. You understand *siladhamma*."

"Meaning precepts inherent in *dhamma*?"

"Yes, morality. Still, one can follow all the precepts, but it does not mean one has morality. *Siladhamma* means correct balance of Nature. For human nature, it means achieving balance between the physical and spiritual aspects of your life. Following precepts like do not kill, do not lie, helps achieve this balance. The principle can be applied to family, nation, environment."

"So *siladhamma* means being and *acting* in harmony with Nature?"

He nodded. "The survival of the forest is necessary for the survival of *siladhamma* in the environment. The forest is the creator and protector of the natural balance. It holds water and insures rain. In the old days our forests were whole and we had enough fish and rice. We were not rich, but we were content and there was material and spiritual peace.

"I tell the villagers: 'The forests are our first home. The home we live in and feel so possessive about is only our second. It cannot be built without the first. Our parents give us life, but the forest sustains it. From it we get the four necessities of life—food, shelter, clothing, medicine. It balances the air we breathe, cleanses the water we drink, produces the soil we grow our crops in. It nourishes the spirit in the same way as it nourishes the body.'"

He paused, his eyes sweeping the greenwood. "I understand and love the forest. I feel gratitude to the forest and its unconditional benevolence toward humans. So I am not afraid."

"Afraid?"

He regarded us with a light smile. "I *must* do what I am doing."

"Can you tell us more about your work?"

He nodded, with the same light, persistent smile. "Two strands need to be worked on at the same time—the educational systems throughout the world and experiencing Nature. The world's educational systems are converging on one track—'success' and consumption. When you become tied to the 'more, more' system, you use up more natural resources. There must be education on the interdependency of life—in Western terms, the science of ecology."

"And what are some of the things you do toward that end?"

"I have spoken at several universities. Many foreign visitors come here. University students come for meditation retreats. I speak with school children who visit during camping weekends. Government officials, especially from the Royal Forest Department, discuss what can be done. Not long ago, 200 doctors stayed in the meditation forest overnight and held a seminar. They decided it was high time to save the forest and government efforts were not enough. Monks, students, and professionals must join forces and press the government to act."

Many monks did understand, Ajahn continued. But others were still afraid to do "wrong." They needed a common awareness of the environmental teachings of the *dhamma*, which say it is their *duty* to act, uphold the balance. Then they could lose their fear of being called "Communist." They could say, "We can do that without the approval of the government."

Yes, monks were also apprehensive about acting against the hierarchy. Some of its leaders found it in their interest to work with certain government officials. Many monks in high positions also felt that new ideas and a new kind of leader meant a threat to their power, and they were giving him "problems." When we observed that all this was very much like the relationship between the Pope and "people's priests" working with base communities, he nodded, adding that base communities were a contemporary idea in the West, but an old idea in Siam.

"How did your project actually get started?"

"In the early 1980s, I began to point out the problem to a few villagers. With the disappearance of the soil came lower water levels, stronger winds, greater extremes of temperature. They listened. Then I related this to other problems brought by the villagers. Some had trouble with neighbors, like competing for good land, or troubles with wives—the stress would come out in quarrels. For instance, the villagers were upset that they had to use more and more fertilizer. I explained why—with the removal of trees, there are no roots to hold the rain, and water rushes off, taking more topsoil with it. So they need more fertilizer for depleted soil."

"He took them up to the ridges, to where the original dense forest remained," interpolated Nunie. "He showed how the deep rich soils there were spongy with water. They saw how it trickled out of these sponges, running down the hill and joining together to make streams. Then he showed them other places where the Hmong, one of the refugee hill tribes, have destroyed the forests on the ridges—drying up the streams to the valley. I will show you tomorrow."

That night we stayed in a hut, set on stilts, in the depths of the forest. Since the only illumination was from candles, we two bedded down on our mats, under mosquito netting, well before eight o'clock. But something compelled us out into the night. The blue-black sky was thick with stars. We stood on the porch, listening. A vibrant silence hung over the earth. There was no light, no sound from the world of humans. Only the sounds of the forest broke the stillness: the call of night birds, the resonant drumming of giant cicadas, the sigh of wind in the trees, faint rustles from invisible creatures on the ground. Other worlds than ours. And yet, part of us, too. Were we not, all of us, stardust?

The next day we visited the area. "We are reclaiming desert land," said Nunie as we made our first stop, a part of the Mae Soi Valley that once was covered with forest and seamed with watercourses. Now we could see only gullies and stony soil in a barren wasteland. Formerly, the farmers had grown three crops a year, yields that included rice, beets, onions, garlic, soybeans, and peanuts. Now they could scarcely reap one yearly crop. As a result, they were being forced into illegal logging and making charcoal. Not far away, however, we could see the first results of carefully planned redevelopment: parts of the valley were planted with its former species of teak, ironwood, and wild mango, and 600 acres of land had been cleared for farming.

At a nursery of some 35,000 seedlings, villagers, student volunteers from Thai universities, and Royal Forestry Department (RFD) workers waved as they tended the new growths they would plant on degraded land. A leader approached and described how reforestation had already led to the return of many animal species, including hares, barking deer, jackals, gibbons, and a black leopard. Two hundred seventy-four families who contributed their labor had been given land for farming from areas of Reserved Forest that had degenerated into scrub.

Along the way, Nunie described the complex, contradiction-filled history of their relationship with the government. The RFD had begun by supporting the project, and had not only released degraded reserve forest land to villagers for farming, but had asked monks to help in forest conservation. Yet for decades it had also granted concessions releasing reserve forest to mining enterprises and logging companies. Was corruption ever involved? Nunie raised her eyebrows.

Moreover, there was friction between the RFD and other departments. The RFD had promoted the idea that all hill tribes in headwater forests, including the Hmong, must be relocated, and in 1989 the Government as a whole had made a decision to that effect. Yet few tribes had been moved. Officials of the Welfare Department, more powerful than the RFD, seemed to find it in their interest to keep the Hmong there. It was convenient to have hard currency flowing in from various foreign aid groups, such as Norwegian Church Aid, which supported a Thai NGO called the Thai-Norwegian Highland Development Project. It was encouraging the Hmong on the ridges to substitute vegetables for their traditional cash crop—opium, the basis of heroin.

Who were the Hmong? We soon saw for ourselves, when Nunie took us to a market in a Hmong hilltop village. Women in black jackets and trousers with striped borders, and wearing elaborate silver jewelry, were selling vegetables, flowers, and bracelets. Of all the immigrant tribal peoples, the Hmong (whose roots lie in China) have long operated on a cash economy and grown opium as a cash crop.[14] Aid groups tried to introduce crop substitution programs—and with them, the idea of farming as primarily a commercial enterprise. This led to far wider forest destruction.

Ajahn and the valley villagers tried to persuade the Hmong at Mae Soi to resettle in the valley. The Hmong were dissuaded by organizers of the Thai-Norwegian Development Project, who told them that Ajahn and the villagers were manipulating them for their own ends.

Meanwhile, the vegetable-growing to which the Hmong had agreed was being carried out with the aid of dieldrin, an agrichemical banned in the United States. "Erosion from slash-and-burn agriculture and poisoning of our streams—foreign countries are paying the Hmong to destroy our headwater forests!" said Nunie bitterly.

Compassion and the Use of Force

Ajahn's attitude toward the encroachment of the Hmong was not one of benign tolerance. We knew this from reading interviews with him, but it came out with particular clarity during our last talk.

We found him under the great mango, talking with a German engineer who had become "fed up" with foreign aid groups in Thailand, and had come here to offer his services. Ajahn greeted us with a nod, and again waited for us to begin. As a barefoot young novice squatted on the ground, listening, we spoke of our visit to the Hmong village.

His lips tightened, but his voice was even. "The United States and other countries have poured in millions upon millions to eradicate opium through programs like crop substitution. But the truth is, *no one* should live on the watershed. And opium grows only at high altitudes. Just moving the hill tribes down would end opium-growing. The question is, Who *wants* it to end?"

"Some people seem to be saying it is not 'humanitarian' to move them."

"Yes. They say the Hmong should not be subject to forest protection laws. We must be good Buddhists, persuasive and understanding. Well, we have tried—and have found good land in the valley for them. But the Hmong do not listen. Why don't these well-meaning humanitarians see that hill tribes should be subject to the same law as the rest of the Thai people?"

"You are thinking not only of human law?"

"Good laws preserve the natural *siladhamma* in society, and in Nature. Some people fail to see this. They cite compassion, which *is* one part of *siladhamma*, yes. But it is not the whole. *Siladhamma* is more. Buddhism teaches us to solve a problem, which is suffering, at its cause. The deteriorating environment is a drastic problem, affecting *all* of life. Extreme problems demand drastic actions. To solve problems, we need wisdom, joined with compassion. Compassion alone is too soft to bring back *siladhamma*. Nor is it suitable for every case."

We were groping for some response. This was hardly what we had expected from a gentle Buddhist monk.

But Ajahn had scarcely paused. "Neither the law by itself, nor *siladhamma* by itself, can solve the ills in society, because some people cannot learn," he went on. "Even if 99.9 percent of the people understood the importance of the forest, the other 0.1 percent could still destroy it. The only way to stop them is, forcefully."

"It seems a bit strange to hear a Buddhist monk talking about the need for using force."

"Oh? Well, what I am saying is, this is where authority comes in. All of us have to work together in our different duties. But the law only punishes, it does not teach people to love and cherish the forest as they love life itself. We should not have a situation where officials empowered by law have become the owner of the forest, and the people, the true owners of the land, are reduced sometimes even to becoming thieves in order to survive.

"*Siladhamma* is the ability to co-exist peacefully in society. We must understand just how the moral values we miss today have disappeared— and why. The times are dark and *siladhamma* is asleep, so it is the duty of monks to bring it back. It would be impossible for me to reject that duty because it is difficult. Government officials cannot recognize this side of *sangha* duty and see it has a place alongside the law. We must understand the *siladhamma* of life, the truth as it exists in Nature. Ways must be found to stop moral problems—deforestation, crime, whatever— from growing. Afterward, development will come."

"To you, development means something different from its Western meaning."

"It means creating the missing factors in one's individual life or the life of society. Conservation is preservation of the good you already have. Together, they make balance."

"Most Americans want to know: what can they do?"

For the first time, Ajahn laughed. Nunie laughed, too. "We are so grateful to America for its great generosity to other countries," he replied. "We only ask, do not damage the environment when you bring projects. We need aid that does not damage, but conserves."

"Americans do not understand very well the principle of balance."

He looked back at us silently, with a faint smile that seemed to express compassion.

"In the U.S., many ecologists say trees are the lungs of the earth."

"Trees. Yes. But the forest is more. The forest is the whole, it is the *life* of the earth. When it dies, we die."

Community. We looked at each other; both of us had been reminded of Thomas Berry's core concept that humans emerged from the primordial earth community, and our own well-being can be achieved only through the well-being of the entire natural world. For several minutes we described Berry's thought to Ajahn.

He listened attentively, nodding from time to time with a resonant "ah-h-hm."

"Do you think, as he does, that we are entering an ecological age?"

"It *must* be an ecological age—or we will perish. We must think interrelatedness."

The Scandal

Events moved swiftly after our departure.

One day in March 1991, villagers from Huay Kaew, near Chiang Mai, approached a forest reserve to gather food, as they, like their forebears, had always done. They were startled to see a sign proclaiming that it was closed and had been leased out to Pramern Shinawatra, a businesswoman and wife of a member of Parliament. Soon workers and bulldozers arrived to clear the forest and plant mangoes. Then trees in watershed areas began to be cut for roads.

The villagers sent letters of protest to the authorities. A week later, Pramern Shinawatra's husband Surapan told villagers that a 1964 law allowed the private sector to lease "denuded forest" for planting trees.

In less than a month, sand and soil from construction and cut trees fell into streams, blocking water flow to farms. Led by village schoolmaster Thaweesilp Sriroeng, the villagers approached Ajahn. He pointed out the causes of the situation and described possible solutions. The idea that they could whip up publicity by getting themselves arrested for sitting down and obstructing the bulldozers appealed to the villagers.

Thaweesilp also approached university students, who joined the villagers; the demonstrations received considerable publicity.

Students, accompanied by reporters, surveyed the area and concluded that not only had Pramern taken more than the allotted land, but this was not all denuded forest. While leaving, they were confronted by armed men who told them to get out immediately.

A day later, hundreds of villagers entered the forest, drove out workers, and began occupying it. Publicity was spreading, together with evidence that the "mango plantation" was actually intended to be a tourist resort or golf course. The Prime Minister himself rebuked Shinawatra, and the latter admitted that "some mistake" had been made—perhaps the man his wife had put in charge of the project had used more land than allowed.

The humiliation of conceding even this little did not sit lightly on this powerful businessman-and-politician, however.

The schoolmaster began receiving death threats. "It's a small price to pay," Thaweesilp told reporters, "if it can save the forest for future generations."

Three weeks later he was assassinated.

Ajahn, too, was receiving death threats. Then venomous snakes were smuggled into his garden and one of them bit him. After weeks of lingering near death, he recovered.

In 1992 Ajahn received the United Nations Environment Programme's Global 500 Award, as well as the RFD's Gold Medal. Tensions eased. But at year's end, they exploded.

On November 18 Nunie received an anonymous letter with a photograph of Ajahn—in *flagrante delicto* with a woman. The letter listed an array of sexual, moral, and financial allegations against the abbot. The next day all the media, except the two English-language newspapers in Bangkok, carried the photo, together with lurid stories.

According to Rod Nelson, an English environmentalist who was visiting the project, that night Wat Palad was a "madhouse," crowded with clerics, journalists, environmentalists, and the curious. Rod was infuriated. Not only was such misconduct completely outside Ajahn's character, but he was now seriously ill with Parkinson's disease and "hardly likely to have deep inclinations for a torrid affair." But how could one contradict a photograph?

Rod was suspicious. He already knew about digital manipulation of photographic images, a new technology that can create "reality" as picturesque as dinosaurs chasing youngsters in a Disneyland park. At the time, it was virtually unheard of in Thailand. Later, however, it was discovered that one man who had access to this very new technology was Surapan Shinawatra, who, among his many business enterprises, was importing state-of-the-art computers.

Colonel Sommart Sukhontipak knew a more intimate side of the story. While working with the Third Army in the Mae Soi sub-district, he became converted to Ajahn's conservation effort. After he retired in 1991, he was asked to become the foundation's secretary-general.

In an interview with Larn Seri Thai, the colonel recalls that on November 18, 1992, he and Ajahn were called away by authorities to answer what seemed a strange allegation: a Foundation worker was encroaching on Forest Reserve land. After clearing the charge, the two returned to Wat Palad—to discover it filled with police, monks, reporters, and photographers.[15]

Ajahn was led into his hut and shown the photograph and letter, which named two monks (who happened to bear personal grudges against Ajahn) as witnesses to the act. Ajahn said nothing; he looked stunned. Then he was hurried into the office by senior monks and officials. "They closed the door and would not let any of us in," says Colonel Sommart. " . . . It was dark when they left, allowing no one to go with them. They took Ajahn away. He just disappeared. . . . Any layman in the same position would have been allowed consultation with a lawyer. Ajahn asked for three days to look into the matter. The Senior Monk refused, and insisted he disrobe immediately."[16]

The next day Ajahn disrobed himself. In a quiet, dignified ceremony he made a statement that he was doing this in order that "confusion and agitation may cease," since "in the opinion of the *sangha*, the problems this affair has caused will best cease by my disrobing." Then he took off his saffron robe, but donned a white one (worn by meditators who are not ordained), all the while maintaining a tranquil composure.

To his followers, Ajahn explained that he had disrobed to preserve the purity of the religion; he had seen how cases of other monks faced with similar accusations had been turned into a media circus. He assured them that the accusations were entirely groundless; he hoped that some day there would be an opportunity to investigate and he would be able to re-ordain.

No plaintiff has ever come forward. No witnesses have sworn testimony. It is not known who took the photograph, or how. The woman's name is still unknown; in the photograph, little of her is visible but the genitals. Yet police, high monks, and government officials arrested and condemned him in a few hours. The case was closed before any charges were investigated.

Phra Surat, senior subdistrict monk (the nephew of the senior district monk) was appointed acting abbot. He interrogated the Colonel, not about Ajahn's moral transgressions but about Dhammanaat Foundation funds. Colonel Sommart observed that the accounts of the Wat and the

Foundation were separate, and demonstrated that everything was in order. Nevertheless, Phra Surat took away all the bank books, then made an order to freeze the Foundation's account. The Colonel knew he had no authority to do so and proved to the bank that this was illegal. "As for the Wat's account, almost 40,000 baht (10,000 dollars) had been withdrawn for an unspecified reason," says Sommart. The only people then with authorized access to the account were the District Education Officer and the senior monk of the subdistrict, Phra Surat.[17]

Ajahn was replaced as abbot by Phra Santeu, a monk chosen by the Senior District Monk. Known as the "Mad Monk," Santeu has been described by many witnesses as a man who holds seances, boasts about owning a revolver, has been involved in a knife fight with another monk, goes on drunken binges during which he sometimes threatens to kill "that damned Pongsak," openly makes coarse sexual advances to young women, and imprisons, in steel cages, wild animals who once roamed the forest. He is also wealthy. Displaying fat rolls of banknotes, he boasts of coming from a family of billionaires—then shows snapshots of himself with certain government officials and with the most powerful mafia figure in Thailand.

Ajahn was forced to flee for his life.

The Never-Ending Tension

Ajahn did not quit his mission, however. From a village "somewhere in the hills," he continued to give the movement quiet direction, surrounded by villagers who had committed themselves to defending him at any cost.

Through correspondence and phone calls with Nunie and others, we managed to follow the fortunes of the Project between 1991 and 1995. Although Nunie nearly lost her life one night when someone started a fire in her house—fortunately, soon extinguished—she continued leadership of the Project. Two more dams, four reservoirs, and a new nursery were completed. More firebreaks were constructed; during the dry season, villagers camped out along them 24 hours a day.

By 1994 villagers were able to see that the Mae Soi was the only river, of the eight in the district, that was still flowing during the dry season. More than 80 families then settled into new plots in the valley.

Ironically, success created new problems. As the Project transformed worthless desert into fertile farmland, the area became increasingly attractive to entrepreneurs.

Confusion over government policy persisted. For example, several times authorities said they would allow villagers and monks to take part in forest management, but somehow that decision was never put into action. When villagers applied for formal title to the reclaimed land they had been promised, the RFD informed them that administration of developed degraded forest had been handed over to the Land Reformation Department. The villagers continued to have no formal title—while developers hovered nearby.

Despite government relocation decisions going back to 1989 and public concern over increasing floods and drought, despite the fact that good valley land had been set aside for them and a wholistic resettlement plan worked out, in 1995 the Hmong at Ban Paa Kluay continued to live in headwater forests, slashing and burning—and sometimes setting fire to Dhammanaat Foundation work.

What if relocation of the Hmong at Ban Paa Kluay did become a reality? we asked ourselves. Would it not create a precedent for the termination of other highland projects, hence the loss of foreign aid to various government departments? The proximity of the Thai-Norwegian Development Program to Chiang Mai made it the prime choice to display the efforts of the many government departments and NGOs involved in the programs to halt opium-growing—programs that somehow managed to fail. We remembered Ajahn's words: "Just moving the hill tribes down would end opium-growing. The question is: Who *wants* it to end?"

Is *Siladhamma* Asleep?

In 1995 the concerted campaign against Ajahn appeared to have dissipated. Or was it only lurking in the wings? The cultivation of opium—much of it destined to become heroin in the U.S.—is addictive. Thailand not only grows its own, but far more lucratively operates as the major processing-point for opium smuggled across the border from nearby Burma. The now-fertile fields of the Mae Soi Valley invite the prospect of development into an international resort, a prospect particularly attractive to Chiang Mai's leading businessman-politician, who has enough financial resources to continue indefinitely his efforts to sow dissension among the villagers. Known as a man who never forgets, Shinawatra has not regained face since Ajahn and his followers exposed the scheme to develop forest land into a "mango plantation."

Indeed, the broader campaign indirectly controlled by the forces of development was picking up momentum all over Thailand. In Buri Ram province, for example, conservationist monk Phra Prachak Khuttajito was sentenced to a year's imprisonment for leading "a mob" to occupy forest reserve land, a move that Phra Prachak defended as an effort to protect the forest against the tree-felling that has persisted in the face of a nationwide logging ban.

"The times are dark, *siladhamma* is asleep," observed Ajahn under the great mango tree.

Yes, Ajahn suffered flagellation. But also, that failed to suppress the monks determined to speak for the forest and the people. Indeed, after Ajahn disrobed, many younger monks felt challenged to pick up the cause.

With Ajahn no longer able to give the villagers open leadership, the most significant outcome of all was the flowering of their solidarity and initiative, we learned. When asked what they gained from the project, few mentioned benefits like a new plot of land; most spoke of other gains: "We've learned how to work together for the good of everyone —how to look at problems and work out answers on our own, together. We've come to understand how rivers form and soil erodes, and ways we can improve our soil."

The people in the village where Ajahn was living vowed to protect him with their own lives. Close-knit village committees in the Mae Soi Valley emerged to analyze their situation and plan strategies, particularly in protecting their lands against developers. In 1995 only four out of 229 families in the valley had succumbed to offers that could make them rich by Thai standards.

This is a story, then, of the Ecologist versus the Entrepreneur. The tension between those seeking to continue plundering, and those committed to preserving the natural world. The drama that will dominate the coming decades, Thomas Berry tells us.

And the Entrepreneur can wear many guises: politician, ecclesiastic, bureaucrat.

Ajahn Pongsak and Thomas Berry, two visionaries based in the monastic tradition, dwell at opposite ends of the earth. From their seats under ancient trees, the massive mango and the great red oak, they have contemplated the disorder unleashed upon the planet. And they have each in his own way reached out to engage themselves in the world of action.

Berry speaks of our human story as integral with the larger life-story of Earth and the universe. Ajahn bids his followers remember that the forest gives them life: it is their first home, without which they cannot have their second.

The historian-geologian in the West warns of the imperative need for a creative balance between human activities and other forces functioning throughout the planet. The forest-dweller in the East calls on the people to take care of the natural *siladhamma* of life.

Both speak of gratitude—gratitude to Planet Earth for its gifts—as fundamental to the bonding inherent in the religious impulse.

A desolate Earth will be reflected in the depths of the human, Berry predicts. Beside him, Ajahn reminds us of a truth we already sense but often seek to forget: if the *siladhamma* of Nature is out of balance, the *siladhamma* of the individual and the *siladhamma* of society will sicken and suffer. The Natural Law applies to all life.

Conclusion

In India we reflected back on our long journey beyond the Western horizon.

Mother India. The womb from which Hinduism, Jainism, Buddhism, and Sikhism emerged. Today home not only to these traditions, but to Zoroastrianism (Parseeism), Islam, Bahai'ism, Christianity, Judaism, and faiths of tribal peoples like the Bishnoi and Kameng. A subcontinent so rich and complex that only a book devoted to India could truly describe it.

Hinduism, vast and amorphous, defies reduction into a system of beliefs. One Supreme Reality (called by many names) is worshipped; all sincere paths are accepted. Devotion is manifested in pilgrimage, prayers at home shrines, chanting of hymns, and celebration of festivals in which, as in other Asian religions, vibrant images of nature permeate ceremony.

Mother India. Where one encounters frigid indifference to suffering beside acts of spontaneous generosity even to strangers, religious fanaticism coexisting with an easy openness to all faiths ("We all worship the same God, no?").

Mother India. After visiting Hindu, Muslim, Orthodox Christian, Sikh, Parsee, Jain, Ba'hai, and Buddhist temples and gatherings, and talking with religious, ecological, and political leaders as well as countless people from all walks of life, we began to see this sprawling nation as a microcosm of the conflicting forces we had witnessed in Asia and other parts of the "two-thirds world." More than 800 Indian environmental groups struggle on, some of them—like the Chipko "save the trees" movement led by Sunderlal Bahaguna—inspired with a Gandhian vision.[18] Yet the elite pushed massive development programs like the project at Singrauli, which has displaced hundreds of villagers and destroyed ecologically rich tropical forest, home to creatures ranging from tigers to wild boar. Meanwhile, the population soars, and the gap between the rich and the poor widens, even as their mutual basic support, the ecosystem, weakens each year.

As we saw in other parts of the "non-Western" world, in India the energy to preserve the natural heritage is generated less by middle-class groups than by poor people who experience the deterioration of their land, air, water, and way of life. For guidance, they often turn to environmental organizations or radical activists like ecologist/economist/feminist Vandana Shiva. But the élan and perseverance, the spontaneous creative ideas, come from people at the grassroots.

In India and elsewhere in our travels, the leadership and rank-and-file of secular movements are often animated by a spiritual commitment, which may or may not be closely related to an organized religion. Not all are clearly conscious of this commitment in themselves. Indeed, after talking with us, many thanked us for helping them to articulate an inspiration they already felt.

In many other ways India seemed to mirror the obstacles encountered by the ecospiritual movement, not only in Asia but other parts of the "two-thirds world" we had visited:

- Passivity and despair among poor people who have never experienced anything but powerlessness before those who represent authority;

- The prevalent image of clerics as bearers of a salvific message rather than people who could also take action against powers and principalities;

- Unwillingness of many clerics to forego the security and status from associating themselves with the privileged and powerful;

- Ignorance among religious leaders of the root causes, complexity, and pervasiveness of environmental pollution, to say nothing of insensibility to problems like global warming. For example, Jains we met in Delhi called their faith "very ecological," followed strict vegetarianism, and took great pains to cover their mouths lest they harm insects—yet seemed indifferent to the fact that only two-thirds of 1 percent of India's towns and cities had even partial sewage facilities;

- Reluctance to give up age-old ways of thinking. In Nepal, for example, Rinpoche Teche's reply to our question about the responsibility of religious leaders for the planet was that "bad *karma* has taken over everywhere," but he and his followers were praying for peace;

- The simple reality that the dense forests, the remote retreats in misty mountains so celebrated by religious mystics for contemplation, are virtually disappearing.

Yet we found some grounds for hope. In all of these countries, there was a growing comprehension of the enormity of the crisis we face. In all of them, growing numbers of spiritual leaders were engaging in action. Moreover, even in the face of worldwide fascination with new! new! technologies, respect endures for the values of tradition—values which in Asia and Africa are inextricably interwoven with religion.

A sense of the human being as belonging to the cosmos, a sense of union with the land and the creatures upon it, somehow survives. As one Hindu woman put it: "There is even a temple in Rajasthan where mice still go free. To us, even the worst of animals can be godly."

To be sure, this abiding consciousness will not be enough to save the planet, as the clash between the Ecologist and the Entrepreneur grows ever more fierce in the "two-thirds" world. But it provides a bedrock for people who seek to heal the consequences of the rift between humans and the forces of Nature.

8

A GLOBAL PERSPECTIVE

A Milestone Meeting of Faiths

When participants gathered for the 1993 Parliament of the World's Religions, marking the centenary of the parliament that was held in conjunction with the 1893 Chicago World's Fair, many considered it the most significant religious event of this century. The 1993 eight-day assembly also convened in Chicago, drawing 6,000 leaders and lay followers of over 100 faiths. With hundreds of speeches and symposia, as well as prayers, films, music, and dance, the atmosphere was one of a solemn but joyous festival. Bearded, turbaned Sikhs and Hindu women in gorgeous saris mingled easily with German Lutherans, American Indians in full ceremonial regalia, and Goddess-worshippers in flowing white dress. Many participants reported afterwards a feeling of being on a week-long high.

To be sure, tensions emerged, especially over the presence of "neo-pagan" religions. Fundamentalist and evangelical Christians declined participation on theological grounds. Four Jewish organizations withdrew over the inclusion of Louis Farrakhan, Nation of Islam leader.

But there was evidence of new developments in the realm of religion and the world at large: a strong presence of Asian religions, especially Hinduism; a substantial contingent of American Buddhists, including many nuns with shaved heads; and a marked (although not equal) presence of women, including Muslims. The rituals conducted by various

Earth-centered faiths drew full-to-overflowing attendance and enthusiastic participation in the dancing. Many at the gathering were searching for their own fusion of faiths, describing themselves as Buddhist Christian, Catholic Hindu, multi-denominational, or Jewish Hindu witch.

To the surprise of many, there was a notable emphasis throughout the week on living at peace not only with fellow humans of differing faiths, but also with Earth.

The organizers must have known they were taking a chance when they chose not a religious leader, but a nuclear physicist, Gerald Barney, founder of the global issues think-tank Millennium Institute, to deliver the keynote address. "We are here because we sense that Earth and her people are in serious trouble," he said. "Fundamentally, these difficulties are spiritual in nature. . . . We Christians pay lip service to protecting Earth, but at heart feel Earth is insignificant and irrelevant since our real home is with God in heaven—which is not on Earth."[1] Noting that the human population had already reached 5.3 billion, he urged that parents limit their families to two offspring.

Assuming the miraculous—that replacement fertility (two children per couple) could be achieved *throughout the world*, the planet's population might top off at 11 billion or more by the end of the next century.

Yet even if human population is thus limited to 11 billion, the problem would be far from solved. What we really have, he asserted, is a mega-problem: a population-poverty-hunger-energy-trade-atmosphere-waste-resource problem. For example, more mouths must be fed, hence more land cultivated. But the economic cost of bringing it all into production would be prohibitive, to say nothing of the enormous loss of habitat for many entire species and for critically important wild varieties of food species for humans. Soil loss and deterioration, too, have been growing. Even if extraordinary efforts are made to preserve the land, even if soil deterioration (caused in part by dependence on pesticides derived from petroleum) and soil loss (caused largely by competing uses of agricultural land, such as development) can somehow be stopped completely within a century, it will be extremely difficult to feed some 11 to 12 billion people.

Barney continued, demonstrating the interlocking effects of population growth, land use, agricultural yields, species extinction, energy use, greenhouse gas concentrations, and ozone depletion. To them, should be added tuberculosis, homelessness, nuclear weapons, water deterioration, drug trafficking, and many other problems—all of them, in some sense, evidence of the pathology of the human spirit. The breaking of life-sustaining relations in the biosphere parallels the breaking of life-sustaining relationships in the human community, our most critically important resource. We are a species without a vision.

What shall we do? Barney offered an abundant array of economic, political, social, and ethical suggestions involving change and sacrifice, but also offering hope for a sustainable future.

Where can we turn with questions about what to do, with questions of ultimate meaning and direction? Barney asked. He doubted that any faith tradition today was practicing a way of life that could provide a model for knowing ourselves not as individuals but as a species, or provided moral precepts to guide interspecies behavior. Nevertheless, such fundamentally spiritual questions continue to well up in the human spirit. And so, Barney told the assembly, in hope and trust we turn to you, the carriers of our spiritual wisdom.

There followed 36 questions, directed to all participants, concerning the traditional teachings—and range of other opinions—within each one's faith, on topics ranging from the meaning of "progress" to the possibility of envisioning new revelations.

"Let us all listen to and allow ourselves to be guided by the creative energy that shaped and lighted the universe from the beginning," Barney challenged the assembly. " . . . Let us *act* with conviction and confidence!" His voice rang out, but it was trembling, too, and tears shone in his eyes.

The gathering rose as one body, and responded with an ovation that reverberated for more than five minutes. Barney walked up the aisle, the tears washing his cheeks. "That response—" he was heard to say, "I would never have believed it!"

To our knowledge, only one other speaker, of the hundreds that week, elicited a standing ovation: Thomas Berry. He, too, addressed humankind's relationship with the earth. Some of the fundamentals of his thought, together with fresh insights, emerged during his speech, which was even more critical of established religion than Barney's.

The Parliament, he said, had not really focused on the future of Planet Earth, even though the deepest pathos of our time is in the Earth-human relationship. *Earth* is the place where the human and the divine have their primary meeting. From now on, we can do little for the human without saving the earth. Yet the interfaith declaration to be signed spoke only briefly about this.

We must develop a new sensitivity in every field, he emphasized. Take economics. There is a debate as to whether the ecology of the planet is going to be sacrificed to the economy or vice versa. In economics no one speaks of the earth economy. Yet the human cannot survive without air, soil, water, and other elements of Earth's interdependent life-systems.

We fail to realize spiritually that the outer world is necessary to activate the inner world. If we tear the mountains apart, then what is going to evoke in us a sense of the divine? When the planet is trivialized, when the butterflies disappear, when we no longer hear the song of the birds, and the children in the cities cannot see the stars, then the possibility of being truly religious disappears. A person can be taught Scripture, but the true meaning of this cannot enter into the souls of the people, if it is not within the *experience* of this larger context.

Today, Berry continued, there is a need to enter into the universe's sacred story. And we need the traditions more than ever. All religions, all rituals, celebrate the cosmology of things. We do not need a new religion; we need new religious sensitivities.

But the deepest pathos of our time is the inability of our religious people to enter into the new revelatory mode. There is a need to realize that every human, every tree, is irreplaceable. Each thing has its own inner voice. And everything is bonded together in an inseparable relationship with everything else. You can feel alienated, but you can never *be* alienated.

Now we need new liturgies to celebrate the great moments of the universe. We need to feel, to experience, that the human is that being in whom the universe celebrates itself in the deep mysteries of its existence in a special mode of conscious self-awareness. We need to realize that the human community has a distinctive role, but not outside the sacred community. We form a single sacred community with every other mode of being.

Every prophet in history has been denounced by those who wish to hold on to power or comfortable assumptions. Yet these two speakers, one from the scientific and the other from the religious worlds, had evoked an oft-suppressed "Yea, in truth!" among followers of the very traditions they were criticizing. They had found honor even in their own domains—and in that wider country that knows no frontiers, and reaches down to a substratum of consciousness.

Perhaps in part because Berry expressed such disappointment about the declaration to be signed, leaders of the world's major faiths met again several times that week. In its final form, "Towards a Global Ethic," which leaders signed as individuals, spoke from the beginning and frequently thereafter of the abuses to Earth's ecosystems. It spoke of our interdependence, of the community of living beings, and of how the very foundations of life were being exploited today. It linked peace, social justice, and the protection of the earth, and declared that no one has the right to use her or his possessions without concern for the needs of society and Earth. In its conclusion the declaration called for a transformation of consciousness in areas such as war and peace, economics and ecology; for a willingness to sacrifice; for commitment to a global ethic and to socially beneficial, peace-fostering, Earth-friendly ways of life.

Then it invited all men and women, whether religious or not, to do the same.

It did not emphasize, as did Berry, that the deepest pathos of our time is in the Earth-human relationship, nor did it quite suggest, as did Barney, that we need to understand ourselves as a species. "Towards a Global Ethic" avoided their conclusion that we *are* Earth.

Yet coming from so many diverse, often discordant faiths of the world, it was a remarkable testimony—a new revelation in the history of the earth and its major voice, humankind.

The crucial question, of course, is: How have religious leaders been working to make these resolutions a living reality?

Almost immediately the Council for a Parliament of the World's Religions began planning a parliament in South Africa in December 1999, developing a process for creating periodic parliaments, solidifying its working relationship with the Millennium Institute, and arranging a series of programs to help people of diverse faith traditions work together. In Chicago Muslims, Hindus, Buddhists, Jews, Baha'is, and Christians have met for interreligious conferences, "leaders encounters" celebrating diversity, and occasional dialogues on preserving the planet.

Elsewhere, there has been less activity. Recalling our travels, we have been able to grasp to some degree the difficulties of translating visionary goals into doable steps, especially in countries where religious and political tensions flourish.

Such difficulties, we realized, must be essentially similar to those faced by the people we had met in our explorations. As we reflected, the desire grew to revisit some key leaders. We had kept up with them by telephone, letter, and fax. But now we felt the need to see them in person.

By late 1995 our plans were complete. Lacking sufficient time and funds for an extensive trip, we chose our destinations carefully, selecting countries that are centers of religious power. For Eastern Orthodoxy, we chose Greece; for Islam, Egypt; for Judaism, Israel; for Theravada Buddhism, Thailand; for Taoism, Taiwan; and for Shinto and Mahayana Buddhism, Japan. Palestine, too, was included. Although it functions only as an almost-state, in a sense it is the other side of Israel and a crossroads of Islam, Eastern Orthodoxy, and Western Christianity as well.

All these countries are also the centers of political struggles that bear directly on the health of the earth. They are important players in the network of changes that are fast transforming its face.

Far more than any idealistic longing for global harmony and understanding, global capitalism is gluing distinct peoples together, even against their own will. Traditional cultures, especially those closely tied to the land, are weakening. Rural dwellers are seeking survival in urban areas. It has been predicted that before the year 2010, more than half the world's population will be living in cities—a new and disturbing phenomenon in human history.

We had already seen some of these changes at work. But on the journey before us, we would reflect more on the various links between these countries, and on the interconnections among the religious, political, economic, and ecological domains.

When we left the U.S. at the beginning of November 1995, a current of malaise was gnawing at the vitals of the world's richest society.

Despite low unemployment, abject poverty and homelessness persisted; the gap between rich and poor was widening. Hundreds of thousands of middle-class people lived in fear that they would lose their jobs if their employer moved abroad or automation accelerated. Although the shopping malls were full, a general sense of insecurity was pervasive. "The world feels shaky. Out of joint," confided a friend who had a good income but had had to change her field three times. "The people I know have enough money. But they aren't happy. And I—I feel I have no center. I guess what I'd like to see happen would be a Second Coming. I'm ready to buy into someone's philosophy that gives a reason for suffering, that demands personal sacrifice, that promises Nirvana for the earth."

People were hurting. And Earth was hurting, too.

Natural Bonds and Natural Law

By what seemed an almost miraculous coincidence, Oren Lyons addressed a peace symposium at our college, Wilmington College of Ohio, on the day before our departure.

He related the long story of the Great Peacemaker who had brought an end to the strife among the Iroquois tribes. That peace could never have lasted, he concluded, had it not been based on justice and equity and on peace with the earth. Achieving these is never easy. But the kind of lesson the Iroquois learned then is basically the lesson we need to learn now. More than a Bill of Rights, we need a Bill of Responsibilities.

The Iroquois learned that true love means to have compassion with generations to come. And as they planted a tree, they declared, "This tree represents spiritual laws! Let us make our laws accordingly." Today, Lyons continued, we see nations making laws against the natural world. Well, you cannot have peace as long as you make war on the earth. Under the natural law, there is no mercy.

"What can *you* do?" he challenged his audience. "You can seek out your grandparents. You need their experience and wisdom. And they need you. Between elders and the young there's a natural bond that bridges the generation in the middle—those in charge of the world today.

"What can you do? Today the accelerating accent on 'high tech' does not leave time for reflection. You young people need to get away from 'computer-think,' to learn to say 'no,' to find serious time, to be alone and reflect.

"We must think *seriously* about overpopulation. The law of nature tells us that no single entity can grow unchecked. We are part of the earth, subject to the same law. And when there are too many of us?" He shook his head. "We cannot master the outcome—the law always prevails."

We must think seriously about what is happening in the world of high technology, he counseled the students. Taking out *patents* on DNA strains, which contain the genetic code, is an idea that is taking on full force! His voice rose to a passionate pitch. Already Stanford University is working on a patent of the DNA strains—not of First World white people, but of South American Indians. Two weeks ago the National Institute of Health patented the genetic pattern of a native from Papua New Guinea. They are classified "intellectual *property*"! And they will be used for multinational drug companies' profits. The human species is marketing life processes. We will soon manipulate entire species, considering the products to be creations of human genius and thus ownable, saleable. "Is this the kind of future you want?" Lyons asked. "We must think out our values. We must do it quickly. Hard times are coming."

In a talk with us afterwards, Lyons was far from optimistic about the future. "It's been a market-driven world since the 1920s. Today the market has its own direction—*it* dictates politics. "But we will see a reaction from the natural world," he added. "There will be wars not only over oil, but water, food, land. Migrations will increase. We've talked about these things before. But now I see them coming on fast."

"Early in the next century?" we asked.

"It's an unknown. My guess would be, a real crisis by the year 2020. People are talking about the new millennium as a critical point. But the millennium, the year 2000, is no more than a date on a man-made calendar. Unless, of course, humans *act* in a way to make it significant."

A Green Presence in the Eastern Mediterranean

Greece, Egypt, and Israel represent three Semitic religious traditions that have frequently warred with each other. Yet for thousands of years they have been linked by one wine-dark sea and flourishing trade. Although hostilities are more often publicized, today visitors from Israel and Greece travel to Egypt's tourist sites, and Egypt exports oil and petrochemicals to both.

In an area where rapid industrialization has made the Mediterranean one of the most polluted seas in the world, the three nations also have many similar problems. It is no accident that Greece and Egypt should have given birth to Green parties, and that in Palestine, the "other half" of Israel, a fledgling Green Party has been forming.

In 1997 there were 25 Green parties in Western Europe, and at least 20 others elsewhere on the globe. Their political fortunes have fluctuated greatly, but in this decade the voting power of Green parties in countries like Sweden, France, Germany, and Luxembourg has risen. Most describe themselves as purely secular, and none espouse a certain religion.

Of the five Green parties we have visited—German, Italian, Turkish, Greek, and Egyptian—leaders of the first three expressed a belief in a humanism that transcended geographical or religious boundaries; yet many members told us their work was inspired by a "spiritual motivation." In Greece Anna Harrisson, a founder of the country's Green Party, had talked passionately during our 1990 visit about a "green religion" that she and some of her comrades had come to believe in.

Our many attempts to communicate with Anna and other Greek Greens since then had been unsuccessful. How are they faring? That was our first question as we arrived in Athens.

Greece: Bats Rise from the Ashes

The "greening"—or "regreening"—of Greece had a long way to go, we realized almost immediately. Since our last visit, the pollution of air, water, and soil had increased more than ever. Since the 1970s, modern Greece had rushed into industrial growth, making the valleys, particularly, ever more subject to inversions.

In Athens, persistently under a chemical cloud produced largely by cars, the law restricting driving to every other day was ignored by various ruses. During our November visit the skies were still thick with smog. One victim of air pollution was the human species, the hundreds of people regularly sent to the hospital with cardiac and respiratory illnesses. Another victim was the religious and cultural heritage that was the magnet for Greece's tourist industry. Today the famed statues and temples were pocked and discolored by sulfur dioxide.

In the past the rains had been a partial solution, but today they simply washed down the eroded hills surrounding the city. Environmentalists had won a ban on tree-cutting but, periodically, mysterious fires would rage on the hills. It was no secret that they were the work of developers, who were permitted to build on land left treeless for two years.

And yet, Anna told us, the Green Party had dissolved. It had become a "Tower of Babel" because of the members' individualism, their unwillingness to make small sacrifices for the sake of unity. Then, too, she added despairingly, the poor among the electorate seemed preoccupied with day-to-day survival and the others, with individual success.

"However," she went on, "some of us decided to work with the Hellenic Society for the Protection of Nature. Some joined WWF-Greece or Greenpeace, which are new here and strong already. Others joined small groups that try to preserve a certain animal. I chose bats because I understand how they help control mosquitoes and pollinate plants. And no one else wanted them. They are so underprivileged! As head of the Hellenic Bat Society, I speak for them. And I am always being invited to talk at schools. It is wonderful—*children* can see that even bats have an important place in the chain of Creation!

"My husband Richard and I have also launched a pilot project from our summer home on Aegina Island. We work with scientists studying bats' movements over the area—some 1,300 Greek islands."

She laughed. "One of our mottoes comes from Ariel in Shakespeare's *Tempest*: 'On the Bat's back I do fly/After summer, merrily!'"

In the hectic, convivial atmosphere of the Greenpeace office, young staff members described their current major campaigns: against driftnet fishing in the Mediterranean, against Greece's oil-based economy, and against nuclear testing. They had convinced 200,000 Greeks to sign a petition opposing French nuclear testing in the Pacific.

On our visit to World Wildlife Fund-Greece—likewise endowed with a youthful, enthusiastic staff—we learned that among other things, it had produced well-documented, colorful booklets on water management, endangered wetlands, and national parks, which were particularly welcomed by teachers. Perhaps its most spectacular victory was a concerted campaign that had resulted in the High Court's decision to halt construction of the Acheloos river dam—a development project pushed by the European Union—which would have destroyed an ancient monastery, beautiful lagoons, a thirteenth-century bridge, and habitat for many species of wildlife.

Despite all this evidence of concern for the earth, the Church of Greece at parish level was lagging far behind secular environmental groups. (As previously noted, it was, however, cooperating with the Ecumenical Patriarch and WWF-International on significant environmental projects based in monasteries.)

At one time the Green Party of Greece had served this country as a gadfly that pricked the conscience of church, state, and populace.

Would it rise from its ashes and do so again?

Egypt: Pyramids, Police, and the Polluted Poor

The Egyptian Greens, the first Green Party in Africa, was also the first such party in the Muslim world. Unlike Greens in Western Europe, they explicitly acknowledge a religious element, calling their statement of principles and objectives, "God, Man, Environment." Its preamble begins: "God created the universe, distinguished and balanced it in the most accurate system. Then He created Adam with His hands. . . . Then He made him [Adam] in the Universe His viceregent, not to spoil and disfigure it but to safeguard and inhabit . . . ."[2] It continues in a somewhat idealistic and flowing style to elaborate on the religious, political, spiritual, human, social, environmental, economic, national, and international constituents of the Greens' program. The starting point, then, is religious, but nowhere does the document speak of the Qu'ran or Muhammad; clearly, "God" refers to the "God" of many faiths.

Greens here had also suffered a crisis of leadership, we learned. But unlike the Greek Greens, they had emerged stronger than ever. One reason, perhaps, was that the environmental situation here was even more ominous than in Greece. Crises can draw people together.

The problems we witnessed in Egypt now were basically the same we had seen on our first trip, but they had intensified. The population was continuing to grow rapidly, adding to Egypt's burden more than a million new consumers of grain, water, oil, and other scarce resources every year. By contrast, Greece had one of the lowest rates of population growth in Europe.

The two countries did share many other problems. In Cairo air pollution was often more than 10 times what the World Health Organization considers safe. Since our last visit, desertification had not halted in a country where large areas in ancient times were green and wildlife flourished. Water pollution continued unabated. Few tourists, ensconced in hotels heavily guarded by police, seemed more than superficially aware of the environmental and political realities. During the day they were led by guides; at night they dined and wined in hotels and "safe" restaurants. They continued to use great quantities of water—good water—for most hotels considered it "bad for business" to suggest that guests economize.

Despite the political unrest engendered by Muslim extremism and the government's brutal crackdowns, tourism remained a prime source of the foreign currency needed to pay for imports from industrialized nations. But how long could it thrive in a country where tourism itself has caused the Pyramids, the Great Sphinx, and other tourist sites to decay?

The government had good reason to fear religious militants who killed some rich tourists, provided the poor with the health care they could not get from the government, and seemed to be working toward a more equitable society, we reflected as we walked through the city's slums. The air was heavy with dust, rubbish spilled over the broken sidewalks and into ditches, car horns and transistor radios outshouted each other, and children rode atop huge mounds of garbage heaped on donkey carts.

Many of the people in the teeming streets were friendly and talkative. Children playing in the open sewers called to us merrily. Unemployed youths gathered in circles, laughing together, and gesticulating dramatically. It could have made a perfect snapshot of happy-faces-in-the-midst-of-poverty. What were they really talking about? We wondered.

We could not know. But we could see that some of those faces looked bored, restless, impatient, angry. We could see middle-aged "old ones" move slowly and painfully down the streets, their wrinkled faces and arms often marked by the scars of disease. Many lived in dank apartments, sometimes four or five to a room. Others lived in makeshift shacks on rooftops. Not far away, we knew, there were still thousands living in mausoleums, next to the dead. This was the mega-city; the Third World that was growing globally, at a cancerous rate, within the First. Cairo—this Cairo—was a prime example of what lay ahead for the planet in the new millennium.

The Greens we met in their modest office on a crowded side street did not speak of Cairo as a Third World mega-city. Nor did they question—in our presence, at least—the benefits of tourism. They were eager to tell us about the new directions the party was taking.

After Hassan Ragab retired in 1991, the party foundered. Gradually, however, new faces joined those who had resolutely stuck with the group. The new president was expected to be Baha Bakry, a well-traveled professor of environmental engineering with whom we had already talked.

At our meeting with five members—most of them with scientific and technological expertise—they described the worsening environmental situation. Yet they soon changed the subject to Green initiatives already bearing fruit. There were now large member groups in Alexandria and Luxor; branches were expected to cover the whole country soon. Contacts with other Muslim countries had begun; an alliance with the Jordanians looked particularly promising. They were also planning to work more closely with Egyptian NGOs. Most impressive were plans to work at the grassroots: to go into slums and villages to ask people just how environmental conditions affected their lives. "The poor suffer most from pollution. Our students need to really *see* this, and listen to the

Group photo of members of Egypt's Green Party includes the authors.

villagers themselves," explained long-time member Aida Hussein, the one woman present.

They described plans for a tree-planting campaign. "In Muhammad's time they knew trees conserve water and help prevent erosion. The Qu'ran speaks often of trees. Today we also know that a tree contains at least 400 organisms, trees block out noise, and they contribute to biodiversity. Ninety-six percent of Egypt is desert. We need 200 million more trees. With a population of 60 million, if 50 percent plant just one a year in the next five years, we'll have 150 million new trees!"

Women were always important, the men agreed, but in this campaign they were even more qualified than men. They understood the importance of nurturing life.

After our departure, Dr. Bakry did become the new president. A woman was chosen vice-president: Dr. Wasaa Abdullah, a professor of planning and landscape. The Greens also held community meetings in two villages, focusing on teaching women how to preserve food from contamination, avoid insect bites, purify water, and teach their children the importance of protecting their environment. The meetings were so successful that members were planning many others.

We remembered our last exchange, on leaving the Greens' office. "It sounds as if overall, you are optimistic," we had observed.

"Well, not exactly. We are *hopeful*. Without hope, one cannot live."

The Holy Land: Fratricide and Terricide

For the Israelis: Power or Peace?

We arrived in Jerusalem nine days after the assassination of Prime Minister Yitzhak Rabin. The Israelis, still in shock, were reluctant to discuss with an outsider the searing question: How could a Jew murder a Jew?

In part it went back to the perennial question of identity: Who is a Jew? For Israelis that issue is complicated by the paradox that by geography their country belongs to the Levant, the region in the Eastern Mediterranean from Greece to Egypt, including Syria, Lebanon, and Palestine. Yet most Israelis have tended to identify with the West, particularly their nation's patron, the United States.

Beneath all this lay the historical tension between the "unique" and the "universal."

The unique perspective, in its most extreme form, was exemplified by convicted assassin Yigal Amir's insistence that God had ordered him to kill Rabin for ceding Israeli land to Palestinians. It echoed some Zionists' belief that Eretz Israel, Greater Israel, had been deeded exclusively to the Jews through a covenant between Abraham and God, and that if a Jew is about to hand over a Jewish community to a non-Jewish entity, he should be considered a traitor and handed over to death.

The universal was discernible in the support for the peace process launched by Rabin, a reflection of the feeling among growing numbers of Israelis that it was important to see themselves as citizens of the international community, and even accept that they were co-inhabitants, with their Palestinian neighbors, of one land.

Moreover, the government was taking part in more international initiatives, especially those concerned with the environment. High on the agenda of the Middle East peace process was the water issue, although it was hard to see tangible progress. The Ministry of Environment was expanding rapidly. For the first time, environmental units were being set up for the Palestinians living in the Central Galilee (who, in theory, were Israeli citizens). All this appeared to be based on tacit recognition that pollution respected no borders—and perhaps (although it was never stated) that the old vision of Greater Israel was either unattainable or attainable at too great a price.

Significant, too, was the inauguration in 1994 of the Abraham Joshua Heschel Center for Nature Studies, named for the Polish-born American Conservative rabbi known for his "theology of pathos" and his insistence that humans be partners with nature. Unlike other conservation groups in Israel, the Center had an ecospiritual approach. Like Ellen Bernstein, director Eilon Schwartz, an American-born education professor at Hebrew University, believed that the environmental crisis is basically a crisis of values. "We need something more than technology," he told us. "Heschel's ideas were based on awe and wonder and radical amazement—as well as humility.

"It is in the Jewish heritage to *act* on one's belief, as did Heschel. So we engage people in educational projects and work in the field." These projects were wide-ranging: preparing a Jewish environmental curriculum for the mainstream elementary school system; leading a four-month kibbutz program on "Judaism and the Environment" for university students from abroad; running seminars for the Ministry of the Environment; exploring the importance of the Jordan River's sources in Mideast politics; leading camping excursions to places of historical and ecological importance like the Sea of Galilee and Negev Desert. Today, said Schwartz, no place can humble a human as the desert can. "Always we try to be responsive to the needs of the day, to what is happening in Israel and elsewhere. We try to embody Heschel's universalist perspective."

But beside the universalist vision, another vision was growing, calling into question the genuineness of the much-vaunted "peace process." If the Heschel Center emphasized humility, living in harmony with nature, and the limits of human technology, there were mighty forces at work seized by an entrancement with power. One expression of that entrancement was a dream being spun by an elite of technocratic experts. It was called the Israel 2020 Master Plan.

The goal was to create an Israel of Tomorrow perfectly designed from every point of view—economics, environment, education, transport, and energy. It would catch up with—and perhaps surpass—American standards (based implicitly on the philosophy that "more is better") that are referred to in reports on the plan.

The population of Israel (excluding the quasi-desert Negev, which encompasses 60 percent of the land, but only 7 percent of the population) is 50 percent higher than in most densely populated countries, such as Holland. But unlike them, it has a people-count that is growing rapidly, at a rate of 2 percent a year, declares an *Israel Environment Bulletin* report on preparations for the Plan.[3] Thus if present plans continue, within 30 years Israel, north of Beersheba, will be one of the most densely populated countries in the world.

Instead of considering this startling fact a sign that population planning should be promoted vigorously, the experts proceed to plan everything else. Israel's population of 5.5 million will "burgeon" to 8 million, its built-up space will treble, the number of motor vehicles will also treble, and the road network will undergo major expansion to keep pace with Western standards.

This great dream reflected Israel's new affluence. Partly because of American subsidies, its per capita income was becoming one of the highest in the world. At the same time, there was a retreat from the conservation ethic preached in 1990, particularly in the area of water.

To be sure, some Israelis pointed to the ways the highway project would exacerbate the already serious ecological problems in this country, scarcely larger than the state of Connecticut. Some reports in the *Bulletin* emphasize that already land resources are dwindling, ozone levels often reach dangerous levels, and solid wastes, water demand, and water quality are grave problems. Nevertheless, the overall implication is that somehow such obstacles would be overcome through new means of organizing Israel's limited space, a new approach to population dispersion and spatial density, more efficient land use, and innovative building in previously uninhabitable areas like arid zones, mountain slopes, the sea.[4] Nothing, then, would be considered beyond the reach of humans.

In the words of architect Adam Mazor: "[In 30 years] all the building and infrastructure that presently exist is only one-third of what will be built then." Thus would the old Zionist geo-political-religious dream of an expanding Greater Israel—expanding even as far east as the Euphrates and as far southwest as the Nile—be replaced by a dream of expanding in other ways.

Curiously, Palestinians do not seem to figure in this "future image"—although most of the Israelis' groundwater comes from sources in Palestinian land and they share the same sea and sky.

The Trans-Israel highway, central to the Plan, envisions a straight stretch linking the Negev in the South to three points not far from Lebanon and the Golan Heights. Proponents stress that it will relieve congestion, since Israel's motorization rate lags behind the Western world, yet car density is way above Western norms. What is not said is that the highway could speed the movement of troops and also enhance Israel's position as the entrepreneurial hub of a new Middle East.

Opponents have countered that the grand highway will ravage the environment by destroying scarce open land reserves, adding to urban sprawl, encouraging building in agricultural areas, aggravating air and noise pollution, harming wildlife, and further degrading ground water. Cultural and environmental groups, as well as most of the Hebrew press, raised loud protests.

To no avail. By late 1995, the government had approved the central stretch, which includes eight lanes, and a 16-mile stretch with nine inter-changes, each requiring between 49 and 247 acres of land.[5] In 1996 the Cabinet approved the total scheme, even while the Israel Union for Environmental Defense and other Green groups continued to object. Eilon Schwartz joined a huge protest demonstration. Jeremy Milgrom called the plan "insane." Azaria Alon was bitter: "It will be a disaster." Criticizing the Cabinet's decision in the conservative *Jerusalem Post*, businessman Ben Dansker described Israel as "hell-bent on creating a mini-America, on exorcising our inferiority complex upon this tiny postage stamp of a country."[6]

Few rabbis protested. Explained Israeli commentator Israel Shahak, a Holocaust survivor: "Almost 99 percent of Israeli rabbis are Orthodox, and a type who even oppose enjoying nature as a 'waste of time.'"[7]

The Israelis, it seemed, were looking backward—back to a time when it made sense to take literally the ancient biblical injunction: "Be fruitful and multiply and fill the earth and subdue it, and have dominion over the fish of the sea and over the birds of the air and over every living thing that moves upon the earth."

The Palestinians' Struggle to Survive

The people living on the other side of this land had already felt the impact of Israel's auto power. On our visit, the most frequent grievance we heard was that more Israeli roads were crisscrossing the West Bank, and Palestinian land and homes were being destroyed to build them. The number of checkpoints and fortified road blocks, too, had actually increased during the peace process. Indeed, directly or indirectly, the Israelis controlled all roads on the West Bank—a "fact on the ground" that was coupled with the frenetic pace of Israeli settlement building.

One scene in Bethlehem, cradle of Christianity, stands out in our minds. Looking out the windows of Jad Isaac's Applied Research Institute office, we saw a circle of Israeli apartment houses, towering like fortresses. "Almost every day, I see new building surrounding us, closing in, creeping closer," muttered Isaac, a prominent Palestinian Christian and American-educated environmentalist. We had never forgotten the hours spent with him in 1990 in his Beit Sahour home opposite historic Shepherds' Field, after his imprisonment for helping lead the non-violent Beit Sahour "no taxation without representation" movement. His chief "crime" had been to teach Palestinians, deprived by Israelis of their jobs during the Intifada, to adopt various down-to-earth methods of self-suf-ficiency, especially gardening. Yet even then he belonged to a small informal group of Israeli and Palestinian intellectuals working for a better understanding of each other and for a peaceful, cooperative future.

"New building. And the roads!" he continued, with a long sigh. "Unless a Palestinian has special permission, he cannot go from Bethlehem to Jerusalem, less than six miles. Workers commuting from Ramallah to Bethlehem cannot enter Jerusalem; they must use narrow, dangerous roads that circle it and take more than twice the time."

That scene mirrored others on our visit. Everywhere we sensed the Israeli presence. That was the intention, Palestinians agreed: "To keep reminding us of who's really boss."

This was not new. The number of Israeli settlements on Palestinian land had actually *increased* by more than 25 percent during the "peace process," Palestinians told us. The United States (which has been funding Israel with an average of 5.5 to 6 billion dollars a year in grants, interest, and loan guarantees during the 1990s) claimed to oppose further expansion.[8] Yet "the exception committee" of Rabin, that "martyr for peace," had approved it. In 1993 then-Deputy Prime Minister Shimon Peres had announced, "We will build, *but* without declaring it in public." The mushrooming ring of settlements in and around East Jerusalem, home to many Christian and Muslim sacred monuments, and home to hundreds of thousands of Palestinian people, was the core of a frantic rush to create the "fact on the ground" that Jerusalem belonged exclusively to Israel. Thirty percent of the former West Bank was being redefined as Greater Jerusalem.

The expanding system of roads served many purposes—not least, to isolate Palestinian communities from each other, connect the Israeli settlements, which were placed at strategic points, and allow Israelis to be spared the sight of Palestinian villages. Moreover, Israeli military bases in the West Bank were actually increasing as the "peace process" marched forward.

All this was hardly surprising to Palestinians. They remembered that Rabin had encouraged Israeli soldiers to break the bones of young protesters in the Intifada, and maneuvered a "peace agreement" that gave outsiders the impression that Israel had agreed to quit the West Bank. Now Peres was continuing the same hypocritical "peace" policy.

But how could repression continue under accords signed by the PLO? Virtually all the Palestinians we met declared angrily that they had no say in the matter, and a corrupt Yasir Arafat had betrayed his people. There were reports that his men were even using methods of torture on certain members of the extremist group Hamas who were denouncing him as a "collaborator"—methods that had been used on them while prisoners in Israeli jails. As so often in human history, some of the oppressed were becoming oppressors.

As for development—witness its spread in once-beautiful towns like Ramallah. It was the product of investment by rich Palestinians, some of whom had returned from the West with a free-market ideology and by others who were rarely identified. Suddenly, parts of a poor country had become—for the moment, at least—the new frontier for get-rich-quick building schemes.

The new class had been enabled to power by Arafat's acquiescence to the Israelis and their American sponsors, we were told. Privately, we decided to dub him "Yessir!" Arafat.

The ultimate victim in all this was the earth. Driving through the countryside, we watched Israeli bulldozers leveling Palestinian farmland and homes in order to create feeder roads. Almost everywhere, the landscape was losing its pastoral, distinctively Palestinian character. Yes, Jad Isaac told us, today agriculture contributed less than a quarter of the GDP (down from over a third in the early 1970s), a drop caused by many factors, including urbanization and population growth. Linked with this was the decline in water quantity and quality. Israel would not yield control over Palestinian water. Some 80 percent was still going to Israel and its settlements. Settlers swam in swimming pools, watered their lawns with sprinklers, and were not even asked to conserve water— while Palestinian children did not have enough to drink. Israel had promised to "allow" the Palestinians a 25 percent increase, but only after five years, and it remained only a promise.

Hence one of Jad's many goals was to develop "dry land farming," which depended not on irrigation, but on new methods of using rainfall, traditionally sparse in this region. His Institute was working, too, on waste water disposal, transboundary pollution, socio-economic factors influencing the environment, and regional cooperation on water and other environmental issues.

Ramzi Sansur, a Palestinian Christian with an American doctorate in environmental science, was equally concerned about water. As director of the Center for Environmental and Occupational Health Sciences at Bir Zeit University and author of a comprehensive United Nations study on environment and development in Palestine, he had observed the worsening of many problems. Gaza was especially serious.

We knew that today approximately one million Palestinians squeezed into the 140-square-mile strip known as Gaza, making it one of the most crowded places on the planet. Some estimates of unemployment ran as high as 40 percent. The one million Palestinians had access to only 25 percent of the fresh water supply there, while their Israeli settler neighbors (approximately 4,000 to 5,000) were allocated the remaining 75 percent.[9] We knew that the situation had barely improved since our first visit to Gaza in 1988—there were still open ditches and canals reeking of sewage, children often fell into them, and the sewage was frequently pumped back into them so that people drank their own excrement. From

Sansur we learned how Israel's overpumping was a major factor in the deterioration of aquifers; salinity was increasing as more sea water seeped in to make up for the increased pumping. Such water is too salty for drinking and even for irrigating most crops, Moreover, high levels of nitrates, lead, and fecal coliform bacteria had been found, contributing to the dangerously poor health of Gazan children, particularly. "All this will *foil* water conservation efforts," Sansur said wearily.

In the West Bank, he went on, Israeli settlers' pesticides were also polluting the water. Moreover, untrained Palestinian farmers were over-using agrichemicals—including 40 pesticides that were restricted or banned elsewhere. The warning instructions were in Hebrew, and thus could not be understood by most Palestinians.

Developers were tearing the West Bank apart. The wilderness and the creatures who make it their home were disappearing before the on-slaught. A tree-planting campaign, so important in preventing erosion, was badly needed, but Israelis fiercely opposed it.

Water and land, then, remained the key issues. All over the world, they were looming more ominously as interlocking sources of strife. What made the predicament here particularly poignant was that water-sharing between the two peoples, together with some mutual agreement on what constituted *real* needs, could avert tragedy.

For many years, Palestinians were too preoccupied with just surviv-ing to evince interest in caring for the environment. Nor, without a gov-ernment they could call their own, was there a national program to raise environmental awareness. This may change. Thus far, however, the Pal-estinian Authority has had other priorities.

Nevertheless, there is rising popular concern, signaled by the grow-ing number of environmental non-governmental organizations whose concerns ranged from land and water issues to community health and education. Among the latter is an environmental education program be-gun by the Lutheran schools in Jerusalem, and entitled Children for the Protection of Nature in Palestine. Its director, Imad Atrash, was born in the predominantly Christian town of Beit Sahour, and quit his job as lab technician at Bethlehem University in 1992 to dedicate himself to nature preservation and environmental problems. (By 1999, the group was work-ing with 50 schools throughout Palestine.)[10]

Ecological concerns are seldom pushed by Palestinian churches, however. One reason is that they have been struggling just to exist, as Israel has continued to confiscate church property. Few Christians in other countries have protested, and the vast majority of American media have ignored the issue entirely. (One belated sign of hope is the confer-ence of 185 international participants from 25 countries, who gathered in East Jerusalem in January 1996 to discuss "the significance of Jerusalem for Christians and Christians for Jerusalem." Throughout, they emphasized the equal rights of all three Semitic faiths to religious attachment there and urged commitments to action.)[11]

Another reason is alienation among the faithful, because most churches are "colonials." That is, they are controlled by the "mother church"—in Rome, Greece, or elsewhere—and the parent chooses the clergy. Moreover, the parent churches have only rarely spoken out strongly for Palestinians' rights. Hence the faithful seldom turn to the churches for leadership.

Many individual Christian lay persons do recognize the spiritual dimension of the ecological crisis, although they rarely speak of it. For example, in 1990 when he had more hope, Jad Isaac listened intently after asking us to describe Thomas Berry's ideas, nodded fervently, and responded, "It corresponds to what I've been thinking. Almost *completely*!" In late 1995 he refused to discuss the subject. "All I can think of now is struggling on, one day at a time." His tense, tired face and body said the rest: in this atmosphere of Islamic militancy and Israeli infiltration into every aspect of life, it was politic not to be "political" or to talk, as a Christian, of ecoreligious beliefs that might be considered "subversive." Above all, his unique community-based work for self-sufficiency and a sustainable future must survive.

Thus far the Muslims of Palestine have no ecoreligious movement. Some individual believers, like Nafez Assaily, feel deeply the connection between their faith and preserving the natural world. But the leadership needed for a movement has been lacking. This may change as barriers between Palestine and Muslim countries begin to crumble. One hopeful sign is that at the 1990 meeting of the Global Forum of Spiritual and Parliamentary Leaders, Sheikh Ahmad Kuftaro, Syria's Grand Mufti and supreme judge of Islamic civil law, declared: "We have to have birth control for the global welfare, without exploiting it at the expense of one nationality over another."[12]

Since our visit, Hamas has reacted violently to the violence wrought upon the Palestinians with desperate attacks on Israel. Brutal and indiscriminate they have been. Yet not so massive, indiscriminate, or technologically efficient as the destruction of people and land that the Israelis have inflicted on Palestinians, and the Lebanese as well.

Meanwhile, reigning Israeli and American leaders—as well as "Yessir" Arafat—have continued to verbalize support for the "peace process," as if that were some disembodied being that could rise from the ashes. They do not speak of peace based on justice. It might seem strange that in the face of Hamas assaults, Israeli leaders, with all their vacillation, have generally declared that the "peace process" will go on. But how can it be otherwise if that religio-political-economic dream of an Eretz Middle East, presided over by Israel with Tel Aviv as its commercial center, is to have dominion over this corner of Planet Earth?

It is hard to believe that a people as closely tied to the land as the Palestinians can ever be completely subdued. Like the American Indians, they will struggle, in the face of overwhelming obstacles, to keep their identity. The Israelis, in *their* fear, will continue to tighten "security," even as the financial and moral costs become self-destructive. Yet the Palestinians will fight back, sometimes with their wits, sometimes with arms, sometimes with ultimately suicidal weapons like enjoining their people to be fruitful and multiply.

Where will it all end? As Rabbi Jeremy Milgrom observes, even if a Palestinian state emerges it will be barely viable, and will remain subservient to the Israeli economy—which is 25 times stronger than the Palestinian. Israel will continue to exploit the last natural resource left to the Palestinians—their workforce.[13]

Where will it all end? Humans, not destiny, will decide. Humans—and the earth itself, with its limited resources. At this point, it is hard to imagine anything but disaster. Thousands of innocent people on both sides perishing in a war between the children of Abraham, a war that need never have been. Millions of their descendants leading stunted lives as a result of the war against the fragile land that they share.

East Asia

Thailand: New Gods in Green Land

The capital of Thailand, a star performer in the East Asian Miracle, was bursting with the sights and sounds and smells of dynamic growth. In Bangkok new five-star hotels had gone up since our earlier visit, new roads had been built, and in a single five-block area one could choose among Burger King, Dunkin' Donuts, Baskin Robbins, Pizza Hut, and Kentucky Fried Chicken.

To be sure, even on Bangkok's grand avenues near the grand hotels, we inhaled scents of sewage as we made our way over plastic throwaways, broken steps, and gaping holes in the pavement. Makeshift stalls of Thai-made "imported" baubles spilled over sidewalks, hawkers cooked supper *al fresco*, and gaunt flea-bitten dogs and cats lay prostrate underfoot. The air was heavy with grit; the smog seemed even more oppressive than on our first visit. "What can you do?" The hotel clerk shrugged. "They say you can't stop progress."

Siam/Thailand's primary forest, which once covered almost all of the country, had now dwindled to less than 20 percent.[14] (Ironically, the name "Siam" comes from a Pali word meaning "green.") The country's shortage of water was worsening, and was coupled with a recent series of disastrous floods, caused largely by erosion. Many parts of Bangkok had been submerged.

Although Bangkok had created more roads and extended others, the number of vehicles had also grown. Hence the traffic crisis had only worsened. Deputy Prime Minister Thaksin Shinawatra was openly criticized for failing to live up to his campaign promise to ease it, and for his secretive, enormously profitable financial dealings. When we tried to travel from central Bangkok to some outlying area with more breathable air, endless traffic jams forced us to turn back. We remembered Iroquois Chief-of-Chiefs Leon Shenandoah's despairing words: "Mother Earth now, she's nothing but webs of roads around her body, and they're strangling her to death."

Thailand/Siam bore certain similarities with Israel. Both countries had rushed into industrial growth, both suffered from drastic loss of tree cover and consequent erosion, both were faced with critical shortages of water, and both were planting vast networks of roads in the soil. By promising higher wages than those in Thailand, Israel was importing Thai laborers to replace workers from the West Bank and Gaza, holding this as a threat over the Palestinians' heads. This exacerbated Thailand's semi-skilled labor shortage, but the government "solved" it by reaching down the pecking order and using even cheaper workers, illegals from Laos, Cambodia, and Myanmar, whose illicit status served as a threat over *their* heads: "Make no complaints!" And just as Israel served the U.S. as policeman for the Middle East, Siam/Thailand served U.S. interests by exerting its political and economic might over neighbors considered susceptible to instability.[15]

The grand avenues of Bangkok included pockets of squalor, but the fetid sections of people living near garbage-strewn canals and rat-filled gutters were a step downward into a more homogeneous underworld. This Bangkok reminded us of Cairo's slums. These streets, too, swarmed with dispirited-looking women who had probably just emerged from polluted sweatshops; men wearily smoking cigarettes made by U.S.-based multinationals, whose sales were faltering in the domestic market; gaily waving children who might soon be pimps or prostitutes. Perhaps some had been ousted from farms like those we had seen on our visit to Ajahn Pongsak. This was far from the smooth, sterilized world just a few blocks away—the tinted glass spheres of those who worked and lived high above the streets within Bangkok's skyscraper offices and the towering luxury apartments and hotels. But at bottom, it was that towering, insider world that really needed the outsider world teeming around us.

Indeed, as we looked out at the office buildings and elegant apartments, we realized that many were empty. Yet new building continued. How long could such contradictions go on? we asked ourselves. Could this shining miracle of transnational capitalism last?[16]

Outside the capital, we knew, Thailand's "tiger economy" was being nourished by the fast-growing golf industry and its spinoffs: hotels, restaurants, real estate development, new road networks. There were now 200 courses, with a new one opening about every two weeks. They displaced thousands of farmers from their ancestral lands; destroyed forests; infected the water, earth, and air with regular doses of chemical fertilizers and pesticides, including carcinogenic artificial coloring agents; and caused a massive drain on scarce water supplies. During a recent drought, course operators had deprived desperate local farmers of water by drawing it off reservoirs illegally. A typical course used as much water as 6,000 city people.[17]

All this was a manifestation of the golf boom that had erupted throughout the world, especially East Asia. Ecologists like Sreela Kolandai, a leader in Friends of the Earth-Malaysia and a founder of the Global Anti-Golf Movement, called them "green graveyards" because they supported only grass—"no trees, no birds, no insects, no nothing." Entrepreneurs retorted that their courses were "a home in the wilderness," where one could find "conservation and recreation in harmony." And apparently, this was the way that golfers perceived them.

Siladhamma Hibernates

Soon after our arrival, we met with Nunie Svasti to learn more about what was happening to Ajahn Pongsak and to the Dhamanaat Foundation, which, we knew, was facing yet another crisis. Although Nunie was still in great pain from a back injury sustained in an automobile accident while transporting visitors to the project, she met us for a long talk in Bangkok.

Ajahn was still hiding, yet from time to time took a chance and returned to his original meditation spot, the Tu Bou Cave. He seemed to have an uncanny sense warning him when to retreat back to his hiding place among his friends.

Despite the growing number of floods, and the growing recognition of the role of watershed forests in preventing them, the Foundation was being threatened by the prospect of annihilation. "Certain forces" in government and the business world, claimed Nunie, were planning to build a huge dam to help the villagers in the Mae Soi region by supplying more water. Coincidentally, the dam site was planned in a part of the national forest where the Tu Bou Cave stood.

Most villagers were hesitant about being helped. On consulting Ajahn, their suspicions were confirmed. Many large dams in other parts of the world had displaced people, killed fish, flooded farmland, destroyed bird habitat, and threatened rivers. If it were true that a dam *was* needed, they themselves would find a site for a smaller, suitable dam.

Still, government forces pressed the project. It turned out that the central figure in that circle was Deputy Prime Minister Thaksin Shinawatra, who happened to be the nephew of Ajahn's old enemy, Surapan Shinawatra.

Government forces were no monolith, however. The director of the national forest was firmly against a large dam. And there were other opponents. Nunie's idea was to draw together some 20 of the important scientists and government figures who sensed the dangers to Thailand's forests and rivers, for they had been too isolated. Communicating with one another, they could come to realize that in unity there is strength. Already a team of specialists—including a geologist, a taxonomist, and an environmental engineer—was making a feasibility survey. Thus far their findings demonstrated the same conclusion that Ajahn had come to: the rock foundation was so porous that it would not hold water. If all these concerned people could agree on an approach, they could go to the King and ask him to intervene.

It would not be wise to visit Ajahn, Nunie advised us; it could be risky for us, and risky for Ajahn, since two Westerners were highly visible. When her health permitted, she would visit him, and then report on the condition of Ajahn and the project.

We understood. Nevertheless, it was frustrating not to be able to see him. We consoled ourselves with the thought—indeed, the conviction—that somehow Ajahn would triumph. In this quiet man lay power. He was effective because he understood the causes of the sickness afflicting his country, and knew how to explain them to the villagers. He also had the support of someone with absolute faith in him. Nunie had financial means, contacts, administrative ability and, most important, the unwavering determination to put his ideas across—commitment.

RIGHT MINDFULNESS, RIGHT LIVELIHOOD, AND RIGHT RESISTANCE

At the end of our stay, we talked with Sulak Sivaraksa, Siam's best-known Buddhist lay activist. Recently acquitted of lèse majesté charges, and quietly glowing with the news that he was being given a Right Livelihood Award (known as the Alternative Nobel Prize), he was animated and hopeful.

Could democracy succeed in Siam? we asked. His answer was categorical: "Only if it includes a spiritual element."

He was continuing to expand the activities of the Wongsanit ashram he had founded in 1985. Situated near Nakhon Nayok, northeast of Bangkok, it is a "green oasis" set among rice paddies and canals. The people live simply in straw huts, cultivate organic gardens, and find a balance between living a contemplative life and working for social change. In conjunction with the Spirit in Education Movement, which encourages ecological, holistic, and spiritual learning to counter the globalization of Western rational education, the ashram hosts courses in conflict resolution, deep ecology, and community-building, taught by activists and thinkers ranging from Japanese Buddhists to American Quakers.

A new initiative at Wongsanit, we learned, is a worldwide network known as Alternatives to Consumerism, which records the true stories of people inspired by differing spiritual motivations, who have created sustainable alternatives to the Western consumer model.

Since our departure, ecological activity has continued despite the "Asian flu" that has infested Thailand. In 1996, 30 regional coordinators, as well as interested persons from Europe, South Korea, and North America, gathered at Wongsanit to exchange their stories and discuss the way ahead.

Elsewhere, the Project for Ecological Recovery, which has always tried to work with local monks, has continued to support Thai communities in protecting rivers, forests, land, and rural livelihoods. It has also joined with a new sister organization, Towards Ecological Recovery and Regional Alliance (TERRA), which works with grassroots organizations in neighboring Burma, Cambodia, Laos, and Vietnam by encouraging exchange and alliance-building. The two groups, as well as TERRA's magazine *Watershed*, have focused particularly on Thailand's demands for power, especially from dams in the Mekong Delta, and on the eviction of communities and destruction of undisturbed forest caused by the Yadana gas pipeline from Burma. In 1998 Sulak was arrested again for protesting the pipeline. Clearly, as in the Middle East, a consciousness of the regional nature of such ecological problems is growing.

Ajahn's situation has not changed, according to Nunie. She reported "a little progress" with her own efforts to preserve watershed forest, and on the broader front, an encouraging growth in awareness of the importance of Siam's natural heritage.

In the face of continuing harassment from both the government and the Buddhist hierarchy, most of the Siamese ecological monks have managed to persist with their work. True, Phra Prachak Khuttajitto was not only sentenced to a year of imprisonment for leading "a mob" to occupy the Dong Yai forest reserve land, but forced to disrobe. He has been subjected to more lawsuits instituted by authorities who felt threatened by his actions, and has become thoroughly debilitated, physically and psychologically. Nevertheless, other stalwarts continue, and younger monks, determined to serve the country's green heritage, appear on the scene. Indeed, Susan Darlington, who has worked with "ecomonks" in Thailand, observes that the Thai movement is still growing, and becoming more vocal and controversial.[18]

Thus in 1997, Phra Somkidjaranadhamma, working with Northern Farmers Network, mobilized villagers in central and northern Thailand in a campaign to save 800,000 acres of forests by "ordaining" the trees with monks' orange robes to remind people that nature should be treated as equal with humans.[19] Other monks work in other ways to establish protected community forests and protest development projects. They also devise fresh approaches—blessing a river and declaring part of it a fish sanctuary, which fits villagers' needs and beliefs, including spirit beliefs.

New ideas, new initiatives.

As we left Siam/Thailand, it was hard to be optimistic about the future. Arrayed against Ajahn Pongsak, the other ecomonks, and lay "steadfast ones" like Sivaraksa, was a conglomerate host of entrepreneurial forces, rendered even more formidable by the fact that so many of them had an invisible and global dimension.

Yet the spiritual forces persisted. The cry from the forest insisted. It was almost as if the earth itself cried to be heard.

Taiwan: Tiger Power at Any Price

At first, the capital of Taiwan, the third of the tiger states we visited, looked brighter and cleaner than Bangkok. Taipei's streets were lined with colorful shops, and passionate round-the-clock political campaigning added to the vibrant atmosphere. Almost immediately, however, we noticed that many motorcyclists wore masks against the clouds of pollution, and shoppers hurrying down the streets looked weary and harassed.

The shops were filled with expensive merchandise, to be sure. Taiwan was living up to its reputation of having one of the highest per capita incomes in Asia, an achievement in large part based on its exports of consumer commodities, including finished goods and components for products sold by such name-brand companies as Radio Shack, Nike Shoes, and Giant Bicycles.

Less visible were underground "pharmacies" dealing in elixirs made from African rhino horn, American bear gall, Pacific seals, Siberian or Indian tiger bone, and shops marketing panda-skin rugs, jewelry of elephant ivory, and body parts of monkeys and snakes. We had read about Taiwan's distinction as a major international center for illegal trafficking in wildlife. We knew that despite their Westernized secular outlook, many big businessmen pursued salvation and virility through ancient Chinese folk medicines—most of them linked to Chinese folk religions—such as powdered rhino horn. Nouveaux-riches Taiwanese treated friends and customers to state-of-the-art dinners (costing up to $3,000 per head) that began with tiger-penis soup to impart the sexual potency of tigers. Meanwhile, the global population of tigers was declining rapidly.[20]

GROWING RESISTANCE FROM ENVIRONMENTALISTS

Although conservationists like Dr. Lucia Severinghaus, whom we had first met in 1989, were continuing their efforts to protect endangered species, that issue seemed remote to most Taiwanese. They were profoundly worried, however, about the persistence of environmentally induced diseases of the human species, which hit the poor most of all. Childhood asthma, for example, was rising. Cancer was still the leading cause of death. A close connection with the island's nuclear plants (now numbering three, each with two reactors) seemed undeniable. The Taiwanese we spoke with talked angrily about the discovery of radiation-contaminated rivers, buildings, roads, and farm fields—and the series of accidents that had plagued the reactors from the beginning. How much longer, we asked ourselves, could the sources of life—water, air, land—on this still prosperous but tight little island be poisoned before a day of reckoning arrived?

(After our departure, cancer continued to mount. In 1999, National Taiwan University physics professor K.L. Chang wrote us that "as for cancer death rate, it goes up steadily: 121 in 1996, and 169 in 1998 per 100,000 population." He also revealed that there had been three serious accidents at Taiwanese nuclear plants in the short period July 31, 1998 to February 25, 1999 alone.)[21]

The center of opposition to nuclear power was still the Taiwan Environmental Protection Union (TEPU), whose founder, Professor Chang, we had met in 1989. This time he recounted a long list of popular protests, including a thousand-kilometer march across Taiwan, and a petition of 300,000 signatures for a plebiscite on the government's demand for legislative approval of billions more for reactors.

He described the persecution and harassment that he and his colleagues continued to suffer. The law required that any "assembly" (more than three people) obtain official permission seven days ahead, and laid

Dr. K. L. Chang of the Department of Physics, National Taiwan University leads nuclear power protest.

out such complicated rules concerning marches that it was impossible to follow them. Professor C.Y. Kao, the current head of TEPU, had already been convicted for seven cases, and could be imprisoned up to 14 years. Because of public outcry, the cases of both men were being appealed, but the courts kept postponing hearings. However, the threat remained hanging over their heads, including the reminder that in the past, two such demonstrators had been imprisoned.

Were they discouraged? "Sometimes," Chang replied wearily. "But not long." He smiled as if to keep his spirits up. "Some colleagues do leave. But then others take their place."

In fact, TEPU was expanding its horizons. During 1995 alone, it protested Chinese missile tests and French nuclear testing in the Pacific and organized the Third No-Nukes Asia Forum in Taipei, attended by delegates from many countries. Moreover, a Green Party had recently been formed in Taiwan by several National Taiwan University professors.

We returned to Houshan (Monkey Hill) to climb its "thousand steps" and visit its Buddhist, Confucianist, Taoist, and folk temples. As before, the altars were filled with pineapples, oranges, and papaya, and an Earth-loving spirit seemed to radiate through all these holy places. But this time, there were far more tourists, and much more development on the lower reaches of the hill.

Fong Mau Li, the Taoist priest we had met in 1989, told us he had moved to Academia Sinica, but was still teaching Chinese literature and philosophy. His buoyant voice faltered a little as he told us that most of his students did not seem to comprehend his ideas about "living the na-ture life," or "changing our ways with Taiwan and the earth."

He sighed. "What they see, it is not Nature. It is something else. But a few students see the Way. That they will *live* it—that is my hope."

RESISTANCE AMONG THE TAOISTS

On our return home, we found in our mail an article from the Alliance of Religions and Conservation (ARC), telling how Taoist monks in China had become horrified by the way their sacred mountains were being threatened by tourism and the entrepreneurial culture. Traditionally, the sacred mountains have been places of retreat from the world, refuges for wildlife, and models of co-existence with the natural world. Intended to be difficult to climb, in order to instill humility, these sacred places can be reached today by roads or cable car. Hotel complexes and heli-copter ports on the summits have been proposed. Visitors invade even the temples that cling miraculously to the sides of perpendicular rock cliffs.[22]

Accompanying the article was the first statement on ecology in the Chinese Taoists' long history, issued in May 1995 at a meeting in Bei-jing's White Cloud Temple. Among other things, it declared that accord-ing to the classic *Tao Te Ching*, "Humanity follows the Earth, the Earth follows Heaven, Heaven follows the Tao, and the Tao follows what is natural." This means, said the statement, that all humanity should obey Earth's rule of movement. We should let Nature be itself. Moreover, peo-ple should take into full consideration the limits of nature's sustaining power.

Perhaps the most remarkable assertion was that "Taoism has a unique sense of value in that it judges affluence by the number of species."[23]

In past years Chinese Taoists have engaged in protecting orchards, planting trees, and protecting the nearly extinct Chinese fir. Now, work-ing with ARC, the International Consultancy on Religion, Education, and Culture (ICOREC), and UNESCO's World Cultural Heritage Pro-gram, the Taoists are planning projects that include a periodical to edu-cate people about protection of the environment; more tree-planting, using temple grounds as the basic unit; and a study, intended to influence the authorities, surveying the impact of tourism and development on the

Taoist cave temple suspended on the sheer side of the Northern Heng Shan mountain in China. (Courtesy CIRCA Photo Library; photo by Tjalling Halbert-
sma)

holy mountains.[24]

    Was this a completely new turn in a tradition known as one empha-
sizing passivity? We remembered Fong Mau Li's words: "From the beginning, non-intervention has not meant no-action, but respect for the
rights of all things." What these plans did represent was a new turn toward organized action.

Japan: Land of the Rising Sun?

Walking down the smoggy, shop-lined streets of Osaka we were forcefully reminded that Japan was the original "East Asian miracle." That very success seemed to be carrying the seeds of its own destruction, however, as cheap labor competitors—Thailand, South Korea, Vietnam, and China—set themselves the goal of catching up with their mighty Nipponese neighbor. At the same time, Japan was suffering from more floods, more contamination of groundwater and soil, more pollution of the ocean that provided the staple food, fish.

Yet instead of seeing all this as a warning, the Japanese (whom Ronald "Progress is our Most Important Product" Reagan had once criticized for resisting consumerism) were charging ahead. There were more automobiles and more paved-over land than ever. There were more Japanese traveling abroad—many of them armed with disposable single-roll cameras. The number of tourists had leaped from one million in 1970 to 10 million in 1990, and continued to multiply every year. Indeed, the Japanese were now seen by eager upscale merchants abroad as "the world's greatest shoppers." While opposition to golf course development had grown so strong that the country was now headquarters for the global anti-golf movement, this business sport— once known as "the rich white man's game"—continued to devour more scarce Japanese land.[25] The English name of a Japanese magazine for women said it all: *MORE*.

As a society, the Japanese were still living high. True, there were many poor who did not share in the "miracle." We had seen them on inner-city streets and back country roads. But they were rendered invisible by an unspoken agreement not to talk about them. All this affluence was a little like the packaging of gifts we had bought: individual chocolates decorated with roses; then wrapped individually in gilt paper; then arranged under a colorfully printed plastic cover; then placed in a box with floral designs; then wrapped elaborately, as a box, in gleaming foil; then tied with bows; and finally slipped into an elegant shopping bag.

The Japanese were still living high on the ecological capital of less-developed countries. They—and we Westerners—were leeches on the backs of ill-paid laborers in Malaysian rainforests, Ghanaian cacao plantations, or Chinese coal mines. We were also drawing on the life-blood of birds, fish, trees, insects, and other creatures in the earth community.

A Return to the Green Kindergarten

We had expected to see Shinto followers and both of the Buddhist "ecological priests" we had met in 1990, Shincho Tanaka in Kyoto and Eisho Yoshida in Kofu City. That plan was frustrated when the persisting illness of one of us worsened, and it was necessary to limit our visit to meeting Yoshida on a Sunday morning and return home quickly that night.

Yoshida lamented the fact that we could not see the children at his "green kindergarten," but welcomed us jovially and ushered us into a room of his temple that overlooked the school grounds and a garden. While widely praised as evidencing "Japanese love for nature," many gardens in this country seemed designed to bend and twist trees and order plants into some human fantasy only remotely resembling the natural world. Yoshida's temple school garden was a joyous, informal array of winter vegetables and sprawling plants, in summer brightened by flowers.

With Rick Davis again acting as interpreter, Yoshida talked of many happenings since our last visit. After recovering from oral cancer by means of a "natural cure," he had begun making calls on hospice patients, "just waiting around to die." He had not played doctor, nor had he acted like a conventional priest. Instead of talking religious abstractions, he had roused the dying by getting them to draw pictures with him, thus stimulating them to talk of their feelings; afterwards, they seemed more ready to die in peace. When parishioners collected aid for people in war-torn Somalia, Yoshida, aware of frequent corruption in delivering aid, had made the trip there in order to present it himself and get to know people directly. And after the Kobe earthquake, he had collected clothing and food, taken them to the ravaged city, cooked meals, and talked with the victims. "Meeting face-to-face, heart-to-heart—" He smiled pensively. "That is what is real, no?"

But Yoshida was most eager of all to talk about his pupils. He brought out pictures of them walking excitedly through the autumn woods, examining crustaceans at the beach, braving the waves in a skiff, and cooking vegetables they had grown, then gathering to eat them.

We were particularly struck by a series depicting their study of silk-making: the silkworm's metamorphosis from worm to caterpillar, the mysterious moment when the caterpillar begins spinning out filaments of viscous fluid from its body to form a cocoon, the entry of humans on the scene to reel the silken filaments and spin them into thread. Later the youngsters themselves wove the thread into lustrous cloth on a handloom they shared.

When the silkworm moths died, said Yoshida, the children were deeply saddened. Then they had an idea. Would their teacher-priest bless the departed insects? "I was astonished! Well, I dressed myself in my vestments and performed a Buddhist ceremony for the dead. It was a sacred moment for them. Afterwards, the children still looked sad, but also satisfied.

"Adults see silk as a *commodity*!" Yoshida added, clapping his hands to his head. "They never imagine where it comes from. But children—

children see silk as a *living thing*. They have raised it themselves—I mean, working along with the parents, the male and female moths.

"Unfortunately—" he let out a sigh. "Unfortunately, when they go to regular school, they have to unlearn all this and prepare to become competitive. The transnational capitalist system is crazy, crazy! The spiritual element is missing!"

He paused for a long meditative moment. "Still—" he said slowly, "My wife and I, we always remember that the parents support what we do. We all work together. And when young people who left the kindergarten years ago come back to visit, we can see that they have absorbed much here—much. Children who say they must have a funeral ceremony for silkworm moths—they will never be drawn to religious cults that deal in violence and death. Because they have seen what is life, where does it come from, how does it grow. They will see what is *real*!"

Wonderland for the Few, Underland for the Many

As we think back on the miraculous "tiger states," it is clear that their smiling has been a mask. In all of them, a tranquil and productive countryside has been turning, by the "inevitable" direction of Progress, into a mere fringe around sprawling, oppressive cities. It is no accident that in environments which barricade human beings against direct experience of the stars and the moon, the sound of the wind in the leaves and of water burbling somewhere in the forest, there should be so much anger and despair.

The World Bank long claimed that most of the rapidly growing economies in the region actually increased the equality of income distribution and dramatically reduced poverty, while sustaining the highest economic growth in the world. Have the poor experienced it this way? In the Philippines, crowds have taken to the streets every time a new government measure is seen as "anti-poor," and in Indonesia the gap between the "haves" and the "have-nots" has caused outbreaks of popular revolt. In Japan ordinary citizens have encountered a new kind of poverty—degradation of the environment and deterioration in the quality of life. Sometimes led by Buddhist priests, citizens have been protesting planned dams, opposing incinerator construction because of dioxin, and forming groups to halt nuclear reactors like the Monju fast-breeder—which, fulfilling the warnings of "Cassandras," suffered a disastrous fire in 1995. And in August 1996, in their first-ever referendum, the Japanese voted against nuclear power.

Both urban and rural dwellers have been expressing their frustration through organized protest, until now a comparatively infrequent phenomenon in Asia. During the spring of 1996, more than 13,000 Thai farmers marched to Bangkok under the umbrella of Forum of the Poor to demand the return of lands taken by the state and private corporations. In 1997 they returned, demanding tangible action on the promises made the year before. There was so little response from government officials to claims for restoration or compensation that it seemed clear that they expected to control the situation through delaying actions.

Such familiar methods of averting crises came to naught in fall 1997, when the stock market and then currencies in Asia skidded in the direction of a crash. Panic grew worldwide, as the "Asian flu" spread to Russia and touched South America. In Thailand workers rendered jobless have been heading back to the countryside. But what lies waiting? Millions find a land robbed of its productivity by toxic waste, industrial development, tourist resorts, roads, and golf courses.

The development of tourist attractions, of course, was supposed to benefit the poor. Yet, as we have seen, in this global industry—the number one source of foreign currency in the world—it is the educated and the elite who do well. The poor who find work in the industry tend to get seasonal, menial jobs. Meanwhile, the natural resources—the basic capital of the country—are dissipated. Some traditionally self-sufficient East Asian countries, including Japan, South Korea, and Taiwan, have been importing more than 70 percent of all the grain they consume. At the same time, worldwide the base of grainland has been contracting. And by the year 2021, the farmers of the world will have to feed 39 percent more mouths than they did in 1996.

In the U.S. a few environmentalists have begun to question tourism. We have still to hear of a sermon here on the subject. But is tourism a concern for religions? Yes! says the Ecumenical Coalition on Third World Tourism, which publishes *Contours*. In it theologians and other contributors from around the developing world debate questions like: Can the advantages of tourism outweigh the damage to our environment and culture? Can we justify a so-called "ecotourism" that cannot market itself without offering comforts comparable to those at home—comforts that often mean depriving local people of essential needs like water and sanitation? If ecotourism is to live up to its name, should it not focus on short-distance travel to places reachable without fossil fuels, and include local ghettos and ecological disaster sites? *Is* there a "right" to travel?[26]

For all of us, including the authors, these are uncomfortable questions with annoying implications.

And the questions spawn others. In an era when camera-clicking tourists invade even Taoist sanctuaries, Mount Sinai is littered with soda cans and plastic rubbish, and our military-industrial complex seeks to use land sacred to American Indians for burial of nuclear waste, what is too hallowed to be violated?

If all faiths cherish the holy, the recesses of mystery, how can religion ever be reconcilable with a global force for which nothing is sacred?

Visitors explore the lower slopes of Mt. Sinai, the "holy mountain," and meeting place of three Semitic faiths. (Courtesy *The World & I* magazine; photo by James Young)

9

CONCLUSION

Love, Law, and Living as if Life Really Mattered

I have set before you life and death, blessing and cursing:
therefore choose life, that both thou and thy seed may live.
—Deuteronomy 30:19

As we look back on what we have seen and learned in the closing decade of the second millennium, we are struck by the persistent growth of the young ecospiritual movement in its diverse manifestations. Perhaps the most clear sign that it was reaching maturity was the conference we attended in October 1998: "Religion and Ecology: Discovering the Common Ground." Convened at the United Nations and chaired by Maurice Strong, Senior Adviser to the Secretary General, it gathered other prominent UN figures, religious scholars, and leaders in major faiths. Their purpose was to address the urgent need to examine the role of the world's religions in helping to solve environmental problems.

The UN gathering, together with other meetings and festivities, was the culmination of a series of conferences held at the Harvard University Center for the Study of World Religions from May 1996 to July 1998. Coordinated by John Grim and Mary Evelyn Tucker of Bucknell University in collaboration with Lawrence Sullivan, director of the Center, the series involved an extraordinary network of some 600 scholars, religious leaders, and environmental specialists from around the world. Exploring how 10 faiths (Judaism, Christianity, Islam, Buddhism, Hinduism, Jainism, Shinto, Taoism, Confucianism, and Indigenous Traditions) view the natural world and humanity's relations to it, they were seeking an alliance that would foster a religious voice in ecological policy. Plans were made for an ongoing Forum on Religions of the World and Ecology.

These conferences represent, for the most part, the work of scholars and religious leaders. Some of the meetings, however, have also featured a dialogue between religious views and the four sectors of business, science, education, and public policy. In other words, the hope is that such conversation will result in partnerships and more action.

That will not happen unless the nitty-gritty business of working at the grassroots goes on. Indeed, the conference would never have come into being without such efforts—the day-to-day labors of action-oriented people who have sometimes despaired, but still refused to accept the widespread belief that "we don't have enough ecological knowledge to speak up or *do* something."

The people in this book are convinced that one need not be an expert to grasp the essentials; it takes but the will to learn them, together with love for this earth. In the words of Sister Pat Monahan, founder of Kids for the Earth: "Anybody can do it. I took an extension course in ecology, read up on the issues, listened to other people tell what they thought needed to be done, and started a project in the setting I know best—this school." The same kind of response could be echoed by Father Dmitri and his wife Tatyana in their struggle against Russian town authorities who had allowed factories to pollute the water; by Reverend Tanaka and his wife Tomoe in their campaigns to prevent a damaging dam near Kyoto; by Eilon Schwartz as he built the first ecoreligious movement in Israel; and by countless others who invent new strategies daily.

To be sure, today some matters require consultation with experts who have proved their competency. They are often happy to give their time. But the cardinal point is that the basic information is there for those who seek it, are skeptical of easy "feel-good" solutions, and care enough to keep learning.

To start at the level of rediscovering the beauty of the Creation requires no great expertise. Here members of the ecospiritual movement have been particularly imaginative. To cite a few examples in this country alone: at the instigation of laypersons and/or pastoral leaders, congregations have created wildlife habitat on temple or church property; established a nature center within the house of worship, including a library of books on trees, wildlife, and biblical plants; and laid out meditation trails. Some have sung music composed by their pastor to communicate the value of oceans and the dangers of water pollution, or even participated in a local ecojustice task force.

In the U.S., clergy and laypersons have found help with ideas for activities and scriptural references to illustrate their religious significance through their own research, ecoreligious publications, and the National Religious Partnership on the Environment (NRPE). In poorer countries such resources are limited, but groups rely on their creative imagination and traditional stories.

Emerging Trends

The late 1990s have witnessed a number of encouraging developments. In this country alone, new groups spring up every year, ranging from Sisters of the Earth (founded at the Grailville Community) to Floresta (emphasizing tree-planting) and the Christian Environmental Association (oriented to college students).

Small but increasing numbers of women and men, often secular and religious people working together, are developing alternative programs that offer models of a viable nature-human relationship. They spring up in Palestine, Israel, Japan, the U.S.—virtually anywhere. They focus on developing truly sustainable models of meeting human needs as varied as energy, housing, waste disposal, health care, and the production, packaging, and distribution of food. Often the programs operate in the context of community, especially spiritual community. The activities of Genesis Farm, Earth Connection, Grailville, Michaela Farm, and Villa Maria in the United States, of Wongsanit in Thailand, and Project Ormylia in Greece have already been described.

Faith-based networks that focus on action to preserve the Creation are growing. The Episcopal Environmental Coalition, Presbyterians for Restoring Creation, and the United Church of Christ's Network for Environmental and Economic Responsibility (NEER) are but three examples. NEER has awarded "Whole Earth Church" certificates to several hundred environmentally active United Church of Christ congregations. All three are becoming involved in practical steps like promoting legislation. Moreover, the National Council of Churches, representing the mainline Protestant churches and most of the Orthodox, is taking up more and more issues of social injustice that are based on abuse of the ecosystem. They are implicitly political issues, such as the grave dangers small children face from the more than 60,000 commercial pesticide products today.

Some ecospiritual groups are decentralizing, producing small local progeny that operate autonomously. Every year John Seed, co-founder of the Council of All Beings and a leader of the Rainforest Information Centre in Australia, conducts Council sessions in many parts of the U.S., Canada, and Europe. As described in the section in Chapter 3 about Miriam Theresa MacGillis, "Celebrating the Earth," a major focus is for each participant to identify with some threatened species, meditate on its joys and sufferings, and speak to the other species about its plight. Seed encourages participants to learn how to conduct such workshops; in this way a new kind of consciousness, a sense of kinship with all forms of life, is being planted in many parts of the world.

Simultaneously with the movement toward decentralization, one can see a trend toward closer collaboration. For example, in 1997 Green Cross, the World Stewardship Institute, and the Christian Environmental Association teamed up to sponsor "Opening the Book of Nature." It features retreats in nature preserves where participants can pitch tents or lodge inexpensively, take prayerful nature walks with reflection stops at beautiful spots, and gather around campfires to picnic and sing and recall the long religious tradition of cherishing two paths toward understanding God: the Book of Scripture and the Book of Creation. Today Opening the Book of Nature Programs function quite independently all over the United States.

The trend toward closer collaboration often draws together groups with widely varying philosophical outlooks and approaches. The Religious Campaign for Forest Conservation, launched at Redwood National Park in 1998, is a case in point. Although it was conceived by religious groups, its 26 sponsoring organizations include groups like the Earthjustice Legal Defense Fund, the Natural Resources Defense Council, and the Native Forest Council that are affiliated with no religion, yet often draw strength from inner sources they would call "not so much religious as spiritual."[1]

In varying degrees, all the groups described have shown a new willingness to make themselves heard in the world of politics. Evangelicals, particularly, have surprised many. For example, a campaign launched by the Evangelical Environmental Network, which has a power base of some 30,000 evangelical churches and is part of NRPE, was an important actor in the successful 1996 initiative to preserve the Endangered Species Act. Calvin De Witt, co-founder of the network, declared vehemently: "People in their arrogance are destroying God's Creation, yet Congress and special interests are trying to sink the Endangered Species Act. It is the Noah's Ark of today!" De Witt appeared with Interior Secretary Bruce Babbitt (who had criticized the "extinction lobby" in Congress) on nationwide television, and with other network members, addressed a large press conference. The campaign story was carried by TV, radio, and national newspapers.

The Religious Campaign for Forest Conservation is one example of an emerging force that might be called "eco-ecumenism." As we have seen, religious ecumenism has been growing, particularly on the local level. But eco-ecumenism is far broader, for it draws together not only followers of various faiths, but also people with a more secular orientation—scientists (whom some have called "a new breed of twentieth-century theologians"), economists, historians, and others.

Obstacles to New Perspectives

While the ecospiritual movement has made remarkable progress, much work remains. It is important to understand the obstacles that institutional religion and its leaders continue to face.

One obstacle is embedded in its very nature. Although religion has two faces, the prophetic and the conservative, the latter has always been dominant: the mission of conserving traditional Scriptures and traditional practices, linking the present and past, responding to the human need for a Rock of Ages in a changing and hurtful world. All this has provided great emotional and spiritual benefits to humanity. But it limits the ability to respond to new crises and encourages concern with the individual self, to the exclusion of the wounded world.

As we have seen, institutional religion generates power structures, which foster passivity and responses like "The Lord will provide" or "The Buddha taught us to accept that the world is full of suffering." Out of conviction or convenience, many religious leaders foster such pietistic persuasions.

Ministers, priests, rabbis, imams are buffeted by ceaseless demands—weddings, funerals, sick calls, speeches, board meetings, counseling, mediation, community meetings, and more—quite aside from preparing and delivering the sermon. It is extremely difficult to find time to reflect on ideas that, in any case, many believers are likely to find uncomfortable.

Nor do many religious leaders live on a holy mountain; they are themselves caught up in the mystique of growth. They are inclined to measure success in large part by expansion of their following. And a dwindling flock generates fear.

Other fears pursue them. In male-dominated hierarchies, particularly, fear of the feminine element in life and the presence of real women in positions of authority. In Abrahamic religions, the abiding fear of "paganism"—often a catch-all term for new and threatening forces. In all faiths, fear that valuing other religions as equal will weaken the distinctiveness and strength of one's own.

Religions the world over are facing crises of survival and relevance—which in turn generate fears of change and surrendering identity. This was clear in the tense encounter between Orthodox Christian male hierarchs and female theologian Chung Hyun Kyung at the 1991 WCC conference in Canberra. Parallel clashes occur at other ecumenical conferences, such as the 1993 Parliament of the World's Religions and the 1993 "Re-imaging God, Creation, Community, the Church," a conference principally designed for women to express new ways of understanding God. For some peoples of the world, losing religious identity is linked to a fear that their distinctive culture is crumbling before the homogenizing power of capitalism and its servant, the global mass media.

I = P x A x T

To convince a religious congregation that concern for the earth and its creatures is a concern for people of faith is difficult. But the religious leader or lay person who has taken long, solitary, meditative walks through woods and fields is likely to be the one who can best lead people back to the primary experience of seeing the divine in the natural world— an experience increasingly rare in the ersatz world of television, Internet, and Disneyland. It is a good beginning.

To convince people of faith that political action is necessary is even more difficult. The usual response is "Let's not confuse the political with the spiritual!" This, despite the reality that religion has always been "political," and Jesus, Muhammad, Gautama Buddha, Handsome Lake, and many founders of sects spoke out against the principalities and powers, the societal behavior of the time.

But most difficult of all are the issues that form the bedrock of our predicament: population growth, overconsumption, the changes that big technologies are making in ways we perceive and experience reality, the conflict between individual and societal rights, and the radical alterations needed in our day-to-day lives. The great majority in every community of faith seeks to avoid these issues—in a sense, to deny them. Sometimes they are discussed, most often in a gingerly way, by top religious leaders or scholars, but rarely are they addressed from the pulpit.

Particularly uncomfortable is the issue of overpopulation. Reproduction issues are sometimes discussed in places of worship, but seldom does discussion focus on the population explosion. It is usually cast in secondary terms: the human rights debate over the right of a woman to make the first decision about an abortion, or the human ethics issue of whether each human sexual act should be open to bringing new life into the world. Only in very "liberal" faith groups is it put first as the stark question: How many humans can Earth support?

Even more rarely is the issue framed in terms of the blunt reality that Britain's Prince Philip has described so succinctly: "The increase in human population has been matched by the decrease in the populations of other forms of life. As people move in, wildlife has to move out."[2] Society as a whole has acted on the underlying assumption that even non-essential human needs are paramount. And religious and academic institutions have tended to do likewise.

Many liberal-minded men and women—including religious people committed to social justice—regard overpopulation as a non-problem. If only we redistribute global resources equitably, and the poor in developing countries thus improve their standard of living, the population problem will take care of itself, they maintain. This is, of course, a response of compassion or guilt to the accusatory assertion by many people in poor countries that overpopulation per se is not a threat; rather, the problem lies in waste and overconsumption, particularly among Westerners. And the reality is that the U.S. alone, with 5 percent of the world's population, owns 22 percent of its wealth, and is responsible for 25 percent of its emissions.

Still, one might ask: does the existence of one cause of a crisis rule out another? Of course overconsumption is a vital issue of both social justice and survival of the ecosystem. Of course we need more equity. But on a planet where Nature's resources are diminishing, the number of newborn consumers is expanding rapidly, and the expectations of people in poor countries are expanding even faster, it is hard to see how merely redistributing global resources could solve our collective dilemma.

Is it not more realistic to see overconsumption and overpopulation as intertwined? Thus we can recognize the birth of an American baby as up to 100 times greater a disaster for Earth's life-support systems than the birth of a baby in a poor country.[3] In this sense the U.S. is the most overpopulated country in the world. Then let us factor in the toll exerted by modern technology on life-support systems. The "ecological problem" has swollen.

Anne and Paul Ehrlich express the interlocking nature of these three factors in the equation $I = P \times A \times T$. The Impact of any group on the environment can be seen as the product of its Population size multiplied by its per capita Affluence (measured by consumption), multiplied by the damage done by Technologies supplying each unit of that consumption. Thus Impact is more than the sum of its parts: it is the ever-multiplying product of interacting variables.[4]

As population increases, per capita damage done by technologies that support consumption also increases. For instance, food, water, and goods need to be transported from more distant sources, while crops are grown on land with declining aquifers and requiring more synthetic fertilizers and pesticides. Thus, T increases with P, as more technological effort must be expanded to supply each unit of consumption.[5]

Indeed, virtually all environmental problems are connected to each other and to overpopulation. Furthermore, while profligate consumption is most damaging to earth-processes, even frugal consumption has impact as population and technologies expand.

A major point made by the Ehrlichs is that the human economy is supported by an array of *services* supplied by natural ecosystems. They include moderation of the weather, regulation of the hydrologic cycle that provides fresh water in a way that minimizes the occurrence of droughts and floods, preservation of fertile soils, pollination of many crops, and maintenance of a vast "genetic library."[6]

Today homo sapiens is not supporting itself on income—instead, it is digging into its natural capital. The most crucial issues surrounding the availability of natural resources are the decline of viable soils, of usable water supplies, and of biodiversity.[7]

The Ehrlichs emphasize that we still are not talking about the principal *causes* of decaying life-support systems. These include not only overpopulation, rising consumption, and use of inappropriate technologies, but also inequitable distribution of wealth and resources, and government inaction.[8] In other words, causes embedded in social justice and politics. Causes over which we all have some degree of leverage, if we determine to overcome our inertia.

Environmental writer Bill McKibben (who happens to be a very religious man but speaks from a scientific point of view) sees the essential equation as I = P x A x T, but adds some disturbing considerations. He poses three basic questions: How many of us will there be in the near future? How "big" are we? How big is the earth?

They provide a useful framework. The following presents a brief summary of some of his ideas, supplemented and reinforced by those of others.[9]

McKibben tells us that there *is* good news: United Nations analysts say that the rate of population growth has slowed, and offer the mid-range projection that the world's population, presently about six billion, will top off at ten to twelve billion before the next century is out.

Good news, except that this is just an optimistic scenario, resting on the far-from-certain assumption that women in the developing world will average two children apiece, the rate at which population stabilizes. At the end of this century, 33 countries, 25 of them in Africa, still had a fertility rate of six children per woman, according to the Population Institute.[10] And if fertility worldwide remained at its present level? It would reach an absurd 296 billion in just 150 years.[11]

How big are we? Another way of putting this is to ask the question posed by Mathis Wackernagel and William Rees: What is our ecological footprint? The answer involves great variances in how much food, water, energy, and minerals we consume. Certainly, as a species we are ever more voracious consumers. But some of us are bigger than others. Wackernagel and Rees say that 20 percent of the world's population consumes over three-quarters of the world's total output.[12] McKibben points out that the average American uses 70 times as much energy as the average Bangladeshi, and that we use nearly seven times as much water as our forebears in 1900.

But have Americans not developed all sorts of energy-saving devices? Certainly. But since 1983, U.S. energy use per capita has been increasing almost 1 percent per year. There are also more of us—in 1998 the U.S. population was approximately 270 million, 36 million more than in 1983.[13]

Indeed, according to the U.S. Census Bureau, by 2050 the number of Americans (i.e., consumers) will have increased to almost 400 million, half again as many as in 1998. The populations of European countries will have begun to decline, but in the U.S. (which tends to see population as a problem solely for the Third World) we shall be growing.[14]

How big is the earth? That is, how many humans can it support? Estimates differ, for the variables are numerous. It depends, in part, on one's requirements. McKibben says that while the average hunter-gatherer used about 2,500 calories a day, all of it in food, a modern human uses 31,000 daily, mostly as fossil fuels. And the average American uses six times that much. Cornell biologist David Pimentel concludes that the earth could support no more than two billion people over the long run on a middle-class American standard of living; he believes we are *already* too crowded. Wackernagel and Rees emphasize that preliminary estimates suggest that consumption by the 1.1 billion comparatively affluent people alone (some one-fifth of the earth's present population) already exceeds global carrying capacity of the planet.[15]

True, we have expanded food production through use of agricultural chemicals and now—perhaps—genetic engineering. But between 1945 and 1990, annual losses of productive land averaged just under two million acres, according to World Watch Institute's *State of the World.*[16] Gerald Barney adds that of the 14 billion acres of land on the earth, only 3.3 billion are potentially arable, and most of the best lands are already in use for agriculture. Agricultural land also is becoming ever more subject to devastating floods. Moreover, doubling the amount of land in production would lead to massive extinctions of species. It would cause enormous environmental damage.[17]

We have also produced an ever-expanding variety of baggage, things that in the West we cannot imagine doing without. We consider them just part of normal life. But they are coming in such great quantities, says McKibben, that they overwhelm the planet.

As everyone has come to realize, the earth is getting warmer. The 1990s have been the hottest decade on record. At the same time, the unusual climate patterns have brought colder weather to some areas. Why these changes? Because of great increases in nitrogen, methane, and carbon dioxide, says McKibben. Nitrous oxide traps solar heat and stays there a century. Human activity has doubled the amount of NO_2 in the air. Methane concentrations, too, have doubled as a result of increased activity: raising more cattle and chopping down more tropical forest (causing termite populations to explode).

Carbon dioxide is the most dangerous of all. It is deceptive. It is clean, and unlike carbon monoxide, cannot kill humans directly. CO_2 is the inevitable product of combustion, and the combustion engine [Mobil Oil reminds us] makes the world go round. Before we began burning fossil fuels, the atmosphere contained some 280 parts of CO_2 per million. That figure is likely to become 500 parts by about 2050.

Far more than even methane and nitrous oxide, then, CO_2 causes global warming and other climate change. As a result, the Poles are warming, and there are already 20 percent more bad storms in the United States than in 1900.

Why are we experiencing not only severe storms but droughts? Because a hotter planet means greater rates of evaporation, which leads to more rain and snow, even as comparatively arid regions like the American Midwest, breadbasket of the world, become drier. Furthermore, forest fires triggered by the heat intensify global warming by releasing CO_2 locked up in trees into the atmosphere. It is a vicious cycle. Barney also points to the sea level rise that would be expected during the second half of the twenty-first century, forcing resettlement of hundreds of millions of people.[18]

These are only a few of the effects. The nub of it all is that while members of the human species have always changed the places where they lived, now they are changing even the places they do not inhabit. They are changing the way the weather works, and they are changing other species, the plants and animals at the Poles and deep in the jungles. In the ordinary rounds of their daily lives, they are changing the face of the earth.[19]

As Berry puts it, we have altered the very chemistry, the biosystems, the topography, even the geological structures of the planet.[20]

As McKibben puts it, from a new heaven filled with nitrogen, methane, and carbon dioxide, a new earth is being born—Earth II.

And we, homo sapiens, have assumed the role of Creator.

Population. Affluence. Technology. Are these, then, religious and spiritual concerns?

Most of the people who appear in this book are convinced that they are spiritual in a very fundamental sense of the term—rooted in how we look at ourselves and our place in the world, in how we relate to other humans, other species, and generations to come. But at this point in time, they seem to be only a prophetic minority.

True, there is movement among mainline religious leaders to rouse people to the significance of climate change and similar politically sensitive issues. Religious groups were an important contingent of the non-governmental organizations (NGOs) at the 1992 Earth Summit in Rio, as well as the 1997 UN Conference on Climate Change in Kyoto.

(For example, the World Council of Churches sent a large delegation to Rio; Buddhists, Muslims, Jews, Hindus, native peoples, and other people of faith were also present. Prominent among the U.S. delegations was the long-standing Eco-Justice Working Group of the National Council of Churches (NCC), together with missions from member churches. Since then, these leaders have worked diligently to arouse public awareness about the progress and failures of Rio and Kyoto. Their struggle is a difficult one. They stress uncomfortable conclusions that bear on the Affluence factor in the I = P x A x T equation. Among other things, curtailing greenhouse emissions *will* cost money and change the way we in the West live; developing nations are unwilling to reduce their emissions until industrial countries in general, and the U.S. in particular, take the first step in dealing with a situation they are primarily responsible for creating; and political action is essential. Thus in 1998, 22 member churches of the NCC, together with Jewish groups, launched an active campaign to persuade the Senate to approve the Kyoto Protocol, and NRPE made plans to lobby senators. Efforts are also being made to involve large corporations. On a related front, these religious groups have been working diligently on the Earth Charter.)[21]

Clearly, progress on these issues will be difficult. The Population factor, particularly, is an extremely sensitive issue. But religious leaders do know they are in a unique and powerful position to influence decisions about it. For centuries, they have taken stands (heeded or not) on the subject. While Buddhism and Taoism have been comparatively reticent, the three Abrahamic faiths have not. The Roman Catholic church has traditionally enjoined the faithful to have large families. Muslim and Orthodox Jewish leaders have preached the same. For Jews, it has been justified as ensuring the survival of the people and the religion. For Christians and Muslims, it has also rested on *propagation* of the faith.

The political dimension, the urge for power, is clear. Today the issue is complicated by the fact that although they rarely say it publicly, many religious and political leaders see population growth as an important ingredient of the power of their nation or faith. And if the urge to grow is rooted in long oppression at the hands of the Goliaths of this world, it is hard for people concerned with social justice to condemn resorting to the "poor man's weapon." The social and political causes of the oppression need to be addressed as a priority.

For millions of poor families, too, many children represent security. Moreover, many true believers still take literally the divine mandate to be fruitful and multiply. It is hard for them to recognize how much the world has changed since their religions were founded.

It is a hopeful sign that today some religious leaders see that population growth can eventuate in self-destruction for their own group and the global community. For example, Aubrey Rose of the Executive Board of Deputies of British Jews points out that for the tiny population of Jews, the problem is one of survival rather than population; and Jews, particularly Orthodox Jews, try to follow God's injunction, "Be fruitful and multiply." Nevertheless, he says, if population explosion can only lead to the destruction of nature and human dignity, another view must now be considered, on the basis of the traditional Jewish precept, "Thou shalt not destroy."[22]

As we have seen, some Muslim, Christian, and American Indian leaders have also voiced strong forebodings about the population threat. The World Council of Churches has issued a statement on the dangers of overpopulation. A number of church leaders have taken courageous stands—notably, the United Church of Christ delegation to the preparatory discussions for the 1994 Cairo conference on population. The problem is that these views are rarely discussed by congregations; the issue seems too explosive. Religious leaders need to work more closely with environmentalists and other secular groups to reach their own people.

On the other hand, rank-and-file believers are often ahead of their leaders. Pope John Paul's condemnations of artificial contraception have failed to convince many Catholics in industrial countries; and Italy, Spain, and Poland have some of the lowest birth rates in the world. American Catholics often report that their parish priests refrain from counting birth control as a sin.

Overconsumption has always been a religious concern. Jews and Christians can find "Give me neither poverty nor riches" in Proverbs; Muslims, "Poverty is my pride" among Muhammad's sayings; Taoists, "He who knows he has enough is rich" in the *Tao Te Ching*; and American Indians, "Miserable as we may seem in thine eyes, we consider ourselves much happier than thou, in that we are very content with the little that we have," from the sayings of a Micmac chief.[23]

It is doubtful that sermonizing against "materialism" or "greed" can be effective. We tend to recognize only the other guy, further up the ladder, as materialistic or greedy. On the other hand, we can hardly deny the power of consumerism in our lives. Individually and in discussion groups, we can pose questions to ourselves. What forces are driving us to consume more and more? How is our buying behavior connected to the mountains of waste, much of it toxic, that have been rising to unprecedented levels? How is our consumer behavior related to the use of agrichemicals that help produce the cheap food that we feel is our due? Are "rights"—like deciding how to use *our* land, or traveling anywhere that funds permit—part of the problem? How do our life-styles affect the lives of people in poor countries? What are we to make of the finding that since 1970 there has been a 47 percent increase in per capita consumption in the U.S. alone—yet for the same period, Americans report a *decline* by 51 percent (measured by several variables) in the quality of life?[24]

Magazines ranging from the Christian *Target Earth* and *Earth Letter* to *Hinduism Today* and the Buddhist *Seeds of Peace* have begun to look at consumerism in concrete ways and make suggestions about action. NRPE reaches out to congregations with booklets and sponsors a Consumption Project.

It is harder to discern movement toward open discussion of modern technology. We tend to assume that "technology" automatically saves resources. Some technologies do. But not all. And there are often unintended, graver consequences—the surgery is successful, but the patient sickens or dies. Consider that production of a six-inch silicon wafer, for example, may require nearly 3,000 gallons of water.[25] Big technology has assumed a momentum of its own, an aura of untouchability. Computers are being replaced by "better" ones—capable of whisking money around the world at a Houdini-like pace—requiring exploitation of more natural resources, and more investment, more skills, more time to master the new complications. Today some marriages are in peril because one partner spends so many hours before the entrancing screen.

As we pointed out earlier, biotechnology is only rarely discussed by top religious dignitaries. Even then it is generally confined to developments that affect *human* health or *human* reproduction. Seldom is it the subject for congregational discussion. Grassroots discussion of such topics as in vitro fertilization and cloning, however, does emerge in the pages of some religious periodicals like the *National Catholic Reporter*. And at least one international meeting, largely led by religious people, has focused on the subtle influences and broad implications of modern technology. Somewhat misleadingly called the Second Luddite Conference,[26] it gathered together a spectrum of people united around the urgency of the question: "How much of this stuff do we really *need*?"

Despite the paucity of discussion, technology troubles increasing numbers of people with whom we have talked. We think particularly of the conversation, during our second global trip, with Egyptian Green Party founder Hassan Ragab. He had experienced a conversion.

"Since retiring, I read even more, especially history, economics, science," he said. "The world—it is in disintegration. Technology—modern industrial technology, not the marvelously efficient simple technologies used by ancient Egyptians—is moving so fast, we can't seem to stop it. It has brought nuclear, chemical, and biological weapons. It is the source of pollution, the source of our trouble. Perhaps you are surprised to hear an *engineer* say that. But I see what is happening.

"Many think renewable energy will be an answer. That is mistaken. It doesn't pollute of itself, but the products and inventions coming out of its new technologies will create another pollution. So more raw materials will be exploited, to give consumers more gadgets. There is no hope." He sighed deeply. "Because there is no hope of stopping modern technology. Whoever advocates that is called 'crazy.' Or a heretic. Technology is the world religion today."

Ragab had not given up entirely. "The Greens still consult me. And they are the party of the future."

But he could never shake off the conclusion he had reached so reluctantly. "New technology for machines takes away jobs, especially in poorer countries. So it makes people idle. Their minds become infected. The minds of those who create and worship technology become ever more polluted. That leads to more pollution of the planet through mindless actions. It is a vicious cycle. You will ask what would wake people up? Perhaps, a catastrophe."

Alternatives

An apocalyptic catastrophe. Today there seems to be a growing sense that it is inevitable. On an unconscious level, some seem to long for it, as if that would put an end to the disturbing practical decisions we must make. It is indeed a real possibility. Ecologists tell us that the population explosion might well lead to an uncontrolled and massive explosion of deaths. And the scriptures of many religions speak of apocalyptic finales.

But let us start with the most likely possibility among the alternatives before humankind. In our own musings we see five.

The first would be to muddle along much as we are is doing now— patching up here, compromising there, but always subconsciously aware that we are drifting toward the end of life as we know it. Not an explosion, but slow, relentless deterioration. Not a bang, but a whimper.

Another way would be to seize more desperately on modern technology, "superized" into even faster and more complex know-how. We can remember that the Green Revolution has destroyed diverse agricultural systems adapted to the diverse ecosystems of the planet. Or that, especially when overused, miracle antibiotics developed through state-of-the-art technology have a nasty way of developing mutant strains resistant to its magic properties, so that ever-more powerful miracles have to be dreamed into being. Yet it is hard to give up believing in miracles.

Still another way is to retreat into a cave of despair. An 86-year-old farmer neighbor of ours puts it simply: "I've declared this farm a nature preserve. Developers come by, I tell them, 'Forget it.' Well, I've done my bit. But when I look at the world—what's the use? . . . Every night I read history. Gives me a lot to think about during the day. All this—," he gestures toward the ripening grain and the forest beyond, "all this is headed for destruction. Maybe not in our lifetime. But it's bound to happen. Man is destroying himself. And he'd *better.* If he doesn't, everything else will be destroyed."

A fourth possibility is the great catastrophe. Instead of working with nature and learning from its technologies, we cast it even more into the role of Satan until it fights back even more bitterly and defensively. Already it is on the counterattack, with the increasingly "weird" weather that has become the norm in the 1990s. We like to blame it all on that disobedient child, El Niño.

And then there is the hard way, the hardest way of all for the human species. It would involve no magic bullet, no super-technology. Instead, it would consist of really looking at what we do know now, although always searching for more understanding and wisdom, then organizing it all with the big picture in mind. Absence of more data is not the basic problem. What our species has lacked is the will.

The implications from the "big picture" *are* intimidating. McKibben says that if we followed the recommendation of the 2,000 prominent scientists on the Intergovernmental Panel on Climate Change (IPCC) to cut world fossil fuel use by 60 percent—the amount that would stabilize world climate—and then shared the remainder equally, each human would get to produce 1.69 metric tons of CO_2 annually. Today that would allow you to drive an average American car nine miles a day. By the time world population reached 8.5 million, we would be down to six miles a day. If we carpooled, we'd have about three pounds of CO_2 left in our daily ration. That could be enough for a highly efficient refrigerator—but we would have to forget our computers, TVs, stereos, stoves, dishwashers, water heaters, microwaves, and water pumps.[27]

Every one of the interlocking variables (P x A x T) should be addressed simultaneously. That prospect, too, is daunting. But limiting population can be a most significant factor. McKibben urges Western—especially American—couples to consider limiting their progeny to one child.[28] He and his wife Sue Halpern made that decision and have experienced great satisfaction on a number of levels. Among other things, this would show Third World people that we recognize that population is not just their problem, but ours.

Such decisions are always difficult, nevertheless. One needs a sense of purpose, and the feeling of being part of a community that shares the same purpose. Indeed, only when groups act can decisions to make certain sacrifices be effective. And so we come back to the point that what our species has lacked is the will.

A New Way of Looking at Spirituality

How to acquire that will, that élan to move as a society? We believe it can come only through recognizing, and in some way experiencing, the spiritual dimension of the task.

This may sound too quixotic for a society to deal with. But perhaps it is time to re-think "spirituality." It has always carried ambiguous meanings. Today it is generally used to "describe those attitudes, beliefs, practices which animate people's lives and help them to reach out to supra-sensible realities," according to the *Westminster Dictionary of Christian Spirituality*.[29]

This Christian dictionary makes the somewhat surprising assertion that spirituality is not simply for the inner person, it is as much for the body as the soul. "Indeed," it adds, "our love, like God's, should extend to the whole Creation." And it cautions that spirituality "cannot deliver us from the sometimes unbearable tensions, dangers, and sufferings of the world of action."[30]

What shape would a new way of looking at spirituality take? How would it mold our outer actions as well as our inner persons?

It would not exclude the mode of spirituality exemplified by the hermit's withdrawal into the desert, nor Charlene Spretnak's definition as "the focusing of human awareness on the subtle aspects of existence, a practice that reveals to us profound inter-connectedness."[31] But the new mode centers on reaching into every aspect of ordinary lives. Environmental educator David Orr calls it "hard-edged spirituality." What he means is best seen through his work, for example, designing a building that provides much more than shelter. At Oberlin College, Orr has engaged his students, as well as leading green designers, in helping him create an environmental studies center that—among other things—discharges waste water at least as pure as the water taken in, generates more electricity than it uses, incorporates no material known to cause such hazards as cancer or hormone disruption, and is surrounded by pleasant landscape that promotes biological diversity.[32]

Such a building gives concrete form to ethical attitudes and beliefs, to feelings about the beauty of the Creation. Orr sometimes calls this work "applied spirituality," as well. And it is more than a dream, for it already exists—not only in Orr's work, but in that of others. For example, the labors of Sister Paula Gonzalez to construct sun-powered homes that use technologies of nature.

But the concept is not limited to such visible forms. It could also describe the efforts of Oren Lyons to build an international movement of native peoples, of Eisho Yoshida to nurture his Green Kindergarten, of Al-Hafiz B.A. Masri to waken Muslims across the world to the rights of animals. Indeed, the story of virtually everyone in these pages illustrates the same fundamental idea or, perhaps better put, the basic urge to live in harmony with the Creation, the natural world. Theirs is an earthy spirituality. They rejoice in the diverse forms of life on this planet, and seek to demonstrate that the complex web of life can indeed be preserved. But to accomplish this requires thought, discipline, humility, "letting-go" of certain conventional expectations, and understanding the strength of the forces arrayed against one's efforts. Love is not enough.

Hard-edged spirituality can embrace the profound insights and many of the beliefs coming from the world of religion, but it is more all-embracing. The Dalai Lama observes that true religious believers number perhaps one-fifth of the world' population.[33] But he speaks of compassion with all creatures as being within the reach of all. After long research, entomologist E.O. Wilson came to a belief in "biophilia," an urge to affiliate with living things. He sees it as beginning in early childhood, and inscribed in the human brain itself. This does not mean that it cannot become distorted. When the mind is removed to purely artificial environments, and deprived of "beauty and mystery," it will "drift to simpler and cruder configurations," threatening sanity itself. Moreover, biophilia competes with the "audaciously destructive tendencies of our species" that also appear to derive from "archaic biological origins."[34]

Is biophilia shared by other creatures? Darwin himself believed that "all animals feel wonder." And Orr tells us that primatologist Jane Goodall and others have observed animal behavior that seems to reflect awe and wonder.[35]

Biophilia alone is not spirituality, to be sure. But awe, wonder, reverence for life form the primal basis for meaningful spirituality. And in a world that increasingly reflects virtual reality, one source of hope that we can rediscover the "really real" is the growing testimony from the scientific domain that biophilia, or passionate love of life, is innate, and that, to some degree, we humans share feelings of awe with other species.

An expanded spirituality—Earth-based and both tough-minded and tender-hearted—can be liberating. But it can also force us to re-examine assumptions we have taken for granted.

Spiritualized Ideologies

The need for a hard-edged spirituality becomes even more clear if one recognizes that people all over the world today are being inculcated with covert indoctrinations that could be called "spiritualized ideologies." One example is "economic growth" (or, often, simply "growth," which a consumer society is expected to identify with economics). The mantra is repeated so frequently, and with such moral overtones, that it becomes the basis for a creed.

"Sustainable development" is another magical incantation. The very definition of "develop" is "to become fuller, larger, better." Today we stress "larger" rather than "better." But how can the earth sustain the consequences of more growth, or even today's rate of resource depletion?

Capitalism, which has unfortunate associations, is renamed "market forces"—transcendent, almost etherealized, entities that are quite separate from the human beings who originate and perpetuate them. Thus "free market" becomes another facet of the creed. Free? Freedom for whom? For the poor in our deunionized factories or Third World sweatshops, working to make products that the rest of us often have to be indoctrinated into viewing as needs? Or freedom for the multinational empires that operate as secretly as possible, control 70 percent of world trade, pressure governments into agreements which diminish autonomy, and by their very nature can only prosper and grow if they continue to ransack the planet? Free trade is *not* anti-protectionist, declares Vandana Shiva, the Indian physicist, ecologist, and feminist; it is protection of the strong and the powerful.[36] Yet the so-called First World is automatically identified with democracy, therefore with "reform" of those societies that do not agree with our free market ideology. The holy empires of corporate enterprise do not quite proclaim "God is on our side," but that is the subliminal message.

One feature of the corporate strategy is the North American Free Trade Agreement (NAFTA), which has already led to the exodus of U.S. jobs to Mexico and contributed to ecological deterioration in both countries. Negotiations have been launched to expand the agreement to all 34 countries in the Western Hemisphere as the Free Trade Area of the Americas (FTAA). Another feature has been the General Agreement on Tariffs and Trade (GATT), now replaced by the larger and hence more powerful World Trade Organization (WTO), which in 1999 had 135 member countries.

Still another feature is the Multilateral Agreement on Investment (MAI), which would provide extensive rights to foreign investors while undermining the ability of signatory nations to pass laws considered discriminatory against foreign corporate inverstors—including those nations' environmental laws. Several WTO member countries have been attempting to fold the MAI into WTO. Typically, such negotiations are conducted in virtual secrecy, and receive little publicity in the U.S. except in the Global Trade section of Ralph Nader's group Public Citizen, and in independent media frequently labeled "radical." Thus allegiance can be effectively shifted to "market forces" from elected governments, which might have had the power to curb exploitation and the international anarchy following deepening scarcities of Earth's resources.

The lack of publicity is hardly surprising. Part of the transnationals' strategy is to grasp control of the mass media. In the U.S., particularly, they are being merged into conglomerates. Authors' contracts have been broken because executives of the conglomerate ownership decide the book embraced an uncomfortable message. Some books have made it to publication, only to be withdrawn because the multinational (often a big polluter) threatened the publisher.[37] Sometimes whistle-blowers feel forced to pay damages, even when their allegations have not been disproved, because never-ending lawsuits would drain their resources. A major weapon for the corporations is fear.

It would be too easy to see this "Mutually Assured Collaboration" as one giant conspiracy. This is more insidious, diffuse, and slippery. What seems to be operating is a set of game plans, some of them loosely affiliated through interlocking lobbies at every governmental level. But it is the public affairs/public relations firms that do the heavy lobbying in Washington and reach television.

What unites these forces is dedication to propagation of the true faith. The average person may harbor doubts about the doctrine of growth (which is never portrayed as growth in the sense of community—or growth in the quality of life), but is likely to repress them quickly. We two have observed this all over the world, including the once-rural Ohio county where we now live. Our efforts and those of a few like-minded people to generate active resistance to rapid land development have met with some successes. But it is a tough fight; most residents, even those directly threatened by this runaway growth, only sigh: "What you gonna do? You can't stop progress!"

Looking Toward the Future

Envisioning an Ecology-Centered Society

When asked our vision of a "sustainable society," we think of Earth Day founder Randy Hayes' observation that "ecological society" would be a better term because it emphasizes the totality of life's relationships and means that technologies would abide by the cycles of nature and principles of ecology.

Would this be an impossible dream? David Orr has concluded that the ecological crisis comes from the failure of people today to think about ecological *patterns*, *systems* of causation, and the *long-term effects* of human actions. He also points to the failure of education about the natural world, which emphasizes technical efficiency over conscience, neat answers instead of questions, theories not values.

We see these obstacles as challenges. But we cannot offer a definitive picture of an ecological, or ecology-centered, society. The actual contours of each will emerge out of the soil, the trees, the water, the wildlife, the human culture, the needs of the inhabitants of that bioregion. To find an ideal "model" for all is difficult.

Yet despite the differences in our circumstances, humans have but one planet. We share common ancestors—the sun, the stars, the seas, the soil, the birds, the mammals, and other forms of life—in our awesome evolution from the original "flaring forth." Like other creatures we respond to cycles of seasons, of day and night, and to five basic senses; like them, we are endowed with a will to live. We share with other humans a need to love and be loved, to find meaning in life, to feel secure, to be part of community, to experience the beauty of this wondrous planet.

So it is possible to trace the broad outlines of a society that would offer satisfaction of basic human needs and, at the same time, refrain from stomping humans' heavy hob-nailed boots on the earth. Thus in an ecology-centered society:

- Everyone sees that the principal goal must be to reduce the human impact on the earth.

- Every person feels the importance of greater equity between rich and poor nations, and between people with the luck to be born in comfortable circumstances and those less fortunate.

- *Prevention* of ecological damage is recognized as the most effective route to pursue.

- Leaders and populace practice the principle of "think globally, act locally."

- They are guided by a new concept of progress—one more sustainable than our present dream, rooted as it is in exploitation of both people and the earth. Progress is measured more in terms of quality of life and how well it meets fundamental needs—ranging from clean water to work (paid or volunteer)—that is of value to oneself and society. People with basic security are less likely to seek material riches or to dominate others.

- Action is taken to ensure elimination of chemicals that destroy the ozone layer and to make drastic cuts in emissions of greenhouse gases—with the U.S. taking the lead. This is carried out through an orderly transition to non-CO_2 sources of energy that even poor people can afford, and conservation measures in which everyone takes responsibility. Special pressure is put on big polluters through moral persuasion and tough laws.

- The usefulness of modern technologies is appreciated, but open discussion of their appropriateness to the task at hand is encouraged. Technologies are as simple, long-lasting, and energy-frugal as possible. They correspond to the resources of people using them and value inventiveness of so-called ordinary folk.

- The importance of biodiversity is widely understood; soils and species are preserved.

- Each community sets aside large areas for parks and, where possible, nature reserves.

- Education emphasizes the interdependence of life-systems, and provides opportunities for experiencing and learning from the natural world.

- Basic health care is a right. Prevention and the relationship between healthy bodies and a healthy environment are stressed.

- Voluntary but free programs teach measures to reduce human fertility and stress their importance.

- There is a continuing forum, from local to international level, for discussion of common problems. Special efforts are made to include religious and spiritual voices in the discussion.

In the end, we are talking of conversion to a new set of *values*, new in the sense that they have not operated at the center of "dynamic" societies today, but old in the sense that they have always operated in the human psyche—values like "participation" and "community." Today we often forget how much we need them and how much they stimulate thought and feeling. Values like transcendence of one's immediate gratifications for the sake of one's children and, by extension, their grandchildren's grandchildren. Throughout human history every society and every faith tradition has asked its members to forego some pleasures for the well-being of the whole.

Values such as dignified self-reliance, compassion, sharing. They do not come from simply willing them into being; in times of famine, widespread destruction, pestilence, and death (the Four Horsemen of the Apocalypse), they often diminish and even disappear.

Conversion

While there are no living examples of societies where all these things have come to pass, we can briefly describe some that are moving in that direction. In varying degrees and ways, all have gone through what might be called "conversion."

Conversion simply means basic change and can take many forms: change of the economy, of the society, of a technology, of religious belief, of the spirit. As its deepest level, it means re-formation of both the way one looks at life, and the way one acts in the world. It is always difficult. And it is always dynamic, for it leads to new visions of possibilities and to new challenges. "Integrating the values of natural harmony into our daily life," says John C. Elder, "calls for a spiritual reorientation so fundamental as to be, at heart, a conversion."[38]

In Curitiba, the tenth largest city in Brazil, Jaime Lerner, an architect who became mayor in 1970 at the age of 33, and a team of imaginative men and women have worked together to convert a rapidly growing, congested city into a pleasant, indeed exciting, place to live, while thinking small and cheap. For example, they have cut traffic snarls and air pollution through a fast, innovative bus system (in lieu of expensive subways); integrated all modes of transport, including a 90-mile bike path; transformed the central street into a colorful pedestrian mall, and created 350 square feet of open space per person—three and a half-times as much as New York City. Recovering alcoholics and homeless men work together to sort out trash to be recycled and recycling is practiced by 80 percent of the people. Day care is free for children over three months old. Small businesses "adopt" street children by employing them for light duties. Work programs for the poor enjoy widespread popular support. There is *community*.[39]

Gaviotas, in the barren eastern savannas of Colombia, is the realization of an "impossible dream" spun by visionaries and technicians who believed that in the future humans would have to learn to live in harsh conditions. They set out to prove it could be done. Since the early 1970s, technicians, health workers, peasants, street children from Bogotá's slums, and Indians have joined together to form a sustainable community in an inhospitable environment not far from guerrilla warfare and drug-trafficking. They have invented solar collectors that function even in the rain, windmills that can convert mild breezes into energy, pumps powerful enough to tap deep aquifers but so simple that they operate by being hooked up to children's seesaws, and many other appropriate technologies. They have used the Neem tree as basis for many natural medicines. And an unexpected miracle has occurred: the regeneration of an ancient rainforest. All this has been accomplished through a spirit of togetherness. There are no rich or poor here—there are only hard-working but hopeful people united by a purpose.[40]

There are also examples of countries that have achieved partial but notable success in fulfilling an ecological vision. Holland, for example, in 1989 passed a National Environmental Policy Plan, requiring 223 policy changes, a plan that involves all sectors of society. Among other things, the green plan has contributed to sizeable reductions in emissions of noxious gases, such as sulfur dioxide, and spurred plans to plant 99,000 acres of forest and restore 800,000 acres of wetlands.[41] New Zealand has passed the Resource Management Act, which is principally designed to regulate the key industries—agriculture, fishing, forestry, and mining—through an integrated plan. One of its many achievements is that commercial forestry has been steered into intensive tree farming, so that the remaining original forest can be set aside as part of the national reserves.[42]

Norway, Sweden, Canada, and Austria are other examples of countries where green planning has begun. In the United States, such a national plan still seems utopian, but some states—New Jersey, Oregon, and Minnesota, for instance—have launched statewide green strategies. In all these plans, industries, to some degree, have cooperated in the process.

These examples have been of secular communities. But there is another level of conversion, one stirring within communities of faith and reaching out to the rest of society. Let us look at two recent examples.

After years of growing concern over the plight of the Mediterranean and other endangered seas, in September 1995 Eastern Orthodox leaders astonished many people with an unprecedented initiative: a symposium entitled "Revelation and the Environment." On board a "latter-day ark," over 150 people (including women) from 30 countries sailed from Istanbul to Patmos, where St. John the Divine recorded the Book of Revelation nearly two millennia ago. Despite centuries-old resistance of many elements in this conservative church to ecumenism, the symposium included religions from Islam to Zoroastrianism. The conference was eco-ecumenical as well. Co-sponsored by Britain's Prince Philip in his capacity as president of World Wildlife Fund-International, it gathered economists and environmentalists, such as Herman Daly and Sierra Club President Robert Cox—as well as scientists, industrialists, and American and Asian government officials— into dialogue with religious leaders and each other.

Pious optimism was notably absent. Rather, the common search was for *preconditions* of hope. Thus even the religious leaders emphasized *change*. Roman Catholic Cardinal Etchegaray declared, "One can never say enough that the Apocalypse does not describe the end of the world, but rather, the *new* creation of the world." Calling for a new partnership, Ecumenical Patriarch Bartholomaios asserted that "science saves faith from fantasy" and "faith generates the energy for a new world," and outlined several steps for action.

For the Christian Church, the most important development was Metropolitan John of Pergamon's declaration that environmental damage should be considered a *sin*. "We are used to regarding sin mainly in social terms. But there is also a sin against nature." For the assembly of diverse callings present, perhaps most important was the "revelation" that the plight of the environment topples the barriers between differing faiths and between science and religion.

For future generations, most significant was the agreement that "This is only a beginning; it is action that counts, action that will make the next millennium a green millennium."

The new revelation continues to unfold. In September 1997, the Orthodox convened a similar conference on a boat sailing the Black Sea. Two months later, Bartholomaios made a 16-city visit to the United States and was welcomed by huge audiences everywhere. The "Green Patriarch" met with Vice-President Gore, was awarded the Congressional Medal of Honor, and in Santa Barbara, California, presided at a symposium on religion and the environment.

In June 1998 more than 500,000 people gathered on the dried-up shores of Lake Chapala, outside Guadalajara, Mexico, for a day of prayer to end the record-setting drought caused by El Niño and global warming. Cardinal Sandoval Iniquez, head of the Archdiocese of Guadalajara, told his audience that scientists declared the drought to be some of the first evidence of global warming, and added, "But this is also a divine sign that society is on the wrong path."[43]

Organizers were surprised at the enormous turnout. But these were extraordinary times. The poor, especially, had suffered from the devastating forest fires, air pollution, and wave of deaths from respiratory ailments. Many made the long trip on foot.

Fred Krueger, North American program coordinator for the Mexican Interreligious Council, declared that religious institutions have failed to address the ethical issues surrounding climate change; nowhere was this more true than in churches and in preaching of the clergy. Calvin De Witt of the Au Sable Institute emphasized that the drought was an indicator that we have to seek to do God's will and make profound changes in our behavior. He also made arrangements for a dozen Mexican church leaders to attend a seminar at Au Sable to learn how to develop more effective environmental education programs. The goal is that every Mexican parish become a center for activity. Carlos Agnesi, president of the Cruz Verde (Green Cross) in Guadalajara, declared that this event began a nationwide program to get all religions involved in environmental concerns. The Interreligious Council of Mexico began planning, for 1999, the first Mexican Congress on religion and ecology, bringing together leaders of all faith traditions, as well as scientists and government leaders, to map action on a broad range of ecological issues. One speaker was expected to be His Holiness Bartholomaios.

SEED

Still another level of conversion is that of transforming ourselves into men and women who go beyond "studying about" the Third World, to a point of empathizing with its people. Thus we can begin to comprehend the integral connections between poverty, environmental destruction, cultural degradation, ethnic violence, and a globalization bent on bypassing local laws and on sanctifying the free flow of capital. Truly empathizing with those most victimized by the breakdown of life-systems can help us understand better the essentials of living as if life really mattered.

Third World people who speak in these pages know the interconnections well. Another voice, now known all over the world, is that of ecologist Vandana Shiva, who heads the Research Foundation of Science, Technology, and Ecology in Dehra Dun, India, and now heads a move-

Economist/feminist Vandana Shiva is one of India's leading environmentalists. (Courtesy *Synthesis/Regeneration*; photo by Cindy Taykowsky)

ment launched in 1992, known as the Seed *Satyagraha*.[44]

It is a struggle in the Gandhian tradition against the patenting of seed—and more broadly, against oppression of the poor and nature itself through biopiracy, the appropriation by multinationals of natural processes and traditional forms of knowledge. Since 1992 the movement has grown, and joined with like-minded groups around the world; today they represent a stubbornly growing force of resistance to the dazzling claims of the biotechnology industry. Such claims rest on advances in transgenetics—inserting material from one species of plant, bacteria, virus, animal, or fish into another, unrelated species, with which it would not naturally breed.

Farmers in highly industrialized agricultural systems seldom replant commercial hybrids (on the market since the 1920s), so demanding are the requirements of machine-harvesting and food processing for crop uniformity. In poor countries like India, however, many resourceful farmers, particularly women, have learned to isolate useful genetic characteristics in second-generation hybrids as breeding material for blending with their traditional varieties. Thus multinational seed traders like Cargill, Pioneer Hi-Bred, Rhone-Poulenc, Hoechst Schering Agr Evo, and Monsanto could be frustrated in their goal of preventing farmers from following the 12,000-year tradition of saving and breeding seed.

In the 1980s, however, U.S. Supreme Court decisions began permitting patents on DNA, whether hybrid or non-hybrid crops were genetically engineered. They became "intellectual property." Hence multinationals could now add to their existing claim that the wonder seeds they have created will bring higher yields and quick prosperity—that is, they could also insist that farmers who save and replant seeds with patented biotech traits are subject to prosecution. And many cases of prosecution have occurred.[45]

The very patent claim is a kind of "creation myth," says Shiva. The truth is that the desirable traits are in the seed that has been selected and maintained by farmers over many generations. All the industrial breeders do is to take that trait and mix it somewhere else. No one can make these traits. Even the farmers have selected them out of Nature's traits. A co-production and a co-creation take place, in which farmers work with Nature to select seed most appropriate for a certain niche.[46]

For traditional farmers, seed is sacred, she says. In India they go through a beautiful ceremony of exchanging seed at the beginning of the agricultural season. It is a symbol of recognition that seed is not a private but a common resource, not an economic commodity but a gift you exchange *freely*. "And seed," she adds, "is not just a gift between humans, it is a gift from Nature. You have to remember that multiple exchange between Nature and people, and people and people, at every point in time is the basis of a sustainable agriculture."[47]

In contrast, forcing farmers to go back to the seed market every year forces a dependency on the corporation. Moreover, it blocks the basic freedom of the seed.

Shiva also leads a fight against another biopiracy: exploitation of the Neem tree, known for millennia among poor farmers as a contraceptive, biopesticide, and medicine. In some parts of India, the Neem is worshipped as sacred. Yet today foreign firms have taken out patents on Neem-based medications. She supports biopesticides as an alternative to chemical pesticides such as Sevin—the pesticide manufactured at the Union Carbide plant in Bhopal, India, where the disaster of 1984 killed thousands of Indians and disabled 400,000.[48]

The latest development is the Technology Protection System, dubbed Terminator Technology. In March 1998, the U.S. Department of Agriculture (USDA) and Delta and Pine Land Company obtained a patent permitting its owners to create sterile seed by selectively programming a plant's DNA to kill its own embryo. Then USDA and Delta and Pine Land applied for Terminator patents in 78 countries through licensing agreements. Monsanto jumped in and began negotiations to buy Delta and Pine Land. Thus poor farmers could be automatically prevented from using patented seed.

Along the way, Monsanto has bought up half a dozen other seed companies and become the most politically powerful of such multinationals. (In Washington there is a revolving door between its core of lobbyists and U.S. regulatory agencies.)

It also happens to be the enterprise that brought us Agent Orange, a defoliant used in the Vietnam War and known as the most toxic of dioxins; PCBs, chemicals that have caused birth defects among children of women who had eaten fish from PCB-contaminated waters; recombinant Bovine Growth Hormone, which scientific studies link to cancer; and Roundup (glyphosate), the world's most widely sold herbicide. It also discovered a bacterium with a gene immune to that herbicide and introduced the gene into Roundup Ready seed. Presto! Soaring sales of both products are assured!

Monsanto's ventures into bioengineering had not been smooth sailing before the invention of the Terminator. To cite two examples. In 1996 it had to recall 60,000 bags of rape seed (the basis of canola oil) that contained an unapproved gene. In 1998 some Roundup Ready cotton in Mississippi developed deformed bolls.[49] In 1998 the U.S. fined the company $225,000 for mislabeling containers of Roundup on 75 occasions. French research has revealed that some strains of transgenic canola (rape) can harm bees, a farm's most effective pollinator, by destroying their ability to recognize flower smells. In India, Mahyco-Monsanto, in which Monsanto held 26 percent interest, persuaded one Basanna Monsole into try-ing—free—a wonderful new variety of cotton. Somehow it forgot to tell him it was genetically altered. Basanna found that it reached less than half the height of his traditional varieties and was infested with boll weevils. The case added fuel to the rage among Indian farmers that Monsanto could so arrogantly assume they were easily fooled. "Operation Cremate Monsanto!"—burning genetically altered cotton plants on test sites—began to spread rapidly. It has been joined by "Monsanto Quit India!"[50]

Despite alluring claims, transgenics represent a host of dangers. As British geneticist Ricarda Steinbrecher explains, "a gene may behave differently according to its environment, its location on the chromosome, and the presence of other genes. The transfer can yield completely un-predictable, and unstable, characteristics."[51]

Unpredictable consequences have already occurred. For example, the transgene for herbicide resistance inserted into engineered rapeseed can spread to weeds, producing transgenic weed-like plants. Genetically al-tered plants have been shown to kill some beneficial insects.[52]

Shiva adds that in the Third World, breeding crops resistant to her-bicides destroys biodiversity. What are weeds for the transnational seed companies are food, fodder, and medicine for Third World farmers.[53]

Could the Terminator terminate the problems that Monsanto and its fellow transnationals have created? Although in 1999 the technology was only in the laboratory stage, the most likely scenario is one of increasing problems. For example, biologists point out that the Terminator could infect the agricultural gene pool of a neighbor's crops and of their weed relatives. As Terminator-type genetic modifications flow into the ecosys-tem, non-transgenic varieties of soy, corn, wheat, and rice could later become sterile. Its gene cocktail increases risks that new toxins and allergens will show up in our food, animal fodder, and bodies.[54]

But still, does bioengineering not always produce higher yields? No. Seed-saving movements have been growing all over the world, revitalizing degraded farmland with organic agriculture, and recovering biodiversity—the key to food security. In 20 Third World countries, such farming is producing tripled or doubled yields on over 10 million acres, matching if not surpassing intensive agrochemical agriculture.[55]

Meanwhile, bioengineering companies, of which Monsanto is only the most aggressive and most hated, have taken out expensive ads portraying themselves as friendly benefactors who will reduce the need for agrichemicals. They will solve the global food crisis emanating from inevitably growing populations, especially in the hapless Third World. All this will be accomplished through application of the "life sciences," which their ads manage to equate with biotechnology.

Life? In the U.S., the Council for Responsible Genetics has issued a "No Patents on Life!" petition, and international conferences like the St. Louis "Biodevastation: Genetic Engineering" (with Shiva as keynote speaker) are increasing. In India the supposed beneficiaries of bioengineering stage mass rallies protesting seed patenting, and seed banks run by local communities have been set up. Delegates of 19 African countries at FAO's negotiations on the International Undertaking for Plant Genetic Resources strongly opposed "gene technologies that kill the capacity of our farmers to grow the food we need." In Bangkok a global gathering to develop a response to the increasing privatization of biodiversity, especially as driven by the Trade Related Intellectual Property Rights (TRIPS) agreement of the WTO, has declared its "total and frontal opposition to the extension of intellectual property rights to life forms, be it on humans, animals, plants, microorganisms, or their genes, cells, and other parts." Many European countries—and now, growing groups of Americans—have been fighting for laws to label genetically engineered foods. The U. S. is finding it increasingly difficult to argue convincingly that such laws would be a danger to free trade.

Free? What is more basic—the freedom of multinationals, or the freedom of all people to know and choose what their bodies ingest? What is more important for the future of the human and other species—the long-term survival of small innovative farmers and the land itself, or short-term profits?[*]

---

[*] In response to falling grain exports and a groundswell of criticism—from even U.S. agricultural secretary Dan Glickman—in late 1999 Monsanto announced it would not market seeds that produce infertile crops. However, Delta and Pine Land, which originated the Terminator that Monsanto had been trying to buy, reaffirmed plans to go ahead with this research, and Monsanto and some other biotech companies continue to work on similar "gene protection" systems.

"I have set before you life and death, blessing and cursing; therefore choose life, that both thou and thy seed may live. . . ."

Earth Fights Back

The poison of the serpent shall descend
Pestilence and four piles of skulls; living men lie useless.
A dry wind blows. Locust years.
>   —*Native American Almanac of the Dead*,
>   as re-created by Leslie M. Silko

The time has come . . . for destroying those who destroy the
earth.

>   —Revelation 11:18

Climate change causes not only drought, floods, and famines, but
increases airborne pollen and spores that aggravate respiratory diseases,
asthma, and allergy. Bacterial, viral, and parasitical diseases, such as
malaria, dengue and yellow fever, encephalitis, and cholera that thrive in
warmer climates are likely to spread. Pestilence.

All these are diseases which we humans will have helped to spread.
In the end, will we be able to control them?

A reading of *The Coming Plague* and *The Hot Zone* suggests that we
suffer delusion if, in our hubris, we believe that we necessarily have the
last word on the fate of the earth.

Richard Preston's *The Hot Zone* points out that when an ecosystem
suffers degradation, many species die out, but a few survivor-species
experience population explosions. Viruses, which are adaptable and mu-
tate fast, can come under extreme selective pressure, and jump among
species of hosts. For example, as humans enter a tropical rainforest to
clear it, viruses emerge—carried by survivor-hosts like rodents, insects,
soft ticks—thus encountering the two-legged intruding species. The HIV
virus is but one example; other rainforest viruses are likely to spread
swiftly around the world.[56]

Laurie Garrett's *The Coming Plague* describes the surge of infectious
diseases, ranging from the bubonic plague and AIDS to toxic shock syn-
drome, and relates it to recent human social and technological developments. They have actually increased the reach, variety, and deadliness
of dangerous microbes, she maintains. Witness the growth of mutant
strains of microbes, resistant to all or most treatment, that has followed
the extensive use of antibiotics and other drugs once regarded as miracles. Ultimately, she concludes, humanity will need to change its per-

spective on its place in earth's ecology if it hopes to stave off the coming plague.[57]

Love and Law

Is there, perhaps, a curious connection between the fact that the 1990s have witnessed a dramatic increase in severe storms and drought; a worldwide growth in AIDs, tuberculosis, and "newly emerging" diseases; and a euphoria of speculation (made possible only by the magic of computers) followed by the "flu" that has been plaguing the world's interlinked economies?

Is it possible that humans have transgressed some fundamental law?

Love and law are implicit in every faith tradition. Christianity emphasizes the all-forgiving, all-healing power of a divine love that has no limits. Judaism, Islam, Buddhism, Taoism, Confucianism, Hinduism, and native religions all place greater importance on law than does Christianity. Indeed, as we have seen, early Judaism emphasized that if the people of Israel pollute their land, an angry Yahweh will cast them out of the land in order that it can return to its healthy state.

In all these traditions, "law" has emanated from a primal perception of the universe and its story. It is the "law of nature," the basic principle that every expansive life force requires that limiting forces be arrayed against it, if it is not to suffocate other members of the life community.[65] There is no allowance for voluntary compliance to the law, for the human system is but a subsystem of the earth system. Today many members of the human family all over the world forget that basic principle. But our early ancestors, whose genetic imprint we bear in our being, understood the law well.

And so, too, does a child, even today. In the beginning, there is wonder before the sights, sounds, and smells, the touch of the fascinating world it is discovering. Then comes a slow-growing, sometimes ambiguous, love for the forms of life it encounters.

But love is not enough. At last comes law, a dawning recognition that just as living in a family means one cannot always follow one's impulsive desires, the world out there harbors retribution. Life demands reciprocity, life demands balance. There are limits.

Twilight of the Gods

In our more fanciful moments, we imagine the following scenario:

It is the year 2000-plus. The human species has somehow managed to muddle through Y2K, despite an unexpectedly large number of accidents. Still, its fascination with computers abides. Meanwhile, many other species continue to vanish. All those species that remain on the planet have gathered somewhere on the equator, in an enclave of a beleaguered rainforest, for an alternative Earth Summit. Unlike that conference of high-powered dignitaries, this one embraces a truly democratic—or rather, biocratic—representative body. It is called the Parliament of All Creatures.

"Hallelujahs!" go up as Bald Eagle, Chinook Salmon, Gray Wolf, Giant Panda, Prickly Ash, Oahu Tree Snail, California Yew Tree, and a file of other haggard-looking stragglers enter the area. "We were so worried!" their friends shout in relief.

But many others are missing. The delegates decide to hold a mass funeral for all their sisters and brothers who in the past decade have been consigned to oblivion—forever—at a rate that has risen to nearly four species an hour. It is the achievement of a single parliament member, the one uniquely endowed with a superior gift known as "human intelligence." Many are the lamentations for the departed dead, for they were once members of a close-knit, though oft-battling, extended family. But the human delegate hears them not.

The others gather in small caucuses, their faces solemn, for the decision they face is an awesome one, tantamount to regicide. But after long deliberation and prayers for guidance, each member following its own tradition, they reassemble in their meeting place, a vast vacant space in the forest conveniently clear-cut by developers, and commence their plenary discussion. Arriving by consensus at a decision to prosecute, they call on the accused: "To the stand for your trial!"

Human, who has been sleeping in his chair through all of this, is startled when the others shake him into a rude awakening and thrust him before the motley tribunal. "Okay, human species, you've had your chance!" the prosecutors accuse. "The 1990s were supposed to be the Decade of Decision. You were going to turn things around. But you have been fruitful and multiplied to the point that everywhere on the globe you are encroaching on our fragmented pieces of territory and depriving us of our very sustenance. You can eat virtual food; most of us depend on the yield of our natural habitat. Your lust for consumption leads to mining the seas of our kin, choking not only your prey but innocent by-swimmers like dolphins. You hide yourselves within air-conditioned ether, but already global warming stalks amongst you, bringing climate changes that set our forest homes on fire and destroy migration patterns, wreaking havoc with our ways of life. Need we go on? During the Decade of Decision alone, some 300,000 of us were annihilated. And you were going to be our voice—the species who spoke for us! Now, make your own defense."

Human nods, then begins to moan, then splutters out a confession. But he implores his accusers—whom he cannot quite bring himself to call his "fellow creatures"—to have pity upon him. He was not really his own master, he was only the servant of Lord Progress.

The others listen respectfully, but they are visibly tense. They withdraw to deliberate, and 10 minutes later return. "You were warned," they begin. "You've had your chance. Your plea for clemency comes too late. Now, to borrow a phrase from your elegant language, the worm has turned. We have been banding together with the rallying cry, 'Don't agonize—organize!'"

Human stares back. For once, he is speechless.

"So we have organized a pro-life movement," they continue, eying Human coldly. "And, now, are you ready for the verdict?"

Human shakes his head. The jury members shrug. "Guilty of ecocide!" they announce.

Without further ado, the judge pronounces the sentence: "Death by a weapon of war that you humans have brought to state-of-the-art. We have chosen two species and their many subspecies to speak for Earth. Bacteria and viruses, come forth and do your work!"

The summoned ones—strong silent types—emerge and explain tersely, "We speak not with words, with elegant speeches promising prosperity or salvation. By our deeds shall we be known." Whereupon they set to, and begin to carry out the sentence of the assembly.

With much wailing and gnashing of teeth, the more than six billion humans represented by their delegate struggle against the armipotent pandemic. "Tell them we only meant well!" they cry out to him. "We needed more time for further research! Besides, some of you we did *love*, and pet, and protect in special parks and zoos!"

But the other species, who once thought of themselves as subjects, even sometimes as sisters and brothers of the condemned, rise wrathfully to their feet. "So it's gratitude you want? When have you ever expressed gratitude to us for bringing you life? No—you think you give yourselves life. It has all come to a peak with that wondrous invention, cloning. It is the creation of the Holy Trinity: Business, Science, Technology. And of these, the greatest is Supreme God Business. In the past, scientists—even agnostics like Einstein—had some sense of the sacred. But you imagine that you are some species of deity. Alas, you are only mammals—endowed with certain remarkable gifts, to be sure—but mammals, like many you would submit to cloning."

"We d-debate—" Human stutters, then falls silent.

"Yes. You carry on a great *demo*-cratic 'cloning debate'—without thinking on *us*. Your debate is all about human identity, human rights. And you imagine that eventually, you will have the power to toss out all of us who are not serviceable to you. You will create new creatures, but only those that can be patented and assessed in terms of the market. How do you even *know*, how can you measure our value to you now and in the future? And who are *you* to decide which of us should live and which should die?

"No. Now *we* are making the great decision. We shall be released from our bondage. Now we can envision a Second Coming!" And the other creatures cover their ears against the human wails and heed them not.

Then from the four corners of the universe, from the heavens, from the hills, from the fields, from the bowels of the earth, a mighty voice thunders out to the latest species condemned to extinction: "The Law ye were given. But ye heeded it not."

Beginnings

There is another scenario to be imagined. It would be grounded in the view that for the foreseeable future, homo sapiens will enter into every phase of the coming era. In that future we would begin again, begin to reach back to our origins and recognize, as did our ancestors, that we are primarily earthlings. That we can learn to think like Earth, to act like Earth, to *be* Earth.

From the birth of human time, people have asked themselves, "Who are we? Where do we come from? Where are we going? Where do we fit in the universe?" A child asks the same questions today. They emerge again with special force at threshold moments in our lives: as we fall in love for the first time, as we read our first book of philosophy, as we experience the birth of our first child, the death of a young friend, the loss of a parent, the passing of a partner in life. We experience them as we lie on a quiet hillside or some great beach, gazing up at the stars.

All faith traditions have asked these questions. Ultimately, they acknowledge the divine mystery: the power out there is too vast, all-encompassing, and primal for us to truly comprehend.

Yet we can all sense that we are held in the vast net that embraces the horizons, the mountains, the seas, the human eyes gazing upwards.

Today the industrial pollution of our cities and the "security lights" of our industrial parks, shopping malls, highways, and megafarms seem almost designed to blot out our perception of the heavens. Television, computers, and electronic games keep our eyes indoors, focused on some virtual reality.

Still, we long for something wilder, something greater. As naturalist Henry Beston once put it, "The world today is sick to its thin blood for lack of elemental things."[58] By day we are masters, or fancy that we are, but we fear the mystery of darkness, the nocturnal calls of animals and insects we cannot see or control. Yet through all this there comes an ancient urge, a call to go out into the night and participate in the mystery.

Who can heed this call? At some point, anyone can. But some of us bear more privilege, hence more responsibility than others. Born at a time when the planet is perhaps not quite overcrowded, and aware of our sheer luck not to be living in the numbing megacities of the world, where children may never see the stars, some of us can still walk beside the sea or climb hills like prophets of old and experience the Great Curve of the Cosmos. We are poised, at this significant moment in the unfolding of the evolutionary universe, at a threshold where, leaving behind the Cenozoic biogeological era, we can enter either an Ecozoic period, when, in Thomas Berry's words, "humans will be present to the planet in a mutually enhancing way"—or a time when present trends will harden into a Technozoic period.

At this juncture, we can still take a quiet contemplative walk on the sea's shore, which biologist Rachel Carson once described as "the place of our dim ancestral beginnings." We can remember Beston's solitary year on Cape Cod, without electricity or running water, at the outermost shore of the Atlantic coast of the United States. Like Beston, we may still see animals descend by starlight to the beach: muskrats, sand-colored toads, moles, deer; witness myriads of tiny fish being spilled onto the sand in the moonlight; sight a meteor blazing across the heavens. We may hear the rhythmic roar of the breakers sound through the dark, the winds churning the sky, and as night fades into day, birds celebrating the ancient ritual of the return of the sun.

We can still lie on our backs on a quiet field and see planet Venus, the evening star, rise in the west, and then watch the appearance of Orion the Great Hunter and of the Milky Way, that vast arc reaching from one horizon to the opposite side of the world. Some native peoples of North America learn that it is the path trod by the newly deceased to the Great Beyond. In childhood most of us learned to see it as a galaxy of some 300 billion incomprehensibly remote entities.

Indeed they are. But they are also our cousins, the new story of the universe tells us. It is a story founded on twentieth-century science, but in some sense it also represents the wisdom of ancient traditions. Although lacking today's scientific instruments, many faiths, including Buddhism, Hinduism, and the three Abrahamic religions that emerged among nomadic peoples in the desert, offer insights in many ways congruent with this cosmology.

Some indigenous people of South America teach that to become human "one must make room in oneself for the immensities of the universe," observes Brian Swimme in *The Hidden Heart of the Cosmos*.[59] We need to focus on learning how to "read" the universe in order to enter and inhabit it as a communion event, this mathematical cosmologist goes on to say. We are all embedded in a living, developing universe. And at the same time, we can learn modern science's new discovery that it is omni-centered. While "the center of the cosmos" refers to that place where the great birth of the universe happened at the beginning of time, "it also refers to the upwelling of the universe as river, as star, as raven, as you, the universe surging into existence anew."[60]

That discovery, pregnant with possibilities, is awesome. But it must be incarnated. It must be *experienced* by individual women and men and incorporated into our institutions.

If the essential truths of religion were expressed within the context of the dynamics of the developing universe, they would not suffer belittlement. On the contrary, they would find a far vaster and more profound form. Science does not reduce the mystery but actually enhances it.

And so we return to the proposal put forth by Berry and Swimme in *The Universe Story*: that we celebrate through poetry and song, drama and dance, the great historical moments in the unfolding of the universe, cosmic events that constitute psychic-spiritual as well as physical transformations. Such celebrations might begin with the primordial "flaring forth" and the supernova implosions, and go on to embrace the advent of photosynthesis, followed by flowers, then trees, birds, mammals, humans, and other expressions of this awesome evolution.

Such ceremonies would be communal events, but inner celebrations as well. They represent our evolution as humans, and reflect the natural world that we need in order to activate the sense of wonder without which life is meaningless.

There are also private moments when we seek healing—to be whole again. We can walk a great beach and listen to the eternal but ever-changing sounds of the waves; or meander through a forest of trees that have towered there for centuries and watch the tiny creatures that nurture the soil and giant trees and in turn are nurtured by them; or lie on our backs gazing at stars that are really light perceived thousands of light years after it left home. In moments like these, we feel the urge to express gratitude for the gift of life, the urge to reach out and embrace the world. It is a fundamental impulse that gives rise to religio-spiritual bonding.

Various faith traditions have found ways to describe that experience. But essentially it is beyond words. At that moment, in some recess within, we know who we are. The center of the universe is out there, but it is also within ourselves.

We sense that the natural world needs us to respect and preserve it, but we also need it in a physical sense and in the psychic-spiritual sense of feeling fully alive. We sense that we are part of some great community.

Many Hindus and Buddhists would say that it is the Great Self calling the small self.

Navajos, believing that the balance of an ill or depressed person is restored only in relationship to the universe, call the sick one to health through a ritual connecting him or her to the power source—the land.

Still, those moments for communion with the power sources will not be available to us forever. The sea itself will always be there, but the sea community that lends it wonder and meaning already is changing. The great beach at Nauset, where Beston speculated on humans' place in the order of things, is evidencing erosion, and the waves spew up waste. Although the Bible tells us that God made his covenant between him and humans and every living creature, humans seem to have forgotten it; forest communities are dwindling—not only trees, but animals, insects, and birds whose destinies are intertwined with the trees. Holy mountains, where sages meditated on eternal truths, are beginning to crumble under the weight of human too-muchness. Eternal truths, as we have known them, will not be revealed to us eternally.

We can renew them, but only through effort. For every woman, man, and child, there is work to do.

Joy and community and creative work go together. Even when the intoxication of the "Millennial Moment" recedes, we can plan planet-wide ceremonies, uniting people of many faiths and walks of life. Joyous they can be, if we make them so. A high point at the 1993 Parliament of World Religions came when a moment of great discord was transformed: someone began a snake dance, which grew and grew until Jews and Muslims, Christians and neo-pagans, Vedantists and Rastafarians—until representatives of more than a hundred faiths were dancing and singing and laughing together.

The challenge before us is far more awesome. We shall have to choose whether it will be a Technozoic or an Ecozoic era that we enter. We shall have to decide whether to cling to the naive twentieth-century dream that Earth will yield its gifts to us forever—or reach for a new way that means dwelling within the laws of nature, yet opens new possibilities of living true to the core of our being and in harmony with the earth community.

NOTES

INTRODUCTION

1. Paul Ehrlich in a conference sponsored by the National Academy of Sciences in Washington, D.C., September 1986.

2. Published in *A Directory of Environmental Activities and Resources in the North American Religious Community* (New York: Joint Appeal by Religion and Science for the Environment, 1992), 158-159.

3. William J. Freburger, "A Deeper Clerical Problem than Sex," *National Catholic Reporter* (16 April 1993).

4. Aldo Leopold, "Thinking Like a Mountain" in *A Sand County Almanac* (San Francisco: Sierra Club/Ballantine Books, 1970), 137-141.

1. A PROPHETIC VOICE: THOMAS BERRY

1. Thomas Berry in dialogue with Thomas Clarke, *Befriending the Earth: A Theology of Reconciliation Between Humans and the Earth* (Mystic, CT: Twenty-Third Publications, 1991), 143.

2. Thomas Berry, *The Dream of the Earth* (San Francisco: Sierra Club Books, 1998), 2.

3. *Ibid.*, 132.

4. Berry with Clarke, *Befriending the Earth, op. cit.*, 143.

5. Statement of the Catholic Bishops of the Philippines, "What Is Happening to Our Beautiful Land?" in *Amicus Journal* (Fall 1988), 8.

6. The works of Thomas Berry include: *Thomas Berry and the New Cosmology* (Mystic, CT: Twenty-Third Publications, 1987); *The Dream of the Earth* (San Francisco: Sierra Club Books, 1988); *The Great Work* (New York: Bell Tower/Random House, 1999); and two collaborative works: Berry with Clarke, *Befriending the Earth*; and Berry and Swimme, *The Universe Story: From the Primordial Flaring Forth to the Ecozoic Era* (San Francisco: HarperSan Francisco, 1992). Berry also published privately a series of essays entitled *The Riverdale Papers* (10 vols.) that are currently out of print.

7. Brian Swimme, *The Universe Is a Green Dragon* (Santa Fe: Bear & Co., 1983).

8. Berry and Swimme, *Universe Story, op. cit.*, 29. Reprinted by permission of Ned Leavitt Agency, literary agents for Berry and Swimme.

9. *Ibid.*, 25.

10. *Ibid.*, 38.

11. *Ibid.*, 40.

12. *Ibid.*, 219.

13. Berry with Clarke, *Befriending the Earth, op. cit.*, 114-115.

355

14. *Ibid.*, 76.

15. From a conference at the Cincinnati Nature Center, March 15, 1993.

2. JUDAISM

1. Ellen Bernstein, *The Trees' Birthday*: *A Celebration of Nature* (Philadelphia: Turtle River Press, 1987).

2. *Ibid.*, see Preface.

3. Barry Holtz, *Back to the Sources*: *Reading the Classic Jewish Texts* (New York: Summit, 1984).

4. Marc Swetlitz, ed., *Judaism and Ecology*: *A Sourcebook of Readings* (Philadelphia: Shomrei Adamah, 1989).

5. Ellen Bernstein and Dan Fink, *Let the Earth Teach You Torah*: *A Guide to Teaching Ecological Wisdom* (Philadelphia: Shomrei Adamah, 1992).

6. Neal Joseph Loevinger, "(Mis)reading Genesis: A Response to Environmentalist Critiques of Judaism," in *Ecology and the Jewish Spirit* (Woodstock, VT: Jewish Lights, 1998), 33.

7. Stephen S. Schwarzchild, "The Unnatural Jew," *Environmental Ethics* 6:362 (Winter 1984).

8. See Martin Buber, *I and Thou* (New York: Scribner, 1958, 2nd ed.).

9. Norman Lamm, "Ecology in Jewish Law and Theology," *Faith and Doubt* (New York: KTAV, 1971), 173-175.

10. David Weiss, "The Forces of Nature, the Forces of Spirit: A Perspective on Judaism," *Judaism* 32:477-487 (Fall 1984).

11. David Ehrenfeld and Philip Bentley, "Judaism and the Practice of Stewardship," *Judaism* 34:301-311 (Summer 1985).

12. Samuel H. Dresner and Byron L. Sherwin, "To Take Care of God's World: Judaism and Ecology," *Judaism*: *The Way of Sanctification* (New York: United Synagogue of America Press, 1978), 131.

13. Marc Sirinsky, "The Land of Your Soul," *Ecology and the Jewish Spirit* (Woodstock, VT: Jewish Lights, 1998), 121-124.

14. Everett Gendler, "On the Judaism of Nature," *The New Jews*, eds. James A. Sleeper and Alan L. Mintz (New York: Random House, 1971), 239.

15. Everett Gendler, "The Earth's Covenant," *The Reconstructionist* (November/December 1979), 28-31.

16. See Buber, *I and Thou, op. cit.*, 1-34.

17. Lamm, "Ecology in Jewish Law and Theology," *op. cit.*, 178.

18. Samuel H. Dresner, *The Jewish Dietary Laws*: *Their Meaning for Our Time* (New York: Burning Bush Press, 1965), 10.

19. *Ibid.*, 24.

20. Eliezer Diamond, "Jewish Perspectives on Limiting Consumption," *Ecology and the Jewish Spirit* (Woodstock, VT: Jewish Lights, 1998), 80-87.

21. Ehrenfeld and Bentley, "Judaism and the Practice of Stewardship," *op. cit.*, 310.

22. Barry Freundel, "Judaism's Environmental Laws," *Ecology and the Jewish Spirit* (Woodstock, VT: Jewish Lights, 1998), 214-224.

23. Aryeh Carmell, "Judaism and the Quality of the Environment," in *Challenge: Torah Views on Science and Its Problems*, eds. A. Carmell and C. Dombs (New York: Feldheim, 1976), 518-519.

24. David Ehrenfeld, "Environmental Control and the Decline of Reality," *The Churchman* 32(2):5-19 (1990).

25. *Ibid.*, 18.

26. Arthur Waskow, "From Compassion to Jubilee," *Tikkun* 5(2):78-81 (1990).

27. Letter to the authors from Everett Gendler.

28. Rosemary and Herman Ruether, *The Wrath of Jonah: The Crisis of Religious Nationalism in the Israeli-Palestinian Conflict* (New York: Harper & Row, 1989), 244-248.

29. *Ibid.*, 232.

30. Arthur Hertzburg, ed., *The Zionist Idea: A Historical Analysis and Historical Reader* (New York: Atheneum, 1973) in Hertzburg's Introduction, 45-72.

31. See William Orme, "International Study on Water in Mideast Leads to a Warning," *New York Times* (3 April 1999).

32. Telephone conversation with Thomas Naff, University of Pennsylvania.

33. *Israel Environment Bulletin* 18(4):10 (Autumn 1993).

34. Pamphlet given to the authors by Peggy Brill.

35. Azaria Alon, *Plant and Animal Life in the Land of Israel*, 12 vols., in Hebrew (Tel Aviv: misrad ha-bitahon; ha hearah le-haganat hateva' 1982-1988).

36. See Leonard Fein and Rabbi David Saperstein, eds., *To Till and to Tend: A Guide to Jewish Environmental Study and Action* (New York: The Coalition on the Environment and Jewish Life, 1995).

37. Tikva Frymer Kensky, *In the Wake of the Goddesses* (New York: The Free Press, 1992), 100-107.

3. WESTERN CHRISTIANITY

1. Thomas Berry, "Our Children: Their Future," *Riverdale Papers IX* (New York: Riverdale Center for Religious Research, 1982), 1.

2. B. J. Przewozny, "Ecologica Francescana" (Rome: Quaderni Francescana (13) 1987), 223-225 (in English); "Il Problema Ecologico," in *Quaderni de L'Osservatore Romano* (6 December 1989), 81-89.

3. Joseph Campbell, *The Masks of God: Oriental Mythology* (New York: Viking, 1964), 3.

4. Lynn White, Jr., "The Historical Roots of Our Ecologic Crisis," *Science* 155:1205 (10 March 1967). Reprinted by permission.

5. *Ibid.*

6. *Ibid.*

7. *Ibid.*

8. Arnold Toynbee, "The Religious Background of the Present Ecological Crisis: A Viewpoint," *International Journal of Environmental Studies* 3:145 (1972).

9. Jürgen Moltman, *God in Creation: A New Theology of Creation and the Spirit of God* (San Francisco: Harper & Row, 1985), 244.

10. See Vine Deloria, Jr., *God Is Red* (New York: Grosset & Dunlap, 1972).

11. Anand Veeraraj, "Christianity and the Environment," in *World Religions and Environment* (New Delhi: Gitanjali, 1989), 75-76.

12. Rosemary Radford Ruether, New Woman, *New Earth: Sexist Ideologies and Human Liberation* (New York: Seabury, 1975), 18.

13. See Marjorie Casebier McCoy, "Feminist Consciousness in Creation," in *Cry of the Environment*, eds. Philip Joranson and Ken Butigan (Santa Fe: Bear & Co., 1984), 142.

14. Evelyn Reed, *Women's Evolution: From Matriarchal Clan to Patriarchal Family* (New York: Pathfinder, 1975), 137.

15. *Ibid.*

16. Carolyn Merchant, *The Death of Nature: Women, Ecology and the Scientific Revolution* (San Francisco: Harper & Row, 1980).

17. Benjamin Farrington, *Francis Bacon: Philosopher of Industrialism* (New York: Shuman, 1949), 62, 129-130.

18. Ruether, *New Woman, op. cit.,* 13.

19. Max Weber, *The Protestant Ethic and the Spirit of Capitalism* (New York: Scribner, 1930).

20. Veeraraj, "Christianity and Environment," *op. cit.,* 89.

21. H. Paul Santmire, *The Travail of Nature: The Ambiguous Ecological Promise of Christianity* (Philadelphia: Fortress Press, 1985), 15.

22. René Dubos, "A Theology of Earth" (booklet), n.d.

23. Jacques Ellul, *The Technological Society* (New York: Alfred A. Knopf, 1964), 64.

24. Santmire, *Travail of Nature, op. cit.,* 197-198.

25. *Ibid.,* 177.

26. Paul Wiegand, "Escape from the Birdbath," in *Cry of the Environment*, eds. Joranson and Butigan (Santa Fe: Bear & Co., 1984), 148-156.

27. Matthew Fox, *Original Blessing: A Primer in Creation Spirituality* (Santa Fe: Bear & Co., 1983).

28. René Dubos, *The God Within* (New York: Scribner, 1972), 168-172.

29. Richard Woods, "Environment as Spiritual Horizon: The Legacy of Celtic Monasticism," in *Cry of the Environment*, eds. Joranson and Butigan (Santa Fe: Bear & Co., 1984), 67-68.

30. Wesley Granberg-Michaelson, ed., *Tending the Garden: Essays on the Gospel and the Earth* (Grand Rapids: Eerdmans, 1987), 87.

31. John Cobb, Jr., "Process Theology and an Ecological Model," in *Cry of the Environment*, eds. Joranson and Butigan (Santa Fe: Bear & Co., 1984), 329-336.

32. Sallie McFague, *The Body of God: An Ecological Theology* (Minneapolis: Augsburg/Fortress, 1993), 236.

33. *Weekly World News* (8 February 1994), 8-9.

34. McFague, *Body of God*, op. cit., 162-163.

35. Ian Barbour, *Religion in an Age of Science: The Gifford Lectures. 1989-1991*, Vol. 1 (San Francisco: HarperSan Francisco, 1990) 1:240-241, 269-270.

36. Santmire, *Travail of Nature*, op. cit., 217-218.

37. McFague, *Body of God*, op. cit., 162-163.

38. *Ibid.*, 165.

39. Veeraraj, in "Christianity and Environment," 109-113.

40. *Ibid.*, 161.

41. The Catholic Bishops of the Philippines' Pastoral Letter "What Is Happening to Our Beautiful Land?" *Amicus Journal* (Fall 1988), 8-10.

42. Statement issued by Bishop Anthony Pilla from the Archdiocese of Cleveland, "Christian Faith and the Environment" on the Feast of St. Francis of Assisi, October 4, 1990.

43. Albert Schweitzer, *Out of My Life and Thought* (New York: Henry Holt, 1949), 133.

44. Committee on the Environment, *Human Values on Spaceship Earth* (New York: National Council of Churches, 1966).

45. *End Times News Digest* 14:6 (1990).

46. Albert Fritsch and Iadaria Fox, *Eco-Church in Action* (San Jose: Resource Publications, 1992).

4. EASTERN CHRISTIANITY

1. Larry Rasmussen, "Toward an Earth Charter," *Christian Century* (23 October 1991), 966.

2. Paolos Mar Gregorios, "New Testament Foundation for Understanding the Creation," in *Tending the Garden: Essays on the Gospel and the Earth*, ed. Wesley Granberg-Michaelson (Grand Rapids: Eerdmans, 1987), 87.

3. Message of the Ecumenical Patriarch Dimitrios on the Day of the Protection of the Environment, "Orthodoxy and the Ecological Crisis" (Istanbul: The Phanar, 1989), 1. Reprinted by permission of the Patriarchate.

4. *Ibid.*, 1-2.

5. Anuradha Vittachi, *Earth Conference One: Sharing a Vision for Our Planet* (Boston: Shambhala, 1989), 104-105.

6. Stanley Harakas, "Ecological Reflections in Contemporary Orthodox Thought in Greece," *Epiphany Journal* 10(3):46-60 (Spring 1990).

7. Feodor Dostoyevsky, *The Brothers Karamazov* (New York: Random

House/The Modern Library, 1937), 349-354.

8. James H. Billington, *The Icon and the Axe*: *An Interpretive History of Russian Culture* (New York: Random House, 1970), 426-428.

9. Dostoyevsky, *Brothers Karamazov*, *op. cit.*, 334.

10. G.P. Fedotov, *The Russian Religious Mind*: *Tenth to Thirteenth Centuries* (New York: Harper & Brothers, 1946), 369.

11. Billington, *Icon and the Axe*, *op. cit.*, 18-19.

12. *Ibid.*, 403.

13. *Ibid.*, 403-404.

14. Wilfred Royer, "Nature Mysticism in St. Seraphim of Sarov and St. John of Kronstadt," in *Christian Ecology*: *Building an Environmental Ethic for the Twenty First Century*, ed. Frederick W. Krueger (San Francisco: North American Conference on Christianity and Ecology, 1988), 52-53.

15. Mircea Eliade, *Patterns in Comparative Religion* (New York: Sheed & Ward, 1958), 355.

16. Billington, *Icon and the Axe*, *op. cit.*, 20.

17. Fyodor Dostoyevsky, *The Possessed* (New York: Random House/The Modern Library, 1936), 144.

18. Frederick W. Krueger, "Christianity in the Soviet Union," *Firmament* 2(4):19 (Winter 1991).

19. By 1998 the life span of Russian males had fallen to 58. *The World Almanac, 1999* (Mahwah, NJ: World Almanac Books, 1999), 836.

20. Aleksandr Baranov, "A Real Threat to the Nation's Future," *Russian Social Science Review* 39(4):4-13 (July-August 1998).

21. Vladimir Andreev, "Leave a Little Bit of Soup for Me," in *Russian Social Science Review*, 39(4):14-18 (July-August 1998).

22. Boris V. Dubin, "Orthodoxy in a Social Context," *Russian Social Science Review* 39(3):51 (May-June 1998).

23. Jim Forest, *Pilgrim to the Russian Church*: *An American Journalist Encounters a Vibrant Religious Faith in the Soviet Union* (New York: Crossroad, 1988), x.

24. Prince Philip in a talk at the Summer School Seminar on Chalki Island (also known as Heybeli), June 1, 1992, and sponsored by Worldwide Fund for Nature.

25. Rasmussen, "Toward an Earth Charter," *op cit.*, 966.

26. This account is largely based on Paul Burks' "Confrontation, Reconciliation, and Renewal at the 7th Assembly," *Sequoia* (May-June 1991), 4-5. See also Mary Evelyn Tucker, "Expanding Contexts, Breaking Boundaries: The Challenge of Chung Hyun-Kyung," *Cross Currents* (Summer 1992).

   For a different viewpoint, that of a woman delegate from the Orthodox Church of America, see Valerie Zahirsky, "Are the Orthodox That Far Apart?" *The Ecumenical Review*, 43/2 (April 1991), 222-225. While lamenting the fact that others did not seem to understand the Orthodox teaching about women, she called for a mutual ecumenical understanding of possible new or renewed ministries for women in the churches, not limited to ordination.

27. Dostoyevsky, *Brothers Karamazov, op. cit.*, 342-381.

5. ISLAM

1. R. Marston Speight, *God Is One: The Way of Islam* (Albany: SUNY Press, 1985), 32-45.

2. Charles Le Gai Eaton, *Islam and the Destiny of Man* (Albany: SUNY Press, 1985), 1.

3. Speight, *God Is One, op. cit.*, 67-70.

4. *Ibid.*, 31.

5. *Ibid.*, 50-53.

6. In recent years, many books on "the woman question" have been published. We list a few of the more significant: Mahnaz Afkhami, *Faith and Freedom: Women's Human Rights in the Muslim World* (Syracuse: Syracuse University Press, 1995); Margot Badran and Miriam Cooke, eds., *Opening the Gates: A Century of Arab Feminist Writing* (London: Virago Press, 1990); Elizabeth Fernea, *In Search of Islamic Feminism: One Woman's Global Journey* (New York: Anchor Books, 1998); Fatima Mernissi, *Beyond the Veil: Male-Female Dynamics in a Modern Arab Society* (Revised) (Bloomington: Indiana University Press, 1987); Suha Sabbagh, ed., *Arab Women: Between Defiance and Restraint* (Brooklyn: Interlink, 1996); and Bouthaina Shabaan, *Both Right and Left Handed: Arab Women Talk About Their Lives* (Bloomington: Indiana University Press, 1991).

7. See Laleh Bakhtiar, *Sufi Expressions of the Mystic Quest* (London: Thames & Hudson, 1973).

8. Seyyed Hossein Nasr, *Islamic Art and Spirituality* (Albany: SUNY Press, 1986), 114-147.

9. Gilbert Herdt, "Homosexuality," *Encyclopedia of Religion* (New York: Macmillan, 1998), Vol. 6, 447.

10. We have used the translation of the Qur'an of Abdullah Yusuf Ali, originally published in 1934. Our copy is the second U.S. edition (Elmhurst, NY: Tahrike Tarsile Qur'an Inc., 1988).

11. See Mawil Y. Izzi Dien, "Islamic Ethics, Law and Environment," in *Ethics of Environment and Development: Global Challenge and International Response*, eds. J. Ronald Engel with Joan G. Engel (Tucson: University of Arizona Press, 1990), 188-198.

12. This section is based on B.A. Masri, *Animals in Islam* (Petersburg, UK: Athene Trust, 1989); and Masri, "Islam and Experiments on Animals," in *International Animal Action #18*, Hertfortshire, England, n.d.

13. This brief summarization of some aspects of Nasr's thought is based on his *Man and Nature: The Spiritual Crisis of Modern Man* (London: Allen & Unwin, 1968); *Science and Civilization in Islam* (Cambridge, MA: Harvard, University Press, 1968); *Sufi Essays* (Albany: SUNY Press, 1973); *Knowledge and the Sacred: The 1981 Gifford Lectures* (Albany: SUNY

Press, 1989); and *Religion and the Order of Nature: The 1994 Cadbury Lectures* at University of Birmingham, England (New York: Oxford University Press, 1996).

14. Nasr, *Knowledge and the Sacred, op. cit.*, 12.

15. Nasr, *Man and Nature, op. cit.*, 12.

16. The Hamdard Institutes compose not only an Institute of Islamic Studies, but also a faculty of Unani medical science (herb-based practice combining traditional methods of Arabic, Chinese, Greek, and Indian schools).

17. *Spirit and Nature* with Bill Moyers was produced by Public Affairs Television, Inc., June 5, 1991. See page five of the printed transcript.

18. Nasr, *Knowledge and the Sacred, op. cit.*, 110.

19. *Ibid.* See Chapter Four, 130-159.

20. Martin Palmer, Anne Nash, and Ivan Hattingh, eds., *Faith and Nature* (London: Hutchinson/Century, 1987), 67.

21. Fazlun Khalid, "Islam," in *Encyclopedia of the Environment*, eds. Ruth A. and William R. Eblen (Boston: Houghton Mifflin, 1994).

22. Fazlur Rahman, *Islam and Modernity: Transformation of an Intellectual Tradition* (Chicago: University of Chicago Press, 1983), 131.

23. *Ibid.*, 153.

6. THE WAY OF NATIVE AMERICANS

1. Thomas Berry, *The Dream of the Earth* (San Francisco: Sierra Club Books, 1988), 184.

2. "The Land Is Sacred to Us: Chief Seattle's Lament" (Philadelphia: Wider Quaker Fellowship, 1989), a leaflet.

3. Kent Nerburg and Louise Mengelkoch (comps.), *Native American Wisdom* (San Rafael: New World Library, 1991), 31.

4. Paula Gunn Allen, *The Sacred Hoop: Recovering the Feminine in American Indian Traditions* (Boston: Beacon Press, 1986).

5. Jose Maria Arguedas (edited by Ruth Stephan), *The Singing Mountaineers: Songs and Tales of the Quechua People* (Austin: University of Texas Press, 1989), 39.

6. Mary Evelyn Tucker and John A. Grim, eds., *Worldviews and Ecology* (Lewisburg: Bucknell University Press, 1993), 42.

7. Jamake Highwater, *The Primal Mind: Vision and Reality in Indian America* (New York: Harper & Row, 1981), 189.

8. Allen, *Sacred Hoop, op. cit.*, 210.

9. John A. Grim, "Reflections on Shamanism: The Tribal Healer and the Technological Trance" (Chambersburg, PA: Anima Books, 1981). *Teilhard Studies* 6:2.

10. Vine Deloria, Jr., *God Is Red* (New York: Grosset & Dunlap, 1973).

11. *Ibid.*, 73.

12. "Land Is Sacred to Us," *op. cit.*, note 2 above.

13. Stan Steiner, *The New Indians* (New York: Dell, 1968), 139-140.

14. T.C. McLuhan, *Touch the Earth: A Self Portrait of Indian Existence* (New York: Outerbridge and Lazard, 1971), 23.

15. Ernest T. Seton, *The Gospel of the Red Man* (New York: Doubleday, Doran, 1936), 58-59.

16. McLuhan, *Touch the Earth, op. cit.*, 63.

17. Steiner, *New Indians, op. cit.*, 105-106.

18. See "Handsome Lake," *Encyclopedia of Religion* (New York: Macmillan, 1988), Vol. 6, 191-192.

19. Edmund Wilson, *Apologies to the Iroquois* (New York: Farrar, Straus & Cudahy, 1960).

20. "A Public Declaration: To the Tribal Councils and Traditional Spiritual Leaders of the Indian and Eskimo Peoples of the Pacific Northwest," *The NARF Legal Review* (Winter 1988), 3.

21. "We the First Americans" (Washington, D.C.: Bureau of the Census, 1993), 6. By 1998 it was estimated by the Census Bureau that the Native American peoples had increased to two million, or 1 percent of the U. S. population. *The World Almanac, 1999* (Mawah, NJ: World Almanac Books, 1999), 373.

22. Susan Shown Harjo, "I Won't Be Celebrating Columbus Day," *Newsweek*, special issue (Fall/Winter 1991).

23. James Welch, *The Indian Lawyer* (New York: W.W. Norton, 1990).

24. Leslie Marmon Silko, *Almanac of the Dead* (New York: Simon & Schuster, 1991).

25. Philip Yellowhorse Minthorn, "This Earth," in ed. Joseph Bruchac, *Songs From This Earth on Turtle's Back: Contemporary American Indian Poetry* (Greenfield Center, NY: The Greenfield Review Press, 1983), 156.

26. See Letty Lincoln, "Becoming Somewhat Shawnee: The Appropriation of Cultural Content." Paper read at 1994 Annual Meeting, American Anthropological Association, 93rd meeting, at Atlanta, GA.

27. N. Scott Momaday, *The Names: A Memoir* (Tucson: University of Arizona Press, 1987), 135.

28. *Ibid.*, 142.

29. *Ibid.*, 156.

7. BEYOND THE WESTERN HORIZON

1. This section is based on H. Byron Eckhart, *Japanese Religion* (Belmont: Wadsworth, 1982); and Ian Reader, *Religion in Contemporary Japan* (London: Macmillan, 1991); as well as three visits by the authors.

2. Donald Swearer, "Buddhism in Southeast Asia," *Encyclopedia of Religion*, Vol. 2 (New York: McGraw-Hill, 1988), 396.

3. Marjorie Hope, "The Reluctant Way: Self-Immolation in Vietnam," *Antioch Review* (Summer 1967), 149-163.

4. Helen Cordes, "Buddhism American Style," *Utne Reader* (January/February 1995), 16.

5. Today some self-immolations still occur in resistance to the present government's attempts to control Buddhism. See "Vietnam Monks Lead Protest to Repression," *Christian Science Monitor* (November 21, 1994).

6. Joanna Macy, "In Indra's Net: Sarvodaya and Our Efforts at Peace," *Paths of Compassion: Writings on Socially Engaged Buddhism*, ed. Fred Eppsteiner (Berkeley: Parallax Press, 1988), 174-179.

7. *The Japan Environment Monitor*, an English-language environmental publication commenced publication in 1988. The staff was made up of volunteers. It suspended publication in December 1998, mainly because of the necessity of making a living in this expensive nation.

8. *The New Road* was founded in 1988 as the bulletin of the WWF Network on Conservation and Religion. At one point, it had a worldwide distribution (free) of several hundred thousand. Unfortunately, the Worldwide Fund for Nature ran into financial problems. In 1993 *The New Road* was the victim of this crisis.

9. The foregoing is drawn largely from Seri Phongphit, *Religion in a Changing Society: Buddhism, Reform, and the Role of the Monks in Community Development in Thailand* (Hong Kong: Arena Press, 1988).

10. Chatsumarn Kabilsingh, *Cry From the Forest* (Bangkok: Thammasat University Press, 1991).

11. Buddhadasa Bhikku, *Dhammic Socialism*, trans. and ed. Donald K. Swearer (Bangkok: Thai Interreligious Commission for Development, 1986).

12. *Ibid.*, 14-28.

13. Cited in Thomas Berry with Thomas Clarke, *Befriending the Earth: A Theology of Reconciliation Between Humans and the Earth* (Mystic, CT: Twenty-Third Publications, 1991), 114-115.

14. See Alfred W. McCoy, *The Politics of Heroin in Southeast Asia* (New York: HarperCollins, 1973).

15. Larn Seri Thai, "Yantra in Pongsak: The Yellow Robe Must Be Washed White," *Manager Daily* (in Thai) (14 February 1995), 6-7.

16. *Ibid.*, 6.

17. *Ibid.*, 10.

18. Thomas Weber, *Hugging the Trees: The Story of the Chipko Movement* (New Delhi: Penguin, 1989); and Vandana Shiva and Jayanya Bandhyopadhyay, *Chipko: India's Civilizational Response to the Forest Crisis* (New Delhi: INTACH, 1986).

8. A GLOBAL PERSPECTIVE

1. Gerald Barney with Jane Blewitt and Kristen Barney, *Global 2000 Revisited: What Shall We Do?* (Arlington: The Millennium Institute, 1993).

2. "God, Man, Environment." Issued by the Egyptian Green Party (14 April 1990).

3. Ministry of the Environment, *Israel Environment Bulletin* 18(2):5 (1995).

4. See Zev Naveh, "The Value of Open Landscapes as Life-Supporting Systems," *Israel Environment Bulletin* 20(4):21-24 (1997).

5. Yaakov Garb, "The Trans-Israel Highway," *Earth Island Journal* (San Francisco) 12(2):28 (1997).

6. Ben Dansker, "Concrete Realities," *Jerusalem Post* (11 February 1996).

7. Letter from Israel Shahak.

8. Lucille Barnes, "In Allocating Aid to Israel, Congress Has Lost All Sense of Proportion," *Washington Report on Middle East Affairs* (Washington, DC) 15(1):45 (1996).

9. Ziad Abu Nada and Aymara Jadallah, "Water for Settlements: The Gazan Water Crisis," *Palestine Report* (5 February 1999), 8-9. See also Nina Sovich, "The Drought in Palestine," *Palestine Report* (3 March 1999), 5.

10. Muna Hamzeh-Muhaisen, "Bethlehem Man Leads Crusade for the Environment," *Palestine Report* (17 October 1997), 6-7.

11. Rosemary Radford Ruether, "Israel Keeps Stranglehold in Jerusalem," *National Catholic Reporter* (March 1995).

12. "Islamic Stand on Population Lauded by Religious Press," *Shared Vision* 4(7):13 (1990).

13. Jeremy Milgrom, "A Sophisticated Colonialism," *Sojourners* (January/February 1998), 31.

14. Thailand's original forest amounted to 125,191 acres. By 1990 the acreage had fallen to 32,793 acres, and in 1995 it had dropped to 28,793 acres. *World Resources 1998-1999: A Guide to the Global Environment* (Washington, DC: World Resources Institute, 1998), 292.

15. See Israel Shahak, "The Replacement of Palestinians by Imported Workers"; also Anat Tal-Shiv, "They Pay Me $120 a Head." Both in *From the Hebrew Press* 8(4):5-8 (1995).

16. The Thailand Crisis did not take place until July 1997. However, our second visit to Thailand in late 1995 told us that a crash was inevitable.

17. The Thailand currency and real estate debacle in 1997-1998 hit the golf industry hard. Over 200 golf courses have been built. Fourteen were built by Jack Nicklaus Design Company at a cost of one million dollars per course.

18. Susan Darlington, "The Ordination of a Tree: The Buddhist Ecology Movement in Thailand," *Ethnology* (University of Pittsburgh) 37(1):1-15 (Winter 1998).

19. *Ibid.*, 7-11.

20. Sam La Budde, "Unmade in Taiwan," *Earth Island Journal* (San Francisco) 8(2):36-38 (Spring 1993).

21. Communication by fax from K.L. Chang, February 26, 1999.

22. Martin Palmer, "Saving China's Holy Mountains," *People and the Planet* (London) 5(1):12-13.

23. *Ibid.*, 13.

24. *Ibid.*

25. Gar Smith, "No Golf Day," *Earth Island Journal* 8(2):17 (Spring 1993).

26. The current address of *Contours* (as of April 1999) is c/o Christian Confer-

ence of Asia, 96 2nd District, Pak Tin Village, Mei Tin Road, Shatin, N.T., Hong Kong, China. Tel: 852-2691 1068; Fax: 852-2692 3805; E-mail: cca@hk.super.net.

9. CONCLUSION

1. In early 1999, 40 members of the Religious Campaign for Forest Conservation (including one of the authors) traveled to Washington. They visited their elected representatives, sponsored a prayer breakfast with Interior Secretary Bruce Babbitt, and talked with Chief of Forestry Service Mike Dombeck. Ten days later, Dombeck issued an order declaring a moratorium on road building in national forests.

2. *New Road* 16:2 (October/December 1990).

3. Charles Hall, et al, "The Environmental Consequences of Having a Baby in the United States," *Wild Earth* 5(2):78-87.

4. Paul Ehrlich and Anne H. Ehrlich, *Healing the Planet: Strategies for Resolving the Environmental Crisis* (Reading, MA: Addison-Wesley, 1991), 7-10.

5. *Ibid.*, 7.

6. *Ibid.*, 15-30.

7. *Ibid.*, 30-37.

8. *Ibid.*, 8-9.

9. See Bill McKibben, "A Special Moment in History," *Atlantic Monthly* (May 1998), 55-78.

10. Desikan Thirunapuram, "Institute Overview Asserts: Population Explosion Is Far from Over," *Popline* (January/February 1998), 1, 4.

11. McKibben, *Special Moment, op. cit.*, 56.

12. Mathis Wackernagel and William Rees, *Our Ecological Footprint: Reducing Human Impact on Earth* (Gabriola Island, B.C., Canada: New Society, 1996), 102.

13. *The World Almanac, 1999* (Mahwah, NJ: World Almanac Books, 1999), 873. In Europe, for instance, Italy currently has 57 million people. This is projected to fall to 38 million by 2050.

14. *Ibid.*, 863.

15. Wackernagel and Rees, *Our Ecological Footprint, op. cit.*, 102.

16. Lester Brown, "Feeding Nine Billion," *State of the World 1999* (Washington, DC: Worldwatch Institute, 1999), 121.

17. Gerald O. Barney with Jane Blewett and Kristen Barney, *Global 2000 Revisited: What Shall We Do? The Critical Issues of the 21st Century* (Arlington: The Millennium Institute, 1993), 18-19.

18. *Ibid.*

19. McKibben, *Special Moment, op. cit.*, 71.

20. Thomas Berry, *The Dream of the Earth* (San Francisco: Sierra Club Books, 1998), xiii.

21. The objective is to involve diverse groups around the world in articulating a shared vision of ecological integrity and building a just, peaceful, and sustainable world community. It is hoped that a final version of the Earth Charter will be issued early in the year 2000, and that it will be endorsed by the UN General Assembly by the year 2002. See "Earth Charter: Benchmark Draft II, April 1999," *Resurgence*, 12:7-9 (July/August 1999).

22. Aubrey Rose, "Judaism," *The New Road* 16:2 (October/December 1990).

23. Alan Durning, "Asking How Much Is Enough?" *State of the World 1991* (Washington, DC: Worldwatch Institute, 1991), 166.

24. *The Index of Social Health: Monitoring the Social Well-Being of the Nation* (Tarrytown, NY: Fordham Institute for Innovation in Social Policy, 1998). Now available in a book, *The Social Health of the Nation: How America Is Really Doing* by Marc Miringoff and Marque-Luisa Miringoff (New York: Oxford University Press, 1999).

25. McKibben, *Special Moment, op. cit.*, 76-77.

26. The Center for Plain Living, located in Barnesville, Ohio, sponsored The Second Luddite Conference, April 13-15, 1996. The keynote speaker was Kirkpatrick Sale. In June 2000 a new session will take place with Wendell Berry giving the opening address.

27. McKibben, *Special Moment, op. cit.*, 11, 19.

28. Bill McKibben, *Maybe One: A Personal and Environmental Argument for Single-Child Families* (New York: Simon & Schuster, 1998).

29. "Spirituality," entry in *Westminster Dictionary of Christian Spirituality* (Philadelphia: Westminster Press, 1985), 361-363.

30. *Ibid.*, 362.

31. Charlene Spretnak, *The Spiritual Dimension of Green Politics* (Albuquerque: Bear & Co., 1986), 41.

32. David W. Orr, "Architecture as Pedagogy II," *Conservation Biology* II(3):597-600 (June 1997).

33. Dalai Lama, "Keeping Faith with Life," in eds. Stephen Rockefeller and John C. Elder, *Spirit and Nature: Why the Environment Is a Religious Issue* (Boston: Beacon Press, 1992), 186.

34. E.O. Wilson, *Biophilia* (Cambridge, MA: Harvard University Press, 1986).

35. David W. Orr, Earth in Mind: *On Education and the Human Prospect* (Washington, DC: Island Press, 1994), 138-139.

36. Vandana Shiva, *Biopiracy: The Plunder of Nature and Knowledge* (Boston: South End Press, 1997), 113.

37. Marc Lappe and Britt Bailey, *Against the Grain: Biotechnology and the Corporate Takeover of Your Food* (Monroe, ME: Common Courage Press, 1998). Three days before the book was scheduled to go to press, the original publisher pulled out due to a letter received from Monsanto declaring that the book was 'defamatory' and potentially 'libelous.'

38. John C. Elder, "Brooding Over the Abyss," in eds. Rockefeller and Elder, *Spirit and Nature* (Boston: Beacon Press, 1992), 199.

39. Bill McKibben, *Hope, Human and Wild: True Stories of Living Lightly on*

the Earth (Boston: Little, Brown, 1994), section on Curitiba, see 57-115.

40. Alan Weisman, *Gaviotas: A Village to Reinvent the World* (White River Junction, VT: Chelsea Green, 1998).

41. Steve Lerner, *Eco-Pioneers: Practical Visionaries Solving Today's Environmental Problems* (Cambridge, MA: MIT Press, 1997), 392-393.

42. Information obtained from Professor John Scott, Department of Agriculture, Wilmington College, formerly in the same position in New Zealand.

43. Interreligious Council of Mexico, Fred Krueger, North American Program Coordinator in Santa Rosa, CA (a six-page press release).

44. Vandana Shiva, "Freedom for Seed," *Resurgence* 163:36-39 (March/April 1994).

45. Jennifer Kahn, "The Green Machine: Is Monsanto Sowing the Seeds of Change or Destruction?" *Harpers' Magazine* (April 1999), 70-73. A letter from Monsanto to a farmer is reproduced on these pages outlining the penalties for "pirating" Roundup Ready^R seed.

46. Shiva, "Freedom for Seed," *op. cit.*, 37.

47. *Ibid.*, 38.

48. See Ward Morehouse and M. Arun Subramanian, *The Bhopal Tragedy: What Really Happened and What It Means for American Workers at Risk* (New York: Council on International and Public Affairs, 1986); and J.R. Chouhan, *Bhopal: The Inside Story* (New York: The Apex Press, 1994).

49. Kahn, "Green Machine," *op. cit.*, 71.

50. Paul Kingsnorth, "India Cheers While Monsanto Burns," *The Ecologist* 29(1):9-10 (January/February 1999).

51. Ricarda Steinbrecher and Pat Mooney, "The Terminator Technology: The Threat to World Food Security," *The Ecologist* 28(5):277 (September/October 1998).

52. *Ibid.*, 273.

53. Vandana Shiva, "Monsanto's Roundup: A Recipe for Soil Erosion and an End to Diversity," *The Ecologist* 28(5):272 (September/October 1998).

54. Steinbrecher and Mooney, "Terminator Technology," *op. cit.*, 279.

55. Mae-Wan Ho, "The Inevitable Return to a Sane Agriculture," *The Ecologist* 28(5):318 (September/October 1998).

56. See Richard Preston, "Crisis in the Hot Zone," *The New Yorker* (26 November 1992), 58-81.

57. Laurie Garrett, *The Coming Plague: Newly Emerging Diseases in a World Out of Balance* (New York: Farrar, Straus & Giroux, 1994).

58. Henry Beston, *The Outermost House* (New York: Viking, 1928).

59. Brian Swimme, *The Hidden Heart of the Cosmos: Humanity and the New Story* (Maryknoll: Orbis Books, 1996). Reprinted with permission of publisher.

60. *Ibid.*, 112.

INDEX

369